Sensory Worlds in
Early America

PUBLISHING FOR THE WORLD
125
Years
THE JOHNS HOPKINS UNIVERSITY PRESS

Sensory Worlds in Early America

PETER

CHARLES

HOFFER

The
Johns Hopkins
University Press
Baltimore &
London

2 4 6 8 9 7 5 3 1

The Johns Hopkins University Press
2715 North Charles Street
Baltimore, Maryland 21218-4363
www.press.jhu.edu

Library of Congress Cataloging-in-Publication Data
Hoffer, Peter Charles, 1944–
Sensory worlds in early America / Peter Charles Hoffer.
p. cm.
Includes bibliographical references and index.
ISBN 0-8018-7353-3 (acid-free paper)
1. United States—History—Colonial period, ca. 1600–1775.
2. United States—History—Colonial period, ca. 1600–1775—
Historiography. 3. United States—Social conditions—To 1865.
4. Senses and sensation—United States—History. 5. Senses and
sensation—United States—Historiography. 6. Perception—History. 7. Perception—Historiography. 8. Social psychology—
United States—History. I. Title.
E188 .H75 2003
973.2—dc21   2002152160

A catalog record for this book is available
from the British Library.

Contents

Preface

NOT LONG AGO, I was sitting at my desk looking over the convention program of one of our national historical associations. In recent years, these programs have become subjects of controversy. Students and proponents of public history and political history (which includes diplomatic and military subjects) argue that they have been slighted in favor of cultural and social historians. There's demonstrable truth in the claim, but its significance is unclear. Whatever hypothesis one wishes to propose for the rise of social and cultural history and the relative decline of political history in academic circles, the shift seems to run counter to popular interest in history. One look at the shelves devoted to military history at the giant bookstore chains demonstrates the continuing popularity of the Civil War, World War II, and the Vietnam War. Political history, in particular accounts of presidents and would-be presidents, is not far behind in shelf space. Publishers know this, and for every cultural or social history they produce, there are a dozen books on war and as many political biographies.

Why then offer readers what appears on its face to be an arcane study of the senses in early America? What difference will it make? Any argument I make here must be self interested, in the sense that it will justify my ten-plus years' labor on the subject—but not crassly self-serving, I hope. Instead, I want to make a larger and less personal claim. We who study, teach, and write American history have transformed our subject matter over the past century, broadening it from the military and political narrative that dominated the nineteenth century by stressing the importance of class, race, and gender. When we emphasize these themes, we are able to include the powerless, the put-upon, the oppressed, and the hitherto overlooked in earlier writings. We restore to American history its diversity and ambiguity and return to ordinary people the agency they had to remake, if not the whole world, at least their small corner of it. Modern American historical writing reminds us that family homes and workplaces are just as much a part of our history as the White House and the halls of Congress.

But until very recently, we had largely overlooked a fourth theme that those very people on whom we now focus our attention would have immediately recognized: the importance of the senses. Looking over the convention sessions I am delighted to find that other scholars and teachers are recognizing this gap in our depiction of the past. Sessions on the body, clothing, food preparation, home decoration, and the smells of the streets—the very topics that political historians find so unimportant—dot the program. But even these may not go far enough, because, although rich in depiction, depiction in them is still a literary device, a way to enhance the account though metaphors and anecdotes. The next step is for us to consider the sensory world for itself, to try to discover how the world presented itself to people in the past and then ask what impact the reports of the senses, mediated to be sure by cultural norms, had upon human action and thought. We must, in short, think about the sensory quality of events and about how sensation and perception might have acted as causes. When we begin this project—for this book is really no more than a set of exploratory essays—we will see that sensory history plays into all the realms of the past, political and military as well as social and cultural.

But my purpose, and the contribution of this book, is a little less ambitious and a lot less pretentious than a revision of all our historical ideas. I have two aims, and though they fit together (one is evidence for the other), their jointure is not perfect, and I do not want to argue that both are equally original or important. First, I want to show that sensation and perception affected some of those great events whose cause and course we historians conventionally attribute to deep cultural structures and overarching material forces. Indeed, viewed in this fashion, the study of the senses reunites social and cultural history with political and military history as, simply, past experience. The second contribution is a revisiting of historical sites and a rereading of primary source texts to uncover the sensory in them. Travelogs through past worlds are staples of cable television and a major component of popular history, but here sensory detail has a purpose beyond mere entertainment. From all evidences, the report of the senses was of immense importance to the people who lived in early America. It should be so to historians.

These two overlapping purposes could have been served by examining a single episode in our early history. Such microhistories have proven themselves both exciting and revelatory. But I began writing this book immediately after finishing a textbook of early American history, and I wanted to retain the sweep of the textbook. Thus, *Sensory Worlds in Early America* begins with the first encounter between Englishmen and Indians and concludes with the establishment of a new nation. Its four chapters address the conflicts at Roanoke and Jamestown at the outset of colonization; the Indian wars and witchcraft crises in seventeenth-century New England; slave rebellions and the Great Awakening in the middle of the eighteenth century; and the rise and fall of the revolutionary mob.

This project has a long trajectory, passing through years of travel with sketchbook and camera and more sedentary perambulations through texts. Along the way, Bernard Bailyn asked me what was important about the senses—what difference did they make? I did not have a very good answer then. Perhaps the following pages will supply that want.

•

A note on the treatment of primary source texts. After wrestling with the question, I decided to modernize spelling and punctuation slightly. A number of years ago, historical editors and literary editors argued with one another about how much change was permissible in an edited text. There is no particular virtue, in my opinion, in retaining the spelling variations (sometimes within a single document) or the contractions and abbreviations of early modern writing, as long as the changes made are consistent from one document to the next and do not alter the meaning or literary flavor of the writing. Applying modern rules for commas, periods, and capitalization enables the ordinary reader to understand what the author of the old document meant to convey.

•

I fear that I have taken so long to finish that the kind archivists and curators at the sites and museums I visited may already have retired. Still, my thanks to the folks at Colonial Deerfield; the Peabody Museum and the Essex Institute, Salem; Plimouth Plantation and the Pilgrim Hall Museum, Plymouth, Massachusetts; Jamestown Historical Park, Jamestown Settlement, and Colonial Williamsburg, Virginia; Roanoke Island National Historical Park, North Carolina; the South Carolina Department of Archives and History, in Columbia; Strawberry Banke in Portsmouth and the Fort at No. 4, Charlestown, New Hampshire; the Museum of the City of Newport, Rhode Island; the Philadelphia Museum of Art and Independence Hall National Historic Site, Philadelphia; Historic New Castle, Delaware; the Old Barracks

Museum, Trenton, New Jersey; Colonial Annapolis, Maryland; the Cahokia Mounds Museum Society, Collinsville, Illinois; the New-York Historical Society and the Museum of the City of New York, in New York City; the Guilford Historical Society, the Keeney Memorial Cultural Center, Weathersfield, the Mystic Seaport Museum, Mystic, and the Pequot Museum on the Mashantucket Reservation, outside of Mystic, all in Connecticut; and Popham State Park and the York Historical Society, York, Maine. The librarians at the Library Company of Philadelphia, the University of Georgia Library, Rutgers University Alexander Library, New York University Bobst Library, and the University of Pennsylvania Van Pelt Library were unfailingly courteous and helpful.

I am especially grateful to my editor at the Johns Hopkins University Press, Robert J. Brugger, who supported the endeavor during my many tacks in approach, and to Barbara Lamb, for her expertise in line editing. I am indebted as well to Virginia DeJong Anderson, Karen Ordahl Kupperman, and Peter Mancall, who encouraged me at an early stage of the project; Mark Huddle, who shared with me references on "passing"; and to colleagues who have read portions of the manuscript or allowed me to use their work as I pondered mine, including Joseph Conforti, Richard Godbeer, Allan Kulikoff, Wayne E. Lee, Daniel Mandell, Daniel Richter, Claudio Saunt, and Michael Winship. My thanks go to my colleagues Josh Cole, Tom Cleaveland, and Thom Whigham, for help with my introduction. Vincent Brown, Matthew Dennis, Ann Kirschner, Allan Kulikoff, Wayne Lee, Mary Beth Norton, Laurent Turgeon, Cynthia Van Zandt, and Gordon Wood shared unpublished manuscripts and references with me. Such collegiality is one of the joys of being a historian. Williamjames Hoffer, now a member of "the profession" in his own right, contributed judicious comments on an early version of the manuscript, and N. E. H. Hull read many versions of the work thereafter, the most recent contribution to a collaboration now lasting over thirty-three years.

-⟨⟩ ☀ ⟨⟩-

New Worlds for Historians

The Realm of the Senses

IT IS one of the peculiarities of our language that the word *history* has two very different meanings. It denotes what people did and said, felt and learned and taught in the past. History also means what scholars have written, and are writing, about the past, the latter an activity that occurs in the present. All historians are aware of the paradox that this peculiarity of speech presents: the attempt to write about something when much of our subject recedes from us even as we study it.

My object in this book confronts the paradox directly. I have set out to recapture pieces of the most ephemeral of past worlds—the record of the senses and the impact of sensuous experience on the larger course of history. One might object that such an undertaking risks falling prey to naive realism. Surely among historical subjects, nothing is so fleeting as the report of the senses, so mediated by cultural conventions particular to time and place, and therefore so suspect when reported in historical texts. In this heyday of textualism, poststructuralism, and other creeds of reading, only the most uncritical realist would claim that it is possible to recover the sensate past.[1]

But historians–like everyone else—are all naive realists when it comes to sunsets and dog droppings. Looking up and out at the horizon at day's end, at the purples and oranges of a spectacular sunset, we are overwhelmed by color and the emotions it produces. We do not see the sun hidden below the horizon but infer its presence from the refraction of its rays through the dust and moistured filaments of clouds. Looking down at the turd, we smell and see the waste and infer what happened. How inconsiderate we think the owner not to have used a pooper scooper. Like the past we recount in our books, the recessional of the sun and the brief stopover of the pooch were finished before we knew to look for them. Only the effects remain. But the use of our senses and our powers of perception has allowed us to appreciate and write about what happened.[2]

Can we use our senses to replicate sensation in a world we have (almost) lost? Can we use our skill as interpreters of texts to get inside the perceptual apparatus of people who lived long ago and recover how they made sense of their sensations? Can we go a step further still, and reconstruct from evidence of past sensation and perception some causal theories about important events?[3] I think the answer is yes, and perhaps more important, the project is worth the effort. "The witnessed and experienced particular" is our lodestone—every historian wants to go back and see it as it was—but that world "intersects ours at only a few points that we can now experience directly."[4] We find ourselves wanting to write history the way that Susan Sontag depicted Howard Hodgkin's artistry: "The idea is to put as much as possible, of color, of feeling, into each picture. It's as if the pictures need their broad border to contain so much feeling. As if they need to be painted on something hard." We know that the task is difficult, and our "sense of vulnerability has not diminished. Nor has the sense of gratitude: for the privilege of feeling."[5] A sensory history should convey to the reader the feel of the past.

But first things first. In this introduction, I confront the claim that all sensation is culturally bound, relative, and thus that all historical narrative is no more than a gloss on texts. I deal with the caveat that in all written primary sources the authors used their senses and perceived the world in a way so different from our own as to be unrecoverable now. I respond to the challenges raised by commercial re-creations of the past and popular re-enactments of events and concede the limitations of even the most sympathetic and knowledgeable historians' readings of sensory documents. But in the end, I conclude that none of these important methodological difficulties presents an insurmountable obstacle to a sensate history of early America. The gateway to sensory history is always open.

The Senses as Cultural Artifact

Many scholars have persuasively insisted that the very idea of the senses is a cultural convention. Consider that we have five distinct senses—sight, hearing, smell, touch, and taste—only because that is how we define sensation. Our senses do not define themselves; they never did. The number and definition of the senses in Western culture comes from a classical philosophical text, Aristotle's *De Anima*.[6] Aristotle's ukase did not prevent rivals from contesting the field. According to the Christian theologian Origen, humans had five spiritual senses to match the material ones—memory, instinct, imagination, fantasy, and common sense. For Origen and the devotees who followed, the five innate senses were just as real as the five material senses. Well into the seventeenth century, some philosophers clung to the notion that "innate ideas" governed the senses, while religious writers insisted on the reality of visions and voices that only the blessed could see and hear.

But by the time of the eighteenth-century Enlightenment, Origen's five innate senses had become mere ghosts in the perceptual machine. John Locke's notion that "all ideas come from sensation," a continuous bombardment of mental faculties by sights, sounds, and touches, was gaining ground as higher education, scientific experimentalism, and polite religion were embraced by elites. His new philosophy of "perception," of how the mind transformed sense data into thought, became the common sense of the subject.[7] The next step was easy. In 1785, Thomas Reid divided our responses to sense data into the categories of sensation (what I feel and see) and perception (what I know is causing me to feel and see as I do). Reid argued that we have the dual apparatus that allows us to "sense" sensations and also to "make sense" of them. Thus, we feel the heat and see a pulsing orb in the sky and can then identify a distant star as the source of the heat and the light that we call the "sun."[8] Of course, Reid's assumption that behind the perception is a real world governed by ascertainable scientific laws is as rooted in early modern Western culture as the notion of five senses was rooted in classical Greek ideas, but too much of this cultural reductionism would lead to the argument of Reid's predecessor, the Anglican Bishop George Berkeley, that all we know are our own sensations. The eighteenth-century literary wit and lexicographer Samuel Johnson's famous refutation of Berkeley—Johnson kicked a stone and announced, "I refute it thus"—is the position that most historians would take in the quarrel.[9]

To return to the culture of sight, this one sense dominates the rest of the senses not only because Aristotle placed it first and the Enlightenment scientists explored its facets but also because we westerners are a people of written texts. The sense of hearing, basic to all oral cultures, made a run for the rank of prime sense, because we "heard" the word of God recited in our churches, but the Protestant requirement that all Christians read the Bible for themselves gave sight the pride of place once again—on top of which stood the triumph of the science of light, color, and optics in the eighteenth century. Laws for the diffraction of light became a proof that all of nature was ruled by laws that men could discover and publish.[10] It was not coincidental that the central intellectual event of the age was called the Enlightenment. Today the eye is aided by photography, motion pictures, and computer internet technologies. "Seeing," as the script for one television documentary on art proclaimed, "comes before words."[11]

As sight stands atop our pantheon of the senses simply because our culture places it there, so the meaning of images is also culturally mediated. The Micmac of Nova Scotia have passed down a legend of how they met French mariner Jacques Cartier's little fleet off the coast in 1534. Of course, the dates and the identity of the newcomers were not part of the Indian story. One morning, the Micmac people gathered on the bank and saw a peculiar little island, with trees on it, float close to the shore and then stop. In the trees were bears. But when the Micmacs ran to the edge of the water with their bows and arrows to shoot them, the bears magically turned into men and climbed into a strange-looking canoe to row to shore. Only when the French took a number of the Micmacs aboard the ship did the Indians realize that it was manmade. Even then they must have regarded the metal work and the planking as we might regard the interior of an alien spaceship.[12]

The French recorded that encounter as well, and what they saw was quite different from what the Micmac saw, just as their culture was different from the Micmac's. The French assumed that the "two fleets of savage canoes," which approached them on July 6, 1534, had a warlike purpose. In Cartier's words, though the natives "all came after our longboat, dancing and showing many signs of joy, and of their desire to be friends . . . we did not care to trust to their signs and waved to them to go back . . . and seeing that no matter how much we signed to them, they would not go back, we shot off over their heads two small cannon. On this they began to return towards [the shore], after which they began to come on as before. And when they had come alongside our longboat, we shot off two fire-lances which scattered among them and frightened them so much that they began to paddle off in very great haste."[13]

The Micmac hunters and the French explorers reacted to what they saw and later recalled, in entirely different ways precisely because their prior experiences and technologies were so different. Both accounts were fully sensate, both purporting to be accurate observations, and as different as any two accounts could be. What is equally important, and will become a major theme in the chapters of this book, is that each groups' sensations and perceptions conflicted with the other's and became a cause of contention.

Sight is not the only sense that has left an impression on the historical record, however. Mark Smith's wonderful essay on sounds of plantations and industrial plants in the antebellum South and North takes aim at our "ocular-centrism." Smith argues that we have given up too soon on the historical importance of sound—the importance it had to our forebears and should have to us—because it is so "ephemeral."[14] The planter South had its characteristic soundscapes–the rising and falling chants of slaves, the crack of whips on mules and men's backs–which whites and blacks understood intimately, a world of sound different from the thump and whine of mill factories and the wall of street noise in northern cities familiar to Yankees. Yet it is the very immediacy of sound that makes it so important in understanding the past. In oral societies, the speaker and the auditor depend upon sound production and the common understanding of sound's meaning. At Second Creek in the Mississippi Delta on the eve of the Civil War, a small circle of slaves talked about what they would do if they had power, falsely secure in their belief that their masters could not hear them, that black voices did not travel to white ears.[15]

In some cultures smell is the predominant sense.[16] Odor recognition is a chemical process. We can distinguish about ten thousand different odors, which not only warn us of danger or remind us that mealtime is near but are able to entice, depress, sadden, and elate us as well. Odorous molecules, unlike light and sound, go directly to the brain, but their meaning is mediated by memory and social learning. Indeed, smell is more closely linked to memory than sight or hearing, so recognition of a particular smell will bring a more immediate response than a light or a sound. Among many cultures, social status is directly related to odor. Pastoralists look down upon fishermen, because fish offal is malodorous (while, to the herders at least, cattle dung is not). Early modern French doctors identified certain odors as signs of disease, and at the end of the eighteenth century, the French Royal Medical Society commissioned a study of dangerous shipboard odors to determine their origins. In nineteenth-century American culture, to smell bad (to be "odorous") was to exhibit invidious social inferiority. Slaveholders in the antebellum South justified their "peculiar institution" in part by recoiling from the "stench" of African Americans. Among some African peoples, evil spirits invisible to the eye make their presence known by their fetor. Today the "great unwashed" are objects of fear, scorn, and derision. Derogatory olfactory language is often gendered; for example, the Spanish word for prostitute, *puta,* is an insult that derives from the Latin for putrid smelling.[17]

In still other cultures, touch remains the primary way to know about the world. When Europeans encountered Native Americans, for example, they were struck by the latter's use of touch to establish intimacy as part of the rituals of greeting. The novel and hence potentially dangerous thereby became familiar and could be incorporated into the rest of the ceremony of welcoming strangers. In 1536, Alvar Núñez Cabeza de Vaca, marooned on the coast of

Mexico, meeting a group of Indians who had never seen Europeans before, re-called that "after becoming somewhat accustomed to us [a party of two Span-iards and one African] they [Caddoan-speaking Indians from the Gulf of Mexico] reached their hands to our faces and bodies, and passed them in like manner over their own." A bad idea as it turned out, for the newcomers brought with them all manner of invisible pathogens, which carried off the populations of entire native villages.[18]

The Historical-Minded Use of Our Senses

If in the past our predecessors' use of the senses was culturally bound, how can we, bound as well by our culture, recover what others long ago saw, heard, and smelled? Must we concede the inevitable presentism in every sensory history? Perhaps we can consider the problem from a wholly different perspective. Even today, the child learns to perceive through a process of social education of the senses. That process, as old as history itself, applies to adults as well as children. Indeed, we even alter the sensate environment to conform to learned priorities of sensation. Medieval gardeners sought to improve the odor of the rose because everyone knew that the sinner stank but that the saint had a per-fumed aura. Modern campers and tourists in Northern New Mexico are struck by the explosion of colors at sunset—the purples and pinks of land and sky. Cloud formations rushing over the mesas have a multilayered texture of whites, greys, and blacks that visitors from the east coast have never seen. The starry night visible from the plains of the Zuni Pueblos of New Mexico draws the observer into the sky itself. But one searches in vain for such observations in Pedro de Castañeda's account of Franciso Vázquez de Coronado's two-year sojourn in this same place, four hundred and fifty years ago.[19] Cabeza de Vaca wandered over the Gulf Coast, the Texas plains, and the desert of southern New Mexico for eight years, but his journal of "things seen and heard" is lit-erally colorless. Of the Rio Grande, Cabeza de Vaca merely commented, "We forded a very large river, the water coming up to our breasts . . . the river ran between some ridges." In hindsight, we can excuse his relative color-blind-ness—for men of religious learning in his epoch, color was dangerous. Piety was austere, and artists were ordered to celebrate light, shadow, and design over bold pigments.[20] In our eagerness to return to nature, to seek out wilder-ness, we have taught ourselves to distinguish the minute varieties of color that older cultures, more concerned with shelter, warmth, and sustenance, did not have time to savor.

At the same time, we know that the receptivity of the senses—that is, our ability to describe what we have sensed—can be expanded with experience. As early as the 1760s, Adam Smith taught his students that they had to learn the correspondence between what they saw and what they read. So it is with touch. Where we may feel only soreness, a trained massage therapist can feel muscle tone, fluid rhythms, and tissue damage. Under his tutelage, we become more "in touch" with our bodies.[21] The neophyte wine sampler can smell fruit and taste sweetness or dryness. With the same sip, the expert can tell the difference between violets and sage in the bouquet of a wine and distinguish green apples from plums in the front of the palate. Over time, and with study, the neophyte becomes a connoisseur of these aromas and tastes.[22] The Apollo astronauts had to learn how to perceive a landscape the way a geologist reads it in order to carry out geological experiments on the surface of the Moon. For this, their senses had to be tuned during walks through the great geological formations of the Southwest, tutored by a leading field geologist.[23]

There is no more striking historical example of the education of the senses than early modern Europeans' efforts to come to grips with the discovery of the climates, landscape, flora, and fauna of the New World. As Sabine Mac-Cormack has written, "The first Europeans to reach America expected to find there things that they already knew."[24] But when they arrived, they had to re-educate themselves. The Jesuit José de Acosta, tutored by Aristotelian texts to expect that the seas in the torrid zone around the Equator would boil with "violent heat," reported with surprise, "when I passed the equator, which was when the sun was at its zenith there, I felt so cold that I was forced to go into the sun to warm myself. What could I do then but laugh at Aristotle's *Meteorology* and his philosophy?"[25] Indeed, New World visitors like the Dominican friar and reformer Bartolomé de las Casas claimed that eyewitness accounts trumped biblical and classical texts precisely because first-hand experience had tutored the senses of the visitors. Anthony Pagden calls "these discourses of privileged visions" the "autotopic I" and argues that critics of the Spanish treatment of the Indians, like Las Casas, defended the authenticity and objectivity of their accounts by elevating the eye that saw the New World above all the learned authors who had never been there. Only first-hand experience could educate the senses, and only educated senses could see through the differences in Indian and Spanish ways of life to the essential similarity of peoples on both continents.[26] Cabeza de Vaca may not have described the colors of plants and the landscape, but he became a superb reader of minute distinctions of dress and hair arrangement among the various clans and villages of the Indians he encountered, because distinguishing a friendly people from an unfriendly one was a matter of life and death. Surely historians can follow this path, becoming historically minded about sensations even as they concede that perception is not the same as sensation.

Going Back in Time

But even if historians can expand their senses, can they do more than approximate the immediate sensory experiences of people long ago? "Humanistic" geographers offer us some help in this regard. They suggest that we can begin to make distinctions between landscapes, the actual forms of the land, and scenery, what people said they sensed.[27] At base, this is a variant of Reid's theory, but it takes us a step closer to recovering past sensation. If we assume also that we have the same perceptual apparatus as the people we are studying in the past, and can sense the world as they did, we are another step closer to our objective.[28]

Still, one can ask how the historian hunched for days over the flaking, yellowed pages of parchment rolls in the archives, scribbling penciled notes on five-by eight cards (or nowadays tapping lightly on the keys of a laptop personal computer), can begin to re-educate his or her senses to recapture that sensory past? Might we filter out the clutter of modernity that stands in the way of every historical flight by using our senses like a child unburdened by the weight of modernity?[29] Perhaps we can do this if we follow children and their parents to the living museums that dot our country.

Commercial enterprises dedicated to recapturing the sensate past abound in the United States. Every battlefield saved from the developer's tract housing and the concessionaire's theme park is an example of the assumption that the past can "live again." Across the land historical restorations and re-enactments bring the past to life for tourists, school children, and teachers. Attendance at some of these—millions a year at sites like Colonial Williamsburg, Virginia— demonstrates that people want to revisit the past. If one is disinclined to leave the chair in front of the television set, cable stations like the History Channel, the Learning Channel, and the Discovery Channel regularly offer historical programs. The grainy documentary films, "talking heads" of scholars, and re-enactments of events "where they actually occurred" bring a simplified version of history into the home. The re-enactors speak English of course, so that American audiences can understand them, or do not speak at all, allowing narrators to tell us what is happening. Camera angles, often from below, prevent the viewer from seeing how much the landscape has changed over time and how few re-enactors are necessary to reproduce a scene. Documentary filmmakers like Ken Burns rely upon an additional technique, the slow pan over a photograph or an artist's depiction while a famous voice reads from diaries, letters, and official reports, a fife or fiddle playing dolefully in the background.[30]

In the course of research for this book, I journeyed to many of these historical sites, restored and renovated, re-created and repopulated, and spent hours in the company of curators, interpreters, and guides. I took along a tape recorder, sketchbook, and camera to capture impressions of people and places, material goods, and climate. I met dedicated re-enactors justifiably proud of the historical verisimilitude of their grounds, buildings, and re-enactments, men and women whose fund of knowledge was almost inexhaustible. But all the while we knew the difference between the original and the re-creation.[31] Some otherwise splendid re-creations, like Plimouth Plantation and Jamestown Settlement, lie just far enough away from the original site to make picky scholars a little uneasy. Even at Colonial Williamsburg, a "living museum" on the site of the colonial Virginia capital, many of the colonial buildings had vanished by the 1920s, when Rockefeller funds and preservationist researches rebuilt the town on its old foundations.[32] Much love and historical research went into these reconstructions, but some remain conjectural.

Attempts to recover old dialects have been equally problematic. The accent that British expert Martin Waklyn taught the first re-enactors (called firsthand interpreters) at Plimouth Plantation is a version of English supposedly spoken in Ireland at the beginning of the seventeenth century and still spoken there. The current crop of re-enactors learn the accent from tapes. But visitors journeying to the restoration from Lincolnshire, England, the home of many of the Pilgrims, expecting to hear the men and women "playing" those settlers speak with a familiar northern English burr, are disappointed. "That's not right," they told one of the curators, "we don't sound like that."[33]

Or look like that. Take the case of Old York, Maine, now a picture-postcard-pretty adjunct to a thriving seacoast resort. In the 1880s, when well-to-do vacationers discovered the pleasures of summering on the south coast of Maine, York's colonial village still existed (it dated from the 1640s), but it was careworn. Bypassed by the industrial development and demographic growth of southern New England, its colonial buildings still stood because there were no resources to replace them with more modern structures. Nevertheless, it had a history and a will to beautify itself. Around the burial ground, the old church, and the colonial tavern the villagers fashioned what historian Joseph Conforti called a "quaint antiquity." Prodded by the Old York Historical and Improvement Society, founded in 1899, the town purchased land and turned it into a commons green, to which in later years were hauled colonial buildings from other locations. The village was "tidied," historical memorials erected, the church and tavern refurbished, walking paths cut and the landscape spruced up. The old jail was transformed into a museum.[34] When I first visited the historical society library and walked the green in 1996, I found what appeared to be a typical New England colonial town that was almost entirely an artifact of a much more recent historical consciousness. My notebook entry at that time waxed eloquent about a pristine colonial village untouched by time. There is such a thing as too naive a realism.

There is another, more disturbing because more purposeful, side to reenactment and restoration that may misrepresent and even misuse the past. Many restorations and living museums are commercial as well as scholarly and public-spirited ventures. As such, they sell a vision of historical process, of the way that people lived, as well as provide a replica of the artifacts of the past. Within the staff of curators, interpreters, and business vice presidents, there is often a tug of war over which facts to stress. Should the harsh side or the heroic side be shown to the public? Should the emphasis be on great men and their families or on ordinary people? Colonial Williamsburg, for example, has come far from its 1950s sanitized self. Then, one had to look hard indeed to find evidence of slavery—the labor system that permitted the wealthy of the town to gain and keep their riches. Now, slave re-enactors are everywhere apparent on the streets, but there is still a gap between what one might call the "high" story of the elite and the "low" story of the slave. The "historical interpreters," guides on the "Patriots' Tour" at the capitol building, where Patrick Henry spoke against the Stamp Act, do not mention the hypocrisy of a planter elite bewailing England's plan to enslave the colonies. The largely white re-enactors inside homes like the Wythe House avoid the topic of miscegenation even though the owner of that house, lawyer and law professor George Wythe, was reputed at the time to have had a child with his ex-slave Lydia Broadnax, after the death of his wife. Wythe later became one of the most outspoken advocates of the rights of free men and women of color, and he freed his slaves. Meanwhile, as you stroll along the streets outside, the African-American Interpretation and Programs guides on the "Other Half Tour" not only tell you the tale as you might have heard it in 1775 but use it to explain the politics of master-slave relations. More important, the two stories never quite meet. There is no incontrovertible factual evidence (that is, no document) to prove the story of Wythe and Broadnax, and the interpreters are loathe to go beyond what can be documented.[35]

The interpreters working in these situations face a unique set of problems; they are employees of a business and so may not send visitors away with a bad taste in their mouths. For that reason, much of what the interpreters say is scripted, and the script is designed to appeal to audiences. Yet the interpreters have opinions of their own, and personal approaches to the historical events they depict. A first-hand relation of the problems of the interpreters of slavery at Williamsburg from one of their number, Karen E. Sutton, explains how these multiple concerns shape the performance: "The challenge of representing eighteenth-century black chattel slavery is to strike a balance between being truthful and being tasteful. To be truthful means to relate enough of the story to be accurate without overloading the visitor with information. To be tasteful means presenting the information in a way that may unsettle, but does not offend the visitor . . . I try to paint a vivid picture of slave life, one that affects the audience's emotional sensibilities—but not so vivid they want to run for the nearest exit."[36]

There are other, more mundane ways in which neither the original site nor the restoration captures the essence of the original. On hot summer days, the first Jamestown settlers suffered terribly from thirst. The brackish water of Jamestown Island made everyone ill, and the supply of beer and cider from England, when it came, was soon gone. There were no bathrooms then, and human waste congealed in the shallow water table. But visitors to Jamestown Settlement, a stone's throw upriver from the original site, can enjoy bottled water and visit restrooms in an air-conditioned museum and gift shop. The interpreters are knowledgeable and dressed in period custom—but the bus loads of visitors swarming over the landscape deny the experience any verisimilitude. Nearby Jamestown National Park is far quieter, and its archeological recoveries are striking evidence of the first settlers' world, but the serenity and openness of the site are in their own way the very opposite of what Jamestown must have been like at its inception.

For those who are trying to recover the everyday sensory world of the past in these living museums, the effort to close the gap between then and now can be vexing, as Ms. Sutton discovered when one visitor complained about Sutton's presentation. The visitor did not want to hear about the pervasiveness of slavery, or the way in which the Williamsburg economy depended on its bondsmen and women. It would have overwhelmed her, and she could not bear the thought of it. Indeed, going back to the past, for example, as a Civil War re-enactor, can be an overwhelming sensory experience. As Howard Mansfield wrote after joining the Sixth New Hampshire Regiment at the re-enactment of the battle of Antietam, "In all my dreams, I'm marching to the drums. Long lines of union blue stretch over a hill into the morning light . . . to stand shoulder to shoulder in a line of forty or so men and fire in unison, as thousands fire, to wheel and move as a unit, the whole spectacle stays with you." On the anniversary of the battle, Mansfield and his comrades strode into the cornfield, where, in the space of a drowsy late summer morning more than one hundred thirty years earlier, eight thousand men had been killed or wounded. "It's smoky, misty, dark, mysterious . . . cannons flare orange-red . . . shake the earth, smash your ears. The Confederate gray blends into the low-lying fog and the gun smoke. Long gray lines of soldiers appear and disappear . . . lost at one moment, and then at the next rapidly gaining definition. They are charging forward, the fog seeming to reform itself as men with muskets." Indifference to the gap between then and now can be dangerous, however, for all the immersion in the rites of Civil War soldiering that the re-enactors practice. Mansfield: "Fifty feet from us, I can read the eyes of a Confederate captain. His sword held high, he charges his men toward us. He is screaming. If he had live ammunition he would kill me."[37]

It almost happened to Clinton Wakefield Epps.[38] On July 1, 1998, more than twenty thousand men converged on Gettysburg to begin the largest re-enactment ever of the 1863 battle. Wearing the clinging woolens of the Confederate troops, shouldering his six-pound Enfield rifled musket, Epps, a twenty-two-year-old re-enactor from Charlottesville, Virginia, had looked forward to the gathering in the lolling fields of south-central Pennsylvania. He basked in something like the comradeship of General George Pickett's Virginia Division of Lee's Army of Northern Virginia and knew, at least for a moment, the exhilaration of the fateful charge up Cemetery Ridge. Re-enactors are the ultimate "explornographers"—voyeuristic seekers of long-lost explorers' experiences. "In its classic hard core form, explornography is the depiction of genuine voyages of discovery" with rescue nearby.[39]

Unfortunately, someone had actually loaded a lead ball in one of the pistols and discharged it on the battlefield, causing injury to Epps. Fortunately, the ball missed the arteries in the neck, and the wounded man recovered after surgery in a nearby hospital. Before modern medical treatment, such a wound might have been fatal or at least crippling. At the scene, many observers agreed that greater care would have to be taken to prevent future mishaps. But the lesson for us is unmistakable: The re-enactment could begin to approximate the past reality. In historical fact, more than twenty-five thousand men were killed, wounded, or missing in action after the battle, and only the exhaustion of both sides, followed by a week of downpours, ended the carnage.

The sensory experiences of the combatants filled their diaries and correspondence. At Gettysburg, the heat approached 100 degrees Fahrenheit. Men collapsed from heat exhaustion and thirst or wandered away from their units in search of water. In combat, clouds of discharged black powder, with its high saltpeter content, made already parched nasal passages and throats sting like fire. The smoke burned the eyes. Together the screeching of the attackers and the shouts of the defenders, the agonizing cries of the wounded, the roar of cannon, the buzzing of near misses, and the terrible thock of iron balls the size of large marbles tearing into flesh overwhelmed the ears. Even those who walked away intact took days to breathe, see, and hear clearly, and years to sleep free of the remembered horrors of battle.[40]

Thus, for all their shortcomings, the living museums and historical re-enactments do capture essential sensory truths. My own experience with living history is less dramatic than Epps', but one episode stands out. While working on a book on the witchcraft trials in colonial Salem, Massachusetts, I journeyed to Danvers, the site of many of the supposed bewitchings.[41] When night came, I left the lighted areas and wandered out into a field. The heat of the summer day had dissipated, and I was alone with my thoughts and the night sounds. As a mental exercise, I convinced myself that I believed in Satan and all his evil works, that witches could make pacts with the devil to bring harm to innocent people, and that some of the women and men in the homes around me might secretly be those witches. The more I threw myself into my fantasy, the more menacing the night became. A dog's barking nearby—perhaps at my scent—became ominous. I knew that animals could be "familiars"—the go-betweens—of the devil and his crew. The rustle of the leaves in trees that bordered the field raised prickles on my skin. Then, out of the corner of my eye, I imagined (I think) that I saw an opaque humanoid shape sliding out from the trees toward me—and I abruptly ended my thought experiment and quick-stepped back to the street where I had parked my car.

Sweating, my breath coming in raspy gulps, but comforted by the familiar array of dials and switches of the dashboard, I laughed at myself. After all, it was only a complex of soccer fields behind the memorial the town erected to the victims of the witch hunt. Still, the moment of terror was real. As a scholar, I had long conceded that in 1692 people might well fear witches' malice. For a few moments in that field, I too knew with absolute certainty that witches could journey through the night in spectral form to do their mischief. I believe that when all the qualifications are entered and all the caveats filed, the re-creations and the re-enactments, the interpreters and the travels to historical sites do enable us to sense a little more of the world we have lost.

Conveying Sensate Experience in Words:
Some Precedents

Even if historians can satisfy themselves that they can recover the sensory world of their ancestors, can they convey that sensory past to their auditors and readers? Here we have a version of the "lemon" problem. I can taste a lemon and savor the immediate experience of my senses; I can recall the taste after I have thrown away the fruit; but can I use words and pictures to convey to another person exactly what that sensation was? Must that person find and taste a lemon to fully understand what I am saying or, rather, to get at the reality behind my words? As the exiled Bolingbroke, urged to remember happier days in England, raged in Shakespeare's *Richard II:* "Who can . . . cloy the hungry edge of appetite, By bare imagination of a feast." But imagination it must be, for conveying the life of the senses in the past to present-day readers cannot be a science.

Immersion helps. Consider Laurel Thatcher Ulrich's prize-winning *A Midwife's Tale, The Life of Martha Ballard, Based on Her Diary, 1785–1812* (1991), which transformed a slender and terse diary of midwife, mother, and businesswoman Martha Ballard of Hallowell, Maine, into a source that enables us to imagine the entire range of women's activities in early modern New England. We feel the cold of the winters' nights and the rough textures of homespun because Ulrich lived the story. She spent enough time on the upper Penobscot to enter Ballard's world.[42] Ulrich's prose conveys her own intimate experience. She claims that the diary speaks for itself—"One might wish for more detail, for more open expressions of opinion, fuller accounts of medical remedies or obstetrical complications, more candor in describing physicians or judges, and less circumspection in recording scandal, yet for all its reticence, Martha's diary is an unparalleled document in early American history. It is powerful in part because it is so difficult to use, so unyielding in its dailiness."[43] In fact, it is with Ulrich's eyes, not Ballard's, that we see Northern New England at the end of the eighteenth century.

Ulrich's ability to see and hear the past directly is heir to two great nineteenth-century depicteurs, Henry David Thoreau, a naturalist, essayist, and amateur historian, and Francis Parkman, the foremost of the romantic chroniclers of the "golden age" of American historiography, and one of our own more immediate progenitors, Samuel Eliot Morison. We know Thoreau as the man of letters whose travel journals have become memoirs of New England at mid-nineteenth century. He was also a student of history. In July 1845, stepping out from Concord, "the oldest inland town in New England," where from "a hundred hills I can see civilizations and abodes of man afar," he searched for the signs of the Indian predecessors of the New England farmers. "I have not seen one on the Musketaquid for many a year [save] . . . A lone Indian woman without children, with her dog . . . insulted by school children, making baskets and picking berries . . . wearing the shroud of her race . . . Not yet absorbed into the elements again; a daughter of the soil; one of the nobility of the land."[44]

Thoreau walked in two eras at the same time, seeing the Indian village as an overlay on the New England towns. But even Thoreau, who never doubted the power of his imagination to make the leap back in time as long as he could stand in the place where the Indian once stood, worried that he could not know what the Indian knew. "Our scientific names convey a very partial information only; they suggest certain thoughts only . . . The *arbor-vitae* . . . is but a word . . . but there are twenty words for the tree and its different parts which the Indian gave, which are not in our botanies, which imply a more practical and vital science. He used it every day . . . A rumor has come down to us that the skin of a lion was seen and his roar heard here by an early settler. But there was a race here that slept on his skin."[45]

I am not arguing for a license to invent wholesale the report of senses past,[46] but I believe that the historian who travels to sites to see and hear what the historical record merely sketched, can, like Thoreau, trust his or her imagination. The model for us all (shorn, one hopes, of its ethnocentrism) is Francis Parkman's travels to historical sites. There, as though "he were present on the historical scene, observing people in action;[47] he stretched his powers of sensory empathy to the limit.

For example, in 1842, Parkman spent his sophomore year's vacation from Harvard touring historical places in the Adirondacks. With notebook in hand to record his impressions, he imagined how the scene must have appeared in 1757, in the third year of the French and Indian War.[48] One of the most melancholy relics of the war was the ruins of Fort William Henry, whose siege and capitulation the final chapters of James Fenimore Cooper's *Last of the Mohicans* immortalized. Cooper's fanciful account had little historical truth,[49] but Parkman's imagination was stirred by it: "I went this morning to see William Henry. The old fort is much larger than I had thought; the earthen mounds cover many acres. It stood on the southwest extremity of the lake close by the water. The enterprising genius of the inhabitants has made a road directly through the ruins, and turned bastion, moat, and glacis into a flourishing cornfield, so that the spot so celebrated in our colonial history is now scarcely to be distinguished."[50] Forty years later, Parkman burnished the memory of his trip in the first pages of his account of the siege: "The earthen mounds of Fort William Henry still stand by the brink of Lake George; and seated at the sunset of an August day under the pines that cover them, one gazes on a scene of soft and soothing beauty, where dreamy waters reflect the glories of the mountains and the sky. As it is to-day, so it was then; all breathed repose and peace"[51]—a peace soon shattered by war whoops and puffs of musketry as Montcalm's force of French and Indians fell upon the garrison. Time and romantic convention obviously had embellished Parkman's recollection of the fort, but his visit in 1842 gave authority to his later, imagined, eyewitness account of the events of August 1757.

Morison, a poor relation of Boston Brahmins, was the most luscious historical prose stylist of his day (which spanned the middle half of the twentieth century). An avid sailor, he was the greatest chronicler of the European explorers of the New World and, not incidentally, Parkman's editor and intellectual debtor. In the preface to his final volume on the voyages of discovery, Morison wrote that "T. S. Eliot's injunction in his *East Coker*, 'Old men ought to be explorers,' has appealed to me; and I would add, 'Young historians, too.' In the 1930s I followed Columbus across the Atlantic and around the West Indies in barquentine *Capitana* and ketch *Mary Otis* . . . I cannot claim to have followed the discoverers of the River Plate under sail; but I have flown over that great inland waterway where the adaptable Spanish rowed, towed, and kedged, their *bergantinas* for thousands of miles. There is nothing like a personal visit to newly discovered lands to bring home to one the pioneers' dangers and difficulties."[52] Whatever his Eurocentric prejudices may have been, Morison's eyewitness confidence and deep sympathy for the navigators and mariners of the early modern world lent to his accounts of the voyages an intimacy and authority they could never have otherwise had.

If hardly anyone can live up to the standard of a Thoreau, a Parkman, a Morison, or an Ulrich, these writers offer models of descriptive vigor and imagination.[53] They inspire us, but how are we to duplicate their feats? The answer is, by accepting their invitation to recover the intimate sensory details of the past. Consider one more recent effort. From a terse entry in Ralph Lane's report of his journey up the Roanoke River in 1586 with a small number of troops and his Indian guide, Manteo, anthropologist Lee Miller has fashioned a compelling scene just before an Indian attack. The text of the source document is in italics in her book, alerting the reader to the extent of her invention. "The wherries ride alone in the river. The soldiers' rations are now utterly spent. As evening shadows stretch across the water, suddenly *we heard certain savages call, as we thought, Manteo*. And then a profound silence. Not a rustle along the bank. Not a stirring. At Lane's insistence Manteo shouts back, as a song eerily floats out of the forest. The men confidently conclude it was *in token of our welcome to them.* Manteo knows otherwise."[54] Some of this scene can be inferred from the surviving documents, but some, including the stillness, is dramatic license, and dramatic license is the use of historical imagination.[55]

Of course, even the most imaginative attempts to conflate direct sense experience and historical evidence have obvious limitations, particularly when the site no longer resembles its historical predecessor. The banks of the Roanoke are still overgrown, but the visitor need not fear a shower of arrows. We have to imagine what Lane saw. In February 1995, a Fort Lauderdale, Florida, newspaper reporter and photographer attempted to retrace the voyage through the Everglades that reporters from a New Orleans paper had made in 1883. Instead of the islands of mangrove and other semitropical trees, set in a sea of sawgrass, the modern travelers found a system of dikes, canals, water drainage pumps, and flat farmland. The word *Everglades* still existed on the map, but the physical reality—and the historical setting—had just about vanished.[56]

A caveat of my own: How far can we go beyond those documentary sources to re-create the past as it "might have been"? Can we follow Simon Schama to the edge of the novella? "Pure inventions, based, however, on what documents suggest"?[57] At the other end of the spectrum are historians who treat documentary evidence as no more than literary texts, from which one must draw out semiotic connections in groups of symbols and signs. One of the foremost modern exponents of semiotic study of texts put its purpose simply: "Semiotics is not about the 'real' world at all, but about complementary or alternative actual models of it . . . thus semiotics never reveals what the world is, but circumscribes what we can know about it . . . it is the interplay between 'the book of nature' and its human decipherer that is at issue."[58] In other words, historians adopting the semiotic pose regard written evidence of the past as a system of messages, a code, or a script, which intimates interpreted in contemporary terms. But even in this arcane effort of translation, the historian must assume the possibility of reading from the text what the people then tried to put in it. We do not need semiotic circularities to tell us that Schama is right to this extent: As historians we invariably claim the authority to touch (yes, to sense directly) past reality.

Sensory History

Let me summarize. To begin to recover the lost world of the senses, to read back from perceptions to intimate, immediate past reality, we can visit the sites and trust our senses "in situ," we can stand with the re-enactors in the living museums, we can read the documentary evidence with our minds open to sensory cues. We can transmit something of this lost sensory world to our readers.

What, then, are we to make of what we have found? What story are we to tell? Can recovery of the sensate world we have lost have other uses than the purely depictive? The answer is yes, though sometimes we may not recognize this. As precedent, I cite one memorable example. In a famous address at the Chicago World's Fair in 1893, then young historian Frederick Jackson Turner called the frontier experience the most significant fact in the evolution of American institutions. He wrote that "the wilderness masters the colonist. It finds him a European in dress, industries, tools, modes of travel, and thought. It takes him from the railroad car and puts him in the birch canoe. It strips off the garments of civilization and arrays him in the hunting shirt and the moccasin."[59] Turner may have gone too far in claiming that American social and economic development derived from the repetition of the frontier experience throughout our history, and historians have not taken the "frontier thesis" seriously for a long time.[60] But in his desire to depict the change in manners and mores in a graphic and striking manner for popular audiences, Turner's frontier thesis rested upon a theory of sensory causation—a facet of his remarkable work that we have yet to explore. It was a highly sensate experience that Turner was describing, in which a continuous immersion in new sights, sounds, and smells induced Europeans to reinvent themselves as Americans. Sensation caused change in political habits, social ways, and cultural understandings.

The French historian Lucien Febvre inaugurated the modern, self-conscious study of the senses. He saw it as a gateway to a history of "sensibilities," the mental equipment by which people in the past organized thought and emotion.[61] As Alain Corbin, Febvre's successor, now teaches us, sensory evidence can be a superb introduction to the study of social and cultural conflicts. Consider the sound of church bells: "It is not easy to picture the emotional power wielded by bells at the end of the Old Regime [in France]." People later remembered the multiple, overlapping "rings" (sets of bells), the various peals (the notes) and tones of individual bells, with a sense of nostalgia and loss. Some towns had special sets of bells, whose distinct tones announced themselves and were a source of pride to the denizens. Important religious centers had many churches and their the bells spoke to one another. But some in the society contested the very use of the bells.[62]

Can we go farther still, to argue that sensation and perception played a causal role in broader and more complex events? That contested readings of the sensuous world caused change in it? I think so, and offer the following four extended moments, four episodes in our early history, as proof that sensory history can be as important to our understanding of certain major episodes in our early history as are the more conventional political, economic, and social explanations. There are times when sensory experience is so highly charged and perception of the sensory material so exigent that it motivates people to act in ways they would not have acted otherwise. Sensation and perceptions then become contested events, markers of differing group identity and values. Sometimes these sensuously charged occasions alter the way that sights and sounds are interpreted over the years and decades thereafter. Such sensory events are both cause and effect, changing the course of history and the working of the senses.

The very first encounters of the English and the Indians in North America constitutes the first of my explorations of sensory history. The New World for the English was filled to overflowing with sensory stimuli, and for a time managing these sights and sounds occupied them more than any other project. So, too, the Native Americans were struck by new sights and sounds when the English appeared, almost as if by magic. The way in which the two peoples tried, and ultimately failed, to mediate their perceptions of each other led to violent confrontations and a series of gruesome massacres.

Transplanted English Americans possessed a robust conception of a supernatural world. In part, the contest between the English and the native was explained as the intervention of God's hand in this invisible world. At the same time, the English perceived specters, demons, and ghosts at the edge of the visible spectrum. These terrors spilled out into the everyday world during the Salem witchcraft trials, when fears of witchery had the power to turn ordinary perceptions into spectral nightmares. The excesses of the latter and the rise of a more scientific sensibility—a sensibility of numbers and abstract laws—pushed the sensory world of supernatural wonders to the margins of American culture.

Over the course of the first hundred years of slavery in the English-speaking colonies, Africans and African Americans introduced their own sensory presumptions into a hostile world. But the English saw the African as a dangerous other, and in the slave rebellions of mid-century that ready sensory categorization of otherness became even more vivid, as color came to mark danger. The suppression of the rebellions had a high sensory cost: Skin color would become a boundary to social and cultural integration—the beginnings of Jim Crow.

The religious enthusiasms of the evangelicals during the Great Awakening posed similar sensory challenges as those in the slave uprisings. Opponents of the Awakening decried the sights and sounds of the revival. At the same time, the "auditory," or audience, of the itinerant preacher and the visible signs of revival opened the door to wider sensory experiences and striking visual and auditory performance. The two sides contested the meaning and uses of the senses, and in the decline of enthusiasm, an expansive and vivid accreditation of sense data was lost.

Finally, the anti-British government protests of the 1760s and early 1770s overwhelmed the senses of contemporaries. During the course of the eighteenth century, a sensuous provincialism had emerged whose refined, genteel features visibly and audibly defined status and rank. In the 1760s and 1770s, mobs took aim at these sensory markers of privilege. The mob's purpose was first and foremost to cow officials into compliance by shows of defiance that no one could overlook. But at the height of its success, the revolutionary leadership demanded that the rich variety of voices and displays of the common people be supplanted by an orderly and respectable republican sensory etiquette. A highly vivid and auditory campaign led, through an ironic chain of events, to a dampening of the role of the senses in public life.

The foregoing are the four episodes or extended sensory moments that I selected for this book. There are many more that might have been chosen—some, I do not doubt, better examples of the genre. What motivated me in part to make the selection that I did was another, nonhistorical set of questions that long ago gave rise to my interest in sensory history. In 1965, I wrote my first graduate school seminar paper for Ernest May and Akira Iriye on American businessmen and the Japan trade from 1935 to 1939. In it I tried to apply Kurt Lewin's field theory to the way that businessmen looked at a little piece of their world.[63] From that time to this, I have been drawn to the way that sensation and perception work in our everyday lives.

In the course of my reading for this book, four problems, or (if one prefers the glass half full to the glass half empty) four opportunities for study, repeatedly suggested themselves. First, how we deal with novelty, with things, settings, and people we have never directly encountered before? Second, how do we make sense of the unseen and unheard worlds that appear to some among us—what our forbears would have called "the invisible world"? The third is how we comprehend and respond to people we perceive as "other" because they appear different from us. The fourth is how the senses tell us where we belong in society and how we should behave: sensuous etiquette. Employed as introductory devices in the four chapters that follow, these questions help focus our attention on key moments in larger historical events.

One last introductory matter before we begin. As I recounted each of the episodes, it seemed to me that, at their outset, a diversity of sensory skills and approaches was in play. Competing ways of sensing and parsing sensation allowed the protagonists to make sense of the world in their own way. In the course of each of the stories, however, diverse sensations became warring perceptions, in which one sides' way of sensing the world gave way to the other's. Something valuable was lost as one culture, or people, or system, or ideology won out over its rivals.

CHAPTER ONE

Brave New Worlds

English-Indian Encounters

How do we deal with novelty, the unexpected, the unforeseen? When our senses alert us that we face a new situation, how do we respond? Insofar as our senses are tutored by our culture, our reaction to the unfamiliar is scripted. The intonations are our own, but the words are those that every other actor in the same role recites. Such preset cognitive patterns are psychologically necessary. In every culture and for every individual, cognitive frameworks do not operate willy-nilly on novelty. Our minds work hard to fit the new into the old.[1]

To avoid cognitive dissonance, the mental friction produced by discordant perceptions, we play tricks on sensuous novelties. We can, for instance, deny novelty by categorizing the new as something that we already knew about. Or we might denigrate the new as inferior and so reduce its power to force reordering of old perceptions. We can perceive the novel in a particular or partial way, altering our interpretation of what we sensed to make it less disturbing. Or we may handle dissonance in reverse fashion, by making the new an immediate and catastrophic threat, demonizing what we cannot immediately place in a reassuring perceptual category.[2]

In general, modernity welcomes novelty and embraces change. The new and improved model is always better than last year's. Indeed, for us the word *novelty* has gained a second meaning. Surf the web for *novelty* and you will find a bewildering variety of jazz music groups, nouveau restaurants, high-tech electronics supermarkets, and low-tech party favor shops—anything to amuse, shock, and keep the party rocking. We are unafraid of what lies just ahead; convinced that we can master what we have not yet met. In fact, we regard encounters with novelty as opportune starting points for rational calculations about advantage. We confidently propose answers to questions like, In what sort of setting do we want to live? In what environment do we prefer to work? What sights and sounds and smells so please us that we desire to journey to them?[3]

But our early modern predecessors did not share our optimistic view of change or our sang-froid in its presence. Originality was frightening and the unknown could be deadly. The European explorers of the New World and the Indians who inhabited that world gave the highest priority to a swift and reliable reading of novelty. In this chapter we will ask what novelty meant to English and Indian men who met one another for the first time on the coast of North America. How did they handle the singularity of their encounters? How did sights and sounds dictate their conduct toward one another?

Some of the English who came to the Americas at the end of the sixteenth century and the beginning of the seventeenth had already traveled abroad, and more of them had read accounts of other European travelers' experiences. But much of this literature was from Spain, France, or Portugal, England's rivals for empire, and was treated with suspicion and derision in England.[4] The English decided to find out for themselves about the new plants, animals, and peoples that European visitors brought back from the Americas.[5] English demands and expectations—including the need to prove English superiority over native cultures—structured these perceptions.[6] The English approached the problem of explaining the new in terms of the old, already prepared, niches.[7] "Confrontation with novelty served to magnify a people's cultural bias: migrants saw the new environment through eyes that had adapted to other values."[8]

The Native Americans who greeted the English had either already met Europeans or had heard about them. Systems of trade up and down the coast were also news networks. Stories about Verazzano in 1524 and the Spanish slave incursions in the same decade, followed by word from the interior of the invasion of hundreds of haughty men riding tame animals as fast as deer (De Soto's expedition), all merged into a composite picture. The men with shiny hard vests and crested headdresses walked or rode in packs like wolves, spoke in harsh gutturals, and were easily offended. They demanded tribute and called themselves sons of the one true god.[9] The coastal Indians conceded that the newcomers had spiritual power—they were "manitou."[10] But the newcomers looked and sounded unlike any newcomers the coastal peoples had known.[11] Indians turned to sensory managerial skills different from those the Europeans employed to fit the new into the familiar. Thus a contest of the senses began.

When they met, what would the two groups do? Over and over, simple divergences in perception would lead to larger errors in social intercourse. But not always, and not at first, for novelty has a charm as well as a cutting edge.[12] The English and the Indians were capable of genuine wonder and even delight in the recognition of differences. But the English soon came to regard the Indians as dangerous, and they acted in aggressive anticipation of the Indians' savage nature.[13] For their part, the Indians' amiable curiosity quickly turned to injured bewilderment at the demeanor of some of the English. Some Indians tried to remain accommodating, others took flight, and many chose to resist with arms.[14]

Novel Encounters

That the novelty of the first encounters between Indians and the English would soon give way to misunderstanding may have been inevitable, because the two peoples employed their senses in such profoundly different ways. We can glimpse the differences in two accounts of encounters, the first a story that a Delaware Indian told to a Moravian missionary sometime in the early nineteenth century, the second a report that Thomas Harriot (sometimes spelled *Hariot*), a young university-trained scientist, wrote of his stay among the Roanoke Indians, in 1584 and again from 1585 to 1586. From these, we will turn to the ways that Indians and English New World visitors tried to make sense of the novelty of meeting one another for the first time, that is, how they tried to organize their respective sensory experiences. Over time, these sensory experiences not only influenced the actions of both parties when they met but also shaped the enfolding of the longer course of events. Curiosity gave way to animosity and violence, and in the end, one set of sensory experiences came to dominate the other, impoverishing the common sensory store of both the Indians and the English.[15]

What the Delaware Said

In the early 1800s, John Heckwelder, a Moravian missionary long stationed among Ohio's native peoples, wrote down a story told him by an old Delaware Indian about an encounter between Indians and Europeans.[16] The Delaware of New Jersey were among the first east coast Algonquians to greet the Dutch and later the English, although by the end of the colonial period most had moved from New Jersey to the Ohio country or to Canada.

Word pictures and mental impressions of the newcomers traveled wherever native peoples met.[17] The oral culture of the natives was rich, encompassing and facilitating pedagogy, diplomacy, and adjudication of disputes as well as entertainment.[18] One of the preeminent figures in that culture was the story-teller. The storyteller is the custodian and the living library of custom, ritual, identity, and meaning in social intercourse. Storytellers embellished their offerings with every telling. Leslie Marmon Silko, a modern Pueblo storyteller, recalls of one of her predecessors: "The old teller had been on every journey and she knows all the escape stories, even stories told before she was born. She says, 'with these stories we can escape almost anything with these stories we will survive.' She keeps the stories for those who return, but more important for the dear ones who do not come back so that we may remember them and cry for them with the stories."[19]

The sensory content and the causal role that sensation played in the story are seamlessly interwoven in the rhetorical conventions the storyteller followed. He began, "It was long ago." Indians were not indifferent to precise measures of elapsed time when appropriate; they deployed both linear and nonlinear notions of chronology. When recalling wars, treaties, individual heroics, and migrations, Indian chronologies could be fairly precise.[20] Indians were myth makers as well, setting the origins of social customs and migrations in a time indistinct or immemorial.[21] By convention, the Hopi storyteller starts with "humma-hah," roughly translated "long ago."[22] The Delaware tale, set "long ago," represents the collective recollection of a real event. Indians fishing at the mouth of the "river that flowed into the sea" (the Hudson River) espied "something remarkably large floating on the water, such as they had never seen before." The native observers tried to make sense of what they were seeing. "The whole appearance . . . was to them a subject of wonder." Was it a big house? an animal? an island? As more Indians gathered and chiefs were summoned, they talked among themselves and decided that it was the house of a Manitou, a powerful spirit familiar to Indians, although this one, with its many attendants, was unlike any they knew. In any case, such spirits had to be appeased.

By emphasizing the senses rather than power or dominion, the Delaware's story is an encounter of equals. There was no invasion, conquest, or subjugation of one people by another, and the outcome of the meeting was not foretold.[23] Instead, the story captures the wonder and worry of the Indians at the novelty of what they beheld, leaving all manner of opportunities and outcomes in the air. Of later contact between Indian and European negotiators on the Pennsylvania frontier, James Merrell wrote: "Trailing along behind [the negotiators], crowding in with them as they crossed the threshold [of the meeting places] peering over their shoulders, picking up the snatches of their conversations . . . we can make our way back to where Indian met colonist face to face."[24] So it must have been for the Delaware as they prepared to greet the Manitou. Face to face—seeing, hearing, touching for the first time.

The storyteller's repetition of phrases like "never seen before" gives the encounter a sense of living, immediate drama, as one native after another in the story recounts what he "had observed." The first spectators called others, who then hurried out to see the event that was "astonishing to their sight." They gathered and shared information, then sent runners to tell others, who arrived "in numbers," and "having themselves viewed the strange occurrence, and observing it moving," decided what it was and, even more important, what it meant. The plot line of the story is the sequence of sensory impressions. The Indians' attempts at explanations are the lesson of the tale.

The Indians delighted in the "various colors" the house and its inhabitants exhibited and the ornaments the newcomers sported. The people on the house were white, and the Manitou was dressed entirely in red and gold. Some of the Indians fled, but others stayed because novelty attracted their attention. Why, they wondered, did the Manitou have white skin? Why was he dressed in red and gold? Color and design had distinct and compelling meaning among the Indians. Although some eastern woodlands Indians went about clothed only in loincloth or apron, others wore a mixture of finely wrought pelts and skins. Algonquian speakers had "words for coat, mantle, waistcoat, apron, stockings, and shoes."[25] Delaware male dress included deerskin breechclouts and thigh-length leggings, one-piece moccasins, and in cold weather "matchcoats"—tanned deerskin cloaks draped over one shoulder and belted, or worn vest style. In winter, robes of bear, beaver, and other furs sown together appeared, the more stylish ones featuring turkey feathers. Jewelry made of copper and seashell or whalebone, beaded pouched, belts, garters, headbands, and caps, sometimes dyed red, finished the wardrobe. Men sported tattoos of animal or geometric shapes, and women rouged their faces and painted their hair. Indian moccasins were works of art—tanned, oiled, decorated, and almost waterproof.[26]

Adornment and color went hand in hand in the Indians' design sense. As William Wood described personal adornment among the Indians of coastal Massachusetts, in 1634: "Their longing after many kinds of ornaments, wearing pendants in their ears, as forms of birds, beasts, and fishes, carved out of bone, shells, and stone, with long bracelets of their curious wrought wampom

. . . which they put about their loins . . . Many of the better sort bearing upon their cheeks certain portraitures of beasts, as bears, deers, mooses, wolves." These were tattoos, "a certain incision, or else a raising of their skin by a small sharp instrument under which they convey a certain kind of black unchangeable ink. Other tattoos included "round impressions down the outside of their arms and breast in form of mullets [five-pointed stars] or spur rowels." The Indians did not content themselves with mere depictions of nature. "The sagamore [chief] with a hummingbird in his ear for a pendant, [and] a black hawk on his occiput for his plume" thought himself handsomely attired.[27]

Europeans thought that the varieties of Indian self-adornment marked "the same kind of gender and status distinctions" as existed in European society.[28] Whether or not this was so, individual adornment certainly distinguished leaders from followers and men from women. Indeed, Indians did not need clothing and jewelry to make statements about themselves. As George Percy noted in 1607 of the James River Indians, even when men dispensed with clothing and went "altogether naked [that is, except for their "privities"], some paint their bodies black, some red."[29]

Display was not mere ornamentation. Colors had meaning to the wearer. After contact with European traders, reds and blues were Indians' favored colors for cloth trade goods precisely because they conveyed messages.[30] White connoted harmony and transparency—all that was visible and tangible. White was light itself, an aid to memory and thought and a sign of optimism and power. The Cherokee used white flags as a sign of peace.[31] The white Manitou the Delaware greeted would bring new game or good fortune. Black expressed war and death. English visitors to Maine's coast in 1605 reported that "when a sagamore [chief] dieth, the people black themselves."[32] Warriors on the way to battle blackened themselves to absorb the power of the underworld.[33] Red was the color of the animate world; it suggested both anger and creativity. When Massasoit's leading men visited with the Pilgrims in 1621, the Indians decorated their faces in black dye. They were ready to fight if necessary and prepared to die. But Massasoit had painted himself red, for he was more optimistic about the meeting.[34] Red could also warn of warlike intentions.[35] In later years, the English would call the Indians red, but the origin of this depiction was some Indians painting of themselves with red ointments.[36] Blue was fanciful—a color of sky and flight. Maryland Indians painted their faces "with several colors" including blue.[37] Percy reveled in the visit of a sachem whose "body was painted all with crimson . . . his face painted blue, besprinkled with silver ore.[38] Gabriel Archer, Percy's comrade at Jamestown, thought that Indians always dyed their skin, though he could not decipher the meanings of the dyes.[39] But for any English traveler to the New World, meeting an Indian so adorned was a sensory event in itself.

The Delaware storyteller continued. Soon the moving house was close enough to the shore for the Manitou to speak to the Indians. "They are hailed from the vessel in a language they do not understand, yet they shout or yell in return by way of answer, according to the custom of their country." In the woods, where sight is often limited to the next copse of trees, recognition of sounds was crucial to Indian survival. "Calling the game" required an ability to imitate animal sounds. Hearing the approach of an enemy was a matter of life and death. In such an aural environment, the sounds of nature gained animate identity. Trees and rocks spoke; caves and mountains listened. Thunder was a message, not just a noise.[40]

Words and speech were even more important to the Indian. The modern image of the Indian as a strong, silent type is entirely misleading. Indian villages were noisy places. Women chatted as they worked alongside one another in the gardens or by the wigwams. Children cried out at play. Menfolk swapped stories and sang. When John White sketched activities at the Roanoke town of Secota, in 1585, he depicted many of his Indian subjects engaged in conversation. In the story, even if neither side quite comprehended the other's syntax, the gestures that accompanied the speech were enough to show that both sides were trying to communicate and that communication is important. So, with words and gestures, the Manitou expressed his friendship as he approached the shore.[41]

The Manitou's attendants unloaded the ship's boat. It was filled with gifts for the Indians. The Manitou—being a Manitou (even if he was one that the Delaware did not recognize)—must have known the Indian tradition that all conversations and negotiations begin with gifts. Gifts created reciprocity, defined relationships, and smoothed diplomacy. Gifts were also a matter of personal taste. The Indians also understood that gifts were part of commercial transactions, indeed, a necessary prologue to trade—but gifts were never just material things in the stream of commerce. In later years, the English would forget their manners and mistake the courtesy of gift giving for bribery, but the Manitou realized that the great man gives; he does not hoard and he does not extort.[42]

The Indians became concerned that they must receive the gifts with proper ceremony. The story grows more arresting as the chiefs array themselves in a semicircle to greet the Manitou.[43] They watched his every move, intent on divining the appropriate response. The Manitou took a bottle from a servant,

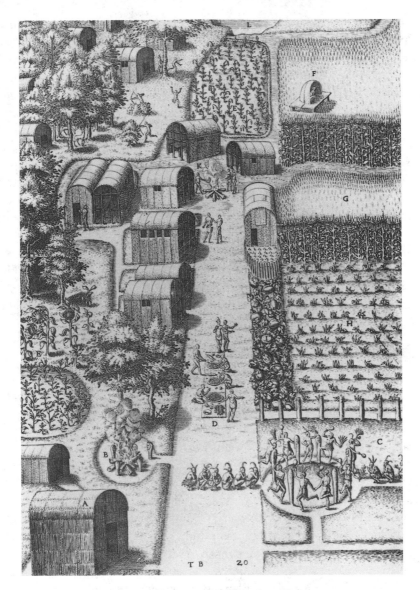

John White, *Secota*, Roanoke Indian Town, 1585

White's drawing of Secota is a composite (note the letters indicating the various sites common to all the coastal villages he visited), obviously contrived. Not only was the village too neat and geometrically regular, but White could not have viewed it from the perspective he used to depict it. It was, like Harriot's prose, an objectification of sensory data. (Published by Theodor De Bry in 1590 as an illustration for Thomas Harriot's *Briefe and True Report of the New Found Land of Virginia*.)

and from it poured liquid into a cup. He drank and then passed the cup to a chief sitting in the circle of Indians. This is remarkably like the calumet (tobacco pipe ceremony) described in French encounters with Great Lakes Indians.[44] The chief touched the cup, turning it in his hands, then smelled the contents, but did not drink, passed it to the next chief, and so around the semicircle.

Here both touch and smell have come into play, as the storyteller mixes excitement with humor, for he knows, and his listener knows, that this is the first time these Indians have been offered an alcoholic beverage. Was it a red wine? Then the Indians thought they saw a cup of blood.[45] What sort of Manitou was this? Indians knew that some of the native peoples practiced cannibalism.[46] Was the Manitou asking them to join in this sanguinary custom? The Indians were wary and skeptical. Potent spiritual figures like the Manitou sometimes played tricks or tested a man's mettle. Such caution grated on one young warrior's sense of honor, and he leapt up and harangued the chiefs. He said that to refuse to drink was an offense against the Manitou who had himself drunk from the cup. If it was death to drink the potion, then one would be all the more famous for dying in such a way.

The orator had as much or more importance in the Indians' councils as the storyteller.[47] Indians spoke in public in the order of their status. The young gave particular attention to the elder orator, as he related "the history of their nation, discoursing of occurrences, and delivering precepts and instructions for their conduct and welfare."[48] Speeches were earnest and sober, and listened to until they ended, sometimes hours after they had begun.[49] The pitch of Indian oratory, sometimes rising to a shriek, accompanied by breast-beating and hand waving, was galvanizing if somewhat daunting to the uninitiated. Even John Smith of Jamestown fame, who by his own account had seen the potentates of Christendom and the Ottoman Empire harangue one another, recoiled at the physical force with which the Indian orators made their points.[50] Some Europeans went further in admitting their bewilderment; to George Percy, the native oration seemed so much howling, stamping, and "antic tricks and faces, making noise like so many wolves or devils."[51] In later years the English, at diplomatic parleys with natives, compared the Indian vocalizations to animal sounds, "howling . . . like wolves," or the demonic, "resembling our ideas of hell."[52] But for the Indians such gestures and tones were ritual speech performance.

Having drained the cup, the young warrior "soon began to stagger, and at last fell prostrate on the ground." He was performing for an audience, and every eye followed him. His collapse was greeted with universal groaning.

Then "he wakes and jumps up and declares that he has enjoyed the most deli-
cious sensations." The cup is refilled and passed around, "and all become in-
toxicated." By adding taste to the story, the teller has brought together the operation of all the sensory organs.[53] Even the wry humor, as the storyteller
warns against the stupefying effect of alcohol, is sensate.[54]

Trade could now follow. The Manitou distributed presents of axes, hoes,
and stockings, along with glass, shell, enamel, or other manufactured beads.[55]
Appeal to the senses as well as practicality dictated preferences among the Indians. They wanted the beads for decoration. The Europeans used them the
same way, but regarded beads as poor imitations of gemstones. Only servants
and laborers wore beads as personal decorations, though those who could afford real gems might also wear a beaded glove or hat, or buy a beaded bed can-
opy or cushion. But beads, particularly those colored white, black, red, and
blue, had far greater value to the Indians because they were so rare. Had they
not come from far away? And traveling that distance, had they not gained a
kind of power that always comes from strangeness? So Indians tied beads to
the deerskin and board pouches in which they carried their infants, in order to
ward off evil spirits; and used tree gum to glue beads to their war clubs, in order to give those weapons power; and wore beads at their necks, hips, knees,
elbows, and ankles, in order to harden the body's joints; and pinned beads to
earlobes, in order to keep evil spirits from entering the body.[56] On one occasion, blue beads offered as a gift to an Indian warrior may have saved an Englishman's life. John Smith, captured by Opechancanough's band of Pamunky
Indians in 1608, gave a necklace of "sky blue beads" to his captor. Indian courtesy forbade the execution of an opposing leader who behaved in such correct
fashion.[57]

In the course of the trading, the two sides conversed in signs, the common
language of traders. Some signs were simply visual: pointing to an item, holding it up, smiling, frowning. Such signs could be matters of life and death,
however. The most obvious sign was the laying down of weapons in sight of
the other party. When Miles Standish and his party of English Pilgrims
wished to parley with approaching Indians of unknown intention, the Pilgrims lay down their muskets and signaled to the Indians to lay down their
bows.[58] One group of Croatoan Indians, desperate to identify themselves as
friends of the English after their return to the Roanoke area in 1587, begged
John White "that there might be some token or badge given them of us,
whereby we might know them to be our friends, when we met them anywhere
out of [their] town or island. They told us further that for want of some such
badge, diverse of them were hurt the year before" by the English.[59] Fifty years

later, when the Narragansett Indians joined with the English in a war against
the Pequots of Connecticut, many of the former were accidently shot by the
English. Roger Williams, advisor to the Narragansetts from his dwelling place
at Providence Plantations, wrote to the governor of Massachusetts, "I understand that the cause why the English hurt so many of the Narragansetts was
want of signs or marks [to distinguish them from the enemy]. You may please
therefore to provide some yellow or red for their heads."[60]

Some signs were understood by both sides. If the laying down of weapons
was a sign of peaceful intentions; the slotting of an arrow signaled a less amiable intent. When the Narragansetts wanted the Pilgrims of Plymouth to leave,
in 1621, they sent a snakeskin full of arrows. The meaning of the arrows was
plain. Snakes were powerful animistic figures, able to move in and out of the
ground, to hide, and to attack from ambush. The Pilgrims got the message
but had no intention of leaving. They sent the snake skin back, filled with
lead musket balls. The Narragansetts apparently understood the reply and
kept the peace with Plymouth.[61] Indians were practiced in "reading" such
signs as belts of wampum, hatchets, and the way in which body parts or weapons were held.[62]

In greeting, signs were vital, and each side used its own. In 1607, when the
English first landed on the tip of Cape Henry, at the mouth of the Chesapeake Bay, the Indians were hostile. Then Captain Christopher Newport,
who had long experience with Indians in the Caribbean, called out in a
friendly fashion and put his hand on his heart. Percy recalled: "Upon that
they laid down their bows and arrows and come very boldly to us, making
signs to come ashore to their town . . . where we were entertained by them
very kindly."[63]

Sometimes signs had to be invented on the spot. In 1602, Gabriel Archer,
camping on Cuttyhunk Island off the coast of Massachusetts, found himself
face to face with dozens of Pokanoket Warriors. Archer cleverly invented a set
of signs to convey his intentions. He clapped his hands to his head, then to his
heart, then brandished his firearm. Was it to be peace or war, he had signaled.
The sachem opposite him replicated Archer's motions, the most common of
all signing strategies, implying that he understood the message. Then Archer
stepped forward and embraced the sachem, which gesture was also returned.
Trading, the purpose of Archer's journey and the Indians' visit to the island,
commenced.[64] South Carolina Indians touched the shoulders of newcomers
to reassure them that they were safe and welcome. Indians in the gulf region
of Mississippi caressed the first French explorers.[65]

Indian Perception: Making the World Whole

For the Native American, making sense of what was seen and heard was a skill taught to children as soon as they could walk and mastered in hard schools of hunting and raiding. Watching the Indians process sensory novelties, Europeans came to believe that the Indians' senses were keener than Europeans'.[66] As one English settler in New England recalled, in 1637 he had "observed that the savages have the sense of seeing so far beyond any of our nation . . . in the sense of smelling they have very great perfection."[67] Trader John Lawson, newly arrived in Carolina and exploring the hinterland with an Indian guide, reported that "we were all asleep, in the beginning of the night, [when] we were awakened with the dismallest and most hideous noise that every pieced my ears: this sudden surprise incapacitated us of guessing what this threatening noise might proceed from, but our Indian pilot (who knew these parts very well) acquainted us, that is was customary to hear such music along that swamp-side, there being endless numbers of panthers . . . and other beasts of prey which take this swamp for their abode."[68]

The report of the senses flowed into every corner of Indian life. Even the names of the peoples were descriptive. Indian place names depicted the scenery and landscape.[69] The Abenaki of eastern Maine were the "Dawn Land People." The Algonquian Indians of the Carolina coast called themselves the Renapoak–"the real men." The Delaware, who spoke another dialect of eastern Algonquian, used the term *Lenapi*. The Wampanoags, who greeted the Pilgrims at Plymouth, were "the people of the dawn," for they lived where the sun rose on the Indians' known world. The Mohawk, who guarded the eastern door of the Iroquois confederation, were the Ganienkeh, the "people of the flint," for the flint deposits on their land.[70]

The Delaware's story reveals that Indians facing novelty applied old categories to new sense data. The Indians might not understand European metallurgy or navigation, but they recognized the power that technology gave the Europeans over nature, so they reasoned that the Europeans must be Manitou.[71] In arriving at this conclusion, the natives combined the report of all their senses, a holistic technique. Studies of modern oral cultures, including those of the Mbuti of the African Rain Forests, the Inuit of Alaska, the Saami of Finland, and the Maori of New Zealand, suggest how peoples living in close accord with nature integrate the various aspects of the senses. They process the sensory in its totality, with the result that the sense data "possess" the observer. The hunter can mimic the natural sounds and see the almost invisible trails of their prey. The wind and the odors it brings become part of this dynamic whole. The senses capture relationships, not objects. Space and form are not abstract calculations of fixed measure but part of living mental maps. Re-creations of such holistic experiences in song and dance were not artistic performances, but literal extensions of the sense data itself.[72]

Thus, when Smith was taken before the chief of the Powhatan confederation, the Englishman was treated to a sensuous performance of the Indians' cosmology. Dancers and singers, "painted ugly as the devil, howling" as they laid down rows of corn and bunches of sticks, drank and feasted. After three days, they explained that the circles of meal signified their country, the circles of corn the bounds of the sea, and the sticks Smith's country. It was the relationships that mattered to the shamans, not the precise boundaries. The dancing and singing tied the story to the past and the future, to nature and the Pamunky people. For Smith's edification, the Pamunky had acted out a creation story, a passion play, an allegory, and a natural history, all of which he dismissed in ethnocentric arrogance as "strange and vehement."[73]

As in the Pamunky ceremony, the Indians' perception was communal—individual Indians heard, saw, smelled, touched, and tasted, but meanings emerged from collective deliberation. When the Manitou in the Delaware story was still distant, the Indians gathered to dance, sing, and converse. An explanation of the novelty before them would arise out of collective effort. When the Manitou stepped on shore, the Delaware chiefs sat in a semicircle so that they could see one another as they gave sensory cues. They were close enough to pass the cup from hand to hand. They groaned as one when the young orator fell to the ground.

The communal assignment of meaning was a social act. For example, Indian shamans healed the sick utilizing shared sensory experience. "The parties that are sick or lame being brought before them," William Wood reported of New England Indians, "the powwow [shaman] sitting down, the rest of the Indians giving attentive audience to his imprecations and invocations, and after the violent expression . . . of hideous bellowing and groaning, he makes a stop, and then all the auditors with one voice utter a short canto."[74] On and on they went, the shaman bellowing and writhing, the Indians replying in chorus. Healing was a communally visible and auditory process—group primal therapy, for want of a better description.

The Senecas of New York have a tale that makes the communality of sense experience even more graphic. A young boy, tired from the hunt, rested his head against a great stone. The stone began to talk. Tired and hungry as he was, he listened, for every hunter knows that spirits dwell in objects. From the stone he learned the ways of the various game animals. He ran to his longhouse with his news, and the people "gathered around the fire and listened intently. As the boy talked, a strange thing happened. The story seemed to warm everyone and drive away the cold and snow. And everyone that night slept well and had good dreams."[75]

As the Seneca boy's tale reminds us, Indians made no sharp distinction between sensations of the everyday and perceptions that came from the spirit world.[76] When the Delaware first observed the European ship, "their conjurers were set to work" and "all idols and images were examined and put in order." The Indian was a sensory animist. The animals that he hunted, the seeds that she planted, the fish in the sea and the birds in the sky were all alive in multiform ways.[77]

A superb example of this overlapping of everyday sensation and perception of the spirit world in the native mind appears in the work of M. Scott Momaday, arguably the foremost Native American poet and novelist of the twentieth century. In his *House Made of Dawn,* a young warrior named Abel shepherds a flock of sheep through an arroyo. "Then Abel heard it, the thing itself. He knew even then that it was only the wind, but it was a stranger sound than any he had ever known. And at the same time he saw the hole in the rock where the wind dipped, struck, and rose. It was larger than a rabbit hole and partly concealed by the chokeberry which grew beside it. The moan of the wind grew loud, and it filled him with dread. For the rest of his life it would be for him the particular sound of anguish."[78] All of Abel's senses operated simultaneously on two levels. He heard the wind and saw the hole; he heard the thing itself—the moaning of the spirits at war with the land. Abel lived in his grandfather's house in a town, but he saw in his mind's eye the house made of dawn, made of all the spiritual things, of pollen and rain, of sky and the different colored clays and sands.[79] A Paiute song captures the same spiritual closeness of person and nature: "Something from there, from down in there, is talking to you. You could hear it if you listen. Listen! . . . When we pray, when we sing . . . we talk with the stones rattling in the ground . . . And the ground is hot and shaking. Something is doing that, and the People know that."[80] Then as now, the Native American spiritualist communicates "through praying, talking, singing, dancing, meditating, touching, smelling" —in a word, by connecting the workaday and the spirit worlds through the senses.[81]

Indians believed that weather and animal behavior warned of future events. Powwows or spirit chasers could gain knowledge of the future from visions and dreams. The eastern Algonquians, for example, believed that every Indian had two souls—a clear soul, resident in the heart, which guided Indians while awake, and the "dream soul," which traveled abroad while the body was asleep. Leaving the body behind, the dream soul could know future and past, paradise and evil.[82] Joseph François Lafitau, a Jesuit missionary among the Mohawks of Kahnewaka, said of his charges: "The soul of the Indians is much more independent of their bodies than ours is" and "take long journeys" during sleep. In dreams, the soul reports on its travels.[83]

The Powhatan people of the Chesapeake were warned by one such pow-wow's dream before the English arrived that "a Nation should arise [in the Po-whatan land] which would dissolve and give end to his empire."[84] When the Pilgrims defaced a Massachusetts' Indian grave site, the Indian sachem whose mother was interred there had a dream: "Before mine eyes were fast closed, methought I saw a vision, at which my spirit was much troubled . . . A spirit cried aloud 'Behold my son, whom I have cherished, see the paps that gave thee suck, the hands that lapped thee warm, and fed thee oft. Canst thou forget to take revenge of those wild people, that hath my monument defaced in despiteful manner?" The dream seemed so real that the sachem called his warriors to his side, told them what had happened, and led them to seek vengeance.[85] Another Plymouth-area Indian found an explanation in a dream for the sudden sicknesses that had beset Indians years before. As he told minister Thomas Shepard, in 1647, "Two years before the English came over into those parts there was a great dying." At the time he had a dream "in which he did think he saw a great many men come to those parts in clothes, just as the English are now apparelled, and among them arose a man all in black, with a thing in his hand which he now sees was a book . . . this black man stood upon a higher place than all the rest . . . and told the Indians that God was angry with them." Only by renouncing their sinful ways would the Indians find safety.[86]

Such dreams and visions helped to organize the experience of the senses. Young Algonquians went on a "vision-quest," which allowed the individual to inhabit the spirit world for a time.[87] The Narragansett Sachem Miantonomi, who with his father, Canonicus, had befriended Roger Williams and his fellow exiles from Massachusetts in the 1630s, saw a new and ominous future a few years later. He shared his vision with the Indians on Block Island, in 1643: "For you know our fathers had plenty of deer and skins, our plains were full of deer, as also our woods, and of turkeys and our covers full of fish and fowl. But these English, having gotten our land, they with scythes cut down the grass, and with axes fell the trees; their cows and horses eat the grass, and their hogs spoil our clam banks, and we shall all be starved." The potency of the prophecy lay in large measure in its sensuousness, though one in Miantonomi's audience warned the English of his disaffection, and they arranged for his assassination.[88]

The Indians managed sensory novelties by fitting them into holistic frameworks of natural behavior. No thing stood alone, just as no sensation existed by itself. Perception demanded integration. Whatever could not fit into the whole must be outside of nature, hence dangerous. Just as the nonconformity of an individual Indian imperilled his kin, so the ill-fitting cognition endangered the people.

What the Scholar Wrote

Thomas Harriot was a member of Sir Walter Raleigh's household. The Roanoke settlement was to be the first outpost of Raleigh's colony "Virginia." The voyages Harriot undertook to Roanoke in 1584 and 1585 became Raleigh's eyes and ears in the colony.[89] Harriot's report on what he saw (and heard and otherwise sensed) was published in 1588 and reprinted in 1590. It carried on in the tradition of literary imperialism begun by the "elder" and the "younger" Richard Hakluyts, both promoters of England's expansion.[90] The sensory part of promotional literature required detailed accounts of people and places to catch the imagination of elite English readers who might in time invest in the colonization effort. But Raleigh's agents had left in the colony more than one hundred and fifty colonists, whose fate Harriot did not know. Thus his *Brief and True Report* has an apologetic as well as a promotional tone, directed to the "adventurers, favorers, and wellwishers of the action, for the inhabiting and planting there."[91]

The *Report* appeared to be meticulously specific, beginning with the dates of the voyages and the names of the principal explorers. Harriot promised to sort through the "diversity of relations and reports" others had already published of the New World, seeking an objective, neutral truth. But proper use of the senses should lead to "certainty." If there was a profusion of reports from the 1585-86 expedition, the reason was that many who went sought only gold or "to pamper their bellies," and others had "little understanding, less discretion, and more tongue then was needful or requisite." Despite the "envious, malicious, and slanderous reports and devices" of these malcontents, a clear eye and a sharp ear—Harriot's—had discovered the real Roanoke.[92]

In precise and detailed prose, Harriot described the plants, minerals, and even the pearls they found in mussels, "of a pale color." There was "shoemake" (sumac), used in England as a black dye, and oad (woad), maize in abundance, beans, peas, and melons. Invariably Harriot compared what he found to European stocks and varieties. His way of describing, like his way of seeing, was essentially Old World—that is, new sensations had meaning through association or connection with a thing that was "called by us" or "about the bigness of our" or "which I take to be a kind of." Indian religion made sense to him as a pale counterfeit of Christianity, with the many lesser spirits like angels, and one chief deity. He assumed that the Indians also worshiped the sun, moon, and stars, the waters and other features of the land, much as the ancients in Europe had done. They believed in the immortality of the soul, the existence of heaven, and even had a creation story similar to that in Genesis—although they believed that God first made women.[93]

Harriot was also a keen-eyed observer of people and behavior. He watched and noted how the Indians planted and harvested their crops, fished, and hunted; what they valued and what they discarded. Above all he observed how thoroughly sensuous their world appeared to be: "All done with strange gestures, stamping, sometimes dancing, clapping of hands, holding up of hands, and staring up into the heavens, uttering therewithal and chattering strange words and noises." The strangeness of their clothing, weapons, and dwelling sites captivated him in large measure because they captured his eye and ear.[94]

Harriot trusted what his eye saw and his ear heard because he believed that the senses could record reality without distortion. This we know is an assumption that was rooted in his culture and validated by his experience. Hired by Raleigh to teach geometry, the foundational skill in mapmaking and navigation, Harriot would become a major figure in his own right in the development of the science of light. His work on refraction, the angular shift in light as it passes into and then out of a medium, such as water or a prism, anticipated Isaac Newton's *Optics* by sixty years.[95] Harriot discovered, by observation and measurement, that each medium through which light passed had a different index of refraction.[96]

In the *Report,* as in his later work on refraction, Harriot believed that he could see the real world directly, peer into its recesses, and from observation deduce its laws. These assumptions were the backbone of the English ideal of empirical, experimental science, which was coming into vogue. Findings like Harriot's would be vital to that empirical movement. For example, Francis Bacon, a scholar and jurist whose essays captured the spirit of the era of exploration, also called for "perspective houses" to study the mathematical and physical relations of light, color, and vision. His *New-Atlantis,* an essay on futuristic education, linked eyewitness accounts' of the New World's novelties to a new, more precise world of measurement and explanation of what the senses recorded.[97]

Neither Harriot nor Bacon demanded that English perception purge itself of all fascination with extraordinary and spectacular events. Even among the educated elite, accounts of the sensible world mixed religion, astrology, and spiritualism with natural observation. The very first occurrence that George Percy recorded on the trip to what would become Jamestown, in December 1606, was the passage through the sky of "a blazing star." For him, it was a sign of great portent.[98] The same English Renaissance mind that refined the mathematics of refraction read the heavens for signs of God's pleasure or displeasure. Sales of almanacs and other works with astrological prognostications were as popular as reports of new plants and animals.[99]

Percy did not regard his observations of celestial movements as superstitious; quite the contrary. What he saw at the outset of the voyage was part of a rational universe of signs which educated men should be able to understand. He continued his "Discourse" by describing the landfall at "Dominico [Santo Domingo] . . . a very faire island, the trees full of sweet and good smells inhabited by many savage Indians." Indians brought fruits, tobacco, and potatoes to the ship; the English gave the Indians knives and hatchets in trade.[100] Percy kept count, according to the instructions that Thomas Palmer gave in a treatise he wrote that same year for pilots, ship captains, and overseas merchants: "Be careful to set down . . . every thing of special note, as countries, havens, creeks, isles, rocks, gulfs, shoals, sands, shelves, and such like: whereby others . . . may make use thereof . . . and when . . . return, to make a true relation (if they be demanded) of every accident during their voyages."[101]

Men like Harriot and Percy assumed that they were observing discrete natural events that could be explained by natural laws, which could in turn be discovered through measurement and experiment. Even the most novel forms of Indian decoration must have a function. Thus Percy remarked of the Indians' red body paint, that it was "to keep away the biting of mosquitos."[102] Sensation was merely the first step in rational enumeration: so many savages, so much arable land, so many useful plants, so much to gain, so much danger in a venture.[103]

The English noted that the Indians lacked the instruments to measure their world precisely. This was a defect of Indian culture. In Harriot's words, "most things [the Indians] saw with us, as mathematical instruments, sea compasses, the virtue of the loadstone in drawing iron, a perspective glass [i.e. a magnifying glass] whereby was showed many strange sights, wild fireworks, guns, books, writing and reading, spring clocks . . . and other things that we had, were so strange unto them and so far exceeded their capacities to comprehend the reason and means who they should be made and done, that they thought they were rather the works of gods than of men."[104] Such awe at simple technologics could easily be manipulated, the English found. John Smith, captured by the Pamunky werowance Opechancanough, impressed his captor with modern European technology. The compass, so important to European overseas expansion, awed the savage, Smith believed. "I presented him with a compass dial describing by my best means the use thereof, whereat he so amazedly admired, as he suffered me to proceed in a discourse of the roundness of the earth, the course of the sun, moon, stars and planets."[105]

In sum, Harriot promised "to deliver freely my knowledge . . . not only for the satisfying of . . . my particular friends but also for the true information of any other whosoever." English seeing and hearing was, for him, objective, neutral, perfect. Harriot conceded that his colleagues' conduct at Roanoke led to the ruin of the colony, but their misbehavior had at its root their sensory incapacity. They were so busy looking for loot that they did not see or hear properly. Their senses were addled by their greed.[106]

English Perception: Calculation and Categorization

Harriot's narrative reveals how the English organized the report of the senses. First, he explicitly rejected the holistic naturalism of the Indians. Instead, he opened with a direct address to the reader, one on one. This was a conventionality of Elizabethan travel narratives, but, like the Indian storyteller's own narrative devices, such literary conventions illustrate sensory modalities. Harriot's appeal to "the gentle reader" emphasized the individuality of both author and reader. This is Harriot speaking, it said, who has "been requested by some of my particular friends, to deliver freely of my knowledge" to you, the reader.[107] Seeing and hearing for him and his readers was individual, precise, and set in a particular time and place.

Second, the English did not regard themselves as part of nature, or regard nature as simultaneously material and spiritual. Eyewitness testimony from English voyagers to America conclusively demonstrates that the English travelers and settlers were overwhelmed by the novelty of what they sensed.[108] William Bradford, elected governor of the Plymouth colony in 1621, feared the novelty: "What could they see here but a hideous and desolate wilderness, full of wild beasts and wild men—and multitudes there might be of them they knew not . . . all things stand upon them with a weather-beaten face, and the whole coutnry, full of woods and thickets, represented a wild and savage hue."[109] Others, equally awed, found delight where Bradford espied danger. Sir Walter Raleigh, journeying up the Orinoco River in search of gold, reveled in the strange scenes and sounds: "Some of the most beautiful country that ever mine eyes beheld . . . the grass short and green and in diverse parts groves of trees by themselves as if they have been by all the art and labor in the world."[110] Arthur Barlow, piloting one of the two barks that Sir Walter sent in 1584 to explore the coast of what is now North Carolina, recalled the odors as the boats neared land: "and was so strong a smell, as if we had bene in the midst of some delicate garden, abounding with all kind of odoriferous flowers."[111]

Feared or embraced, the novel had to be manipulated, fit into familiar English perceptions through easy-to-envision comparisons. The most obvious of these was between the character of the Indians and that of the English. In their natures, the Indians were not inferior to the English. Harriot: "In respect of us they are a people poor, and for want of skill and judgement in the knowledge and use of our things, do esteem our trifles before things of greater value. Notwithstanding in their proper manner considering the want of such means as we have, they seem very ingenious. For although they have no such tools, nor any such crafts, sciences, and arts as we, yet in those thing they do, they show excellence of wit."[112]

Comparison narrowed the gap between the new and the old and reduced the cognitive anxiety of discovery. The dunes of the Carolina barrier islands were like the hillocks of the Downs in southeastern England. Percy, bathing himself in a natural spa on Guadalupe, recorded that he "found it to be of the nature of baths in England, some places hot and some colder."[113] The comparisons extended to the Indians' technology. Although Harriot and those who came after him generally disparaged Indian tools, they made an exception for the bows and arrows. No doubt with England's traditional reliance on its longbow men in mind, English visitors to the New World admired the craftsmanship of the Indians' bows and their skill as archers. The bows were in form "like ours."[114]

In the English processing of sensory novelties, anticipated use directed the eye and tutored the ear. The first paragraph of Ralph Lane's report to Sir Francis Walsingham—the former Raleigh's lieutenant in Roanoke, the latter a sponsor of the voyage and the colony—set this tone. Lane's arrival in those parts "hath nevertheless discovered unto us so many, so rare, and so singular commodities (by universal opinion both of our apothecaries and all our merchants here)."[115] Harriot's *Report* extolled the commercial potential of an outpost in Carolina. "Of the commodities there found and to be raised, as well merchantable, as others for victual, building, and other necessary uses for those that are and shall be the planters there." Take, for example, silk: "The like groweth in Persia, which is in the self same climate as Virginia, of which very many of the silk works that come from thence into Europe are made.

Here if it be planted and ordered as in Persia, it cannot in reason be otherwise, but that there will rise in short time great profit to the dealers therein." Flax and hemp "will grow excellently well, and by planting will be yielded plentifully: seeing there is so much ground whereof some may well be applied to such purposes."[116] In Jamestown, John Smith was similarly impressed less by what he saw than what he foresaw: "All the rarity of needful fruits in Europe, may be there [in Virginia] in great plenty, by the industry of men, as appeareth, by those we there planted."[117] When Winslow spied the whales that frolicked along the Cape Code coast, he thought to himself, "if we had instruments and means to take them, we might have made a very rich return."[118]

But such comparisons had a price, one that the explorers paid. At the end of Smith's table of contents for his history of Virginia he groused: "These observations are all I have for the expences of a thousand pound[s], and the loose of eighteen years of time, besides all the travels, dangers, miseries and encumbrances for my countries good, I have endured gratis: and had I not discovered and lived in the most of the these parts, I could not possibly have collected the substantial truth from such an infinite number of variable Relations."[119] Other venturers paid with their lives.[120] Looking out toward the Atlantic from Roanoke, Barlow viewed the dunes of the outer banks. Sparkling in the sun, the beauty of these living mounds of sand and grasses, like Circe, beckoned the unwary navigator into treacherously shallow waters. The beached ship would then be ripped apart by the fury of the storms that flew out of the southeast. Mariners could not see the warm waters of the Gulf Stream, some forty nautical miles off the coast, meet the tendrils of the cold Labrador current. The jetsam of the first of the unwary vessels—now some six hundred fifty and still counting—was already visible in the treacherous currents.[121]

When comparisons failed and the costs of exploration seemed to outweigh the benefits, the English adventurers extolled a vision of a New World transformed by permanent colonization. These perceptions differed from the Indians' dreams and prophecies. The English imagination did not wander into the spirit world or hear the voices of the forest. Instead, the visitors pictured colonies of busy workers harvesting staple crops for export. On first entering the Albemarle sound, Barlow observed: "I think in all the world the like abundance is not to be found: and myself having seen those parts of Europe that most abound, find such difference, as were incredible to be written."[122] In the same year that Barlow set out for America, Richard Hakluyt "the younger," whose accounts of these voyages in later years made them so popular among the English reading public,[123] called for vast plantings of England's "numbers of idle men" in agricultural colonies. In America they could produce wholesome exports for English laborers to refine, English consumers to enjoy, and English merchants to ship to European markets.[124]

The sights and sounds of the Carolina coast fed dreams of mass migrations and giant company farms. The Albemarle Sound around the island of Roanoke is almost 90 percent fresh water, fed by seven rivers on the mainland. To a visitor standing on the western shore of the island, the water smells sweet enough to drink. The sea of marsh grasses that fringe the islands must have waved a welcome in the unceasing wind. Cut and dried, such grasses would support herds of cattle. Barlow's eye also picked out likely places for gardens in the fields the Indians had already cleared.[125]

But the delights that the English imagined in the novelties of the New World were tempered by later experience. Some wonders were not welcome precisely because they seemed to indicate the difficulty of extracting wealth or establishing English control of a region. Straining his eyes toward the marshes on the mainland, Barlow could not make out any landmarks in what one modern journalist has called the "tangled wilderness" of the early modern North Carolina mainland.[126] It was to the English what, in later years, Pennsylvania surveyor Lewis Evans described as an "ocean of woods" without boundary, markers, or end.[127]

English perception needed boundaries, markers, and definite ends. What had no extent could not be calculated, and that without markers could not be categorized. Distance and impenetrability frightened the English because it prevented aural and visual communication. Too far off, too densely wooded, meant out of earshot. The Elizabethan Englishman lived in a world full of sounds—rural "soundscapes" of birdsong, insect noise, and the bleating and lowing of domestic animals, to which the yelping of dogs added staccato notes. Town soundscapes of traffic were punctuated by the cries of pedlars, the clank of wagons, and the gurgle of running water. Cannon reports and ringing bells struck the ear and compelled attention wherever they occurred. Ships at sea were just as loud, the rigging and sails moaning and snapping, the cargo in the hold banging about no matter how well trussed; sailors grumbling, snoring, coughing, sneezing, and sometimes shouting at the wind. When storms roared, they drowned out all normal sound. In the city one heard a constant blur of voices mingled; in the countryside farmers working side by side in common fields chatted constantly; at the dockside and in the roads, dory men bawled at the top of their lungs. Elizabethan and Jacobean England were talky places. The English had nothing against noise.[128]

When the English found themselves unable to hear or see one another, they panicked. Novelty became unbearable. The screeching and howling sounds of the American forest and the Atlantic approaches terrified the travelers. Much of the forest land of England was gone by the late 1500s, and the remaining forests were home to witches and sprites.[129] Lost in the woods, fearful of a dark bend in the river or a patch of fog-daubed forest, the English quivered with anxiety. Imagination filled in the pictures that strange sounds outlined. When two of the Plymouth Pilgrims got lost chasing a deer in 1620, "another thing did mightily terrify them; they heard, as they thought, two lions roaring exceedingly for a long time together, and a third, that they thought was very near them."[130] The sounds of the "huracan" (Carib for *hurricane*) were equally frightful for their novelty to the voyagers to Virginia in 1609. William Strachey, shipwrecked after one such storm "swelling and roaring as it were by fits," admitted that "the ears lay so sensible to the terrible cries and murmurs of the winds" even the "best prepared" of the ship's company were shaken.[131]

Out of sight of one another, nervous Englishmen in America relied on trumpets and gunfire to signal position and status.[132] Music was pressed into service in emergencies. When John White returned to Roanoke after a three-year absence and set about finding the 130 men, women, and children he had left as colonists, he and his comrades "sounded with a trumpet a call," no doubt a military trumpet tattoo, and then chorused "many familiar English tunes of Songs," but the colonists could not be found.[133] When the infamous "Sea Dog" Sir Francis Drake attacked Spanish St. Augustine in 1586, a musical tune saved a man's life. As Drake's men rowed up the river toward the town, "forthwith came a French man being a fifer (who had been a prisoner [with the Spanish]) in a little boat, playing on his fife the tune of the Prince of Orange his song." Hearing this, Drake's men spared him.[134]

The demands of English perception required that auditory and visual signals not blend into the landscape, as Indians' signs did, but stand out from it in sharp relief. Thus, the trumpet blast identified the English to one another rather than the imitation of birdsong or animal call the Indians adopted. The same was true of visible signals like fire. The Indians routinely used fire to clear their fields. In their store of images, fire was natural. The English regarded fire as an unnatural event that required immediate attention. The Elizabethan English used bonfires to celebrate special events. Such fires were "dangerous and exciting."[135] White reported that the English used lanterns—controlled fire—to keep fleets of privateers together as they chased down stragglers from the Spanish treasure fleets.[136] The English colonizers also used fire as a signal of peril. When the Pilgrims foraging on Cape Cod feared that they were about to be attacked, they set fires to indicate their position to their shipmates.[137] "One special great fire" on the barrier island of "Haterask" summoned Drake to the rescue of Ralph Lane's men in 1586.[138]

Trumpet blasts, songs, lanterns, and signal fires were temporary expedients to manage the sensation of unknown distance and direction. But English perceptual canons of categorization and calculation required that immediate sensation of geography and topography be made stable and permanent. The answer was to draw impressions of the land and directions to landmarks on paper. Mapping made order out of the sensory chaos of novel locations.[139] Often, the first piece of paper the English put to use in the Americas was a rough map of the coast. On it they included natural features. They also brought with them maps that they emended and improved. Every English traveler prized maps; many made them; some voyagers published their charts when they returned to the Old World. In this they shared a mania for maps with other travelers and would-be travelers: "Europeans from all ranks of society were preoccupied with navigation in the sixteenth and seventeenth centuries."[140]

The map's primary functions were relational and directional, reducing vast spaces to measured relationships and giving compass headings and latitude lines to aid in getting from here to there and back again (the latter even more important than the former). Thus space became place and the new became the familiar. The map transformed raw sensations into precise linearity; an intellectualized mastery of the natural world. Such maps were meant to be practical, this-worldly guides, but that purpose did not exhaust their usefulness as sensory managers, for maps and mapping allowed the English to impose a pictorial as well as a mathematical order on New World sights. In the blanks in the maps—where European eyes had not reached or European interest had not lingered—the mapmakers and printers added drawings of natives and animals, coats of arms, and legends. These all conveyed messages. Because the map as a whole was an argument and an aspiration, a place to go, a territory that beckoned, a dangerously empty frontier, the margins and gaps in the map demanded such images.[141]

One of these early English maps is famous for the visuals in its margins. In 1624, John Smith offered his readers a "Map of Virginia," which filled in all the empty spaces. At the bottom was a legend of miles to inches featuring a compass and a protractor. These signs of English technology celebrated the superiority of the English over the natives. By reducing the terrain to precise dimensions, the map trumped panoptic memory. Smith's own coat of arms (granted to him for his service to Christianity during the wars against the Turks) and the coat of arms of the crown occupied additional spaces, visually reinforcing the English claim to the land and his contribution toward that end. Two pictures of Indians appeared at the top corners of the map. They provided viewers with Europeanized versions of Indian bodies—the first of the Powhatan, a werowance, and the second with an Indian warrior. They were exotics—the Powhatan enthroned in a reed-walled house surrounded by his seminaked (hence barbarous) advisors. Smith's artist bedecked the warrior with animal heads and skins—a truly formidable ("giant" the caption says) adversary. Such graphic concoctions did not have to be accurate. They fit instead a much longer tradition in which cartographers filled in space with imaginary monsters.[142]

Unlike other European producers of New World places, Smith did not assign European names to every geographical feature. The James River, Jamestown, Cape Henry, Cape Charles, and other coastal sites were so named because the English were contesting these areas with the Spanish. English names implied English dominion. But to the interior of the land he gave approximations of the Indian names, making it a guide to inter-Indians' political relationships in the region.[143]

The English managed sensory novelty by calculating advantage and categorizing differences. They accepted the notion of discrete material existence and clearly demarcated the human from the natural. They could tolerate individual divergences in men, but not competing material aims; what could not be fit into their promotional scheme had to be subjugated or removed from their perceptual field.

Talking Back: Communication and Sensory Novelty

Two peoples, two views of novelty, two ways of handling perceptions, but still no sensory dominion by either side. The encounters were still exchanges. The English newcomer and the Indian native evaluated one another in sensuous measure. They stared, signed, touched, and shared victuals.[144] Pacific intent was conveyed in gestures: smiling, laying down arms, holding up trade goods. But the only real guarantee of continued friendship was communication with words, and this was no small task.

To the first Englishmen in America, the Indians sounded like wild beasts or men without their wits.[145] To the Indians' ears, the first white men "spoke too fast and too loudly."[146] But some on both sides hoped that, if only they could understand what the other was saying, sensory novelties would disappear and the other side would happily abandon its mistaken perceptions. For the English, this meant that the Indians would willingly begin their transformation to English ways.[147] As Roger Williams wrote during the days when he was learn-

John Smith, *Map of Virginia*

Smith was above all a promoter and a storyteller, and the map abets both functions. It is filled with useful information (such as the Indian town names) and also effectively claims the land for England. Note that the Powhatan and the Susquehannock brave at the top right are both copied from White's Roanoke Indians in the De Bry edition of Harriot. For Smith and his publisher, images of Indians were interchangeable. (From John Smith, *Generall History of Virginia* [1624], in Philip L. Barbour, ed., The Complete Works of Captain John Smith [Chapel Hill, N.C., 1986].)

ing the Narragansett dialect of Algonquian and simultaneously teaching the natives the basics of English reform Protestantism: "They have no clothes, nor books, nor letters . . . and therefore they are easily persuaded that the God that made English men is a greater God, because he hath so richly endowed the English above themselves."[148] The absence of common language, on the other hand, could lead to dangerous missteps. So Ralph Lane mistook the war songs of Indians on the banks of the Roanoke river in March of 1586 as welcoming, until his interpreter Manteo's warning and a flight of arrows from the banks tutored him otherwise.[149]

The first step was "pidgin." Pidgins are rudimentary hybrid languages with simplified vocabularies and grammars. The first historically documented pidgin was the language that the European Crusaders' sailors spoke with the peoples of the Middle East. Because so many of the former were French, the pidgin was called *lingua franca,* and that term for a universal language has passed into common usage. In the fifteenth century, variants of elementary Portuguese like *saber* (to know) and *pequeño* (small) became part of pidgins along the coast of Africa, where Portuguese sailors and traders did business with African merchants and slavers.[150] European slave traders came to rely on Africans who spoke pidgin as translators and assistants.[151]

Another strategy to surmount the language barrier was to kidnap youths and train them as translators. On his first voyage, Columbus abducted a number of younger Taino Indians from the Caribbean Islands and carried them back to Spain; when they had learned enough Spanish, he took them back to the islands to act as his interpreters.[152] The English at Roanoke took two young Indians, Manteo and Wanchese, home for English-language training. Other strategies included leaving young Europeans among the Indians, sometimes as little more than hostages, at other times as students in the care of trusted sachems, to learn the Indian languages. Young Henry Spilman, for example, lived among the Powhatan peoples during the first years of Jamestown.[153]

Traders and Indians in North America developed a variety of pidgins. The so-called Mobilian pidgin (for the region around Mobile, Alabama, where it developed) helped late seventeenth-century French and Spanish traders deal with the Chickasaw, Choctaw, and other peoples of the area.[154] The Delaware fashioned a pidgin out of one of their dialects, Unami. Even non-Unami speakers like the Munsee of Manhattan Island used the Unami-based pidgin to communicate with the Europeans. Johannes de Laet transliterated the basic vocabulary of this pidgin in 1633. The Swedes in Delaware and New Jersey also used the Unami pidgin, and minister Johannes Campanius translated Martin Luther's "Small Catechism" into Unami sometime in the 1640s. The translation was published in 1696. Using such pidgin word books, European colonizers like William Penn, who arrived in 1682, assumed that Indian languages were plain and spare—little realizing how much the pidgins omitted or oversimplified.[155]

A more sophisticated knowledge of Indian speech was hard for Europeans to obtain. The variety of Indian languages was daunting, and Indians were not always cooperative in elucidating the nuances of their speech. James Axtell estimates that there were 221 mutually unintelligible native American languages and countless dialects within each. Often the dialect or pronunciation of the same basic language group varied from region to region and even from village to village. This variability allowed Indians to use language as a marker of local identity, but the same Indians were unwilling to allow Europeans full access to such intimate details of Indian life as insider knowledge of language conveyed. English naturalist Mark Catesby, on returning from his travels in Carolina, noted how "reserved and averse" Indians were "to reveal their secret mysteries to Europeans." Europeans might be permitted to know the outside boundaries of the identity—the pidgin—but not how the language actually worked from the inside. So, when the Dutch missionary Megalopensis asked his Mohawk correspondents for the names of things, one told him the word in the first person, the next in the second person, a third varied the tenses.[156] What was more, among natives, custom dictated that speech not show anger or other inappropriate emotions. The end result was that Europeans never fully understood the nuances of Indian languages or the rich variety of Indian customs and ideas that the languages encoded.[157] The problem was mutual. Even though Europeans tried to teach Indians to speak European tongues, Indians had trouble with the variety of European languages. Some, like the Croatan youth Manteo, became proficient translators and willing go-betweens. Without him, neither Ralph Lane nor John White could have established even their brief-lived colonial settlements.[158] Even when some of the Indians became fluent in a European language, it remained customary to hide the full extent of that familiarity.[159]

If not communication, with its sharing of sensations of sound and gesture, then what would guide the encounter between the English and the Indians? How would the ambiguities of novelty be resolved and its opportunities realized?

Sensory Imperialism

Thus far, we have traced a mutuality of sensory enterprise among the English and the Indians. They both confronted novelty, and although their methods of processing sensations differed, they both tried to see and make sense of the novelty of the other's presence. But within a short time the story changed from one of genuine curiosity, mixed to be sure with some anxiety, to one of asymmetry. Both sides could have striven for generally even-handed relations based on trade, intermarriage, and selective cultural assimilation. As one modern Indian visionary put it, "there was unlimited potential for harmony. The newcomers could have adapted to the hosts' customs and values or at least understood and respected them."[160] Sometimes this happens in history, though the story of empires is usually one of dominance rather than mutuality. The former is what happened on the North American coast. Why it happened constitutes the three-hundred-year-long story of colonization, a story of competing cultures, mass migrations, epidemics and wars, and the ultimate supremacy of English over native. At its outset, however, it was a story about sensory imperialism.

The Asymmetrical Power of Words

For most of the European explorers in America, language was a mark of European superiority and a weapon of imperial dominance. In the 1492–93 diary of his first voyage to what he called the Indies, Columbus recorded that he "spoke to the Indians." He had no interpreter and the Indians had no one who spoke any of the European languages he understood; how then could he record that he spoke to the natives?[161] The answer is simple: He spoke in their presence. It was not important, at first, whether they understood or could reply, for part of the Spanish process for taking control of territory—that is, claiming it for the Spanish crown—was to read aloud a legal document announcing that the Spanish were the rightful owners of the land on which the Spanish conqueror stood.[162]

Columbus and the European explorers who followed him to the New World saw language as a kind of magical way of controlling people and nature. Columbus immediately set out to use that magic by renaming every place where he stopped. Instead of learning and employing the native name, he gave each site a Spanish stamp. Thus, he called the island where he first landed *San Salvador,* and the large island where he built the first European village in the Caribbean became *Hispaniola.* The natives were *indios,* the Spanish word for the inhabitants of the East Indies (Columbus never did realize that he had discovered an entirely new continent).[163]

The English were desperate to talk with the Indians—but in English. In part, the English demand that the Indians learn English was based on religious beliefs. For the English, theirs was the language in which civilized men prayed,[164] so when Lane wanted to explain how he knew the Indians were plotting against the English, he reported that "now they began to blaspheme, and flatly to say, that our Lord God was not God."[165] The majority of the English ministerial fraternity agreed that the Indians must learn English to pray properly. Even those who, like Massachusetts missionaries John Eliot and

Daniel Gookin, wanted the Indians to learn the Bible in their own language, saw the concession as a stopgap measure.[166]

The English, employing the same tactics Columbus had used, either tricked or kidnaped Indians and carried them back to England. The assumption was that total immersion in the English home culture would lead to facility with the English tongue. The captives could then be returned to their homes, in the company of the English voyagers, to serve as bilingual translators. So the young Carolina Indians Manteo and Wanchese were beguiled to travel back to England in 1585. Manteo would perform his expected role in the years to come, but Wanchese represented the other possibility: he would use his knowledge of English and of English ways to thrust out the colonists.[167] The Pilgrims at Plymouth heaved a collective sigh of relief when an Abanaki Indian named Samoset, who had spent time with the English fishermen visiting the Maine coast, walked into their midst. "He saluted us in English and bade us welcome."[168]

When Samoset spoke to the Pilgrims in English, they read it as both God's balm to them and a proof that their civilization was superior to the Indians'. But even pidgin jarred the English ear. The natives must learn English, the newcomers decided. The English language was England carried abroad. Its words matched what they signified—the aural landscape mapped onto a geographical landscape. One student of sixteenth-century English literature called this "logocentrism," and it certainly matched English ethnocentrism.[169] Lane's contemporaries were exasperated and infuriated by the refusal of the Irish to learn English. It proved that the Irish were "beasts," incapable of civilized behavior.[170] Just so the Indians. Bradford at Plymouth was delighted when Samoset brought along another Indian, a Patuxet named Squanto, who had been taken to England and could speak passable English.[171] The Pilgrims welcomed Squanto as they had never welcomed Samoset, giving him a small parcel of land at the edge of the settlement and honoring him when he passed away. The newcomers did not want any more auditory novelty. They wanted to hear Indians speak good English.

Words aloud were not enough for the English; sound had to be reduced to writing. Lane's reports, Harriot's notes, the maps and charts of the navigators, White's drawings–these made the English language different and superior to Algonquian dialects because all that the men said could be sent over long distances and have the same meaning when read as when written. So the English believed. John Smith, in peril of his life at the hands of Opechancanough, reported that he had stunned the Indians by taking out a pocket notebook and scribbling a message to his cohorts at the Jamestown fort. When the James-town garrison behaved as Smith predicted they would, the Indians announced that Smith could make the paper "talk" and paraded him about the Indian towns as a magician.[172]

Smith thought that he had proven his superiority over his captors by flaunt-ing the power of writing. Among the educated English, the written word took precedence over the spoken word. Literacy was the mark of education, and education the sign of high status. Intellectually, writing was deemed superior to material signing, like pictographs, arrows wrapped in snake skins, and tat-toos of animals on a man's body, because writing was capable of abstraction and generality. Abstraction in turn was a hallmark of civilization, of philoso-phy and science—making the supremacy of writing a self-fulfilling concept.[173] As one of the English promoters of overseas empire would shortly write, "amongst men, some are accounted civil, and more both sociable and relig-ious, by the use of letters and writing, which others wanting are esteemed brutish, savage, barbarous . . . by writing, man seems immortal, [and] confer-reth and consulteth with the patriarchs, prophets, apostles, fathers, philos-ophers, historians, and learns the wisdom of the sages which have been in all times before him."[174]

For missionaries, who had the most intimate contact with the natives, preaching the word was vital, but print culture, with religious books at its center, was the cornerstone of all instruction. Clergyman Robert Hunt brought a small library of religious books with him to the first Jamestown set-tlement in 1607, no doubt hoping to teach the Bible to the natives.[175] Even the Indians conceded that writing and reading aloud of words gave them greater authority. Thomas Morton, whose little household at Merrymount in the Plymouth colony was often visited by the Massachusett Indians, recalled that in 1624 or thereabouts, one of his visitors had asked "that I would let his son be brought up in my house, that he might be taught to read in that book [of prayer].[176] Miantonomi, the Narragansett sachem and friend of Roger Williams, told other Indians that the minister "hath books and writings, and one which God himself made, concerning mens souls, and therefore may well know more than we that have none."[177]

One specialized form of writing some of the English had mastered was her-aldry. Heraldry always connoted hierarchy, for in theory it was only the nobil-ity who could have heraldic devices. With their stylized beasts of the jungle and of myth and their elaborate geometric designs and patterns of color, each coat of arms told a story about its martial bearer. By the 1580s, these devices had lost their original prestige, but not their meaning. They could be purchased from the heralds, as Raleigh did, to give to the twelve assistants who would govern his City of Raleigh in his Colony of Virginia. The assistants were not nobility, but they nevertheless received their "honors" for themselves and their descendants.[178]

Assistant George Howe, who joined the 130 men, women, and children accompanying governor John White to the colony in 1587, was to have the heraldic insignia (that is, the coat of arms on a shield) of "a field argent [a background of silver] on [which appeared] a chevron gules [a v-shaped stripe in red] three fuzels of the first [the diamond shaped fusil was a common geometric "charge"] between three wolves heads coupled sables."[179] A busy device, which meant that Howe and his lineage were "armigent"—entitled to carry arms.

The heraldic shield was power emblazoned. Beware, it warned, the lion and the dragon. But the power of these symbols failed to intimidate the Indians at Roanoke. The magnificent coat of arms that symbolized Raleigh's ambitions and Howe's elevation was no use to Howe when, stripped to his codpiece, he went "without any weapon, save only a forked stick, catching crabs" in the marsh on the landward side of Roanoke Island. An Indian would have known what Howe did not—to look for the signs of an enemy lurking near. He noticed neither that the deer had fled from the reeds by the water nor how the reeds themselves rustled, though the wind was still. Having ignored nature's warnings, he had no defense when a band of Roanokes, hunting deer, found Howe instead, and "shot at him in the water, where they gave him sixteen wounds with their arrows, and after they had slain him with their wooden swords, beat his head in pieces, and fled over the water to the main[land]."[180]

If the most elaborate and time-honored of English symbolisms had no impact on the Indians in America, how then could language gain superiority for the English? The Indian hunters had not seen the coat of arms that sultry summer morning when they bushwhacked Howe, any more than they had seen Raleigh's charter or any of the writings the English so prized. They saw just another white man. White men had killed their kinsmen, and for the purposes of Indian revenge customs, all the members of an offender's village were liable for the actions of the misdoer. All Englishmen were at risk in the blood feud.[181] A final irony of this first feeble attempt at sensory imperialism: The Croatoan fishermen upon whom John White's mission to find the lost colonists of Roanoke chanced assumed that the English practiced the same kind of blood-feud revenge as the Roanokes, which is why they asked White for some emblem or sign to show that they were friends of the English.

Roanoke

All the stories of the imposition of sensory imperialism lead back to Roanoke. White's tale of Howe's fate is graphic. From it one can almost imagine the sea of salt-marsh reeds which hid the Indians. But the moral of the tale is clear even to those without imagination. The Indians would not be willing partners in their own subjugation. They must be shown the power of the English. They must stand in fear and give tribute. The model the English had in mind was Ireland; Hakluyt's promotional scheme for America clearly had Ireland in mind, as had Raleigh himself.[182] Raleigh, who served in the English army sent to suppress the rebellion in 1579 and had seen at first hand the effectiveness of the English program to turn the Irish into tenants or landless laborers. First, the English established armed camps. Then the natives were given the choice of accepting English ownership of the land or of fleeing. Either way, the English triumphed. Raleigh intended to put the lessons of the reduction of Ireland to use in his American colony, and Hakluyt was one of his publicists.[183]

Even Harriot conceded that "some of our company towards the end of the year, showed themselves too fierce, in slaying some of the people, in some towns, upon causes that on our part, might easily enough have been born withall."[184] Lane grew worried about the Roanokes' hostility and wrote to Raleigh that Wingina was plotting against the English. But Lane could not see into the forest on the mainland, where Wingina rallied his kinsmen. Lane literally could not see at all, for the warm days of early spring, followed by the cold of the evening, brought mist, and the all-blanketing fog turned his fear into paranoia. Desperate, he sought a safer place for the colony—perhaps somewhere on the mainland. He gathered a company and rowed across the sound to the mouth of the Roanoke River. The Indians, hoping to be rid of him, revealed the secret of their copper ornaments. They came from high in the mountains, at the beginning of the river. Into its dark corridor Lane rowed.

The Roanoke is the second oldest river in the world according to the curators at the North Carolina aquarium, carrying its brown and red sediments from the Blue Mountains all the way down to the Albemarle Sound. When it floods, as it does every spring, it resembles a rain-forest waterway on whose banks the hardwoods overhang the water. From their protection, Lane was set upon by the Indians firing down into his boats. When he and his men landed on the shore to battle the attackers, they "betook themselves to flight." Lane reported, "We landed, and having fair and easily followed for a small time after them, who had wooded themselves we know not where." Fleeing from the mist, Lane and his men were overwhelmed in the forest, beset with sounds they could not decipher and sights they could not arrange or order.[185]

How then to impose the English will on the North Carolina countryside? How to make the Indians see the superiority of the English? The answer was sensory imperialism. Change the way the land looked, alter the terrain, levy an English scenery upon the wild settings of the New World. Begin with fortification. As George Waymouth, who would lead a foray into Indian lands in Maine in 1605, wrote in his manual for colonization, "for that country being as weakly planted with the English, and they more weakly defended from the invasions of the heathen, among whom they dwell . . . subject unto manifold perils, and dangers whereas it being so fruitful a soil, so goodly rivers and things necessary for fortification." Forts were an absolute necessity.[186] Even when the local Indians welcomed the English, as they did the first settlers to

Landscape of Roanoke National Historical Park

Lane could not see into the woods and high grasses. His men, noisy and armor clad, could be heard and seen from anywhere on the island, but the Indians blended into the landscape and moved about unheard and unspotted. For Lane, this was a dangerous sensory predicament and had to be remedied. For the English who came with White the year after Lane left, the inability to see into the landscape proved fatal. (Photograph by author.)

Lord Baltimore's colony of Maryland, it was prudent to have a fort. So in the fall of 1634 the colonists laid aside their garden tools and English seeds "to finish their fort, which they did within the space of one month; where they mounted some ordinance [cannon] . . . and such other means of defense as they thought fit for their safeties, which being done, they proceeded with their houses and finished them."[187]

Lane would have preferred to construct a permanent fortress not on Roanoke Island, which had little commercial use except as a base camp, but at the head of the Roanoke River on the mainland. If, as his Indian informants had told him, its ores were "worth the possession, I would there have raised a main fort." Between the island and the main fortress he would have erected a series of small bastions, "a sconce [that is, a small fort or earthwork] with a small trench [a dry ditch] and a palisade upon the top of it, in the which, in the guard of my boats, I would have left first the twenty or thirty men," and at a march beyond, some "convenient plot," he would have built another sconce, "according to the former, where I would have left 15 or 20."[188]

As he had neither the time nor the men to construct or man these outposts, he had to rely on a fort on Roanoke. He and his troop laid out the structure in the northwest corner of the island, using earthworks and timber palisades. Outside the ditch and wall stood cottages and workshops, as well as houses for the principal men. These were constructed of wood and thatch, as Lane, in recounting what he supposed to be the plot against the English, wrote to Raleigh: "In the dead time of night [two of Wingina's most trusted warriors, with about twenty helpers] would have beset my house, and put fire in the reeds, that the same was covered with, meaning (as it was likely) that myself would have come running out of a sudden amazed in my shirt without arms, upon the instant whereof they would have knocked out my brains . . .The same order were given to certain of [Wingina's] fellows, for Master Harriot's [house] so for all the rest of our better sort, all our houses at one instant being set on fire . . . and that as well for them of the fort as for us at the town."[189]

Apart from grassy mounds, there is no certain evidence today of the exact shape or construction of the main bastion.[190] At the foot of the wooden walls, Lane probably filled in a firing step, so that his men could see over (or through) firing ports in the walls.[191] He himself did not describe the fort, merely mentioning the "new fort in Virginia."[192] David Beers Quinn, relying on early archeological researchers, thought the fort was some forty to fifty yards square in a star shape.[193] But the dimensions of the star were too small to hold the 108 men who had landed with Lane, and archaeologist Ivor Noel Hume suggested that the star may have been one of the bastions at the corners of the curtains of wall. Hume believes that the fort must have had a rectangular or triangular shape.[194]

Lane's fort-building enterprise had native precedents, and the Roanokes would not have been surprised by the idea of a fort. Indians on the mainland had fortified some of their towns. White visited one of these, Pomeiooc, and drew its palisade. To the north, Iroquois villages were sometimes surrounded by walls of upright tree trunks.[195] The Mississippian Indian mound villages and towns of the late woodlands period (1000–1500) had palisades and earthworks of considerable size. The palisade around the great city of Cahokia, a few miles from the eastern shore of the Mississippi opposite modern St. Louis, Missouri, stretched over two miles and required fifteen to twenty thousand oak or hickory logs. The walls may have been protected by clay, to keep out the moisture.[196] Archeologists have recovered a prehistoric Cherokee fort in northwestern North Carolina which also had a double-row palisade. Its posts were on average about four to eight inches apart.[197] We have a contemporary description of a Pequot fortified village, from coastal Connecticut: "They pitch, close together as they can, young trees and half trees, as thick as a man's thigh or the calf of his leg. Ten or twelve foot high they are above the ground, and within rammed three feet deep with undermining, the earth being case up for their better shelter, against the enemy's dischargements. Betwixt these palisades are diverse loopholes . . . The door for the most part is entered sideways, which they stop with boughs or birches [brush] as need requireth."[198] A reconstructed Pequot village palisade at the Pequot Museum had two- to three-inch spacing.[199]

Lane's fortress was different from the Indians' constructions in three significant respects. First, Lane's works stood out from the land, altering its shape and design. Indian horticulturalists altered the surface of the land but not its shape, and Indian settlements did not deface the land so thoroughly or thoughtlessly as did Lane. Unlike the forts of the mound builders,[200] Lane's fort did not surround a town or village. There were barracks and workshops within it, but it was a European redoubt or refuge, a kind of Norman keep rather than part of a settlement for families. Like any medieval keep, its visible imposition upon the landscape was essential to its purpose. Keeps were not only safe places in time of sudden assault or ambush; they established the authority of the lord of the manor over the terrain. Keeps symbolized the authority of the nobility by imposing themselves on eye. By building a fort Lane was telling the Indians, Look and see. This place is ours, not yours.

Constructed twenty years later, the bastion at Jamestown conveyed the same message. The restored fort at Jamestown Settlement allows modern vis-

John White, *Pemiooc,* fortified Roanoke Indian town, 1585

Palisades were a common feature of Indian towns in the eastern woodlands. More than twice a man's height, they were about four to six inches apart at their bases. These features were also found in Cherokee and Tuscarora towns. Outsiders could see what went on inside the town, but the only entrance, a portal, could be blocked by brush at a moment's notice. (Published by Theodor De Bry in 1590 as an illustration for Thomas Harriot's *Briefe and True Report of the New Found Land of Virginia.*)

itors walking up the path from the concessions and museum to see something of what Indians might have seen as they approached the original. Although the restoration used milled two-by-fours instead of halved tree trunks, the height and the tightness of the verticals are authentic. Twice the size of a man, blocking out the light and imposing on the eye, they give an impression of mass and solidity meant to deter attack and to suggest the superior will, weapons, and skills of the English.

Second, by claiming the landscape in such an aggressive and artificial manner, Lane did what no Indian fortification would dream of doing: He imposed an alien material structure upon a spiritual landscape. Such effrontery would surely drive off the spirits that dwelled in the land. The native landscape, whether town, village, former settlement, woods, or littoral, was a ple-

The walls of Jamestown. Jamestown Settlement

The settlement is a commercial restoration, about a mile up the James River from the original site. The walls of the restoration differ from the originals (they are milled four by fours instead of debarked tree trunks), but they convey how imposing the fort would have been on the landscape. One cannot see between the slats. A firing step inside the walls allowed the garrison to see and fire over them. (Photograph by author.)

num, full of natural spirits. The remains of things, people, prey, crops, fallow—all were treated with respect because all were part of the whole, and the whole was alive. There was no separation between the material and the spiritual, the human and the not-human; teach infused the other.[201] But the Indians could see that the English had no respect for the spiritual landscape. The English might speak of their God and their Savior, and the Indians might be willing to add these gods to their own, but nothing could excuse what the Indians saw the English doing to the places where the Indians' demigods resided.[202]

The closing off of light earthworks and palisade violated a basic tenet of Indian religious life. Indians believed that almost everything important took place outside the artificial space of buildings, in nature, where the spirit world and the everyday world came together. The Indians lived, danced, sang, worshiped, and tended their gardens in these open spaces. There were exceptions—mausoleums for the dead, seat lodges for purification, and council fires within the chief's wigwam—but these were exceptions. Even in mound cities full of buildings, manmade structures were placed atop mounds so that everyone could see religious rites or political displays. Lane's fort, with its closed-up verticals and clapboard walls, denied sight. At best, that was bad manners; at worst, it might conceal all manner of skulduggery.[203]

The effect of Lane's affront to Indian spirits and his penchant for hiding his acts was immediately felt by the Indians. The Indians soon began dying from diseases whose causes were invisible.[204] It started in Roanoke and on the North Carolina mainland. Harriot reported that in those towns in which the Indians "practiced against us . . . within a few days after our departure from every such town, the people began to die very fast, and many in a short space . . . the disease was so strange, that they neither knew what it was, nor how to cure it; the like by the report of the oldest men in the country never happened before, time out of mind." The Indian werowance Wingina had an explanation based on the Indians' way of seeing, or in this case, not seeing. He assumed that the English could kill from a distance, with "invisible bullets," and he petitioned the English not to practice their magic on him and his people. Survivors from the stricken villages also sought to reconcile themselves with the English. They begged to be shown the way of the English god, that he might not be angry with them. For the English did not die, and this must mean they had some power the Indians did not.[205]

Wingina made sense of what he and the other Indians saw happening, or rather, what they could not see, by attributing the maladies to the intentional English manipulation of the spirit world. He professed that the English had reinforcements coming through the air, "yet invisible and without bodies." That made the English powerful, but that power was dark, akin to witchcraft. The Indians feared witches, and this made them suspect the English, even as they put themselves under the English colonists' protection. Perhaps Lane and his men turned into witches behind their walls, after driving away the Indians' guardian spirits.[206]

Third, Lane's works suggested that the English had more in mind that simply keeping their secrets hidden from the Indians. They brought with them a heritage of thinking about material things completely alien to Indian thought. The fort owed its design to a mathematical revolution in fortification theory and practice then taking place in Europe. The origin of that revolution was the introduction of artillery, and with it came new technological and tactical ways of organizing siege warfare which destroyed natural landscapes and replaced them with artificial planes, ramps, and redoubts.

Even a fortress as small as Lane's was built around its cannons. Cannons dictated a mathematical design that allowed the ordnance, placed on raised bastions at the corners of the walls, or curtains, to fire along the walls. The resulting geometrically precise fort could be a square or a polygon with many sides, but it always had bastions projecting out, in triangular shape, because that was the best shape for covering the approaches to the fort and preventing the enemy from undermining it or scaling the walls. Where they rejoined the corners of the fort, the bastions had short, straight sides that faced one another so that defenders could fire at right angles along the curtain. Fortress builders had, therefore, to calculate angles of fire and the distances or range of fire that muskets or cannon could reach.[207] It was all mathematics, straight-sight lines, elevations and declinations, and nothing of the original lay of the land.[208] Lane knew about these matters of fort construction and their tactical purpose, having served in the English army in Ireland as an officer of infantry and as an equerry, an administrative post.[209] Moreover, he had already built two forts of his own early in the 1585 voyage, when the expedition to Roanoke had tarried in the Caribbean.[210] None of these forts blended into the landscape. They were not meant to blend. They sent the message: See us, we are here to stay.

From all indications, Lane's fort at Roanoke looked out of place in the landscape to the Indians; it hurt the Indian eye, disturbed whatever natural spirits lived on the island, and violated the natural shapes of dune, marsh, grassy park, and woods. But in Lane's mind, the fort was a comfort. Nearly two hundred years later, on the upper reaches of the Susquehanna, another Englishman approached another English fort to await a parley with Indians:

"To [Turbutt] Francis, that fort must have been a pleasant sight. Its palisades and blockhouses, barracks and magazine, officers' quarters and commandant's house symbolized his colony's success in turning back the savage foe and imposing a new order on the frontier. The fifty-five Indians approaching the Forks [of the river] from the other direction on the morning of August 19 [1756] would have seen things differently . . . [Fort Augusta] was a magnet for 'vast numbers' of the intruders, people bent on creating a 'very considerable settlement' with no place for Indians.'"[211] It was as much this visual comfort as the matter of security that set Lane to work.

Wingina hurled words against the physical impositions of the fort. These he used well throughout the winter of 1585–86, building an Indian confederacy to wipe out the English. Wingina had given other villages word to assemble, and at a gathering of warriors, into which Lane barged, the Indians were working out their plan to destroy the English. Wingina had not struck yet, hoping perhaps that Lane's quixotic journey up the Roanoke would finish him off. Lane's unforeseen reappearance in Wingina's bailiwick, as if dead men returned to the world again, dissuaded the werowance and his allies from carrying out their plan in the spring.

What Wingina told the other village headmen we will never know, but we do know that warriors were taught from their childhood to fear shame; hardened by exercise, ritual, and abstinence, they were "expected to increase their hunting exploits over time, receiving new personal names, denoting their achievements." Boys saw war as honorable and adult warriors took part in it. Their sense of honor required them to repay all insults and their courage enabled them to face death stoically. Their culture instilled these values in them.[212]

Readying himself for combat with Lane, Wingina changed his name. The Algonquians of the coast were patrilineal, like the English—one's clan membership passed through the father's line. But names could be changed to reflect a person's character, a life event, or a particular deed.[213] When his brother, Granganimo, who had first welcomed the English to the area in 1584 (and warned them not to truck with his brother on Roanoke Island), died, Wingina changed his name to *Pemisapan*. *Wingina* meant "who looks at things with equanimity," a good name for a trading partner or a host. *Pemisapan* means "he looks out for" or "he inspects" or perhaps "he suspects."[214] Names tell a story, and the story that Pemisapan was telling his allies was that they must wash the dust from their eyes. They must see clearly that the English purpose had always been conquest.[215]

Pemisapan could not look into the fort—the planks or slats the English used to span the vertical posts prevented the Indians from viewing the interior. Still, Lane knew that he was being closely observed, "for in truth they, privy to their own villainous purposes against us, held as good espial upon us, both day and night, as we did upon them."[216] In response, Lane no doubt posted "sentinels and courts de guard [guard houses, or huts]" when they went hunting or camped in Indian country).[217] In every encounter with the Indians the English kept a sharp lookout.[218]

The Indians did not have the benefit of written reports, but they were superb at tracking game and human prey, and the Roanokes tried to keep tabs on every Englishman in their territory. Pemisapan often joined his warriors as they canoed across the sound to hunt deer and wildfowl in the reeds that fringed the island. In the middle of May 1586, Pemisapan ordered the dismantling of the fish weirs he had built for the English. But the English refused to depart. From concealment, the Roanokes watched them plant another corn crop.[219] They counted numbers. As if the English were prey, the Indians studied their habits. Did they put aside their swords to carry firewood? How long did it take them to reload their matchlocks? How good were they with their longbows? The Indians could smell the lighted matches—without them the muskets were useless—but the bows were another matter. Indian archers respected the effects of the longbow. The war of nerves continued, until Lane, never a patient man, could no longer stand the waiting. He sent word that he wished to meet with Pemisapan on the mainland on June 1. He arrived at dawn and assassinated the chief and his councilors.[220] Pemisapan had put words ahead of visions, listened to Lane once too often, believed his ears instead of his eyes, and died for it.

After Lane left North Carolina, the Indians reduced his fort to rubble. Its ruins would no longer trouble the spirits; its walls would no longer offend the eye. The settlers whom John White brought in 1587 rebuilt the fortifications, but when he returned to Roanoke in 1590 to look for his "lost" colonists, he found that the Indians had once more burned the buildings and dug up the foundations. The fort's outlines were barely visible when Carolina trader John Lawson passed though in the early eighteenth century; grassy mounds marked where ramparts had stood. The Indians had deliberately wiped out all visual traces of the English occupation.

One might, in charity to Lane and the English with him, regard his quarrel with Pemisapan as the struggle of two self-willed warriors. It would then have no more general meaning than the circumstances around it required. The English, hungry and virtually besieged, saw the Indians as fiends. The Indians, put upon and disrespected, saw the English as thieves. No need to talk about perceptual strategies or sensory imperialism. What happened at Roanoke Island was precedent confined to its narrow fact pattern.[221] But events at Jamestown, twenty years later, prove that Roanoke's sensory warfare was no fluke.

Jamestown

The same conflicting perceptual processes, the same miscoding of sights and sounds, that had caused friction between the English and the Indians at Roanoke exploded in a series of crises during the first two decades of English settlement at Jamestown. By the close of this era of crisis, both sides would have taken its own measure of the other. After the demise of the Powhatan confederation and the transformation of the Jamestown settlement into the colony of Virginia, neither side would ever see the other in a friendly light. Sensory imperialism would have triumphed, and provided a template for the rest of English settlement in North America.

In 1606, the newly chartered Virginia Company of London hired Christopher Newport, an experienced ship captain who had taken part in the Roanoke voyages to command an expedition to the Chesapeake, north of the Roanoke site. In November 1606, the company of 105 gentlemen, laborers, craftsmen, and four boys set sail, including in its number Gabriel Archer, George Percy, and John Smith, a veteran of Europe's wars against the Turks.

On April 26, 1607, Newport brought his little fleet safely to Cape Henry, at the mouth of the Chesapeake Bay, then sailed up the James River to find a site for the new settlement. The mouth of the river is so wide that Newport must have hoped that he had found the "Indrawing Sea" geographers had predicted would lead to the Pacific. The directors had instructed him to find a place that he could defend against Spanish attacks from the sea and Indian assaults from the land. In effect, the company's conception of the ideal fort was visual—the ability to see the enemy from whatever direction he came. There was no instruction on what the settlement was to look like from the ground up—nothing on the vegetation, the water supply, the lay of the land, none of the features that the natives would have immediately weighed when deciding where they would lay out a village.[222]

Newport chose a potato-shaped peninsula of marsh, woods, and grass connected to the mainland by a narrow isthmus, calling it James Island, after King James I of England. It looked appealing. The water at the river's edge was deep enough for the ships to tie lines to trees on shore and the land was already partially cleared. On May 14, the colonists and sailors alit on the northwestern edge of James Island and began to build the shelters and storehouse of Jamestown. They constructed a "half moon" redoubt, probably a version of a "demilune" with triangular sides, the point aimed at the mainland

James Island from the Isthmus

The site was dictated by instructions from the Virginia Company to Newport: a place defensible from attack by land or sea. The river had to be deep enough to harbor the company's ships (in order to load timber and other raw materials for the English market) and not wider than a cannon shot (in order to hit enemy vessels attempting to sail past the settlement). But James Island's terrain was swampy, and it lay at the confluence of the river's fresh and salt water. Soon settlers were dying from the pathogens in their own waste. (Photograph by author.)

and a half circle at the rear. Behind the first fort, they threw up thatched-roofed shanties much as one would find in poorer rural districts of England. The familiar sights comforted them. After a week, Newport set sail upriver with twenty men, to look for indications of rare metals that might be mined and to open trade negotiations with the Indians farther along the James.[223]

Archer, a member of Newport's party, kept a journal of its progress. A merchant and investor in the company, his perceptions followed his purse. He envisioned in natural abundance the prospect of exportable commodities. The waterfalls were "very fit for the building of water mills [for timber] thereon."

The trees were the "fairest yea and best that any of us ever saw being fit for any use whatsoever, as ships, houses, planks, pale boards, masts, wainscoting, clapboard, for pikes or elsewhat." Much as Harriot had in Roanoke, Archer saw the future in Virginia. "The soil is more fertile than can be expressed," a black sandy mold on top of red clay. Fruits loved the topsoil; the clay would make bricks. The English found an abundance of sturgeon, oysters, and wild crabs, as well as wild fowl, and "broke their fast" on turkeys and blackbirds. The land and its products seemed ripe for the taking by the English.[224] Archer superimposed a template of commercial farming and timbering upon the woods and clearings.

The English on the James River resorted to the same set of rudimentary signs to communicate with the Indians as Harriot and White had used at Roanoke. "By our word of kindness" and "by signs" Newport's men haled Indians in a canoe, one of whom took from Archer a pen and paper and drew a map of the course of the river. The local chief was the vassal of the powerful Powhatan, whose village was further up the river at the falls and whose confederation spread over the entire region. Powhatan arrived, his subordinates forming an honor guard. The Newport crew offered gifts, received offerings from native peoples on both sides of the river, and sailed on to the seat of the mighty Powhatan himself, "whereon he sows his wheat [i.e. corn], beans, peas, tobacco, pumpkins, gourds, hemp, flax, and etc., and were any art used to the natural state of this place, it would be a goodly habitation." Removed to the Powhatan's village, once more the English were feasted, but their "best entertainment [was a] friendly welcome." Powhatan indicated by signs that all the Chesapeake Indians gave him tribute, and Newport "signified" that the English would regard all Powhatan's enemies as their own enemies. "Hereupon he (very well understanding by the words and signs we made, the signification of our meaning) moved of his own accord a league of friendship with us, which our captain kindly embraced." By giving gifts of food, Powhatan was telling the English that he viewed them as allied dependents. The dominant partner gave. The English, reading them as tributes of subordinates, accepted them as proof that the Indians would become the willing subjects of King James. Mistakes all around.[225]

What did the Powhatan make of this array of strangers? He had heard of their coming, their vessels described to him by his allies down river. Now they stood before him, armored and armed. He must have been impressed by the metalwork; Indians had wicker and wooden armor only. Their swords and halberds may also have caught his eye. Perhaps they would give him one—a trophy, a tribute, and a formidable weapon? He did not know how the fire sticks worked, but he and his warriors had heard them, and perhaps their deadly effect was already known, as well. The Spanish had been to his lands years before and the soldiers among them carried such weapons. The helmets, too, were striking, not alone for the protection they would give against a tomahawk blow to the head, but for their display value. Who could resist their sharp crests (though they were too hot for summer wear, surely). All this gave him pause. If the English who stood before him were the vanguard of a mightier force to come (the very argument that Smith would make when captured), it would be well to have them as allies.

Following Richard White's notion of a middle ground of European-Indian accommodation defined by creative misperceptions, this James River ceremony should have established a means for the two peoples to live and work together in some semblance of harmony.[226] But the very effort to bring consonance to so many novel sensations was already leading the two groups in different directions. Powhatan had just completed a furious thirty-year process of consolidation of his confederation of villages.[227] He regarded Jamestown as another town to be assimilated into the confederation. If the English resisted, he knew how to impose his will on them. The English saw an Indian king who was still a savage; surely he would soon recognize the might of the English nation. If he wavered in his promises of friendship and refused to supply the colonists with victuals, the English knew how to subdue him. This was a volatile middle ground, and it soon shook with violence.

Both sides' desires and needs had bent their perceptions of the encounter and its prospects. Powhatan was overconfident and short-sighted. He had brought the entire region under his personal dominion. How much trouble could a few newcomers pose? Unused to such novelty as they represented and accustomed to handle novelty in a holistic, communal way, he was unable to comprehend the dimensions of the English threat. The English were even more perceptually inept. The had, for example, let military considerations dictate the site of their encampment, and immediately suffered for it. Jamestown sat on a natural wetlands crossed by two sluggish streams. The eight hundred acres were mosquito-ridden and the English suffered from malaria, which the mosquitos carried from man to man. Worst of all, the isthmus was situated at the confluence of the fresh and the salt water on the James River, causing the ground water on the island to retain most of the waste that the colonists produced. In no time at all, they were drinking and washing in their refuse and falling ill from typhoid fever, dysentery, and other ailments.[228]

Their inability to read the perils of the terrain was equaled by the English ignorance of its human landscape. Jamestown lay in the territory of the Paspaheghs, unhappy members of the Powhatan confederation. Newport had visited them, and they had "entertained him with much welcome" on the fourth of May, some nine days before the English selected the Jamestown site for their settlement, but the English did not ask the Paspaheghs' permission to land, did not seek their consent to the use of the land, did nothing to placate them. The werowance of the Paspahegh arrived, with a hundred-odd warriors, on the eighteenth, plainly seeking some form of submission or at least of alliance. The English took to their arms, there was a quarrel over a stolen axe, and the Indians left "suddenly away with great anger." Watching with growing anger, the Paspaheghs called in all their allies and plotted an assault on the little settlement. The English did not perceive the danger, and the next day four of them followed a path into the woods, "the ground all flowing over with fair flowers of sundry colors and kinds, as thought it had been in any garden or orchard in England."[229]

Jamestown had not been in place two weeks when its sensory history duplicated that of Roanoke. There were no creative misperceptions, although misperception abounded. The Indians mounted an all-out assault on the little fort, the English drove off the attack; and neither side learned the lessons it might have, because both sides' sensations of the events fit pre-existing, pre-encounter models. We have three versions of the little battle from the English colonists. They differed in outlook and purpose, but together they indicate how English perspectives governed English observations.

Archer's financial prospects depended on the success of the colony. He did not see the battle but recast what others had told him in heroic terms. He believed that Newport and the councillors would always be a step head of the Indians, even though they returned to Jamestown a day after the fighting. Then, more than a hundred Indians had assaulted the fort, overrunning the tents outside the redoubt and killing a man and a boy. But four of the council chosen by the Virginia Company to run the colony stood in front of the fort and discharged their muskets, defying the enemy.[230] The Indians carried their wounded and dead away. "A little after they made a huge noise in the woods, which our men surmised was at the burying of their slain men." The next day, the English busied themselves "palisading" the settlement. On June 8, emissaries of the werowances from up river arrived, lay down their bows to show they meant no harm, and called "Wingapoh," a friendly greeting, but were driven off by mistake. On the fourteenth, they returned, and Newport recognized one of his hosts from the falls of the James. The two men parleyed, the Indians promising to intercede with the Paspaheghs and their allies or to join the English to fight against their enemies.[231] All would be well, Archer was certain.

George Percy kept his own account of these events, an educated gentleman's literary journal. It was Percy who went off gathering flowers in the woods the day after the Paspahegh's demonstration of their collective anger. Later that day he joined in teasing the Indians when their arrows could not pierce a steel target. He had little to say of the actual fighting. He had seen enough of combat in Europe to know that the Paspahegh incursion was merely a skirmish. He did not see the Indians as villains, but as adversaries. The world was full of conflict; who could expect anything less in this howling wilderness? There is, in fact, a bit of the cynic in his journal. He had never liked the site that Newport picked for the settlement, and he did not regard Newport as a hero. Instead, he took a professional pride in the construction of the fort. On June 15 "we had built and finished our fort which was triangle wise, having three bulwarks at every corner like a half moon, and for or five pieces of artillery mounted in them, we had made ourselves sufficiently strong for these savages."[232] An English Renaissance gentleman like Percy, who had traveled through the Low Countries at the height of the religious wars, had nothing to fear from the savages.[233]

Where Archer trusted heroes and Percy trusted himself, John Smith trusted no one. He offered an account based on hearsay, but it was the most sensuously cogent of the three. He opined that there could be no sensate compromise between Indian and English.[234] The English acted in plain sight; the Indians skulked. The English reached out in friendship; the Indians hid their feelings and emotions. "Had not God (beyond all the [Indians'] expectations) by means of the ships at whom they [the crews] shot with their ordinances and muskets, caused them [the Indians] to retire, they [would have] entered the fort with our own men, [who] were then busied in setting corn, their arms being then in [boxes] and few ready but certain gentlemen." The colony had survived by a whisker, though thirteen or fourteen were hurt and one killed. At last the English had the dust cleared from their eyes, and "with all speed we palisaded our fort."[235]

Smith regarded the Indians as opponents from the first, and the defining characteristic of that enmity was sensory divergence. He was not the only Englishman to declare sensory war. The English regarded the naked savage as a mere brute, "vile and stinking" in custom. The Indians saw the English as thieves without manners, intruders who refused to leave when they had overstayed their welcome.[236] Even the English understood the animosity of the Indians at "what may be the issue of these strong preparations, landed in their coasts, and yearly supplied with fresher troops . . . to which they open their ears wide, and keep their eyes waking, with good espial upon every thing that stirs, the *noise of our drums of our shrill trumpets and great ordinance* . . . have bred strong fears amongst them" [italics added].[237] The Indians feared thunder. Perhaps the sound of cannon would cow them as well. The English were waging sensory warfare.

The Indians understood those tactics and would employ them in horrific manner in 1622. Indians on the coast were not unused to newcomers or to changes in their material lives due to trade. The Powhatan country was the site of antimony mines, and the ore, used for body paint, had been exchanged widely up and down the coast long before the Spanish and the English visited.[238] Nor was warfare a surprise to the Powhatans; the confederacy itself was a product as much of war as of diplomacy and kinship. But the impact of the English way of warring and the dispersion and multiplication of English staple-crop cultivators on the land was wholly different and unprecedented. The very sight of the English habitations and tobacco fields became as offensive to the Powhatans as they had been to the Roanokes. Even the words of the English grew hateful. English missionaries eager to convert the Indians to Christianity by first making them civilized, "by fair and loving means, suiting to our English nature," inflamed Indian resentment. The savages had first to be shorn of their "blasphemous idolatries" before the transformation process could take root, which meant that every Indian holy place, every shrine, every relic and tomb must be destroyed and the power of every shaman curbed.[239] The spirits of the land and the waters would depart forever. Nothing would look or sound the same when the Indians adopted the faith of the English.[240]

From afar, Smith envisioned the Indians' chagrin and predicted that they would rise up in anger. He was right. Opechancanough, who had succeeded his half-brother Powhatan as paramount chief, plotted the expulsion of the English from the first time he laid eyes on Smith.[241] Only Powhatan's hesitancy to wage open war, accompanied by the ability of the company to restock the colony with men and material, deterred Opechancanough from carrying out his plan. But by 1622, the werowance had seen enough. His half-brother dead, his allies driven from their villages, he had become the Powhatan and wanted but the occasion to recover the native landscape and welcome the native spirits back.

Opechananough designed the attack on the English to be a sensory event that no surviving colonists would ever forget. It must be visible, audible, and tactile. But to succeed, the attack must camouflage itself. According to Smith,

the werowance knew that the English had grown careless, "their houses generally opened to the savages, who were always friendly fed at their tables, and
lodged in their bed-chambers."[242] The plan, set to begin in the early morning
of March 22, 1622, was simple: At breakfast time enter the homes of the unsuspecting Virginians carrying no weapons but those concealed on their person, engage in friendly conversation over the first meal, then use the English
people's tools to murder their hosts, "not sparing either age or sex, man woman
or child . . . neither did these beasts spare those amongst the rest well known
unto them, from whom they had daily received many benefits." To enforce the
message of the Indians' fury on the minds of the settlers, victims would be
mutilated and then displayed. For example, Nathaniel Powell and his entire
family were decapitated and hanged in plain sight.[243] Some of the gruesome
details in Smith's account resulted from hysterical reports, and some were
propaganda, but the decapitation of enemies was a common sensory tactic
used to heighten the terror of the carnage.[244] Torture of the captives served the
same purpose. It was always highly visible, auditory, and even olfactory. What
is more, it worked in terms of the way that Indians processed the report of the
senses. Its performance and meaning were communal. The whole village participated. The strong, comely, and hardy might be deemed worthy of incorpo-
ration into the village—a confirmation of the importance of the immediate
sensory information in determining the value of a person (and proof of the
highly empirical Indian understanding of the senses). Even in death the valiant
enemy did not show weakness, for showing weakness was the worst form of
weakness, because it was the most sensuous. Throughout the entire process,
there was no clear demarcation line between the spiritual and the mundane—
the victim existed in both the everyday and the supernatural worlds.[245] Cannibalism was an alternative form of sensory warfare. It simultaneously humili-
ated the enemy and stole his inner spirit. He could never gain revenge from the
other world and his strength passed to those who consumed him. Invariably, it
was practiced in the sight of survivors, so it would not be forgotten.[246]

Three hundred and forty-seven Virginians, a quarter of the settlers, died in
the massacre; the rest would always remember what they had seen and
heard.[247] Opechancanough's sensory warfare had worked too well, however,
for the English had a sensory answer for the "massacre of 1622," one that went
beyond burning Indian villages and crops. Typically, after the massacre, the
Indians suing for peace begged to be able to plant their corn.[248] They wanted
to restore their old scenery of village and garden plot. But the English had
another vision of the colony, which would alter the face of Tidewater Virginia.
In the English landscape, the Indian would forever be a foreigner.

Changing the Scenery

English occupation profoundly changed the landscape of Virginia. In the years after the massacre, the speed and thoroughness of the Anglicization of the landscape intensified. Building houses and clearing fields for planting were even more important in the sensory campaign to establish English dominion over Virginia than were the sounds of cannons or war whoops. From Jamestown, in 1608, Smith had begged the company: "I entreat you rather send by thirty carpenters, husbandmen, gardeners, fisher men, blacksmiths, masons, and diggers up of trees, roots well provided, than a thousand of such we [already] have."[249] Smith understood that carpenters would succeed where soldiers had failed in dispossessing the natives, because English houses and English fields would make the landscape hospitable for the English and inhospitable for the Indians. John Smith never got his carpenters, and a year later he left the colony, never to return. But in 1614 Smith visited the coast of what he would call a "New England" and on it he mapped a vision of what Virginia might be were its landscape transformed by English hands. "And surely by reason of those sandy cliffs and cliffs of rocks, both which we saw so planted with gardens and corn fields, and so well inhabited with a goodly, strong, and well proportioned people, besides the greatness of the timber growing on them, the greatness of the fish and the moderate temper of the air . . . who can but approve this a most excellent place, both for health and fertility? . . . The ground is so fertile, that questionless it is capable of producing any grain, fruits, or seeds you will so or plant." Here the homeless and the sturdy unemployed of England, the simple farmers who needed land, and the families who wanted to improve themselves could make a new England.[250]

The plow was the pen with which the English husbandman wrote his name on the land, the furrow the proof of his productivity.[251] When English plows replaced Indian hoes and English furrows Indian hillocks, the victory of sensory imperialism would be ensured. That is what, albeit somewhat haphazardly, the Virginia Company of London finally did, by transforming itself from a merchant venture into a real estate development firm. In early 1609, the company reorganized itself to increase its capital, and the new organization determined that the follies of the past two years would end. Armed with a revised charter that gave to the new "governor general," Thomas Gates, the powers of a military dictator, the company dispatched seven hundred settlers to Virginia. Under its new government, the colonists began to spread themselves up and down the river.[252] Jamestown avoided the fate of Roanoke because the Virginia Company, before its demise in 1624, provided sufficient resources to populate a large area of the James River shoreline and encouraged the planting of a commercially viable export crop: tobacco. Tobacco cultivation in the end would do what trumpets and artillery could not–it would make Virginia look like a little England. A boom time in tobacco production, corresponding to widening demand in England and Europe, enabled the company to recruit emigrants. In 1615, the colony sent home two thousand pounds of tobacco; by 1629 that figure had risen to a million and a half pounds. Everyone from governors to servants devoted themselves to the new crop.[253]

In the wake of the massacre, when the English had begun their campaign to destroy every Indian village in the region, Governor Francis Wyatt wrote a letter defending his stewardship of the colony. It needed some defense, for under his care the colony had suffered greatly, and the Virginia Company of London, on its last legs financially, had collapsed. But Wyatt still had a vision for the colony, a vision ratified when he was continued in power as royal governor under James I. He conceded what no one could gainsay: There had been "starving, bloody and wretched times" even before the Indian uprising. Land distribution policies did not favor the security of the cultivators of tobacco, and disease thinned the numbers of settlers alarmingly. The company should have sent beer and cider, for "to plant a colony by water drinkers was an inexcusable error in those, who laid the first foundation, and have made it a received custom." Indians drank the water, their wild and savage constitutions containing its pestilence. But now there was hope for the English, for "our first work is expulsion of the savages to gain the free range of the country for increase of cattle, swine and etc. which will more than restore us" in health. Then, "our intent was after the massacre to have seated the whole colony, (or most part thereof) upon the forest." In other words, by forever changing the landscape from forest and Indian village to English fields and plantations, the colony could be saved, the colonists enriched, and England reap the profits.[254]

Wyatt had seen the future, a sensory dominion that the English would visit upon the land and its living things. If fort building signaled the English initiation of sensory imperialism, and tobacco cultivation brought that vision closer to fruition, the "expulsion of the salvages" guaranteed that English senses would triumph. The Indian would no more be able to hide in the brush or the forest. The Indians' whoops would no longer terrify the settlers.

The scorched-earth policy the English adopted against the Indians after 1622 should thus be seen as part of a war the English waged against the land itself. When the English arrived, the environment had supported a great diversity of species, in part because Indian farmers' methods of clearing land did not exhaust the subsoil nutrients. The Indians turned forest into garden by "girdling" the trees (slashing and removing the bark of the tree) and firing the underbrush. The old field or abandoned village garden turned to "park land"—grassy meadows, perfect for browsing animals like deer—then back to forest.[255] Ecologists estimate that Indian corn culture resulted in a loss of no more than one percent of all forest lands, although in some regions of the coast, the Indians' intensive cultivation had resulted in some deforestation.[256] By contrast, English farmers set about transforming mixed woodland and fields into tobacco plantations. Not only did the company, and later the farmers, use the timber for houses and fuel, they sold timber products like tar, planks and shingles, and naval products to England and the West Indies. The English did not miss the lost forests, which they regarded as dangerous places to live.[257]

Colonial herds of cattle, sheep, and pigs further damaged local environments. English domestic animals ate their way into Indian gardens and competed with deer for forage. One of the first acts of the Indian raiders during the 1622 massacre was the killing of cattle, and the peace accords of 1628 stipulated that no English cattle were to be harmed in future.[258] The colonists left the trapping of beaver and other fur-bearing animals to the Indians, but by inducing the natives to overhunt fur-bearing animals, the colonists further disturbed the ecology of the New World. Untended beaver dams collapsed, spilling rich soils. Clear-cutting of timber, deep plowing, allowing domestic livestock to range freely over the land, and the extinction of many species of mammal left Virginia far poorer in diversity of plants and animals.[259]

The Powhatan chiefdom, after a decade of English retaliation, was in no position to contest the transformation of the Virginia countryside from grassy meadows and woods to tobacco and wheat farms and cattle runs. The Indians had become a minority on their own land, and what is more, an impoverished minority. In 1644, Opechancanough attempted a last full-scale rebellion, but it was crushed. Surviving Indian villages were soon hedged around by English farms.[260] In 1645 and 1646, the House of Burgesses provided for the construction of a line of blockhouses along the frontier—to keep the Indians in sight. In the meantime, the Indian tribes were relocated behind the falls of the James and the York Rivers, allowing the colony to confiscate more than three hundred thousand acres of Indian land.[261]

By the 1630s, English fields bounded by worm, or zigzag, fences or planted hedges replaced the wild glades that had so delighted George Percy.[262] These hedges and fences were not just statements of ownership, they were highly visible, artificial, and abstract signs. They did not fit into the landscape but struck the viewer—as they were intended to do—by standing out from the surrounding fields and woods. The weather, too, would be changed by the English presence. Deforested, Virginia grew warmer. Even the mosquitoes would diminish as the number of English increased.[263] In time this would be so—as wet marsh and fen gave way to drier field and meadow—though that time was much longer in coming than the English imagined.

The first English arrivals at Jamestown had put themselves in peril by not knowing which Indian village occupied which plot of land, but like the "posted" notices that today warn trespassers not to enter, the colonists' hedge and fence required no local knowledge. These artificial land markers did not distinguish between one claimant and another; deed books and plot books in the county courthouse would do that. It was enough that the eye could tell "this land is mine." Pemisapan and Opechancanough had learned the lesson; the English eye had defeated the Indian eye. English sensory imperialism had turned the novel into the familiar, and introduced into the natural landscape

Restored farmstead at Colonial Williamsburg

The fences of colonial Virginia are ubiquitous and unmistakable reminders of English possession. These zigzag, or worm, fences (also often called "Virginia fences") were easily assembled and erected. They kept cows from wandering and also marked boundaries of farms. Indian gardening was communal and had no need of fencing, so the appearance of fences in any region announced the transformation of native landscape into English scenery. (Photograph by author.)

a perception of absolute individual ownership taken from across the sea. In the meantime, sensory imperialism taught the English that novelty was dangerous. Better to rearrange what one saw and heard, to reproduce what one remembered of the Old World. The Indians, too late, perceived the inverse lesson. The novel encounter with the Europeans ended in death. In this light, Opechancanough's rebellion was a last, desperate gamble born of a sense of irrevocable loss—the loss of a sensate world.

•

There would be times when the English and the Indians would have common interests,[264] but they would never—could never—see eye to eye or hear one another truly. Where the Indians perceived a sacred landscape of woods and water and named the land for its natural features, the English imagined a cultivated scenery of boundary fences and tobacco fields marked on maps by English county, town, and noble names. Indian places where the "land was densely settled" (*Tsenacomoco* in the Powhatan dialect of Algonquian) became Jamestown in Virginia.[265] The Indians' landscape was flexible, and villages moved from place to place; field turned to park land and returned to forest. The English scenery was fixed by invisible lines drawn in deed books. Indian gardens mixed varieties of crops and so resembled the diversity of forest and park; English fields were sown with a single crop, uniform in appearance, odor, and texture.[266]

By the beginning of the nineteenth century, the original clearings of the peregrinating coastal natives had vanished from the settlers' accounts, just as surely as the remnant of the original villagers was melting into memory. As James Fenimore Cooper wrote in 1823, recalling his youth in the Otsego country, "a dreary and dark wood, where the rays of the sun could but rarely penetrate, and where even the daylight was obscured and rendered gloomy by the deep forests" had greeted the settlers in his father's generation. They transformed the natural landscape into pastoral scenery. "The green wheat fields were seen in every direction, spotted with the dark and charred stumps that had, in the preceding season, supported some of the proudest trees of the forest. Ploughs were in motion."[267] What had been a "timeless, wild land of pure nature,"[268] became "schools, academies, churches, meeting-houses, turnpike roads, and a market town . . . neat and comfortable farms . . . and beautiful and thriving villages."[269] Because the eye and ear could no longer perceive them, the sounds and sights of Indian habitation and cultivation vanished as if they had never existed.

CHAPTER TWO

Invisible Worlds

Indian Wars and Witchcraft Crises

WE LIVE in two distinct worlds of sensation. The first is readily and immediately available. We are bombarded by sound, sights, and odors; our palates are treated to foods from all over the world; we told to "reach and out touch someone" every day. The second world is more elusive, in some sense "invisible." Browsing the internet for the "invisible world," one finds thousands of references to microbes and disease. We cannot see or hear these "animalcules," but we touch (and sometimes taste and smell) them all the time.[1] The bacteria, viruses, and prions of the microscopic realm comprise even smaller bits of matter, and these too defy precise measurement.[2] "Too small" is not all that is invisible and inaudible. "Too far to see" and "too faint to hear" are also within the reach of our perceptions but beyond the grasp of our unaided senses. The science sections of our newspapers are weekly filled with reports of stars whose light has taken billions of years to reach our eyes and a "big bang" that no one has ever heard or will ever hear.[3]

Perception of the microscopic and telescopic worlds are matters for machines, our senses technologically enhanced. Our willingness to allow scientists to supply the gaps in direct sensation with causal inferences lies somewhere between a conceit and a faith in modernity. Before the discoveries of germs and quasars, descriptions of tiny animals and distant stars would have seemed fantastic at best and demonic at worst. Long ago, the providers of such tales would have been thought wizards. For in early modern England and its American colonies, the invisible world wore a different cast than it does today. It was just as close—indeed, it overlapped the visible world—but its presence was discerned in a different fashion and its impact felt in different ways.

Today skeptics consign claims of ghosts, spirits, and specters to the category "paranormal" and suspect that its probers and purveyors are fakes.[4] We find plausible explanations for implausible sensations in the chemistry of the brain rather than the supernatural. We liken the sensory content of the paranormal to dreams or hallucinations (also invisible to others) or confabulation—our mind's knack of putting together bits of events, images, and information that in real life are wholly separate in time and place.[5] When the little boy played by Haley Joel Osment sees ghosts in *The Sixth Sense* and says to the psychologist played by Bruce Willis, "How can you help me if you don't believe me? Sometimes magic is real," almost everyone in the audience shivers, but everyone knows it's just a movie.

But many of us do not accept this materialistic depiction of the invisible world. For some, the supernatural is not only close at hand, it beckons. In this conviction, supernaturalists are the true inheritors of the founders of the English colonies three centuries ago. When the English landed in the New World they brought with them a belief in the supernatural. Then, everyone from the midwife and plowman to the gentlewoman and the prince conceded the potency of the unseen. The invisible crossed over into the visible, and the unseen had power over everyday life that manifested itself in solemn judgments. One could read omens and prodigies that the invisible world wrote in "multiplied signs, in heaven, earth, and sea."[6] Shipwrecks, monstrous births, sudden storms, and other unexpected and unnerving events pointed to the clash of powerful forces in another, unseen world. This invisible world harbored ghosts, witches, and demons as well as angels, a shrouded sphere with delights for the pious and horrors for the damned.[7]

The pious believed that God's providence was everywhere, although its Author could not be seen. Renowned experimental scientists like Robert Boyle maintained that the "supernatural" was as real as the natural world, and it contained both "intelligent beings" whose purpose was benign as well as Satan and his demons. Reform Protestant ministers told their congregations to pray for God's assistance and He would aid them. But even the Puritan ministers believed that there were "Evil Angels," and they warned their congregants against the inadvertent summoning of such spirits through magic, divination, or astrology.[8] The warning was not always heeded, for the laity routinely sought the aid of cunning folk to ward off invisible evildoers. What gave the veiled universe such puissance in early modern Europe was not so much a faith in the wonders of the unseen world as the presence in it of the devil. In Christian texts the devil was evil personified, immanent, and incarnate. He was "God's ape," imitating by opposition, turning everything upside down.[9]

He looked the part, too: dark, tawny, or red, with horns, claws, teeth, and leathery skin. He could take the shape of fearsome animals and could roar like a beast of prey.[10] His mouth was sulphurous and his eye fearsome. He took a particular dislike to devout Englishmen, and for them, "the battle with Satan and his hierarchy of demons was thus a literal reality."[11]

The devil's wiles lured the unwary and the corrupt to his side. The devil promised release from the torments of hell, as well as sexual and material gratification in this life. In particular, young women seeking wealth and old women seeking vengeance against those who mistreated them were vulnerable to his seductive allure. They became his witches by sealing a pact with him: their service for his powers.[12] Through his converts he could reach out of the invisible world into the visible one. With these powers, witches could cause pain and even kill those whom they wished to harm.[13] Such a pact was the antithesis of the Christian covenant with God, a particularly odious inversion to radical reform Christians, who saw themselves as the inheritors of Abraham's covenant.[14]

Even the learned believed in the power of the devil, but, in what is surely one of the more remarkable revolutions in Western learned opinion, by the end of the seventeenth century the once vivid and potent paranormal realm had lost favor in educated circles. Popular folk still told stories of sprites that could appear and disappear at will, of the devil's familiars and goblins, but elite men and women preferred to look the other way. Elite opinion preferred science, reason, and experiment over the supernatural.[15] My claim is that a series of sensory crises preceded this shift.

Nowhere in early America did this revolution of the senses appear more striking than in seventeenth-century New England. Burned over by three major Indian wars, the Pequot War of 1636–37; "King Philip's War," from 1675 through 1676; and the War of the League of Augsburg, or King William's War, between 1689 and 1697; and a two-year-long controversy over suspected witchcraft, New Englanders became intimates of the invisible world. At first, its blessings explained victory over the Pequots and the conversion of the "praying Indians." During King Philip's War and the years that followed, the invisible world grew malign. Every dark path through the woods and impenetrable copse at the edge of the village became a hiding place for demons real and imagined. In the Salem witchcraft crises of 1692–93, the devil himself seemed to reach out of the invisible world to terrorize the visible one. Only then did the learned among New Englanders begin to rethink the meaning of evidences of the invisible world.

Indian Wars

The First New Englanders practiced sensory imperialism. They changed the landscape to introduce an English scenery of fields, stone walls, and sturdy domiciles. They cut down the forests, deep-plowed the soil, and let loose upon the meadows their herds of cattle. They imposed treaties on the Indians that stole Indian land for a pittance, and when the Indians protested, they forcibly occupied disputed parcels. Diminished in numbers by diseases to which they had no immunities, many coastal Indians found resistance futile, although some refused to submit or retreat. In wars against these native peoples, New Englanders saw themselves as God's warriors and gave thanks for God's judgment on New England's enemies.[16]

But the devastation of the Indian wars caused soul-searching among devout New Englanders and seemed to teach that God's aid was premised on principles not always clear, even to the most learned and pious. Surely God was testing them, and their innate sinfulness and demonstrable backsliding was responsible for their sufferings. At the same time, the travails of combat and capture produced a disquieting remapping of the invisible world in which victims discovered the traces of the Old Deluder. The invisible world after 1676 appeared as much Satan's domain as God's.

The Pequots and the Puritans

The sights and sounds of war were from New England's inception reminders that the region's native inhabitants did not welcome the English intruders. Hit-and-run raids inflamed borderlands between colonial towns and Indian villages, sending streams of refugees and captives in opposite directions out of the disputed terrain. As visible and audible as the effects of conflict were, neither side saw the other rightly and both feared what they could not see of the other's motives and actions. This was the same sensory warfare that washed over Roanoke and Jamestown, but the contest in New England was different from that to the south.

The Pequots and the Puritans of New England were unlike the Indians and the English in Virginia. The Pequots, an eastern Algonquian people whose territory extended along the northern coast of Long Island Sound from the Niantic River in Connecticut to the western edge of the Narragansett Bay, did not regard the English as a novelty. By the time they came into contact with the Europeans, the Pequots knew that the newcomers wanted Indian lands and that Europeans looked down on natives. The Pequots' control of the whelk and quahog beds (from which Indians made the much-prized wampum) on the Long Island Sound's north coast, gave them an advantage over their neighbors, but that advantage was dependent on trade with the Europeans.[17] The dominant figures among the New Englanders were Puritans, a group of radical religious reformers. They saw themselves as God's chosen people and New England as a new Canaan promised them by God. They saw no novelty in the Pequots, only a people, like the opponents of ancient Israel, whose immoral ways had to be altered and whose dominion over the land brought to an end.

To protect themselves against encroaching New Englanders, the Pequots built two fortified towns near the sound, one at Weinshauks and the other farther east, five miles up the Mystic River. Fortification of villages was not unusual for southern New England peoples, but the new towns staked a sensate claim, visually asserting Pequot dominion over the Connecticut coast. Still, the forts made that claim in characteristic southern New England native fashion. Family dwelling sites rather than keeps, they were filled with dome-shaped reed-mat wigwams. The wigwam, in reality a giant, closely woven basket, kept out all the elements except one—fire. In fact, covered with reed mats or slabs of bark, filled with wooden implements, reed baskets, firewood, furs, and tree shavings, the wigwam was a little furnace. The only difference between the precontact-period village and the Pequots' Mystic River town was that the latter was larger and more heavily fortified with a ten- to twelve-foot palisade.[18]

Within the town/fort, the Pequots clung to traditional ways. Unlike their Indian neighbors, they refused to adopt elements of European culture. Activity in and around the village aroused all the senses. The smell of tobacco and roasting meat and corn greeted the nostrils. The weavers and mat makers worked by feel. Laboring and sleeping so close to one another meant that there was no quiet place to go, no time to be alone. Conversation provided entertainment and information. Song and dance might be spontaneous. At times, activities were fixed by a ritual calendar of planting and harvesting.

But the Pequots' world had extended beyond their villages. Pequot fur traders and wampum dealers talked and listened to their English and Dutch counterparts. Pequot hunters could hear and see the English farmers turning the deer parks into cow pastures and the forests into wheat fields.[19] After a Dutch trader had killed the Pequot sachem Tatobem, the Pequots turned east and tried to reorient their commerce to Plymouth and Massachusetts. This shift in commercial partnership brought tragedy, for the English merchants who carried on the trade in guns and ammunition were among the most unscrupulous in the New World. No Pequot trusted men like John Stone and John

Oldham. From them and those like them, the Indians concluded that fraud, deceit, and lying were the nature of the New Englanders.[20]

Had the smallpox epidemic of 1633 not reduced the Pequots from twelve thousand to three thousand, war against them would have been, at least for the moment, unthinkable, but with many of their warriors dead from the disease, the New Englanders saw an opening to expand their landholdings further into the Connecticut River Valley and along the north coast of Long Island Sound. These New England homesteaders, unlike the English visitors to Roanoke and Jamestown, were in the main profoundly religious men and women, who saw the world in religious terms.[21]

Historians have not fully credited the extent to which that religiosity was sensory. Many of the New England colonists were either fleeing religious persecution or had come with those who fled persecution.[22] These Puritans (the word was originally part of the epithet "hot-blooded Puritans," applied to those who would not accept the lingering influence of Catholicism on the Church of England) imposed a highly visible and audible culture on New England. The center of their towns was the church, and the most important figure was the minister, whose piety and erudition made him a focal point of aural culture.[23]

By their adherence to his spoken words they were gathered into congregations and by his words they understood Scripture. The center of church life was the minister's sermon.[24] As they marched to church and listened for hours to sermons, the Puritans literally saw themselves as a saving remnant, the only true Christians in the world. In England and New England, Puritans tried to set a highly visible moral example for their neighbors by refusing to play, dance, or sing on the Sabbath, by studying the Bible closely, and by observing high standards of personal morality, all the while continuing their attack upon the lax conformist and the vulgar sort who thought that the sacraments, good works, and unreflecting faith were enough to save a soul.

Even as they performed works of piety for their neighbors, the Puritans constantly examined themselves for internal and external signs of God's protection and displeasure. Every act, gesture, and thought became part of an ongoing process of sensory self-consciousness, which meant that the invisible world, wherein God made his judgments, also was never far from their thoughts. The process was collective as well as individual. Often regarded as pious busy-bodies by their critics, the Puritans insisted that their loving fellowship rested upon mutual examination. For the visible gathered, or "called," church, with its meetinghouse, covenant, and membership, was only a pale

approximation of the invisible church, whose members were known with absolute certainty only to God.[25]

The Puritans first established themselves in eastern Massachusetts in 1630.
As they "hived out" in the middle 1630s, the newcomers paid little heed to the
land claims of rival colonizers in England, and less to the land claims of the
Indians, whose territory they overran.[26] By 1635, they had reached the edges of
Pequot territory, where they decided to erect their own forts. One of these
palisaded places, Saybrook, lay at the mouth of the Connecticut River, just inside what is now the border of Connecticut with Rhode Island. There the Niantics had a village, and the Dutch had built a trading post.

The outlines of the English fort remain on a small bluff at Saybrook Point,
the end of what was from 1871 until recently a railhead in the town of Old
Saybrook. The forty-yards-square bastion, with its earthworks and ditch, on
top of which stood a wooden palisade, commanded approaches to the town
from the land and overlooked Long Island sound to the south and the Connecticut River to the east. The palisade was constructed of "heavy wooden
slabs," unlike the slit-spaced openings in the Mystic Pequot palisade. At the
four corners of the curtain of the Saybrook fort stood small square cannon
platforms.[27] Thus the Saybrook fort, like the Jamestown fort, was an imposition on the land, not the outline of a village where people lived and worked,
but the boundary marker of the territory of God's chosen people.

The commander, Lieutenant Lion Gardiner, a Scot, a Puritan, and a professional soldier recalled from the wars in the Netherlands by the Puritan patent-
ees of Saybrook, turned the fort into a veritable mirror of English society, with
houses for people of quality, barracks for the soldiers and craftsmen, and a
great house for worship and holding judicial hearings. Gardiner ruled the fort
like a martinet, training the men in the use of firearms and the discipline of
war. Still, he could not stop his troops from strolling about the little peninsula
on which the fort stood, or from fishing or gathering fruits beyond the range
of the cannon. Some of these wanderers fell into the hands of the Pequots.
They were not seen alive again, though their tortured screams were heard.[28]

The Massacre at Mystic Fort

Although it sputtered on for nearly two years, at its center the war between
the Puritans and the Pequots concerned the battles at Puritan Saybrook and
Pequot Mystic. In these, the visible and the invisible worlds collided. Soon after the construction of Saybrook fort, word reached Gardiner from all directions that simmering hostilities with the Pequots would soon erupt in war.

Roger Williams heard whispers among his Narragansett friends that the Pequots had sought an alliance. This much was true: The Pequots had reached out to the Narragansetts. The delegates had their say, but the paramount sachem of the Narragansetts and Williams' friend Canonicus and his nephew Miantonomi were deadly enemies of the leading Pequot diplomat, Sassacus. The Pequots went away empty-handed. Williams passed along the warning to his friend John Winthrop, formerly governor of Massachusetts, and to William Bradford, governor of Plymouth. In Connecticut, the Mohegans spread similar alarms about the Pequots' intentions.[29] Words of war, like the summer crop of deer-flies, were buzzing and biting.

The Puritans insisted that the Pequots come and explain themselves, which they did, at Saybrook fort, in July 1636. Unable to tell one Indian from another, the Puritan conferees assumed that the same Pequots who smiled false smiles and spoke in honeyed words at Saybrook had given sanctuary to the murderers of New England trader John Oldham, aboard his shallop at Block Island, and of trader John Stone and his crew. The Pequots had no trouble reading the hard faces of the Puritans—how silly of them not to conceal their emotions. Thus war began without a formal declaration. In August 1636, Massachusetts militia colonel John Endicott led a contingent of ninety volunteers against the Indians of Block Island, clients of the Pequots. Endicott could not catch the Indians, but he burned their villages and their corn, an adumbration of the scorched-earth policy the New Englanders would pursue against the Pequots the following year. Two forts; two peoples; two ways of seeing and hearing at odds. Nothing new in that any more.

One may surmise that part of the reason the Indians agreed to negotiations at Saybrook was to scout the fort. They accomplished what the Roanokes and Powhatans had so desired—they saw into the hidden space. In the meantime, Gardiner fumed at the incompetence of the Massachusetts troops sent him, the failure of Plymouth and Connecticut to adequately supply his needs, and the growing danger of massive Indian attack, which he could sense but not see. As autumn approached, the Indians picked off stragglers they found outside the fort, burned the fort's corn fields, and butchered the cattle. The cries of the tortured captives assailed the defenders, but they could do little to help. Frightened, some threw down their arms and tried to run away, but Gardiner threatened to hang all cowards and the danger of wholesale desertion faded.[30]

On the other side, ambush whomever they might, the Pequots could not breach the fort, for they did not have artillery. So, throughout the autumn, from the concealment of the marsh grass they taunted the garrison, "Come and fetch your [captured] Englishmen's clothes . . . come out and fight . . . you are like women." In a lull, sometimes the Puritans and the Pequots would parley from a distance, out of arrow shot but close enough for the garrison to recognize that the Pequots wore clothing belonging to slain soldiers. Through translators, the Pequots asked, "Have you fought enough?" and the Puritans answered, "We know not yet." "Did the English use to kill women and children?" "We should see thereafter." The Pequots closed the conversation: "We are Pequots. We shall go to Connecticut and kill men, women and children." The parley ended abruptly, with a discharge of two of the cannon in the direction of the Pequots.[31]

The visual display of power coincided with the verbal taunting, and the Indians were not the only ones parading in their martial finery. When the Saybrook garrison was relieved by troops from Connecticut, the New Englanders, "displaying our colors," marched "completely armed, with corslets, muskets, bandoleers, rests [for their muskets] and swords."[32]

But the Indians had gone a step beyond the Puritans by stripping their victims and donning their clothing, an insult to the dead that infuriated the Puritans. English cloth was itself a valued possession among the Northeastern Indians, and in times of peace it was a consumer item avidly sought. Moreover, the stripping of a dead enemy was a time-honored display of the heroic honor of the victor long antedating the Pequots. (For example, in the *Iliad*, Achilles strips Hector and drags his naked body around the walls of Troy.) Thus the Indians' stripping of the dead New England soldiers was a typical warrior display comparable to cannibalism, the decapitation of the foe, or the mounting of the slain enemy's head on a pike or pole. Stripping the dead and wearing some part of his clothing demonstrates power over the spirit of the enemy. The most notorious case came from the Abenakis' sack of York, Maine, in January 1692. Minister Shubael Dummer's killer stripped the dead man and put on his clothing during the march back to Canada with the captives of the raid.[33]

The Pequots kept their word about killing women and children. On April, 22, 1637, they paddled their canoes through the morning mist up to the Connecticut River town of Wethersfield, south of Hartford. The settlement lay along a half-circle bulge in the river, much of which was a ten-acre meadow. Though they lived in "English wigwams" with little more personal property than the Pequots, the settlers counted themselves fortunate to farm the land and graze their cattle. Indeed, a family's wealth lay in its livestock, and the riverside grasses were vital fodder for the herds. But haying required common labor, and the Indians had watched as the settlers put aside their weapons and their caution to cut and stack the first grasses of spring so they could dry.

Bursting upon the unsuspecting haying party, the Indians killed fourteen men and women before the New Englanders could react. The warriors raced west through the meadow and reached the road running north-south through the town, scattering along the way the terrified survivors and gathering up whatever tools and weapons the settlers had abandoned. When they reached the center of the town, where Main and State Streets now cross, they captured two teenaged sisters, the Swains, and retreated to the canoes. The "long shout" of the advancing Pequots, the bellowed orders and frightened cries of the fleeing colonists, and the groans of the victims mingled in the by-now-familiar orchestration of war. To it the captured girls added their plaintive cries and the Indians their chant of victory.[34] They had proved they could do what they told Gardiner and the garrison at Saybrook they would do—strike anywhere, kill and cause terror, and then retreat without casualties.[35]

One sound was not recorded. Like the dogs in the night in Arthur Conan Doyle's "Silver Blaze," the settlers' dogs did not bark a warning. Anyone who bicycles down a rural lane knows that the passage will be marked by the yelping and growling of farm dogs. Why were the dogs of Wethersfield silent? It may be that the Indians had chosen to mount their raid when the wind was blowing out of the west, when they would be downwind of the dogs. Or, it may be that the Indians killed the dogs; they often slew the dogs of their enemies before advancing on the enemies' village. Or it may be that the dogs did bark, but they were always barking at something, and the settlers, intent on cutting and stacking the grass after the cold hard winter, simply ignored them. The English mastiff was a formidable weapon and much feared by Indians, but a mastiff is not a working dog, and the herdsmen and farmers of Wethersfield no doubt preferred smaller working breeds to guard dogs.

Despite the concealment of their approach, the Indians' purpose was not to hide. Quite the contrary. In this sensory battle within the war, whose sole aim was to show off superiority and loudly and visibly taunt ones' enemies, the Indians' raid on Wethersfield was primarily intended to mock the Saybrook garrison. The Indians did not attempt to destroy Wethersfield; that was not how they waged war. Instead, they put the two girls they had taken prisoner in canoes, paddled down the Connecticut River to the Saybrook fort, and teased the garrison with the sight of their own inability to protect their children—a grisly version of the children's game of show and tell.

Even as the Pequots were flexing their muscles, the New England forces gathered themselves for a concerted counterthrust. Nearly one hundred Connecticut and Massachusetts militiamen assembled under the command of John Mason and John Underhill. The Mohegans, who lived to the north of the Pequots, sent fewer than seventy-five men, but these were led by Uncas, who proved loyal to the New Englanders. The Narragansetts sent more men, but they were not eager to do battle with the Pequots, and hung back. The Niantics reluctantly joined the spring offensive, but played little part in the fighting.[36]

The mood and motives of the attackers can be gauged from various sources. The letters of two of their ministers give a clue. Writing to Governor John Winthrop of Massachusetts to urge expeditious dispatch of men at arms to fight the Pequots, Hartford's minister Thomas Hooker pressed Winthrop "not to do this work of the Lord's revenge slackly."[37] Thomas Shepard, Hooker's son-in-law and the pastor at Cambridge, Massachusetts, wrote as well: "'Tis much desired, that our countrymen's blood might not rest unsatisfied for; our eyes are very much upon you and the Lord in you to devise some speedy execution which may end with honor and quiet to the state and terror to all the rest of them" [those without the state—the Indians].[38]

On May 26, 1637, the militia and Indian auxiliaries surrounded the Pequot fortified village of Mystic. The New Englanders attacked at half-dawn, catching the Pequots off guard, and burned the village, proceeding to kill not only all but fourteen of the hundred fifty or so warriors therein but also nearly every woman and child. Many children were butchered as they tried to escape the flames.[39] Hundreds—we will never know exactly how many hundred—perished.[40] Afterward, with the cries of the dying still echoing in their ears and the stench of the scorched dead reeking in their nostrils, the attackers retreated. Exhausted and afraid that the main body of Pequot warriors would suddenly emerge from the woods, the Puritans gathered up their twenty wounded and the seven prisoners and made their way to the shallops sent to carry them away.

What really had happened? Perhaps intending to overwhelm the Indian fort with surprise and firepower, the New Englanders' instead lost control of the situation. They could no longer clearly see or hear what was transpiring. Inside the palisade, Indians flashed up and down the alleys and in and out of the smoking wigwams. The smoke and flames from the fires that Mason had set so obscured the fort that neither Mason nor Underhill could control his troops by shouted or visual commands. The troops themselves could hardly distinguish the war whoop of the warriors from the wailing of the women, old people, and children.

We often read of the blurring of shapes and colors in battle—the enemy loses his individuality and becomes a single hated and feared mass. The soldier is unsighted by the sensory overload; the sounds, smells, and sights of combat merge into one. At Mystic the retort of the muskets was loud enough to deafen the shooter. The pall of smoke from the black powder, added to the windswept smoke of the fires from the reeds and bark, made precise determinations of targets in the half-light impossible. John Gabriel Stedman, a soldier of fortune of Scottish and Dutch origins, serving with Dutch troops quelling a rebellion of Surinam slaves in 1775, describes one raid upon a maroon (runaway slave) village: "Upon the whole, to draw this picture were a fruitless attempt, thus I shall only say that the incessant noise of the firing, mixed with a confused roaring, halloing, damning and sinking, the shrill sounds of the Negro horns, the crackling of the burning houses, the dead and wounded all weltering in blood, the cloud of dust in which we were involved, and flames and smoke ascending, were such a scene of beautiful horror."[41] That is what happened at the Mystic fort. The massacre did not follow the battle but was inseparable from it.[42]

How did the commanders of the troops at Mystic perceive what they had seen and heard? Shortly after returning to the Bay Colony, Underhill, a "big lusty man" (so big he could not fit into the brush-enclosed opening at the rear of the palisade), penned an account. A devoutly pious member of John Cotton's Boston congregation (and so associated with Cotton and others in the doctrinal stew that would bring crisis to the colony in 1637 and 1638) and a sometime professional soldier, he turned to Scripture. Underhill would leave the colony in 1638, shortly after writing his account of the war. It was published in London.[43]

Underhill depicted Pequot diplomats as "ingenious and witty" and admired the "courage" of the Pequots in defending their towns, but the scriptural version of the victory of David over the Philistines was the pervasive metaphor in Underhill's vision of his role. The Indians were "the devil's instruments." Across the face of the "garden" of New England, "the old serpent, according to his first malice, stirred them up against the church of Christ . . . so insolent have these wicked imps grown, that like the devil, their commander, they run up and down as roaring lions, compassing all corner of the country for a prey."[44]

Mason, the commander-in-chief of the Connecticut contingent, was a Connecticut landholder who had arrived in New England in 1635 at the invitation of the founders of the town of Windsor. Tall and portly, he had some military experience in the Netherlands, though probably none of combat. He wrote at the start of the 1670s, at age seventy or so,, so his memory may have been poor, but he recalled many details of his own participation in the campaign distinctly. He promised his readers and the legislature of Connecticut a "plain and

Massacre at the Pequot Mystic town

The New Englanders' use of firearms is evident, but the illustration hardly does justice to the smoke, fire, and confusion of the fighting. The Pequots' wigwams were not laid out in rows, like English village streets, nor did the militia array themselves neatly around the palisades. (John Underhill, *Newes from America* [London, 1638].)

easy" discourse, with little "high stile." Much of what he wrote was just that. He recalled how the exhausted troops had laid their heads on rocks the night before the battle and listened to the Pequots singing derisively about the New Englanders. He reported with dramatic precision the attack on the village; how he had pulled aside the brush that barred the entrance to the palisade and been hit by two arrows (though neither wounded him). He took credit for the decision to fire the town, after which he burst into one of the wigwams and grabbed a firebrand to set it aflame. He gloried in the exploits of his men as they chased the enemy down smoke-filled alleyways in the town (he himself "out of breath"), slaying forty of them with the sword, and told of how a "dreadful terror" had come upon the once haughty and prideful Pequots. But his acts had been directed by an invisible hand: "God was above them."[45]

For Underhill and Mason it was the invisible but sure hand of God above, rather than the crackling fast-spreading fires below, that had determined the outcome of the battle. "The [Indians] were taken in their own snare . . . to the number of six or seven hundred . . . Thus was God seen in the Mount, crushing his proud enemies and the enemies of his people." Did Mason see God in his glory and his wrath on the bluffs of the Mystic River? Hardly. He saw what he took to be God's work—God's design, God's purpose for New England. The reference to the Mount recalls the Old Testament God of the Mountain and connects it with the hill on which the Pequot fort stood. With this allusion, Mason cloaked the actual scene with a virtual one and replaced the work of the sense organs with a fictive sense. God, invisible to the Indians, sensed only through his providence by the New Englanders, had crushed their enemies.[46]

Behind every human action was the invisible hand of providence. The New Englanders won because, "in a word, the Lord was as it were pleased to say unto us, the Land of Canaan will I give you." The Pequots, like the Canaanites, were "a great [numerous] people, being strongly fortified, cruel, warlike, munitioned," while the New Englanders, like the biblical Israelites, "were but a handful." Only "God's providence" prevented the Pequots from building a general conspiracy against the New Englanders. In battle, "special providences" saved the lives of individual New England militiamen. Of his own role, "What shall I say? God led his people through many difficulties and turnings yet by more than an ordinary hand of providence brought them to Canaan at last." Mason was God's instrument in chastising the Pequots.[47]

For the New Englanders, the massacre at the Mystic fort was part of a divine plan. The Puritans could not see it all, but they knew that God and the devil battled over the fate of the New England colonies. As Shepard put it, writing four years after the massacre, "I cannot omit the goodness of God as to myself, so to all the country, in delivering us from the Pequot furies." When Mason set the wigwams on fire, it was "most dreadful to the Indians, some burning, some bleeding to death by the sword, some resisting till they were cut off, some flying were beat down by the men without, until the Lord had utterly consumed the whole company except four or five girls."[48] No mention of mothers or children—the girls were not daughters—and the slaughter was the work of the Lord. Shepard believed in the many mercies of God; God favored his children,[49] and the Pequots were not his children.

For Puritans like Underhill, Mason, and Shepard, the massacre became a proof of what they could not see—an extension of the biblical story—a "typology" in which New Englanders are the Israelites. If "down fell men, women and children" (note the passive voice—the New Englanders are not doing the killing any more), Underhill loftily reminded his readers that "sometimes the Scripture declareth women and children must perish with their parents." This shift from the visible to the invisible world, from the present to the past, from the reality of the carnage at Mystic to a holy analogy in which the New Englanders saw themselves continuing in the footsteps of the biblical patriarchs, gave the invisible world priority over the visible one. "We had sufficient light from the word of God for our proceedings." The light of the word replaced ordinary light and sound.[50]

No one knows for certain how the Pequots saw the battle or the war. The film *The Witness,* shown every hour at the Pequot Museum, attempts to portray the massacre from the Pequot side, but it is at once too romantic and too bloodless. (Or perhaps modern viewers have become too reliant on the special effects of modern movies.) The visual and auditory impact of the movie's Pequot point of view cannot be mistaken, however. This was Pequot homeland, wrenched from them by force. It was a holocaust. At the time, the Narragansett Indians, allies of the colonists, empathized with the defeated Pequots; this was a kind of war they had never seen and found terrifying. For the Narragansetts circled around the fort heard what the militia did not. They perceived the carnage, as it were, from the inside out, heard the cries as if they were their own. To the New Englanders, the Pequots sounded like animals; to the Narragansetts, the Pequots' last words sounded a perfectly clear lament for the fate of all the coastal natives.

The Narragansetts came to Underhill and berated him about the New Englanders' way of war. "It is naught, it is naught, because it is too furious, and slays too many men." In reply to Miantonomi, the Narragansett sachem, Underhill scoffed: The Indians' "fight is more for pastime, than to conquer and subdue enemies . . . they may fight seven years and not kill seven men." Underhill admitted that others might ask, "should not Christians have more mercy and compassion?"[51] But he preferred, with Mason and in opposition to the Narragansetts, to bleach out the appalling sensate detail of the massacre in the fabric of divine retribution.

Like Shepard and the two commanders, other New Englanders concluded that at Mystic the divine presence in the invisible world had stretched out his hand to aid his chosen people. They did not have to see the carnage to understand this meaning in it. When he received news of the massacre, Governor

William Bradford of Plymouth wrote in his journal, "it was a fearful sight to see [the Pequots] thus frying in the fire . . . and horrible was the stink and scent thereof," remarks that might lead a reader to think Bradford had been there. Instead, the word "see" had morphed from actual sensation to typological invocation. He was able to imagine the fire and its effects because he likened what he was told about the battle to what he read in the Old Testament. In the Pequot War, as in the wars of the Israelites, the New Englanders "gave praise to God, who had wrought so wonderfully for them, as to enclose their enemy in their hands."[52]

Gathering the account from his Indian sources and passing it on to Governor John Winthrop of Massachusetts, Williams adopted the same language as Bradford. Williams did not countenance the slaughter of women and children. "I much rejoice that . . . some of the chief [Puritan captains] at Connecticut . . . are almost averse from killing women and children. Mercy outshines all the works and attributes of him who is the father of mercies."[53] But the Pequots and their allies were the tools of the devil. When the leader of the Pequot resistance, Sassacus, was slain from ambush by a kinsman put up to the deed by the New Englanders, Williams saw "the righteous hand of the most high judge."[54]

Minister Philip Vincent's *True Relation of the Late Battle* (1638), prepared at a hundred miles' remove from the events, reported that the savages were by nature cowards, despite their choleric nature, and they cried out piteously when the New Englanders assaulted the Mystic fort. The "whole work"—a job, not a massacre—ended within an hour of sunrise, a proof of the superiority of Puritan ways and of God's judgment. Now the colony was safe.[55]

Contemporary historians of the events, like Edward Johnson, whose *Wonder Working Providence* (1654) was the first history of New England, offered portraits vivid with ersatz sensory detail because they drew inspiration from analogies to the Old Testament and to stereotypes of the devil. The soldiers, Johnson opined, could not pierce the Indians' bodies with swords because "the devil was in them." Thus the New Englanders had to fire the town. But the "women and children set up a terrible outcry," and the Puritans took pity on them, and spared them.[56] Johnson had confused the Mystic battle with a latter confrontation and erased the massacre from his history—it did not speak well of God's plan that his chosen people should be so bloodthirsty.

In his *Supplement Concerning the War with the Pequots* (1677), minister William Hubbard repeated much of what Mason had written about the Mystic town massacre, but when it came to the slaughter of the women and children fleeing the fires, Hubbard merely reported "many of them issuing forth were suddenly slain, by the English or by Indians who were in a ring without [i.e. outside of] us, all being dispatched and ended in the space of an hour."[57] The fearsome visage of the Pequot warrior had vanished, been effaced, erased; as one Puritan missionary tract reported in 1643, "the name of the Pequits (as of Amaleck) is blotted out from under heaven, there being not one that is, or (at least) dare call himself a Pequit."[58]

The Goodness of the Invisible World Touches the Spirit of the Indians

As the features of actual Indians enemies faded from the Puritans' minds, the image of the Lord's providence grew sharper. The advantages of otherworldly depictions of the Pequot War over literal recountings grew more apparent with the passage of time. The former traveled across the generations well, because they fit into a shared perceptual schema of a cosmic religious drama. In the script of that drama, the enemy was not human, it was satanic, so it was not what one saw in the visible world but what one divined in the invisible world that mattered. Even when human memory of the events had faded, and the generation that had led in the conflict passed on, the invisible world had staying power denied to the immediate work of the senses. The New Englanders were not taking refuge in a literary metaphor; they believed the invisible world was real, even if they could not directly sense it.

Furthermore, they welcomed their former enemies to share in this celebration of the invisible world. Indian conversions reassured the Puritans that ethnic sensory cleansing was a righteous act. Before he would minister to them, John Eliot told his Massachusett friends that they must "first be civilized, by being brought from their scattered and wild course of life, unto civil co-habitations and government." They must, like the Puritans, live "in a town." In Natick they built their first church, and in Roxbury, in 1654, they consented to be "examined in their faith. There Eliot asked, "What is God?" and they replied, "God is eternal, infinite, wise, holy, just." God was invisible, but known; his words were written in a book, but He could hear them.[59]

True converts gained the power to hear the word of God as if it were spoken to them. As Monequassum confessed at Roxbury, "I heard that Word." He did not read it. He heard it—a small still voice in his own head. In fact, the congregational auditory was part of the Puritan formula in the search for salvation, the beginning of the stages on the way to conversion. God did not actually speak. The convert heard Scripture as if spoken. At Roxbury, Eliot did not put the words in the praying Indians' mouths, nor did he invent the Indians' speeches. He was there, with translators, and he heard with his own ears

Indians confessing their sins with their own lips. Prayer was speech that God heard. The convert heard and spoke the word of God—sensory evidence that conversion had begun.[60]

When Indians prayed, they acknowledged that sound in the visible world passed into the invisible world unchanged in meaning and that the sounds of the English language were the ones most pleasing to God. When Indians "prayed well," God heard their prayers.[61] But some Indians did not pray, for as one convert reported, "Satan speaks to them, and bids them not believe."[62] In this the converts echoed the fears of ministers who were hesitant to accept even the evidence of their own eyes and ears that Indians could be true Christians. As Shepard wrote in 1648, it was "a special finger of Satan resisting these budding beginnings" when Indians refused to live in the towns that the General Court provided for them.[63] Like the skeptical ministers, even the most willing of Indian converts knew that there were snares all around them. Like Natick's Ephriam confessing to Eliot, they could not "see" all their sins, and so might transgress without knowing of it. Some accepted English ways simply to remain with loved ones or stay in familiar places; they said the words but did not have the faith.[64] Without faith, they were prey to powers in the invisible world not so well disposed toward Indians—or their Puritan tutors, for that matter. Like the old animistic world of the Indians' traditional religion, the invisible world of the Christians was not without its dangers.[65]

Much as the missionaries wanted to disabuse the Indians of their animal raiment and religious animism—marks, in the educated English mind, of savagery—the project required the missionaries to navigate some contradictions. The first was to chart a course between faith in the spiritual power of God and rejection of traditional Indian spiritualism. The second was to convince the Indians, without falling into crude materialism, that English science rather than Indian magic controlled nature. While the missionaries and their sponsors struggled to explain the distinction between soul and body to the Indians, the Indians struggled to keep body and soul together. Thus complex Restoration intellectual notions about spirits did not always weather the trip from the library to the wigwam.[66]

Still, missionaries like Eliot reported to their sponsors in England that Indians yearned for the comforts of true faith. As they groped toward an understanding of the goodness of the invisible world, the converts looked and sounded more like the New Englanders.[67] The missionaries were pleased that converted Indians attended church, cut their hair, practiced monogamy, put up dividers between men's and women's quarters in their dwellings, and became year-round farmers. In abandoning their "naked" state and their greasy deerskin breech cloths and shawls, they had visibly renounced the savage and adopted civilized ways.[68]

In 1674, Gookin counted eleven hundred sincere conversions, though other ministers hesitated to regard these "praying Indians" as full communicants and insisted upon a longer apprenticeship. Still, the impressive sensory evidence of the willingness of many to abandon their old ways convinced Eliot and others that the reformation was genuine.[69] With an irony that the missionaries probably mistook for proof of the benevolence of the invisible world, it was an old Pequot, a survivor of the war, who came to epitomize the absolute submission of the convert to the Christian way. On his deathbed, Wequash seemed to the Puritans to embrace the Almighty's absolute power over all things: "If Jesus Christ say that Wequash shall live, then Wequash must live; if Jesus Christ say that Wequash shall die, then Wequash is willing to die."[70] In fact, Wequash's deathbed fatalism was exactly the same as that of the Pequots' who chanted their death songs in the conflagration at Mystic. Whether Wequash embraced Christianity in his heart we will never know, but his last words were soothing to the Puritans, who transcribed them because they saw him as proof that Indians could be objects of God's succor. The conversion of the Indians was "like a spiritual garden, into which Christ might come and eat his pleasant fruits."[71]

The visible and audible conversion of the Indians not only proved to the Puritans that the missionary enterprise was worth England's support but also gave evidence that God's invisible hand went everywhere, even into the Indian camp. The Puritans need not demonize what God was making holy. If some Indians remained stiff-necked, the Puritans could always close their eyes and hold their noses around the greasy animal-skinned unregenerate remnant. If warfare resumed, surely the result would be the same as in 1637, for God was still with them. As Increase Mather wrote in 1676, the victory of the New Englanders "must be ascribed to the wonderful providence of God, who did (as with Jacob of old, and after that with the children of Israel) lay the fear of the English and the dread of them upon all the Indians. The terror of God was upon them round about."[72]

King Philip's War

After the Pequot War most Indians refused to play the part assigned them in the New Englanders' divine drama. The natives were not a faceless, homogenous chorus singing hosannas to their new masters and their masters' God; nor were they Satan's defaced minions. Some were genuine converts and remained loyal to the New England governments. Others sought to fuse Christian ways with older Indian religious traditions. Holy men like the Pennacook (Maine) leader Passachonoway and his son Wannalancet tried to keep a foot in both worlds. Other Indians, like the Saco sagamore Squando, hid their animus against the English, pretending that God had told them to adopt English ways while conspiring to maintain Indian independence. Some, like the Penobscot Madockewando, made little pretense of their hope that the English would vanish into the eastern mists from which they had come.[73]

The reason for Indian anger might be a particular incident (Squando's son was allegedly killed by the English) or more general abuses, as it was for the Wampanoag sachem Metacom. Though his father and older brother had been friendly to the English, the friendship had brought only ill treatment and patronization. Throughout the 1660s, Metacom chafed at Plymouth Colony's increasing control over the Wampanoags. Through purchase and fraud, Rhode Island and Plymouth farmers nibbled away Wampanoag territory and stole Indian cattle.[74] Metacom's attempts to frighten off the settlers led, in 1671, to the colony's disarming his warriors. In June 1675, three of Metacom's aides were convicted of killing a Christian Indian. After their execution, Metacom struck at the town of Swansea, burning houses and corn cribs. Plymouth appealed to Rhode Island and Massachusetts for aid and marshaled its troops to chase the Wampanoag chief. Metacom fled, killing ten New England settlers in his path.[75]

What had been little more than a brush fire now became a conflagration: All the tensions simmering beneath the surface boiled over. One of Metacom's allies explained: "Thou English man hath provoked us to anger and wrath and we care not though we have war with you this 21 years for there are many of us [who] . . . have nothing but our lives to loose but thou hast many fair houses cattle and much good things."[76] The powerful and formally neutral Narragansetts gave refuge to the Wampanoags, and the colonists chose to attack the Narragansetts rather than negotiate for the surrender of Metacom. The colonists' decision led to a devastating civil war in which many hitherto friendly Indians sided with Metacom, although the Pequots and the Mohegans, long rivals of the Narragansetts, as well as Indians who had been converted to Christianity by Puritan ministers, fought on the side of the New Englanders.

The war raged from the summer of 1675 to the summer of 1676. With the Wampanoags and their allies starving, Metacom retreated to his old town, Mount Hope, Rhode Island, in search of food. There he died in an ambush. By the time the hostilities ended, half the native population had been slain or driven from New England. Whole regions were devastated, the cattle killed, the houses burned, the crops unharvested, pillaged, or fired, and the fields gone fallow. For Puritans who compulsively examined every event, natural or human, for evidence of God's design, and in particular for God's plan for New England, the catastrophe seemed a test of their faith and a punishment for the wayward and backsliding ways of their congregants.[77]

We do not have to ask what the Puritans saw and heard. All the anecdotal evidence, the first-hand accounts, and the letters and diaries that survive indicate that the war overwhelmed the Puritans' senses to the same extent that the New World had dazed the first English visitors. Here the analogy ends. The Puritans of 1675 and 1676 beheld with horror scenes of gore. Though some of the accounts were printed in England, as was Harriot's, none of the authors found good things to say about the Indians or the prospects for commerce. Indeed, so bitter were the accounts that they eschewed calculation and categorization in favor of stock depictions of the "filthy lusts" of the marauding natives (though none of the captives reported rape or even "incivilities" of that kind).[78]

Other derogatory and misleading sensory details included the claim that Indians always lived in swamps.[79] In fact, the New England Indians who fought the confederated colonial forces did not site their villages on swamps, but on fields, bluffs, hillocks, and other open spaces near water.[80] The Indians chose places that were fertile and defensible, but above all liveable. It was only when the militia struck at them that they decamped, and even then they preferred to avoid swamps.[81] The "miry swamp," to quote the memorial stone in the woods just outside of Bristol, Rhode Island, where Metacom was slain, is damp and low-lying, but hardly a mire. The Indians' choice of such relatively impenetrable landscapes as refuges is thus one measure of the dislocation of Indian life caused by the conflict. At the same time, the Puritan authors' use of the word *swamp* is less an accurate depiction of landscape than a literary device to emphasize the savagery of the Indians. *Swamp* meant a wild place for a savage people.[82] As Increase Mather would write in his history of the war, "their cruel habitations are the dark corners of the earth." Indians lurked in the swamps, like Grendel, hidden from the sight of men until they struck.[83]

The war heightened the Puritans' senses: trying to see into the high grass or behind the copse of trees; listening so hard for footfalls that the facial muscles around the ears began to spasm; smelling the acrid sulfur of burning houses and barns; knowing that the mutilated bodies of the defenders must be nearby. Time and repetition would dull the emotional responses to such sensations, but not the importance of the sensations themselves.[84]

Some of these depictions remain as striking now as when they were written. In January 1676, Quannapaquait, a Nipmuck held at Deer Island with other

Indian converts, volunteered to spy among his former people. He was welcomed by Metacom's forces, and reported back that the Indian camp held many Christians. Indeed, mistrusted by both sides, the deacons among the praying Indians in Philip's camp "daily read the Bible" looking for comfort.[85] Or take the corpse of Metacom as viewed by his pursuer, Benjamin Church. In death, covered with swamp muck and his own gore, Philip was "a doleful, great, dirty, naked beast." Church, recalling how Philip's men had mutilated their victims, ordered another Indian, "an old executioner," to "hew" the corpse into pieces. The hand of the rebel, scarred from a youthful firearms accident, went to Alderman, Church's Indian scout.[86] Church carried the head on a pike into the town of Plymouth on August 17, 1676, where it was displayed, the face of the devil[87]–or so young Cotton Mather thought when he visited the skull on its resting place in the town and pulled off its jaw bone. "The blasphemous exposed skull of that leviathan" had frightened his waking hours and afflicted his dreams. Would that the demon's master were so easy to dismantle.[88]

But the war did not persuade the Puritans to adopt a brand of literary naturalism any more than it made them cynical apostates. They yearned for the old certainties that had drawn them to New England in the first place. Where was the invisible but everywhere potent hand of Providence? Had God turned his eye from their plight? If so, then the invisible world would hold only terror. As it had after the Pequot War, the ministerial fraternity rushed to reassure the laity that God had not abandoned New England.

Increase Mather, the intellectual spokesman for the Boston ministerial association, offered the first and in many ways most persuasive of the wartime attempts to integrate the visible and invisible worlds.[89] Modern scholars have found his account a "fundamentally antihistorical" mythology, indifferent to the actual sufferings of Puritans as well as Indians. He reduced Indians to a "metaphor for the guilt of the English, [that] must be purged."[90] Mather conceded that ordinary history took a back seat to "exhortation . . . speaking what I believe God would have me speak,"[91] but he was not indifferent to the suffering of real men and women. Instead, he was attempting to resuscitate the style of the chroniclers of the Pequot War. He wanted to blend the visible and invisible worlds seamlessly.

Mather's Indians are less manikins than superstitious primitives easily duped by the devil. They mistake the devil, whom they take to be "a tall man, [dressed] in black cloths," for God. They forsake the "blessed design" of peace and conversion that their fathers had adopted.[92] In this, Mather was engaging in an ongoing debate with the missionaries. In vain did missionaries like Daniel Gookin insist that the praying Indians were "always found ready to comply cheerfully with all commands of the English authority." They presented themselves willing to scout, stand guard, and "range the woods from town to town" in search of the rebels, but "a spirit of enmity and hatred conceived by many against those poor Christian Indians, as I apprehend without cause, so far as I could ever understand, which was . . . a very great occasion of many distressing calamities that befell both" [the praying Indians and the colonists].[93]

Gookin did not understand that his vision of the Indians, developed out of the hopes and hard labor of the missionaries in the interwar years, was as chimerical as Mather's imagery, reflecting the Pequot era. Both men had dressed the Indians for parts in a Puritan story, a story about white New England's past and future. In this contest, Gookin needed the praying Indians' conversion to be genuine to prove that God still loved the colony. Thus, he divided Indians into the "wicked," who "proved treacherous and perfidious," and the true converts.[94] Instead, Mather needed the Indians to be the devil's tools to prove that the destruction of Indian homes and fields (including the praying Indians' towns) was part of God's plan.

Throughout, Mather's recounting of the travail of the New Englanders was an Exodus- like honor roll of "prudent and careful" captains and lieutenants and "pious and prudent" goodwives. Mather the "impartial historian" gave dates, places, and numbers of combatants, but often these are a combination of hysterical rumor and wishful thinking. His impartiality lay in his divination of God's purposes, not in the numbers of houses and barns burned in each raid (numbers he invariably rounded off). For example, when the Indians died, they passed by the tens, fifties, or hundreds, never by precise numbers.[95]

The blood and gore in his pages reflected the reality of the suffering, but the immediate sensory experience of the sudden fights and terrible bloodletting invariably paled before his invocation of the invisible. For example, "God saw we were not yet fit for deliverance" in the first months of the war; that is why so many settlers were caught unawares by the Indian raiders. In this inversion of the ordinary meaning of narrative, the story is God's, of how He brought peril to the heedless and then allowed the New Englanders to relearn the meaning of their mission. "Had we mended our ways as we should have done, this misery might have been prevented." The triumph was thus not of the Puritans' arms but of their spirit.[96]

Mather's attempt to reclaim the benevolence of providence inspired other chroniclers. Thomas Wheeler, who commanded a small garrison under siege at Brookfield, celebrated "the providence of God towards us in his ways about us were too remarkable in our sore exercises, and gracious deliverances that they ought never to be forgotten by us." The Lord stepped in, unseen, to frustrate Indian plans time and again.[97] As minister Samuel Nowell, who marched with the armies sent to scourge the Narragansetts in 1675 and 1676, argued in a 1678 sermon, the Puritans had "Israel's title to Canaan" in the wilderness. When all seemed lost, God was beside them, "he appeareth eminently [immanently] in the day of the battle," even if no one could see him.[98]

William Hubbard, from his pulpit in Ipswich, rehearsed the same arguments in his full dress *Narrative of the Troubles with the Indians in New England* (1677). The Indians were "wild creatures," whose animal nature was easily deceived by the devil. "The devil . . . had so filled the heart of this savage miscreant [Philip] with envy and malice against the English" that war was inevitable. Only "special providences" saved individuals from disaster.[99] Nothing new here, save that Hubbard took direct issue both with Mather's assertion that the Indians were God's scourge of the Puritan backsliders and with the notion that conflict with the Indians should be dignified with the word *war*. Trouble, yes, but one could have trouble with wolves or bears.[100] Hubbard nevertheless acknowledged the same one great truth that Mather recognized—the war was an omen of the satanic peril under which the Puritans, and all men, labored.[101]

Captivity Tales

Young Cotton Mather, with his mandible trophy in hand, might think that he had seen the defeat of corporeal evil and the triumph of providence, but his father and others realized that the events of the war had revealed an invisible world that the ministers could neither control nor explain. The most striking representations of this chaotic prospect were the so-called captivity narratives.[102] During the war the Indians took hundreds of New Englanders captive. The majority were ransomed or returned, but all suffered and most could not understand why they had been chosen to watch their families' slaughter.[103] In the one-dozen-plus short but highly charged accounts of New Englanders spirited through the woods by Indian raiders, the invisible world reappeared, but now it was upside down. The narrator was not the victor, but the vanquished. The story was not one of vindication through might, but of survival through faith. The storytellers were not men of the cloth or commanders of troops, but ordinary people.

The threat to the ministerial ordering of the unseen in these men's and women's tales was subtle. The captivity narrative was overwhelmingly visceral, a raw account of harm, wounds, pain, and death. Its narrative structure, the memory of the raid itself, the capture, the treatment on the march away from the settlements, the experience of living among the Indians, and finally escape or redemption (usually by the paying of a ransom), lacked apparent reason and order. The captive could only make sense of the terror of the experience by referring to it in religious terms, that is, by adopting the ministers' meta-narrative. "Captivity was God's punishment; redemption was His mercy."[104] The captive might concede his or her sinfulness and believe that the ordeal was a test.[105] But this abject submission to the will of God was not what made these accounts so compelling, or so well read. It was the other story—the story of the unknown twist of fate, the unknowable mind of the Indian captors, the unpredictable future—that made the narratives bestsellers. Where then was God's plan? In the caprice of the captor? In the randomness of the captives' survival?

Against the sensory impact of the invisible world's tribulations, providential bromides and confessions of sin shielded no one. The invisible world, which should have been a haven from the terror-filled immediate report of the senses, became as impenetrable and inscrutable as the wilderness and the Indian marauder. Providence in these tales worked in blood, whim, and deceit. When Hannah Dunston slew the children of her captors; when Mary Rowlandson stole food from the hungry; when other captives wished evil on those who treated them humanely, the lesson was not one of loving-kindness but of paying back the devil in kind. In this invisible world, the captives' fury came to resemble their captors' savagery.[106]

Mary Rowlandson's narrative was the first and in many ways the model for all the captivity tales that followed. Born in England, she had been brought to the colonial town of Wenham as a small child in the 1630s. In 1653, her family relocated to the Nashua River frontier town of Lancaster, surrounded by Nipmuck Indians. The Indians seemed friendly, and the local sachem converted to Christianity. There Mary White married the English-born minister Joseph Rowlandson and began a family. As the population of the New Englanders in Lancaster increased, relations with the Indians grew testier. Joseph Rowlandson did not help with the missionary work in the town, and he saw the Indians as disreputable characters. In the meantime, Puritan cattle trampled Indian gardens, Puritan land-jobbers pressured Indians to sell their land, and merchants used Indian indebtedness as a wedge to buy the land out from under the native dwellers. Nor were the New Englanders convinced that so called praying Indians could be trusted.[107] The Nipmucks joined the rebellion in the fall.

Rowlandson's agony began on February 20, 1676. Her description of the attack on her fortified house is heartrending, and more so her account of the death of loved ones. Her sister, hearing that her son was dead and Mary was wounded, cried "'and lord, let me die with them,' which was no sooner said, but she was struck with a bullet and fell down dead over the threshold"–providence with a grisly, almost ironic, twist. Recalling that day after her release from captivity, Rowlandson mused upon the state of her sister's soul. "I hope she is reaping the fruit of her good labors, being faithful to the service of God in her place," for in her younger years "she lay under much trouble upon spiritual accounts." The God that Mary hoped would take her sister to his bosom was there, in that place of carnage, "and by his almighty power preserved a number of us from death." Yet Rowlandson knew that it was the Indians—not God—who had chosen whom to take as captives and whom to kill. Providence would not be so arbitrary and callous—would it?[108]

The rest of the narrative is organized by a series of "removes," departures and arrivals with her Indian captors. Each chapter introduces a new scene or setting, giving greater freshness to the report of the senses. In each, Rowlandson measured the distance between perceived reality and assumed providence with bitter, reproachful asides: "When we are in prosperity, Oh the little that we think of such dreadful sights . . . twelve killed, some shot, some stabbed with their spears, some knocked down with their hatchets . . . some here and some there like a company of sheep torn by wolves." The vivid sensory impressions poured onto the page and leapt up to the reader's eye. Watching as the victorious Indians celebrated not a stone's throw from the destroyed village, she recoiled at "the dolefullest night that ever my eyes saw. Oh the roaring, and singing and dancing, and yelling of those black creatures in the night." The metaphor of the dark, hence satanic, Indians was a literary convention, but in fact the Indians did paint themselves black to go to war—Rowlandson was being descriptive, not metaphorical.[109]

As the party moved west, away from the settlements and into the "wilderness," Rowlandson's heart sunk still further, torn between the visible and invisible worlds. God was with her; she felt him "carrying me along." But it was the Indians who carried her wounded six- year-old child on horseback, then allowed her to ride with the child. Reaching the first of many Indian towns in which they would reside, Mary gave thanks to God for deliverance, but for her wound, she employed a folk remedy recommended by a fellow captive. It healed her, but only "with the blessing of God." When her child died of wounds received in the raid, she graphically described her attempts to bury him properly, then commended his soul to the Lord, for He was with her in the wilderness.[110] So she went back and forth between the two worlds.

The alternating invocations of the visible and the invisible gained pace and tension as Rowlandson moved farther away from the settlements. When her ten-year-old daughter was sold away from her sight, she "earnestly entreated the Lord, that he would consider my low estate, and show me a token for good." As if in answer, her teenaged son visited her with the permission of his captors. The son's mistress—that is, the wife of the Indian who had captured or purchased him—brought him to see his mother, a vivid and keenly appreciated kindness, but on reflection Rowlandson was not appeased. "Oh the outrageous roaring and hooping that there was" when a raiding party of Indians joined the main body with which she traveled. In response, she took out her Bible and with other captive women and children began to read Scripture.[111]

Rowlandson's need to juggle the seen and the unseen was common among captives, but because she was a mature woman, the content of her perceptions of the two worlds of sensation distinguished her account from men's. Men viewed the hardship of captivity as a test of masculinity. They took stock of directions and distances, looked for cover, and kept powder dry.[112] Rowlandson located herself in domestic pursuits, replicating in improvised fashion the everyday concerns of New England farm wives. They always kept one eye out for dangers to children. On the trail, she continued to watch over the captive children. Farm women were weavers, sewers, and menders. In captivity, Rowlandson marveled at Indian dress. When her captors adorned themselves for a dance welcoming Puritan emissaries, she reported that the Narragansett sachem Quinnapin, her owner, "was dressed in his holland shirt, with great laces sewed at the tail of it, [and] he had his silver buttons, his white stockings, his garters were hung round with shillings, and he had girdles of wampum upon his head and shoulders." His wife, Weetamoo, was attired in a kersey coat, and covered with girdles of wampum from the loins upward, her arms from her elbows to her hands were covered with bracelets, there were handfuls of necklaces about her neck, and several sorts of jewels in her ears. She had fine red stockings, and white shoes, her hair powdered and face painted red, that was always before black." So, too, as women were the primary food preparers in New England, Rowlandson reported on the Indian menu. In time of scarcity "they would pick up old bones, and cut them to pieces at the joints, and if they were full of worms and maggots, they would scald them over the fire, and then burn them [the joints] and drink up the liquor [liquified marrow] and then beat the great ends of them in a mortar, and so eat them. They would eat horses' guts, and ears, and all sorts of wild birds which they could catch . . . yea, the very bark of trees."[113]

Within the New England "domestic exchange economy," women worked side by side at or near the home while men went off to the fields. Among the Indians, Rowlandson gravitated to the squaws who traveled with her. Sometimes in the company of women she found gracious welcome, at other times cruel jests and threats of a beating. She put aside some of her qualms to fit into the domestic setting of a people at war with her own. Indians who had just returned from a raid on Sudbury, bearing with them the bloody bullet-ridden shirts of their victims, invited her to their wigwam and shared their food with her.[114]

She visited briefly with Metacom—evidence of her high status among the captives. When he asked her if she would smoke with him, she rejected the offer, even though she had taken "a pipe or two" regularly before the raid. He meant it to be the token of a temporary truce between them (after all, he had lived as a good neighbor to many like her from his birth, and he still thought that his grievances against the English were genuine enough for some among them to see justice in his rebellion), but she now regarded the pipe as "a bait, the devil lays." She did comply with his request that she sew a shirt for his son.[115] Thus the devil wore homespun in her narrative. In her sight, he displayed his faux-domestic attributes (sinfully false because it was he and his Indian allies who had destroyed all domestic tranquillity during the war).

The invisible world had become her everyday world, God's grace and the devil's snares overlapping in her perceptions and her dreams. Left to her own devices much of the day, she "had time to examine all my ways: my conscience did not accuse me of unrighteousness toward one or other, yet I saw how in my walk with God, I had been a careless creature." She remembered the good days, before the raid, when she had her entire family, healthy and strong, about her. But this recollection of a past sensory experience faded, for now she had "only a little swill for the body, and then like a swine, must lie down on the ground."[116]

Sometime after her ransom from the Indians but before she and her husband, Joseph, took up his new pulpit in Wethersfield, Connecticut, in 1678, she related her travels to the two Mathers and others, many of whom encouraged her to write them down.[117] As Increase Mather wrote in his preface to Rowlandson's account: "It is no new thing for God's precious ones to drink as deep as others, of the cup of common calamity . . . Take just Lot for instance beside others." For Mather, Rowlandson's tale was "a narrative of the wonderfully awful [full of awe] wise, holy, powerful, and gracious providence of God."[118] But Rowlandson's account did not fit the pattern that Mather's preface cut—the woman of valor whose experiences exemplified orthodox teachings. She had traveled too far into the other world and seen what he had not.

To be sure, if she had claimed to see God, Mather would have been the first to disavow the sighting. The hated and feared Catholics were masters of that genre. Saints had visions; they saw the Virgin Mary. The Roman churches were filled with visual depictions of the deity. Images of saints, appealed to, could perform miracles and alleviate everyday aches and pains. Saints' intercession for sinners was one of the corruptions of the Church that leaders of the Reformation most abhorred. They felt the same about talismans and charms that had powerful magical properties. The English radical Protestants reviled all of this intensely sensory representation of divinity as conjuration and enchantment at best and idolatry at worst.[119]

Indeed, Mather did not see anything that was invisible to others. He knew providence was there; it was vital that it be there; but he had no evidence other than inference. Thus he did not doubt that Rowlandson had been saved by providence, but his belief was a matter of faith, not empirical observation.[120] Here was the disjoint: She did not rely on his faith to interpret her travail for herself or for her audience. Free to reflect on the meaning of her experiences, she averred, "Now I see the Lord had his time to scour and chasten me . . . Affliction I wanted, and affliction I had, full measure . . . yet I see, when God calls a person to any thing, and through never so many difficulties, yet he is fully able to carry them through and make them see, and say they have been gainers thereby." The implications of her claim were striking: Anyone could "see" the invisible world with the help of God.[121] The ministers were helpful, but not necessary.

We should note that much is going on here above and beyond a captivity tale. The decision to publish the narrative raised questions about woman's role in a male-dominated culture.[122] Although the ministers sought to use her narrative to further their blasts against the backsliding ways of their congregations, Rowlandson's discovery of the power of a woman to probe deeply into the meaning of supernatural purposes and report her findings abroad had the potential to cause great upheaval, of the sort that had set the Massachusetts colony on its ear in the 1630s.

Then, during a controversy over the preaching of various ministers, a party in the Boston church had argued that the truly saved must experience inward signs of God's grace to be assured of salvation. Led by the teacher of the church, John Cotton, members of the congregation, including Governor

Henry Vane, cleric Thomas Wheelwright, and his sister-in-law Anne Hutchinson, argued that some ministers based their assurance of salvation simply on appearances of piety. This verged on a covenant of works rather than of faith. For such misguided and weak Christians, the external and visible might be mistaken for proof of conversion. Hutchinson would later be made the scapegoat for what was a far broader movement of dissent, but she never really recanted her belief that assurance could only rest on internal signs of God's love.[123] All might yearn for these, but only those who knew them directly truly belonged to the gathered church. The Boston faction lost, and many of its leaders, including Anne Hutchinson, were exiled from the colony. Some of the implications of Rowlandson's claim to see into the invisible world had revived the essence of that older sensory battle—and the memory of Anne Hutchinson—namely, when Rowlandson's narrative implied that the intervention of the ministry was not necessary for God to reveal himself to his chosen few.[124]

Witchcraft Trials

Rowlandson's tale had revealed an invisible world that frightened as well as tutored her fellow Puritans. In it, demons lurked. Anyone might enter it and not return. Such accounts as Rowlandson's might with effort be bent to the purposes of the clergy, but their authors and their readers were not just the learned clergy.[125] Instead, the tales were read by the same men and women who nailed horseshoes to their barns to ward off evil spirits and made cakes with the urine of animals to ferret out suspected witches.[126] But even these countermeasures to supernatural evil did not help New England. By the 1690s, "the devils were walking about our streets with lengthening chains making a dreadful noise in our ears, and brimstone, making a horrid and hellish stench in our nostrils."[127] In the witchcraft crisis, the invisible world would invade the visible one.

Increase Mather and Cotton Mather
Try to Map the Invisible World

In 1681, the Boston ministerial association decided to revisit a thirty-year-old project of gathering and commenting on the most "illustrious," that is, most illustrative, examples of prodigies, witchcrafts, possessions, and supernatural occurrences.[128] These "eminent" men of God asked Increase Mather to do the job. He did, in *An Essay for the Recording of Illustrious Providences,* published in Boston in 1684. His preface to the work explains why it was necessary and why best that a minister undertake it: "In order to the promoting of a design of this notion, so as shall be indeed for God's glory." He wrote not for popular titillation or to rehearse every "fabulous story" but to demonstrate the efficacy and the omnipresence of "divine judgments." The wonders of the invisible world would then be understood as they truly were, "illustrious providences." To complete this project ministers had "particular advantages," because they were best equipped by learning and disposition to "diligently inquire into and record such illustrious providences." But it was not just for theological reasons that Mather accepted the charge. He saw it as a "service for his country" so lately in fear of God's judgment on it, a logical continuation of his history of King Philip's War and a quiet revisitation of what Rowlandson had written. The ministers would again become the gatekeepers of the invisible world.[129]

Mather did not see or hear the events he included in his anthology. Unlike Rowlandson's, his authority was not autotopic. Some of the illustrious providences he took from Bible, others from medieval and early modern written sources. Some were recent, and for these he relied upon "credible persons who have been eye witnesses of it." He solicited accounts from ministers he knew and trusted, for he was adamant that the tales not be taken as fables or products of fevered imagination. He was no superstitious "popish priest" who credited what is "beyond the power of creatures to accomplish." When it came to ghost stories, he was highly skeptical: "Some indeed have give out, that I know not what specters were seen by them; but upon inquiry, I cannot find anything therein, more than fantasy, and frightful apprehensions without sufficient ground." He did believe certain stories of apparitions, however, and credited that the devil could take the form of persons, even godly persons, to do mischief.[130]

Mather thus relied upon and found reliable various types of what may be termed derivative or secondary sensation. This included spectral evidence—accounts of spectral forms having power in the physical world. The essence of spectral evidence is that it cannot be seen by everyone even when the specter is present; one simply has to be believe an informant that the specter is doing something. The only verifiable component for those who cannot see the specter is the effect of the specter's intervention in the material world. But Mather suspended disbelief in some of these cases, when they came from reliable (to his satisfaction) sources.[131]

A second type of secondary sensation that Mather credited was hearsay: the repetition of what a correspondent had told Increase another person had seen and heard. Such hearsay is today invalid in courts of law but is a staple of gossip and rumor. Gossip is the sharing of information of the type "I heard that."

Rumor has the same origin, but adds to gossip a narrative structure—rumors have beginnings, middles, and ends, motives and causal themes. Puritan New Englanders told one another not to indulge in rumor and gossip, and New England laws forbade malicious and disrespectful speech to officials, parents, and neighbors. Men and women not only policed their own tongues but also busily eavesdropped on their neighbors' conversations lest words of common ill fame disrupt entire communities.[132] But Mather readily included hearsay in his account.

Ministers were especially wary of hearsay-spread accounts of supernatural events. Mather and others warned that the unlettered interpretation of omens and prodigies summoned the devil instead of holding him at bay. "I have not mentioned these things," Mather qualified his own writing, "as any way approving of such desperate covenants [with spirits]. There is great hazard in attending them. It may be after men have made such agreements, devils may appear to them, pretending to be their deceased friends, and thereby their souls may be drawn into woeful snares." But if eminent witnesses told credible correspondents, who then related to Mather that Satan had possessed a man or a woman against their will, or that a person spoke without moving his or her lips, or became suddenly rigid or flatulent and then relaxed, or performed feats of superhuman strength, or spoke in foreign languages or tongues, he believed the tale, and took it as a sign (not proof, but grounds for suspicion) that an invisible demon had entered the victim's body.[133]

Hearsay was oral, the staple means of communication in a face-to-face society and the chief means of information-gathering even among the literate. Mather could hardly ignore it, though he was far more comfortable with the authority of written sources. Yet the sensory evidence in these was often just as secondary and derivative as in the oral accounts. He again qualified his undertaking: Only those stories "credibly attested" should be believed. For this reason, those disseminated in "popish countries," where "destestable superstition" still reigned, must be rejected.[134]

But Mather credulously reprinted much that other authors had already published. New Englanders in the 1680s were avid readers, and Mather was hardly a novice when it came to writing books for mass consumption. A few years earlier, he and Hubbard had raced one another into print on the war. Thus, what to the ministerial association seemed a project of utmost religious significance, Mather knew to be a contribution to an already popular genre. His standards for inclusion of material were dictated as much by his audience as by scholarly or scientific rigor. Books on ghosts and goblins sold well. The authors unashamedly copied from one another, and the same stories appeared in all of these works. Mather's decision to include all the varieties of derivative sensation proved profitable; London editions of Mather were soon available.[135]

Mather reconciled his inclusion of spectral accounts, hearsay, and popular tales with his concern for authenticity through a particular type of causal reasoning.[136] That reasoning depended upon two assumptions: that the account of the real-world events in any particular case was reliable and that no ordinary explanation for the events presented itself. Take the strange episode at the Morse homestead in Newbury, Massachusetts. During the night stones and bricks flew against the outside of the house, and kitchen utensils and food hurled themselves about within. The local authorities regarded the episode seriously enough to investigate whether the elderly William Morse's wife, Elizabeth, was a witch.[137] How did Mather know that the agency was supernatural? The answer was plain: If stones and bricks dashed themselves against the walls and pots and kettles overturned without a visible hand, the cause must be invisible. It was logic, pure and simple—the causal logic of the invisible world.

Of course, one had to accept both preconditions: the informant's report that the corporeal evidence was sound and that no other observable explanation could be found for the events. Mather's personal circumspection constrained his conclusions. He warned magistrates against crediting outlandish and unsupported accounts. In his son's not-so-cautious hands, gossip, rumor, and superstition led to the exact opposite result—an invitation for the authorities in the visible world to investigate crimes that had their origin in the invisible world.

With Increase Mather away in London on the business of the colony, Cotton Mather was left to collect additional tales of the supernatural. In 1688, Joshua Moody, another Boston minister, went to Cotton with the story of John Goodwin's children. In *Memorable Providences Relating to Witchcrafts and Possessions* Cotton recorded his attempts to understand how four young people of outwardly pious and meek demeanor could have been so afflicted by evil spirits.[138] *Memorable Providences* was the antithesis of his father's *Illustrious Providences,* for Cotton made himself as central to the story as Increase had effaced himself from his accounts. Indeed, Cotton would later claim, "I have indeed set myself to countermine the whole plot of the devil against New England."[139] For Increase, the whole point of the anthology was the demonstration of special providences. By taking one of the children under his roof and experimenting with her, Cotton replaced God's providence with his own ministrations.

Unlike his father, Cotton Mather did not need to rely on hearsay or second-hand accounts of the immanence of the spirit world. His account of the possession of the Goodwin children was no "speculation about magical mysteries" but was based on his "own ocular observation." What he saw both fascinated and horrified him. The afflicted children barked like dogs and mewed like cats. They stiffened, rigid as boards, then flew about the room as though their bones had dissolved. Through it all they saw visions of their tormentors' alternately mocking them and demanding that they give over their spirits to the evil one. The senior Goodwins had wisely rejected "many superstitious proposals" and elected the proper Puritan course of "prayers and tears." But the childrens' agony in the visible world must have had a cause in the invisible one, and to determine that cause Mather took Martha, one of the afflicted girls, into his own household for observation and care.[140]

Mather's chief concern was to pursue and puzzle out the logic of the invisible world—the logic his father merely assumed linked the concealed to the observed. The question was not one of belief or disbelief: "I have related nothing but what I judge to be true." Mather never suspected the children of dissimulation or insanity, and the "hag" who was thought by the magistrates to persecute the Goodwin children, an old Irish washerwoman named Glover, had already confessed. Other victims confirmed word for word what she said she had done to them in her spectral form. But how to explain the cause? The girl he took into his home was little help. When he asked her "who her [invisible] company were, she generally replied, I don't know. But if we were insistent in our demand, she would with some witty flount or other turn it off. Once, I said, 'child, if you cant tell their names, pray tell me what clothes they have on,' and the words were no sooner out of my mouth, but she was laid [as if] dead on the floor." He hesitated to perform more experiments with the child for the same reason that he and his father counseled their parishioners not to practice countermagic: "I did not proceed much further in this fanciful business, not knowing what snares this devil might lay for us in the trials."[141]

"Lay for us" was not a figure of speech, some academic concern about being misled. Angered, the devil might swoop down upon the ministers. Cotton was genuinely nervous. At the same time, the epistemological problem continued to bother him. How did the invisible world work its malignity in the visible world? He already had one foot in the empirical world of science, writing reports on American flora for the Royal Society in England.[142] He took as careful notice of the way that spectral weapons like pins and spindles became corporeal when doctors examined Glover's victims as he did of the characteristics of American plants.[143]

Three years after the Goodwin case, when Cotton had had considerably more contact with suspected witches and their victims, he was still bemused by the power of the unseen to cause havoc in the everyday world. As he wrote in the fall of 1692, "in all that witchcraft which now grievously vexes us, I know not whether anything be more unaccountable, than the trick which the witches have, to render themselves and their tools invisible." After much thought, reading, and experiment, Mather found no explanation in "ancient authors" or basis in "natural expedient" for the causal logic of the invisible world. Only those who entered into a "confederacy with evil spirits" knew the solution, though "our witches do seem to have got the knack." Yet he refused to doubt the efficacy of that induction.[144] Indeed, over a decade after the Goodwin possessions, Mather clung to the logic of unseen causes. After all, "it was found that many of the accused, but casting their eye on the afflicted, the afflicted would fall down and lie in a sort of a swoon"—such was the "fascinating mist of invisibility."[145]

Witchcraft's Marks Revealed

When he wrote about the Goodwin case, Cotton Mather had more than the children's demons on his mind. In his "experiments" with Martha Goodwin, he had to steer a course between the shoals of disbelief (the "Sadducees" he constantly demeaned were the atheists), the rocks of Roman Catholic mysticism and magic, and the whirlpool of Quaker enthusiasm.[146] In addition, perils waited outside his study door. In the middle of the 1680s, with the New England colonies still reeling from their losses in King Philip's War, a second round of crises burst upon the Puritans. James Stuart, crowned James II of England in 1685, seemed to be steering the nation in the direction of Catholicism.[147] In 1684 the royal court of king's bench had rescinded Massachusetts's charter of self-government. In 1686, James appointed a close associate, the authoritarian Edmund Andros, to rule a new Dominion of New England that included all the New England colonies. The Puritans applauded when James II lost his throne, but the new rulers, William and Mary, refused to allow Massachusetts to return to its old form of government.[148] In Massachusetts a provisional government took power while the colony waited for a new charter.[149] What came instead was war. When William and Mary assumed the throne, their first order of diplomatic business had been to renounce the Anglo-French alliance forged by James and to re-establish ties with France's enemy, the Netherlands. The English-Dutch alliance brought England into a European war against Louis XIV and France. In "King William's War" (1689–97), as it was called in America, New York and New England bore the brunt of the fighting. No village on either side of the border was safe, and both sides made war on women and children.[150]

The chaos of war, political instability, and resulting panic opened wide the door to sensory anarchy, and the devil seemed to be everywhere.[151] People were hearing and saying, seeing and envisioning, all manner of evils. Cotton Mather wrote in his diary that he felt beset by squadrons of demons.[152] Worse, the overpopulated and hyperactive invisible world now included the most fearsome of all specters—witches.[153] Everyone knew, or at least assumed, that Indian powwows, or medicine men, "often raise their masters in the shape of bears and snakes and fires."[154] New England ministers also believed that the devil lurked in Roman Catholic rituals.[155] Catholic books of devotions and prayer were the devil's books.[156] For both Mathers, as for all educated witch hunters, the arrival of hordes of witches raised fears of doom that went beyond mere numbers. So many witches gathered in one place might portend the end of the world.[157]

This was hardly the first time that New England courts had heard accusations of witchcraft or that convicted witches had been put to death.[158] But this crisis exceeded all others, for it was not confined to a single locality or a particular suspect. New Englanders believed that witches were everywhere, and the invisible tracery of witchcraft afflicted numerous victims.[159] But even the most portentous events have immediate causes, and as it happened, in Salem township of Essex County, north of Boston, a little crisis was already brewing that would give form to the inchoate fear of witches. From 1689 to 1691, the people in Salem Village, a small farming community on the northwestern edge of Salem township, argued about whether to retain the services of minister Samuel Parris. Two powerful landed clans, the Putnams and the Porters, divided over the issue. The Putnams were a close-knit family of farmers whose political fortunes and influence had waned. The Porters, with ties to the commercial elite of the seaport, waxed more powerful each day. The Putnams supported Parris vocally, while the Porters worked silently to oust him.[160]

Some observers saw the hand of Satan in the quarreling of the villagers. Thus, when Reverend Parris's nine-year-old daughter, Betsy, and his eleven-year-old niece, Abigail Williams, fell ill, followed by other girls in the neighborhood, and the local doctor suggested that the cause might be supernatural, the stage was set for accusations of witchcraft. When twelve-year-old Ann Putnam Jr. joined the sufferers, the Putnams asked the local magistrates to examine the girls, and they began to accuse local women of being witches.[161]

From the end of February 1692 until May 1693, the men and women of Salem, Massachusetts, and the neighboring towns engaged in a manic witch hunt. Between June 2, 1692, and September 21, 1692, nineteen women and men were tried and executed for using their powers of witchcraft to assault the girls. Four other suspects died in jail. One man—Martha Cory's eighty-three-year-old husband, Giles—refused to cooperate with the court and was pressed to death with stones. Hundreds were accused, many of whom languished in jail for months. Most of the accused were women, for witchcraft was traditionally associated with women, but men were among the incarcerated.[162]

In May 1692, with nearly one hundred fifty accused witches crowding the jails (one of whom was a child of four) from towns all over eastern Massachusetts, the danger of an outbreak of disease in the jails added urgency to the crisis. Newly appointed Governor William Phips arrived from England with the revised charter and called a special court of "oyer and terminer" (to hear and determine the cases), with Lieutenant Governor William Stoughton, a veteran politician, as its chief judge. Stoughton strongly believed that there was a devil who contracted secretly with men and women to do his evil work in the colony, and equally important, he coveted Phips' post and intended to use the trials to embarrass the governor.[163]

But by the end of September, after the first round of trials had ended and all those tried had been convicted of witchcraft, many who had been silent began to condemn the haste of the convictions and the uncertainty of admitting in court spectral evidence, based on actions no one but the accuser could see. Leading ministers protested against the proceedings and persuaded Increase Mather to prepare a tract on the dangers of admitting testimony on spectral evidence at trial. He agreed that spectral visitations might be the devil's instrument to fool the credulous and cast blame on the innocent—an argument that some of the defendants had made at their hearing. Phips was convinced by the tract and ordered the trials suspended. He would reconvene them in the winter, but this time spectral evidence would not be allowed. All but three women were acquitted at this new round of trials, and Phips pardoned them, as well as everyone else, by the spring of 1693. Stoughton, furious that he could not finish his work of ridding New England of witches, resigned his commission.[164]

Why had the whisper of witchcraft turned into a deafening roar? Why had magistrates believed and juries convicted so many? And why had the cry of "witch" ended almost as suddenly as it erupted? In retrospect, the answer seems clear. Spectral evidence led invariably to convictions in the first round of trials, but, when it was barred from the trials of 1693, the result was acquittals in all but three of the more than fifty cases heard. The fate of the accused, and the course of the crisis, hung on the reception in court of evidence from a veiled sensory world that only a few could tap. The first interpreters of that world for those who could not penetrate its recesses were a group of girls (although they were later joined by others in the community as witnesses and confessors).[165] What did they see, and why were they believed?

The trial records have not survived, although we have a fragment of five of them, to which we will turn shortly. We do have an almost complete set of examinations and grand jury depositions, however. In these, as in the trials, spectral evidence was crucial, and its evaluation always revolved around the senses. The examination was a sensory event, and the decision to pursue an accusation depended upon sensory considerations. One example will serve. On May 28, 1692, Martha Carrier, the wife of an Andover husbandman, stood before Jonathan Corwin, a merchant, and John Hathorne, also a merchant of the port city of Salem, two of the justices of the peace commissioned for the town of Salem. Hathorne did most of the questioning. Abigail Williams, eleven years old, was Samuel Parris's niece and a servant in his home; Elizabeth Hubbard, Susannah Sheldon, Mary Walcott, Mary Warren, and Mercy Lewis were teenaged women who also served in the Salem Village.

The Examination of Martha Carrier. 31. May. 1692

[Hathorne]: Abigail Williams who hurts you?

Goody [short for "goodwife," an honorific for a married woman, like Mrs.] Carrier of Andover.

[Hathorne] Eliz: Hubbard who hurts you?

Goody Carrier

[Hathorne] Susan: Sheldon, who hurts you?

Goody Carrier, she bites me, pinches me, & tells me she would cut my throat, if I did not sign her book

Mary Walcot said she [Carrier] afflicted her & brought the book to her.

[Hathorne to Carrier] What do you say to this you are charged with?

[Carrier] I have not done it.

Sus: Sheldon cried she [Carrier] looks upon the black man.

Ann Putman complained of a pin stuck in her.

[Hathorne to Carrier] What black man is that?

[Carrier] I know none

Ann Putman testified there was.

Mary Warren cried out she was pricked.

[Hathorne to Carrier] What black man did you see?

[Carrier] I saw no black man but your own presence. [Hathorne was dressed in black]

[Hathorne] Can you look upon these & not knock them down?

[Carrier] They will dissemble if I look upon them.

[Hathorne] You see you look upon them & they fall down

[Carrier] It is false. The Devil is a liar.

I looked upon none since I came into the room but you

Susan: Sheldon cried out in a trance, "I wonder what could you murder 13 persons?"

Mary Walcot testified the same[,] that there lay 13 Ghosts.

All the afflicted fell into most intolerable out-cries & agonies.

Eliz: Hubbard & Ann Putman testified the same that she [Carrier] had killed 13 at Andover.

[Carrier] It is a shameful thing that you should mind these folks that are out of their wits.

[Accusers] Do not you see them?

[Carrier] If I do speak you will not believe me.

You do see them, said the accusers.

[Carrier] You lie, I am wronged.

There is the black man whispering in her ear[,] said many of the afflicted.

Mercy Lewis in a violent fit, was well upon the examinants grasping her arm.

The Tortures of the afflicted was so great that there was no enduring of it, so that she [Carrier] was ordered away & to be bound hand & foot with all expedition the afflicted in the meanwhile almost killed to the great trouble of all spectators Magistrates & others.

Note. As soon as she was well bound they all had strange & sudden ease.

Mary Walcot told the Magistrates that this woman told her she had been a witch this 40 years.[166]

How were the examining magistrates to weigh what the accusers and the defendant said? The magistrates did not see what the girls said they saw, but the magistrates could hear and see the girls' evident anguish. Lying in a felony hearing was a capital offense, but the girls did not hesitate in their accusations. Were they possessed? Then their tongues belonged to demons, but they claimed to be afflicted, not possessed. They fought off the witches' blows and refused to become infected with the witches' verbal poison. Might Carrier's spectral form be assailing the girls silently even as Carrier swore she was innocent? Everyone knew that witches could lie with unlined countenances. They could sound reasonable, even comforting, surely bewildered and guiltless, for the devil taught witches to dissemble. Witches could roar, but Carrier's voice had become a hoarse whisper of denial.[167]

The magistrates had to decide whether to apply the causal logic of the invisible world that the two Mathers had explored. When Carrier looked at the girls, they swooned. Did she have the evil eye, or could some other explanation for the girls' fits be imagined? The same inductive reasoning applied to all of these examinations. Bystanders could not see the corporeal cause, but they could see its corporeal effect. When Martha Cory, another suspect, was examined on March 21, "said Cory did but stir her feet, they [the girls] were afflicted in their feet, and stamped fearfully." When Rebecca Nurse, an elderly farm wife and well-regarded churchgoer faced her examination, "her [bodily] motions did produce like effects" in the accusers' bodies.[168] No one could hear the spectral witches demand that the girls join the devil's covenant, but the bystanders could hear the girls cry out in agony. An inferred causal sequence bridged the invisible and visible worlds.

But why should the magistrates accept evidence of unheard commands from invisible specters? The answer comes when we think about the function of sound in New England towns. Cries of alarm had to be taken seriously, even when their visual referents were not in sight. The "hue and cry" of "stop thief" brought out the posse. The shout of "fire" emptied taverns and meeting houses.[169] The absconding felon or the burning building might not be visible, but the words themselves, by their tone and their conventional meanings, galvanized people to action. The word conjured an unseen event. Sounds were conventionally relied on to bring out the people in times of hazard. The firing of cannons and the ringing of church bells warned of danger nearby even when the danger was invisible.

Because much of the evidence presented at these hearings was spectral— that is, Carrier supposedly assumed spectral or invisible form to assault the accusers—the magistrates faced the same problem the modern reader faces. Did they believe the accusers or the accused? There was physical confirmation of the accusers' accounts: Carrier's spectral pinching and pricking left visible marks on her victims, but these marks could have been made with hidden pins and other implements, as one deponent told the magistrates in a later examination.[170] The agony of the victims seemed real enough, but was it hysterical or feigned? The close connection between Carrier's body movements and the pains the accusers said they felt could be a proof of her guilt or a proof that the accusers were acting in concert to mimic her.

Hathorne and the other magistrates believed that the devil was nearby and that he could give witches the power to become invisible.[171] At the same time, the magistrates knew that the devil might be trying to sow confusion among the good people of Salem by causing the pious and righteous to appear to be witches. Carrier and other accused witches asked their examiners why they would attack their victims at the hearings, in front of the magistrates? If their malice against the accusers so overcame their caution, why did they not also attack the magistrates? Or use their powers to escape from the hearings? The magistrates had no answer to these questions other than to order the suspects chained and imprisoned.[172]

No doubt some of the accusers were having hallucinations, hysterical conversion reactions, possession episodes, or the like.[173] Mary Rowlandson and others had referred to the Indians as "black," and at least one of the girls, Mercy Lewis, had been a victim of the Indian attacks on the Maine settlements—thus the "black man" in their accusations. Perhaps she and others were having hysterical fits whose symptoms included vivid memories of the Indian raids. Other accusers no doubt seized the occasion to rehearse old rumors, spread gossip, get revenge on those they thought had wronged them or their families, perhaps even on those who had abused the deponent physically.[174] Those who doubted the accusations did not doubt that there was a devil, that he had the power to contract with people, and that they could gain from it. In a word, they did not doubt the existence of an invisible world.[175]

Distance and time has not made spectral evidence any more visible to us.[176] To some extent the documentary record is misleading, for it was not verbatim.[177] The variation in accounts when there are more than one, the broken spelling and missing words or phrases in the surviving records, and the clerks' obvious attempts at elision and abbreviation further detract from reliability. Indeed, the sheer effort of taking down the testimony, over many days' time, in cramped quarters, during the cold and illness-ridden late winter and spring of 1692, must have made record-keeping of any kind a burden. Contemporary accounts suggest that sickness of the ordinary sort, chest and throat discomforts in particular, were epidemic. Everyone was sneezing, coughing, and bringing up phlegm. The volume of noise, the confusion of people coming and going, must have made listening and watching even more difficult. Parts of magistrates' questions and defendants' responses were lost in the din. The ministers were pressed into service as court stenographers, and they wrote what they heard, but they could not hear everything.[178]

An Inventory of Horrors

Even if the written record can never convey what those in attendance must have seen and heard, much less how they reacted to what they saw and heard, we can begin to recreate the sensory impact of these stories.[179] The extant record permits us to enumerate an inventory of the people, places, and things that the deponents saw and heard in the invisible world. If we are to understand the sensory impact of these events, we must take the witnesses' words seriously. I disagree with Stuart Clark's argument that "to make any sense of the witchcraft beliefs of the past we need to begin with language," because "witchcraft beliefs are an obvious example of signs that had no referents in the real world." The very opposite was true. The witchcraft threat seemed real to contemporaries precisely because the words of the deponents referred to events that were ordinary, commonplace, and easily conceived.[180]

People were the most common sights in the spectral universe. They were often recognizable persons from the deponent's neighborhood. They had no particular marks or signs of malignity. They were not, for example, horribly disfigured. Thus, for example, Ann Putnam Jr. espied Nehemiah Abbott Jr. in spectral form sitting on a beam in the meetinghouse during Abbott's examination by the magistrates. Whole families could be found in the invisible world. The Barkers of Andover confessed to being there. Mary Barker was told by a fly to afflict her victims, while William Barker Sr. flew on a stick to the back of the Salem Village church, where he joined more than a hundred witches at a mass presided over by a black man. This man, the devil in human form, promised that "all persons should be equal, that there should be no day or resurrection or of judgment, and neither punishment nor shame for sin." A trumpet sound brought all the witches together. William Barker Jr., fourteen years of age, going into the woods one evening saw the shape of a frightening black dog, and the next morning he signed the book of a black man in black clothing using red stuff from an inkhorn. The black man baptized young Barker at Five-Mile Pond.[181]

The pretrial testimony in the case of Bridget Bishop, later tried, convicted, and executed, provided a wide variety of her extrabody appearances. Mary Wolcott, one of the teenaged servants, swore that Bishop in spectral form tortured her; the other girls agreed. Mercy Lewis, the oldest of the girls, accused Bishop of traveling to her house at night to reveal the devil's wishes. Confessed witch Deliverance Hobbs accused Bishop and others of asking Hobbs to join them in eating roasted and boiled meat. Hobbs refused. William Stacy recalled that fourteen years earlier Bishop had given him three pence that vanished in his pocket. Later, at night, when he was ill, her specter sat on the edge of his bed, and the night "was as light as it had been day." She wore a black cap and hat and a red jacket. Still later, this time invisible, she played several "pranks" on him, preventing him from performing his chores in the barn. Samuel Grey testified that about fourteen years before, he had awakened to candlelight in his baby's room and found an apparition of a woman. She came and went through the locked door. As though "greatly hurt," his baby cried out and was never the same thereafter. Some months later, the baby died. Grey now recognized the apparition as Bishop's.[182]

Bishop's specter, like much that occurred in the supernatural, favored the night.[183] John Louder, thirty-two years old, recalled that he too had awakened years before to find the specter of Bishop, "in bright moon light," sitting on his chest and causing him chest and stomach pain, and that she "presently laid hold of my throat and almost choked me." But the specters were not afraid of daylight. The next afternoon, as Louder lay sick, a "black thing jump[ed] into the window and came and stood just before my face, upon the bar the body of it looked like a monkey only the feet were like a cock's feet with claws and the face somewhat more like a mans than a monkey." The monkey spoke to Louder: "I am a messenger sent to you," and it offered Louder peace if he would "be ruled by [it]." Louder shook a stick at it, and it jumped out the window and returned through the porch, although the door was shut. As he chased it he saw Bishop going toward her house; then the monkeylike creature reappeared and leapt over a tree in the orchard and vanished.[184]

Bishop was a busy traveler in the hidden realm. Richard Coman was abed with his wife one night eight years earlier when Bishop and two other specters entered. Bishop, wearing her by-now-infamous "red bodice," choked him. The next night she reappeared, and Coman lost the power of speech. Others could not see her, but he was sure that she was his oppressor. Mary Warren, a servant girl to the Proctors, swore that even after Bishop had been jailed in Salem, she came to Warren, tempting her "to sign the book." Susannah Sheldon, another of the teenaged accusers, averred that Bishop visited her at night. Bishop accompanied a black man in a high-crowned hat. Bishop told Sheldon she had been a witch for "above twenty years," and her first familiar was "a streaked snake." Another of the witches who came with Bishop had a yellow bird in her bosom. They knelt down before the black man and prayed. The next day, they told Sheldon she would not eat, choked her, and laughed at her when she tried to swallow a mouthful of food. For six nights the specters tormented her, but she refused the proffered book. The black man gave Bishop a "black pig with no hair on it" to suck at her breast. When she returned it to the black man, she told Sheldon that she had killed four women, including John Trask's wife."[185]

Bishop's specter targeted the ill abed. John Cooke, eighteen years old, when thirteen, awoke one morning to find Bishop sitting on the window sill. She smiled, then hit him on the side of the head, then slipped out of the room through a crack under the window. Later that day, a Sabbath, as he lay, still ill, with his mother and others in the room, Bishop reappeared and knocked an apple from his hand into his mother's lap, some eight feet away. Neither his mother nor the others in the room saw Bishop.[186]

Some reports about events in the invisible world were hearsay. Minister John Hale of Beverly reported a five-year-old rumor from one of his parishioners, Christian Trask: She told him that she had been bewitched by the specter of Bishop. James Kettle reported that Elizabeth Hubbard, another of the teenaged servant girls who saw specters, accosted him at Dr. William Griggs' house and told him that she had seen two children "laying before her and that they cried for vengeance and that Sarah Bishop (in spectral from) bid Hubbard look upon the children and Bishop said, 'I killed them.'"[187]

Other witnesses' memories were jogged by the examinations. Recalled visions could be quite complex in scene and plot. Samuel Endicott testified that, eleven years before, he had seen a vision of Mary Bradbury floating on the water, she a reputed witch and he a mariner returning from Barbados. The specter was a woman from the legs up, wearing "a white cap and a white neckcloth." The legs, severed, he saw on the other side of the boat. Mary Warren's vision was fresher; for a long time she had been afflicted by the specter of a woman whose identity Warren did not know. At Bradbury's examination, Warren recognized the suspect as her assailant, the one who had told her that she was Mary Bradbury. Richard Carr reported that some thirteen years before, Bradbury had exchanged ill words with his father, and when he passed her gate a "blue boar" flew out of it and leapt at his father's horse's feet. Zorobabbel Endicott confirmed the story. Seven years earlier, Carr himself was sick abed one night when something "like a cat" attacked him. Mary Wolcott, one of the young accusers, added that she had seen the specter of Bradbury afflicting others. Elizabeth Hubbard and young Ann Putnam agreed; they had been afflicted by a specter who told them she was Mary Bradbury. Mary Walcott, another of the young accusers, joined them here; she was choked by Bradbury during the examination.[188]

Confessed witches testified to the quicksilver shifts in appearances in the invisible world. Mary Bridges, a young Andover woman, admitted that a yellow bird had besought her "to serve him," and she had agreed in return for "fine clothes." The bird reappeared as the devil, and she was baptized by him. He next appeared as a "black bird" with a paper for her to touch. Then he appeared as a black man at a general meeting of the Andover witches; she had ridden with him on a pole over "the tops of trees" to the gathering. Her sister Sarah confessed, after some hesitancy, that she too had to make a mark in blood in the book that the devil showed her, that sometimes he came to her as a bird and sometimes as a man. She was to serve the devil for four years (her sister's term was only two).[189]

Supernatural events followed set patterns. The witch struck by stealth, sometimes in her spectral shape, sometimes in her corporeal form, through the invisible medium of curses or spells. Most often the visitation was at night, while the deponent was in bed, often suffering with some ailment. The victim may have been a small child, the deponent a parent or caretaker. The form of the assault mimicked the course of an ordinary illness, particularly in winter—difficulty swallowing, breathing, or digesting food. Sometimes the assault was with the teeth, as when Sarah Buckley "tore . . . to pieces" Susannah Sheldon. Sometimes it was simply "something came in the house and stood by her bed side and breathed on her."[190]

The devil did not smite—he used cunning and threats to seduce and frighten the deponent. Sometimes the account of his approach was first hand, but equally often it was hearsay. Visits in daylight were less common, and they almost always took place in isolated settings, such as empty roads, barns, or fields. Witches and the devil had the power to transform themselves into animals that then attacked the victim. Sometimes the presence of the devil was inferred from the actions of the supposed witch. George Burroughs, formerly minister in Salem Village but more recently of Casco Bay, Maine, was a small man with prodigious strength and foreknowledge—therefore part devil, part witch.[191]

Often the spectral witch named herself or himself, sometimes in the course of attempting to recruit the deponent, sometimes in the process of promising future gains or pains. Ann Putnam Jr., testifying against Burroughs, said that in the middle of tormenting her he stopped and offered her a chance to join the group. "He then presently told me his name was George Burroughs and that the had had three wives and that he had bewitched the two first of them to death . . . and that he had also killed Mr. Lawson's child because he went to the eastward and preached so [i.e. to fulfill his own prophecy] and that he had bewitched a great many soldiers to death at the eastward."[192] To the "eastward" Massachusetts and Maine troops were engaged in the terrible war of raid and counterraid against the French Canadians and their Abanaki allies. Surely the devil was present there.[193]

On a few occasions the visitor was not the witch or her master but the witches' victim, arriving to warn the deponent or to accuse the witch. Burroughs did not need to appear to Ann Putnam Jr., for she had already beheld "two women in winding sheets and napkins about their heads . . . and they turned their faces towards Mr. Burroughs and looked very red and angry and told him that he had been a cruel man to them and that their blood did cry for vengeance against him . . . and as soon as he was gone the two women turned their faces towards me and looked as pail as a white wall, and told me that they were Mr. Burroughs' two first wives, and that he had murdered them, and one told me that she was his first wife and he stabbed her under the left arm and put a piece of sealing wax on the wound and she pulled aside the winding sheet and showed me the place." The ghostly parade before the terrified Putnam child continued with Miss Lawson and her daughter, and Goodman Fuller's first wife, all purportedly killed by Burroughs.[194]

Taking the documentary record of testimony as a whole rather than on a case-by-case basis demonstrates the sensory impact of evidence from the invisible world on magistrates and jurors. First, the attacks were unpredictable. Although some of the victims had irked the witches, others could see no reason why they had been assaulted. Moreover, the witnesses came from all walks of life, not just the elite or the propertied. Anyone could become a victim— inadvertent proof of the anarchy of the invisible world that the ministers had so feared. The witching story duplicated the features of the captivity tale; no one was safe, no one could be sure why they had been chosen to suffer, and anyone could become the reporter of the demonic.

Second, the whole of the testimony surpassed its parts through sheer repetition. In fact, for such inherently dramatic and striking events, the testimony was singularly unimaginative, rambling, and sometimes incoherent. The same words and formulas constantly recurred. Some of this dullness of narration may have been a byproduct of the shorthand of the clerks, reducing the variety of language to simpler stock phrases. Nevertheless, the testimony had a stock-like quality, as through drawn from the same property closet at a summer repertory theater production. On top of the relative impoverishment of visuals, the accounts exhibited a lack of individualizing detail, making one episode much like another, even when they were separated by a decade or more (recalling Martha Goodwin's refusal, in 1688, to tell Cotton Mather how her abusers were dressed).

For example, the man in black clothing with a book or paper in hand might as well be a minister, were it not that he was assumed to be the devil. The face of the man is not described, however, or anything of his physiognomy. He is a generic figure of dread who speaks with a sepulchral, regionless accent. His one visual anomaly was his ability to change color and shape. He could "come white, and vanish away black," or appear as a bird with "great eyes," or carry a little girl to her baptism of evil in his arms when her "pole" broke. How big was his book? "Pretty big," Elizabeth Johnson answered in her confession.[195]

Details of other spectral visitors were just as bland or blurred. When Thomas Boarman testified against Rachel Clenton, he swore she turned into "a cat" and then "a little dog" and then "a great turtle." As striking as her shape-changing was, he could not remember any of the particulars about the animals. The cat that stared with human eyes at John Cole was "a great cat of unusual bigness," and it kept him from his own house, but he could not remember anything else about its features. The witches supposedly struck pins into "images" to afflict victims at a distance, but these images were never described in any detail.[196]

Even the terms of service his converts promised to the evil one were mundane. For example, servant girls who confessed to being witches invariably agreed to serve the devil for a term of years corresponding in number to those indentured servants usually owed to their human masters.[197] With the exception of the hearsay stories wherein a ghost related how the witch had slain him or her, there is little variety in the victims' ailments or wounds. They revolve around the ordinary ailments of dyspepsia and nose, throat, and chest pains, the occasional kidney stone or blocked bowel, the aches and pains of arthritis and badly healed war wounds. The girls showed pinpricks and bruises, often from pinching, but these were also common corporal punishments for ill-mannered children.[198]

Specters in the shape of people behaved like people. They drank, danced, smiled, grimaced, and glared. Sometimes they simply cavorted; on other occasions they did things that people cannot do in the ordinary world but can certainly conceive of doing, such as flying through the air, walking through walls, changing their size, and disappearing at will. Animals were usually recognizable from their shapes (though the occasional "strange and unusual beast" appeared), but when they wee familiars of the devil or the witch, they could change their shapes or suddenly rise up or vanish. Some sucked at the witches' breasts. Animal colors were usually drab—black was the favorite—but some dogs were white and some birds were yellow.[199] One boar was blue. The yellow birds, the only distinct animals in the group, were introduced by

Abigail Williams during one of the visiting minister Deodat Lawson's sermons.[200] Soon the whole Village agreed that "the yellow bird hath been seen
by the children and Titabee [Tituba]."[201]

Dogs and cats and birds could do all sorts of unlikely things or appear in
unlikely places. One cat turned out to be the mother of a confessed witch; the
eight-year-old girl knew this because the cat talked to her. But dogs and cats,
even when they were the devil's shapes, did not have many distinguishing features. They were just dogs and cats.

Objects were not transformed into fantastical shapes, although they could
move around as if of their own volition. Objects in the spectral world rarely
had any individuality save possession—my bed, my pots, my clothing. Nor is
the book that is so important in many of the visions described in any detail,
though in one case a confessor described it as a mere "piece of board" or "a
paper"; a second believed that it was "red," a third noticed that it had no covers, and to another it seemed "to hang upon nothing."[202]

Third, what was absent from the invisible world in the depositions and testimony was almost as important as what was there: no angels, no God, no
providences, no flights to heaven, little of the celestial battle between good
and evil that reform Protestantism was fighting on all fronts.[203] But the absence of divine intervention had an even more ominous consequence: Prayer
and ministerial comfort—the weapons that the Mathers wanted victims to
deploy in cases of Indian captivity and demonic possession—seemed to be
useless against the witches. Suspected witch Giles Cory tried to serve a faux
mass of "bread and wine" to an unwilling Elizabeth and Alice Booth, but the
inversion of the sacrament was hardly a religious moment for them. Nothing
intervened in the devil's quest for souls or stepped between the victims and
the witches' malice. The victims had to rely on self-help or simply suffer.
There was little of the bliss of heaven or even the torments of hell. Even when
a deponent, in this case Mercy Lewis, borrowed from the Bible (Matt. 4:8—
Satan tempts Jesus on the mountaintop), she did not mention Jesus or the Bible; she merely made Burroughs into the tempter.[204]

At the core of this dull repetition was the commonplace origin of much of
the invisible world, and this was the reason its introduction at the trials was so
persuasive. Indeed, the conventionality of the objects in the inventory offers
the key to how this invisible world worked on its own terms. There was no escape from the terrors of the invisible world, because it overlay the visible one.
Everything natural might have a supernatural facet that could appear in an instant. The settings were familiar: homes, fields, roads, barns. The victims were
engaged in the commonplace activities of a farming people, but then some-

thing happened that could not be explained rationally. For no apparent reason, cows sickened, butter rotted, nails and boards on barn walls struck the unwary. Mice and rats spoke, flew, and changed into human shapes.[205]

Witchcraft as a Crime against the Senses

The inventory of the invisible world shows how mundane, ordinary, and omnipresent it was, and therein lay its special terror. The scene of the attacks was the rural New England that the victims and confessors knew, the actors the people they knew, the animals the ones they cared for, and the objects the same they owned. "What were the animals like?" confessed witch Abigail Hobbs was asked. "Like a cat," she answered. Spectral events transformed the comfortable everyday routines of milking the cows, visiting the sick, attending a funerals, or drinking a little too much cider into horrific trials. The witch and the devil changed ordinary sensation into extraordinary visitations.[206]

Looking at the face of another person is the most basic act of social intercourse. When the witch used her evil eye to look at someone else, her look caused harm. "Question: can you look upon Mary Warren and not hurt her? Look upon her now in a friendly way." But when accused witch Mary Lacey looked at Warren, she "struck her down." Then Lacey acknowledged that she was a witch. How did the devil first appear to her? In the night he came, "in the shape of a horse." The devil told her to kill a tinker in her town of Andover, but she would not. Then he appeared to her in the shape of "a gray thing" and promised her that he would make her "afraid of nothing," but he was a liar. She was now afraid of everything.[207]

With good reason. Lacey could not trust her eyes. She could harm another simply by looking at that other. And anyone who looked at her might become her victim. It was the malign magical alteration of the process of perception that made the spectral event chilling to the relator. Mary Lacey continued her testimony. She had seen the specters of those whom the witches had ill-treated: little boys and girls who died suddenly and in great pain, others who were sickened and never fully recovered from the "hot irons and knitting needles, spindles and pins" that were the witches' armory.[208]

The witch always wounded the senses when they were most vulnerable. The assaults happened at night, with the victim in bed, often ill; sometimes alone, sometimes with a wife or husband who did not see the apparition. Both illness and darkness caused perception to be distorted, yet they heightened apprehension. The appearance of the witch or the devil was heralded by a strange noise, a noxious odor, a fireball—a threat to the way the victim sensed and understood the world. Night is the time when people hear all sorts of bumps and groans. Ordinarily, they can easily be identified—the settling of the house, the shifting of the next person in bed, the cough or sigh from another room. It is the unexpected and unexplained thump or light that strains the senses, bids one try to see into the dark or listen with special acuity.

The crime of the witch was thus first and foremost a sensate one, transforming normal perception into abnormal and dreadful experiences. The bewitched imagination turned the rural farmhouse, home for generations, comfortable in its worn woodwork and blackened fireplace, into a hell-hole. The windows over the sink, the stair to the bedrooms above, the apple cellar, became hiding places for hideous imps.[209] The demonization of ordinary landscapes and structures linked the witchcraft cases to the captivity tales. Rowlandson had ended her account: "I can remember the time, when I used to sleep quietly without workings in my thoughts, whole nights together, but now it is other ways with me."[210] The night terrors, unseen but vividly imagined, were the same for the victims of witchcraft. But unlike the witchcraft victim, the captive had been redeemed. "Oh! The wonderful power of God that mine eyes have seen, affording matter enough for my thought to run in, that when others are sleeping mine are weeping."[211] Victims of witchcraft went unredeemed and unrelieved.

Under the witch's onslaught, the victim's sense of her own body's health and well-being crumbled. Choking, distension, and pain turned the victim's enjoyment of her own body into dread. As William Brown described his ailing wife's suffering at the hands of suspected witch Susannah Martin, "then [the pain] would rise up into her stomach with pricking pain as nails and pins of which she did bitterly complain and cry out like a woman in travail [giving birth] and after that it would rise up to her throat in a bunch like a pullet's egg." The witch changed the way Goody Brown and her husband perceived essential functions. Goodwife Brown survived, but Goodwife Best succumbed to the attack of accused witch Ann Pudeator, falling under a rain of "pinching and bruising of her till her arms and other parts of her body looked black."[212]

In this context of sensory assault, the familiarity of objects and settings and the ordinariness of pains made the accusers' accounts more rather than less credible to magistrates and jurors. Had the deponents testified that they had seen the devil's face or apparitions of dragons and monsters officials would have dismissed the testimony as the raving of the unsound or the utterance of the possessed.[213] The performance of the accusation was surely important, but the performance gained verisimilitude because the men on the bench and in the box could visualize the events themselves, even if they did not actually see them. They could imagine witches sitting on the edges of beds or hovering over cribs. They could imagine the witch disappearing and a cat or dog suddenly jumping out from behind a bush. They could even, with a little stretch of the imagination, believe that the specters of women chained in Salem and Boston jails could appear to pinch and prick the girls as they testified in court.

Separating the Visible and the Invisible Worlds

For the ministers who watched these hearings and trials, the terrible ordinariness of the accounts of the invisible assault had dire implications. First and foremost was the sensory anarchy that the ministers feared when ordinary people recounted extraordinary events. In this sense, the witchcraft testimony echoed the captivity tales tenfold. The witches struck at anyone, anywhere; any animal or object could be transformed into a weapon, and even the most pious men and women were potential victims. Where was the safety that came with sanctification of life and faith in God? If the intrusion of the invisible world taught that prayer and piety were useless, what value was the Bible, the church, and the ministry? The ministerial injunction to pray and examine one's spiritual state availed reverend Samuel Parris and his family little, though he followed every ministerial rule and invited his brethren to join him in the effort.[214]

Moreover, the gross physicality of the witches' attacks on the bodies of their victims—pinching, biting, choking, striking—violated that other body that God had given the Christian, the heavenly temple of the soul, the sacred vessel of grace. As Cotton Mather later wrote, it was these divine, spiritualized, ethereal bodies that would gather together at the judgment day.[215] None of the bodies described in the victims' testimony resembled Mather's depiction, just as none of the visitations resembled those in his or his father's accounts of remarkable providences. Over and over, it was the sheer ordinariness of the demonic visitations that the record demonstrated.

What, then, to do with spectral evidence? On June 15 Cotton Mather wrote a letter to the judges to regard spectral evidence most carefully; he then added a postscript, saying that they must flush the devils from the midst of the saints.[216] Two weeks earlier, in a letter declining an invitation to watch the trials, he had written to Judge John Richards, "You do not lay more emphasis upon spectral evidence than it will bear." The devil could take the shape of the innocent, and incautious or credulous reliance on spectral evidence—that is, the testimony of those who claimed to see it—meant that the devil could wreck "most hideous desolation upon the repute and repose" of the innocent. At the same time, Mather was not telling the court to bar spectral evidence if it could be corroborated by "dreadfully real" evidence like bruises.[217] And in an August 4, 1692, sermon, he warned that the devil was so near because he knew that the end of days was coming soon, and he could not bear it.[218] The next day he wrote to John Cotton that "our good god is working of miracles. Five witches were lately executed, impudently demanding of God a miraculous vindication of their innocency. Immediately upon this our god miraculously sent in five Andover witches who made a most ample, surprising, amazing confession of all their villainy, and declared the five to have been of their company."[219] Mather was consistent—his August sermon repeated the conclusions of his treatment of Martha Godwin: Be cautious, but take the sensory evidence seriously.

Ministerial critics of the trials agreed with Cotton Mather that the devil lurked nearby, but they asserted that Satan's greatest triumph would be to set innocent and pious people against one another, thereby subtly manipulating appearances in the ordinary world to fool even the best-intentioned observers. So argued minister Samuel Willard of Boston at the height of the crisis. In his preaching, then in a surreptitiously published tract against the admission of spectral evidence at the trials, he denounced the use of spectral evidence. Willard had visited his own parishioners confined in jail awaiting trial and could not believe that they were witches. He said as much to his congregation during the July and August trials, and then he arranged to publish, anonymously, a dialogue entitled *Some Miscellany Observations Respecting Witchcraft*. In it, he called conviction on the basis of the ordinariness of evidence "contrary to the mind of God." The judges had to have before them matters of fact "evidently done and clearly proved." Even if the judges and jurors believed that the girls were beset by specters, such specters could have been created only by an extraordinary process, not a conventional or commonplace one. In effect, he argued that the devil's plans could not be probed in the same way one ascertained cause and effect in the visible world.[220] Willard was telling the court to demote the sensory in its deliberations, for the devil could pervert the ordinary operation of the human senses.

On August 1, 1692, during a hiatus in the trials but at the height of the furor, the Boston ministerial association turned, as it had in 1681, to Increase Mather. The ministers wanted spectral evidence barred from the trials. He accepted their charge to write on the subject but did not rush into print, as his hopes for continued political autonomy for the colony required that he walk a tightrope.[221] He did not want to discredit the court, whose judges were men of great standing in the community and had longed served in government posts. At the same time, he knew that trials of suspected witches had all but come to a halt in England. The last Salem executions, on September 21, occurred before Increase Mather's *Cases of Conscience Concerning Evil Spirits Personating Men* was read to the ministerial association and circulated in manuscript, on October 3. Still, the use of spectral evidence was effectively ended when Phips read the copy rushed to him.[222]

Phips' demons were more political than spectral, and he was more concerned about his reputation in Westminster than in heaven. He closed the court of oyer and terminer and instructed the Superior Court of Judicature to bar spectral evidence when it convened in January to hear the remaining cases. The General Court (the assembly under the Charter), convened on October 28 and agreed that the regular courts should hear the cases. In the meantime, Increase Mather journeyed to Andover and interviewed a number of the confessed witches. Repentant, they told him they had concocted their confessions to save themselves.[223]

The genre of "cases of conscience" was already a century old when Increase Mather published his work, for Puritanism had a peculiar affinity for the exegesis of alleged possessions, omens, and other evidences of the immediacy of God's providence.[224] In fact, although much of what he wrote was genuinely moving and highly relevant at the time, Mather did not add much to the genre; he even repeated what he had written in *Illustrious Providences.* Then he argued that the devil could impersonate anyone, even a virtuous man.[225] Now he made the argument in stronger fashion: Proof of witchcraft had to be extraordinarily conclusive to cost men and women their lives.[226]

As he later wrote, Cotton Mather regarded his father, Willard, and the other ministerial critics of the trials as "persons of great judgment, piety, and experience," but half of the bench that had pressed the prosecution case so hard were his congregants.[227] He could not bring himself to abandon them. At a dinner gathering the night after the last executions, he had promised them that he would write his own history of the events honoring their work, and he obtained from Stephen Sewall, clerk of the court, its records of the trials.[228] He clung to the arguments that he had made in *Wondrous Providences* and rushed into print to answer his father's arguments.[229]

Again, the striking difference between the work of father and son was Cotton's attachment to the sensory evidence. *Wonders of the Invisible World* opened with a version of Cotton Mather's August 1 sermon arguing (as he had in *Memorable Providences*) that the devil was real, witches were real, and so the invisible world could wreck real harm on men and women. Mather had not attended the trials, so he could not claim the authority of an eyewitness, but the bulk of his work was a repetition of the testimony at trial. In the course of this recitation, he gave full scope and credence to the sensory details of the witnesses' accounts. He believed what they said because he could see, at least in his mind's-eye, what they said they saw. Then, following the causal logic of the invisible world, the accused must be guilty as charged.[230]

Cotton Mather spent the next few years comforting the allegedly possessed, while dissuading them from naming the individuals who supposedly afflicted them. There were demons attacking Mercy Short and Margaret Rule in 1693, but such demons could take on any human shape. Looking for the cause of their malady, he hit on an old, highly visible adversary, the Roman Catholic Church. It replaced witches as the target of Mather's animadversions. When Short, three years earlier a victim of the French and Indian assault on Salmon Falls (later Portsmouth), New Hampshire, fell into a delusive state, Mather ferreted out the cause: As a captive in Quebec, she had spurned the offer to join in prayers from a book of Catholic devotions. Three years latter, home again, having been ransomed by Phips, Short was targeted by the devil for refusing to "sign his book." At last there was a detailed description of the book, for "she described to us the color, the breadth, the length, and thickness of the book with all the exactness imaginable." One of the ministers had it in his library.[231] Like the "book of magic" that old reverend John Higginson of Salem had described to Increase Mather in 1684, this book caused its readers to quake in fear. No need for the logic of the invisible world here; everyone could see the danger in the pages of Latin incantations.[232]

By 1694, Cotton Mather's role in the affair was under attack. Boston craftsman Robert Calef accused Cotton of bringing on the calamity, the inevitable consequence of overreaching "zeal" when ministers and magistrates entered the invisible world. The witches' power was a "fable" better left to "heathens" and papists. The supposed victims were engaging in a "juggle" for attention or to gain revenge.[233] Even Cotton conceded that, in the years after the last trial, the dominion of the invisible had receded. Books of wonder continued to arrive in the colony, but these were part of a rearguard action in England rather than the leading edge of a movement to penetrate the "mists of invisibility." The Puritans had always posited "an intensely intrusive supernatural realm," but Anglicans, deists, scoffers, scientists, and now even some of the Dissenters themselves saw the old stories of prodigies and possessions as antipathetic to "sobriety" in worship and letters. By the early decades of the new century, liberal clerics in New England joined in the attack on the logic of the invisible by asserting that belief in witches was a throwback to "priestcraft" in the Roman church. Were not the witches of the Old Testament "providence men," men who saw the immanence of the spirit?[234] The irony of being lumped together with his old adversary was not lost on Cotton Mather. Bit by bit, he retracted and retreated. At first, he suggested that the cause of the Salem Village outbreak might have been the penchant of the young for "little sorceries."[235] Later, he confided, "there have been errors committed."[236] Finally, he conceded that the confessed witches were only deluded and that the magistrates had gone too far.[237]

The elite ministers, like other elites, had moved toward a more experimental, empirical view of perception and the senses, but folklore in New England continued to feature stories of ghosts, demons, and the occasional denunciation of a witch.[238] Countermagic still survived among the common people. Suspected familiars were still tortured to reveal the witch who had sent them forth.[239] In Salem, "Old Granny Ober" fell under suspicion, but it came to naught. In Littleton, Massachusetts, early in the 1700s, three young sisters acted strangely and denounced a neighbor as their afflicter, but the ministers advised the authorities to disregard the accusation. The invisible world still afrighted the senses of ordinary people, but educated discourse regarded the reports of ghosts and goblins as nonsense. The coming of the Enlightenment had changed the senses. It sharpened the eye and the ear in pursuit of precise, scientific measurement, but it dulled the perception of the invisible world. "Invisible" was equated with microscopic. Visions and auditory out-of-body experiences were most often dismissed as myth, hallucination, or lunacy.[240]

A new generation of ministers agreed; loud sounds like thunder or chimes might still cause unbelievers to quake and converts to renew their faith, but the steady clergyman regarded "this way of revelation, by calls and voices . . . the lowest and most dubious of all."[241] In 1746, Jonathan Edwards reviewed the religious revival, called by some a Great and General Awakening, that had swept through the American colonies. A remarkable thinker who had more than a little to do with starting the revival, he worried that the "enthusiasm" of religious visions, dreams, and prophecies that accompanied the outpouring on spirituality might be mistaken for the return of the invisible world. True Christian experience, he decided, must be fulfilled in visible, everyday practice. He feared the "evangelical . . . hypocrites" who mistook "some kinds of impulses and supposed revelations" for direct sensory experience of the divine. The innocent believer under stress was also vulnerable: "So if the spirit of God impresses on a man's imagination, either in a dream, or when he is awake, any outward ideas of any of the senses, either voices or shapes and colors, 'tis only exciting ideas of the same kind that he has by natural principles and senses." For the body itself in a fevered state can "excite imagery or external ideas in the mind." Such chimeras, whether of true piety or false hope, were not real. "From hence it again clearly appears that no such things have anything in them that is spiritual, supernatural, or divine."[242] Visions and other out-of-body experiences had to be regarded in naturalistic terms.[243] Edwards succeeded where Cotton Mather had failed; order had returned to the invisible world, and one could trust the ordinary functions of ones senses again.

But the cost was high—an entire world of visions, sounds, and impressions was pushed to the periphery of sensory conventions. In religion, the supernatural continued to flourish, and men and women on their deathbeds or in the throes of revelation still had visions of hell and heaven, Jesus and Satan, but such visions were now extraordinary and suspect.[244] The nineteenth-century Transcendentalist philosophers believed in an invisible world, but it was benign and without distinct form. As minister George Ripley wrote in 1836, "The religious man is, indeed, conversant with invisible objects. His thoughts expatiate in regions, which eye had not seen, but which God has revealed to him, by his spirit . . . those higher spheres of thought and reality, to which eternal elements of our being belong." Spiritualism would make a return visit in the nineteenth century, and mysticism would find staunch adherents in the twentieth, but neither movement would occupy the mainstream. In print, the revelations of the supernatural that ordinary people recorded became a specialized genre, grouped by its publishers and readers with works about talking animals and ventriloquism.[245]

CHAPTER THREE

Other Worlds

Slave Revolts and Religious Awakenings

ONE OF the prime tasks our senses perform is the perception of human activity. Early in our lives we learn to distinguish people from background settings, to identify human traits, and to classify human conduct. Our culture instructs us what to make of these perceptions, in particular, how to tell those who are like us from those who are not. In fact, human beings are especially adept at identifying other people. Like all born predators, we have to be able to pick out prey from camouflage, to sense differences in familiar settings. But we are the highest species of predator, and we know friend from foe because we recognize the features of faces and bodies. We see in color, unlike most mammals, and our unique ability to vocalize and hear variations in sound patterns allows us to handle a wide range of auditory cues.

Human culture does not rely on raw perception. It imposes elaborate systems of symbols on sense data, and subcultures employ these symbols as markers of group membership. Such categorization of others saves time and effort, and basing this categorizing on general images and impressions further speeds the process of making assessments. Our categories extend to groups as well as individuals, as "snap judgments" allow us to determine the meaning of others' actions and words.[1]

We rarely regard otherness with complacency or neutrality. Most often, we are wary of others, and wariness lends importance to immediate perception of differences. The report of the senses, filtered through frames of reference learned from childhood, tells us which stranger to shun and which to welcome.[2] Our culture is riven with what Irving Goffman, in a seminal essay on labeling, called "stigma-theory." The dangerous other is not quite human—at least, not as human as we are—and being different in a society that defines its boundaries by punishing "deviance" is a lesson in the pain of being an outsider. At times, the despised and feared other must wear a stigmatizing symbol, be quarantined, even be eliminated.[3]

When the other is recognized through the senses of the observer—by words, dress, features of face or of body—sensory prejudices trigger a prepackaged reading of what we see or hear. The anticipation of the degenerative and debased look, sound, and smell of the other is the self-fulfilling prophecy of prejudice. Even when sensory denigration of the other does not rise to the level of national preoccupation as in Nazi Germany, it can be pervasive, as in modern American gay-bashing and in the profiling of suspected criminals by shade of skin color. An essential part of the stereotyping that empowers the labeler is a sensory paradigm: Gays and lesbians walk, talk, dress, and gesture differently, people of color are more prone to criminal activity. But the gay or lesbian can "pass" by changing appearances, by adopting the manners of the "straights," just as ethnic minorities can pass by assimilation when their color is light enough.[4]

Color and speech have always been the easiest ways to identify and typecast the "other."[5] If written and read without a hint of discrimination, colorful prose makes words into pictures. Consider the characters in Walter Mosley's *Fearless Jones:* Theodore Wally, a young clerk, "medium brown"; Milo Sweet, the bail bondsman with a "complexion of polished charcoal"; a guard at the courthouse, "with a red and chapped face"; Conrad Benjamin Till, a walking corpse, "a light skinned Negro with brown freckles across his wide nose."[6] But for many of us, skin color, slang, and prejudice are inseparable. So, despite the formal legal equality of public access, voting rights, employment opportunities, and membership in unions and other organized groups, the color line permeates all social relationships, divides neighborhoods, defines cultures, defies legal remedies, and distorts the media treatment of "whites" and "blacks" by oversimplifying and stigmatizing.[7] We may speak of the ideal of a color-blind society, but we are still blinded by color. Concepts of race used to "diversify" are caricatures meant to discriminate.[8] Where would constructs like "race" and abominations like "racism" be without color? As Langston Hughes wrote in "Let America Be America Again": "The poor white, fooled and pushed apart/ . . . the Negro bearing slavery's scars/ . . . the red man driven from the land."

Otherness is a two-way street. Every person has his or her own predisposition to judge according to perceived material differences. In 1751, Benjamin Franklin wrote that "the number of purely white people in the world is proportionally very small . . . I would wish their numbers were increased." Too many slaves of dark hue were appearing in the streets of his city. "Why should we . . . darken" the city, "where we have so fair an opportunity, by excluding all Blacks and Tawneys [Indians], of increasing the lovely white . . . but perhaps I am partial to the complexion of my country, for such kind of partiality is natural to mankind." Olaudah Equiano, stolen from his West African village and sold to European slave traders, recalled, "I was immediately handled, and tossed up to see if I were sound, by some of the crew; and now I was persuaded that I had gotten into a world of bad spirits, and they were going to kill me. Their complexions, too, differing so much from ours, their long hair, and the language they spoke (which was very different from any I had ever heard) united to confirm me in this belief . . . I asked [the other Africans on board] if we were not to be eaten by those white men with horrible looks, red faces, and long hair."[9]

The presence of Africans like Equiano in both city and countryside in the mid-eighteenth-century colonies posed an array of sensory challenges to everyone concerned, and on two occasions those challenges led to widespread violence. Near the Stono River, in South Carolina, in 1739, and in New York City, two years later, perceptions of visible and audible otherness led African and European peoples to turn against one another. The result was hundreds dead, some through combat, most through the operation of legal systems that defined and defiled people according to the color of their skin. After the violence had quieted, but long before Jim Crow took over in America, the slave uprisings and their suppression in the mid-eighteenth century paved the way for segregation.

There is a second kind of otherness that divides Americans today, based on easily sensed distinctions that have nothing to do with skin color. Our ethnic diversity is matched by religious diversity. One of the sectarian divisions most important in modern American social and political life goes back to the same historical moment as the Stono and New York City slave uprisings. Some Americans are Born Again Christians, experiencing a state of ecstatic and transforming grace that distinguishes them from others who have not been so blessed or sought such blessing. The modern evangelical movement—a loose coalition of southern and western evangelical preachers and their congregations, numbering between 20 and 40 percent of Protestants who regularly attend church services—creates highly visible and audible communities that are distinct from other religious assemblages.[10] The evangelical movement that sustains these churches originated in the Great Awakening of the mid-eighteenth-century colonies.

In the early decades of the eighteenth century a wave of pietistic enthusiasm swept through Protestant western Europe and the British Isles. Proponents of some of these movements came to America and found its peoples ready for regeneration. Here faint stirrings of revival had already caressed congregations in New England and the middle colonies, where ministers and congregants sought a renewal of old pieties.[11] In the course of this revival, men and women assembled to hear preachers in meetinghouses, on city streets, and in country fields, "as if they were hearing the gospel and seeing the world for the first time."[12] Sometimes those gathered listened in absolute silence. More often, the minister's words were soon accompanied by the groans of the penitent sinner and the outcries of the awakened seeker. Slaves attended some of these revival meetings, and observers noted how emotionally wrought the bondsmen and bondswomen became. As Eleazer Wheelock recalled after a revival meeting in Taunton, Massachusetts, in 1741, "almost all the negroes in town wounded [i.e. awakened to their sins], 3 or 4 converted . . . I was forced to break off my sermon before I had done, the outcry was so great."[13]

But the Great Awakening's critics saw and heard in the convening of the revival similar dangers to those the condemners of slave-gatherings decried.[14] Sensation and perception were as vital to the religious awakening as they were to slavery. Indeed, as Charles Woodmason, an Anglican minister who witnessed revival preaching on the South Carolina frontier, wrote in 1768, "one on his knees in a posture of prayer—others singing—some howling—these ranting—those crying—others skipping, dancing, laughing, and rejoicing" resembled nothing more than a gathering of savages.[15] As dangerous, surely, as the unauthorized assembly of slaves, and certainly as great a shock to the senses of the wary observer.

Deeply imbedded in the evangelical vision of the world then, as now, was a sense of the differences between true converts and those whose worship was mere form—what the most radical of the first Puritans in England would have called legal Christians, going through the motions by going to church, reciting the words without feeling the Holy Spirit.[16] The saved knew who they were through the testimony of the word, spoken aloud, in visible gatherings; they were assured of their salvation through their striving for piety and their rejection of the temptations of heresy and materialism. Their critics regarded the evangelicals as misguided at best and hysterical at worst. Perceptions of otherness again divided communities and neighbors.

If the comparison between the gathering of slaves seeking freedom and the gathering of the pious seeking assurance seems forced, a mere concomitance of chronology and outward appearance, in fact both depended upon what people who thought themselves different from those around them said and heard, and both were condemned by those who saw their behavior as dangerously inappropriate. The slave uprisings failed and the evangelical movement fragmented, but their sensory legacy heralded the future—in the one, the division of American society by race, and in the other, the sectarianism that would make American Christianity so fissiparous.

Slave Revolts

The highly sensate nature of early American slavery distinguished it from slavery elsewhere in the world. Slavery was a old feature of human society when the Portuguese first brought Africans to the Americas at the beginning of the sixteenth century. Europeans had held slaves from ancient times. Some American Indian peoples enslaved their captured enemies. In Africa, slavery was endemic before European buyers appeared in the fourteenth century. Indeed, western Europe was the "anomaly" in not seeking to expand its slave markets even after the great plague of the fourteenth century had killed off a third of Europe's native labor force.[17]

Slaves were always a debased and dishonored caste, but the dishonor was not always evident to the untutored eye. Usually there was some mark or sign that an individual was a slave—chains, shorn hair, or clothing—but skin color did not necessarily matter.[18] Slavery was and always had to be a "we-they" relationship—the essence of otherness—but otherness usually had an internal definition that masters and slaves knew, rather than a sensory one. Until Europeans brought African slaves to America.[19]

While the Europeans' purpose in exporting African slaves to the Americas was to provide a labor force for European mining and agricultural enterprises, the massive scale of the importation (some 12 million individuals between 1500 and 1900) and the necessity of monitoring the conduct of so many slaves demanded that the report of the senses become a defining characteristic of American slave societies. Color changed from an incident of the demography of slavery (white masters, black slaves) to a core attribute.[20] The sounds slaves made had to be heard and monitored as well, lest the slaves conspire to resist their bondage. The sensory features of slaveholding societies defined masters and slaves.

The Color and Sound of Slavery

From the beginning of England's overseas expansion, the odious association of blackness with death carried over from England to the English in Africa and then to England's Caribbean and North American colonies.[21] That prejudice has become so ingrained in our language that, for some historians of colonial slavery, "African presence" equates to "black faces."[22]

Skin color was the first but not the only marker of colonial otherness. Whites would sneer at blacks for the "horrid noise" they made in their revelries.[23] Even evangelical preachers who noted with pride the participation of slaves in worship services found the slaves' vocalization of their faith striking. One Presbyterian evangelical lauded the slaves' "delight in psalmody" but noted that it often erupted in the dead of night.[24] Another winced that "they are commonly more noisy in time of preaching than the whites, and more subject in bodily excess." If not constrained, they displayed an excess of "ecstatic delight" in singing the word of the Lord.[25] The denigration of the sight and sounds of the dark other would linger in the air even after slavery was legally dead.[26]

Color prejudices were deeply embedded in English culture before the English embraced African slavery. The Elizabethan world regarded black as the color of death and immorality. Some English writers compared Africans to the great apes, the unflattering comparison arising as much from English ethnocentrism as from facile associations of African primate's facial features. White was virginal, black was ungoverned sexual passion; white was salvation, black was damnation; white was virtue; the black-hearted villain had none; white was life and beauty, black was death and disfigurement.[27] White was angelic; one's enemy was "black as the Devil." For traders like Edward Shippen of Lancaster, Pennsylvania, a year into the French and Indian War, the Indian enemy, "perfidious and cruel in their natures," had to blacken their faces that they [might] be of the same color with their hearts."[28]

For some English commentators, the color black was the result of the curse that Noah put on his dark-skinned son Ham; for others, it was a mark of physiological degeneration (white being the original color of mankind). Seventeenth-century English writers of a scientific bent debated the origins and reproduction of African blackness, but none doubted that the dark color made Africans suitable for domination by those (like the English) of lighter hue.[29] Some observers hinted that the blackness of the African's skin extended to the internal organs; they must have been as corrupt as the skin of African peoples. The foremost political economist in late- seventeenth-century England, William Petty, opined that blacks were "a brutish sort of people."[30] Black was just not a natural color for human beings, and it marked its bearers as children of a lesser God.[31]

The English came relatively late to the enterprise of slave trading and the use of slaves as agricultural laborers, but they quickly grasped the importance of sensory differentiation between slaves and free persons. The English law of slavery, which originated in the West Indian colony of Barbados in the 1660s and spread to Jamaica and the North American mainland colonies, recited the ways that masters must see and hear everything the slaves did and said. Slaves were not to be allowed to congregate away from the masters' sight, or to assemble in large numbers without the master's permission, or to engage in acts easily hidden, like the practice of medicine, lest they plot or carry out crimes. When the law had to distinguish servants of African ancestry, it called them "negar servants." Indeed, many of these regulations extended to free blacks as well, or, in the language of the legislators, "any negro."[32]

Such laws were invariably captioned "Negro" or "black" codes—color becoming the presumptive sign of slave status. The first Virginia laws to distinguish slaves from servants invariably rested that distinction upon color. For example, "whereas the frequent meetings of considerable numbers of Negro slaves under pretense of feasts and burials is judged of dangerous consequence," slaves at such gatherings were not to carry firearms.[33] "These two words, *Negro* and *Slave*," were "by custom grown homogenous and convertible," one Virginia clergyman wrote in 1680, and opinion that was still held one hundred and fifty years later.[34] In 1702, the New York legislature provided for summary trials of slaves accused of assaulting "white women."[35] The South Carolina slave code of 1740 pronounced that any slave striking or attempting to strike "a white person" was guilty of a serious offense. The assumption of the lawmakers was that no slave could be "white."[36] Dark color was not only a badge of inferiority, it was a portent of future misconduct. As the New York colonial lawmakers prefaced their black code in 1708, "whereas, it is found by experience, that the free Negroes of this colony are an idle, slothful people," masters wishing to manumit their bondsmen had to put up a £200 bond for their former slaves' good conduct.[37] Statute law reflected and reinforced color prejudices.

Even critics of slavery admitted that color made all the difference. Begging the crown to end the Atlantic slave trade, William Byrd of Virginia wrote, "I wonder the legislature will indulge a few ravenous [slave] traders, to the danger of the public safety, and such traders as would freely sell their fathers, their elder brothers, and even the wives of their bosoms if they could black their faces and get anything for them."[38] Byrd's objection was somewhat ingenuous—he was one of the greatest slaveholders in the colony. Herman Husband of Maryland and North Carolina was a Quaker and an opponent of slavery, but his plaint against slavery rested in part on color prejudice. "We destroy one native and in his room import three or ten more from Africa that are more foreign by one half both in nature, shapes, and color," he complained in 1755.[39] Abigail Adams, who hated slavery, admitted that seeing Othello on the London stage elicited a "natural antipathy" to the black-faced tragic hero. She shuddered when the "sooty heretic Moor" touched "fair Desdemona."[40]

Long after the law made blackness a sign of inferiority, enlightened minds like Thomas Jefferson's were still trying to explain how color and condition of servitude were aligned. In response to a question from a French correspondent asking why the revolutionary governments did not end slavery and incorporate the African American into society, Jefferson replied, "the first distinction which strikes us is that of colour . . . the difference is fixed in nature, and is as real as if its seat and cause were better known to us. And is this difference of no importance? Is it not the foundation of a greater or less share of beauty in the two races? Are not the fine mixtures of red and white, the expressions of every passion by greater or less suffusions of colour in the one, preferable to that eternal monotony, which reigns in the countenances, that immoveable veil of black which covers all the emotions of the other race. Add to these, flowing hair, a more elegant symmetry of form, their own judgement in favour of the white, declared by their preference of them, as uniformly as is the preference of the Oran-ootan for the black women over those of their own species."[41] For Jefferson, surface distinctions of color signaled a host of social deformities beneath the skin, including sexual ardor, a sensate rather than a reflective nature, and decreased capacity for memory, reason, and imagination.[42] Jefferson did not disclose that in Virginia, debasement of the black person was the foundation for the alliance of whites of lower- and upper-class status.[43]

But the colors of the Africans in America varied, and although the English seemed to think that black was a unitary color, the masters of slaves in America knew better. John Stedman set the categories of color to verse: "The Sambo dark, and the mulatto brown/The mesti[zo] fair—the well-limbed quarderoon."[44] As Thomas R. R. Cobb, the premier antebellum apologist of American slavery, wrote in 1858, "the black color alone does not constitute the Negro . . . there are a great number of tribes, differing not so much in their physical as moral nature, and adapting them more or less for a state of servitude. This difference was well known among the native tribes long before the Dutch, Portuguese, and English vied with each other in extending the slave trade."[45] The perceptual faux-science told the potential purchaser of slaves that Angolans were dark and amiable but slow-witted; men and women from the Gambian River area were light-skinned and hard-working but rebellious.

The people of the Bite of Biafra, stereotyped by the planter-importers as yellowish in hue, were less desirable than any other group, for they were prone to suicide.[46] The registered appreciation of color differences changed over time as well, as slaves of mixed ancestry entered the ranks of skilled craftsmen and became house servants.[47]

Looking at colors was a major preoccupation of masters trying to decide whether or not to purchase a slave. Unscrupulous slave traders would rub lampblack into the skins of their slaves before auctions to make the slaves' skin glisten.[48] Buyers knew about such tricks, and stared long and hard at their prospective purchases. Indeed, the masters and their agents had gained from long experience a kind of "singular look, peculiar to the buyer of slaves," which took in the "slaves' looks" at a single practiced glance.[49] But the examination did not conclude with a once-over. At auction, "the Negroes were examined as if they had been brutes, the buyers pulling their mouths open to see their teeth, pinching their limbs to find out how muscular they were, walking them up and down to detect any signs of lameness, making them stoop and bend in different ways."[50]

Masters employed a myriad of words to describe the shades of the bondsmen and women—some taken from the spectrum (*purple, deepest black, dark brownish, yellow*), others of cultural origin (*mulatto, quadroon, Negro*).[51] Taken by the charms of a "black angel" in 1728, Byrd confided to his diary that "her complexion was a deep copper, so that her fine shape and regular features made her appear like a statue in bronze done by a masterly hand."[52] Newspaper advertisements for runaway slaves were more prosaic than Byrd's depiction but equally explicit on color. Phyllis was a "mustee" woman who ran from her South Carolina master in 1732. She, like other mustee slaves, might have been mistaken for an Indian. Juno, who took flight the next year, was "of the blackest color," as were three lately arrived Angolans, "Hector, Peter, and Dublin . . . of very black complexions."[53] Masters also believed that slaves changed color when they became sick, growing pale or white.[54]

Did slaves note color as well? Of course they did. Equiano cringed in horror at the red hair and pale color of his captors. Color marked African national origins, as the slaves were well aware. Slaves no less than masters knew that lighter-skinned mulattos, often freedmen and women, had higher status than darker-hued Africans. In Charleston, for example, the great majority of the free people of color were lighter than the newly imported African slaves. Did slaves also have some sense of themselves as "black," in a binary opposition to "white," in the way that whites lumped all slaves together by

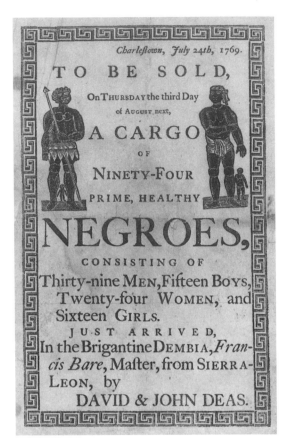

Handbill, Charleston (Charlestown) July 24, 1769

This sheet advertised the sale at auction of a newly arrived cargo of slaves. Many hand-
bills mentioned the nationality of the slaves and, like this illustration, indicated that
the slaves were muscular and healthy. The rude drawings were more like symbols than
depictions; individual buyers were expected to examine the cargo closely before making bids. (Georgia B. Bumgardner, ed., *American Broadsides* [Barre, Mass., 1971].)

skin color? There is a danger here of "upstreaming," of using evidence from
the last years of the century to talk about the earlier incarnations of slavery.
But one piece of evidence cannot be ignored. In the wake of the revolt of the
slaves of Haiti, blacks in Virginia began to speak aloud of people of "our colour."[55] In one of the more telling ironies of slavery, African Americans were
gaining a sense of unity and common purpose by adopting a homogeneous

definition of their color–they were black Americans–at the same time as the
master class was accustoming itself to precise delineation of skin tone among
the bondsmen and women.

Color was the most important sensory marker of slavery. As a definition of
personality imposed by the master, it served to differentiate the slave from the
free white servant at a glance. But those who found in color such an important signifier of status and character did not neglect other sensory cues to the
otherness of slaves. To whites, slaves were as audibly different as they were visibly different.[56]

Masters sometimes gave permission for slaves to gather for funerals, parties,
and other communal events. The noise level at these was often so loud that
passersby complained that slaves were "great and loud talkers."[57] Slaves' voices
were most apparent to whites when bondsmen and women joined in song and
dance, common occurrences in slave communities. Songs often had an African cadence and tonality, even if the words were English. In the dance, with
its African-derived circular forms, its call and response, or "shout," its sharp
drum and fiddle music, everyone could see and be seen, hear and be heard. At
mock elections presided over by slaves in New England and New York, musicians dressed in outlandish costumes, played drums, horns, and stringed instruments, and marched ahead of feather- and jewel-bedecked "kings." Slave
onlookers added their own noise to the parade.[58] Sound expressed emotion,
joy and sorrow, "shouting and clapping hands and singing."[59]

Many vital slave ceremonies involved voices raised in song, shout, or
speech, but the most striking occasions to European observers were funerals.
"Slaves sang all the way" to the funeral site, one observer reported in 1740, and
once there drummers beat out the rhythms of mourning. Whole communities restated their African identity in vocalization at funerals, remembering the
dead with stories, songs, and shouts.[60] We cannot hear those voices now, but a
visit to a modern maroon community in Guyana coincided with a "ceremony
of the dead," when the spirits of ancestors returned to the earth to possess the
living. "The excitement of the crowd grew more intense," the observer wrote.
"Many of the women stood together to one side of the drums . . . They
seemed to be encouraging spiritual stimulation for the men pounding the
drums . . . as the fire blazed large, the drums beat louder and more frantically
and the people grew more excited. Many were chanting songs, some were
dancing, and the children stood spellbound by the entrancing events."[61]

Slaves faced their own auditory challenges, the converse of their masters'.
The spoken word in one's own tongue is the most comforting aural sensation,

but many masters had taken pains to import slaves from a wide variety of linguistic regions and never to purchase many from any one place. Slaves thus had to learn to talk to one another, often in pidgins composed of native idioms and English.[62] They had also lost familiar sounds of now faraway homelands. Some masters allowed slaves time and provided materials to build housing, but the voices in the "quarters" would never fully capture the soundscapes of Africa. Even more frightening, slaves had lost touch with the voices of the powerful spirits that inhabited their homelands. These included ancestors as well as "trees, rocks, and rivers." All could be addressed in supplicating tones, and some Africans practiced magical incantations to summon those powers when the need arose. But now even the spirits of parents and grandparents seemed almost too far away to be heard when called upon.

Still, slaves tried to retain as much of old languages as they could. The words had magical power to comfort and heal."Cornered like this, [the slaves] deepest prayers and desires were expressed through their mother tongue."[63] Hearing their own name, in their own language, mattered. Masters used naming to control slaves, redubbing them with classical, English, or biblical names. But many slaves forced a compromise. Slaves retained their public, or "day names." *Cudjoe* and *Juba* were the male and female Akan (roughly modern Ghana) day names for Monday. *Quaco* and *Cuba* were the equivalents for Wednesday. *Cuffee* and *Quibba* were Friday names, and *Quashee* and *Quashiba* were Sunday. Sometimes an African name was written down as a classical Greek or Roman name merely because it sounded the same, hence *Cato* for the Yoruba (roughly, modern southwestern Nigerian) *Keta*. Sometimes place of origin was added as a surrogate for a family name, like *Congo Tom*, or *Coromantu* (*Coromanti*, for the Gold Coast town of that name) *Cubba*. The acculturation allowed slaves to recall old sounds. Even when these were changed again, anglicized like *Jack* for *Quaco*, *Joe* for *Cudjoe*, and *Coffee* for *Cuffee*, the slave could sound out the old word.[64]

Slave songs, chants, and talk were first and foremost a way to build community, re-establish identity, and simply have fun. But slave sounds were also a form of resistance to the thousands of everyday tyrannies of bondage.[65] Slave singing called out to ancient ancestors or to the Christian Savior to bring an end to suffering. Slave stories, borrowed and adapted from African animal tales, pilloried masters and mistresses or demonstrated how slaves could fool their masters with double meanings and misdirected answers.[66] Slaves manipulated what they said in order to mislead. Landon Carter, a Chesapeake planter, kept a diary in which he featured his dealings with his slaves. He was often exasperated by the extent to which slaves found ways to excuse their negligence on the plantations. Mangorike Willy, Simon the ox-carter, and Bart deflected Carter's fury by playing on words, telling stories about other slaves, and feigning either childlike contrition or simple stupidity. The masters were well aware of the slaves' verbal games and carried on their own side of the contest by teaching slaves English, requiring polite responses, and both rewarding and punishing slaves according to the nature of their vocal conduct. Some slaves were allowed to say more than others or were excused for speaking out of turn, but the verbal jousting went on continuously.[67] Slaves also used silence to wage sensory battle with masters;[68] they refused to answer when called, remained still when ordered to explain themselves, and stubbornly became mute when punished.

Slaves' Sensory Communities

Denied the chance to return to their own homes or create independent communities, slaves fashioned vital, sensory communities. Funeral ceremonies, storytelling gatherings, dances, and songs allowed slaves to build virtual aural environments. Their rhythms and motions were African. As African-American dance teacher and practitioner Pearl Primus wrote, "people who truly dance are those who have never bartered the fierce freedom of their souls." Close their eyes, hear the music, and they could imagine the sounds of home. Behind the big house of the master, but in plain sight, slaves duplicated remembered African shapes. Sitting on the porches of their cabins, slave potters turned clay into the patterns of African bowls and jugs. Turbans, earrings, and other African dress ways persisted in the quarters, connecting the slaves' new world to the old. Slaves laid out their cabins in African fashion, in a circle or in rows.[69] The interiors contained reminders of African ways, including walls facing doors, front porches, and gabled entrances (the origin of the shotgun house, common in nineteenth-century cities).[70]

Not every slave lived in the quarters or in an outbuilding-dormitory; some lived in or near the "dwelling house" of their master.[71] Even living in the master's house, the slaves found sensory ways to remain African. In the mansion's basement rooms allotted to household slaves, just as under the floorboards of slave cabins, archeologists have found the "distant cousins" of a West African diet—calabash gourds and dried fish bones, along with religious objects like cowry shells (used for divining).[72] African burial plots yield jewelry that mourners knew would comfort the dead on their journey home, for Africans believed that the soul journeyed back across the sea to the ancestral land when the body died.[73] Africa was far away, but the feel, smell, and taste of an African world permeated the slave's everyday life.

If the slaves lamented the loss of ancestral holy places, surely there were "spirits all around" in their new home, as well.[74] African folk beliefs carried to the New World held that the invisible spirit world was always close at hand. Material objects could be possessed by these spirits and serve as magical charms. Fellow slaves acted as healers, spell-casters, and herbalists.[75] Some of the magic these men and women produced was evil, and spells had to be warded off (often by going to the same men and women who could cast the spell). The "rangers," free men of color who pursued the rebels in Surinam, all had "amulets and obias to make them invulnerable," but they trusted these magical objects at their peril, as one slave raider discovered in Surinam: His amulet did not protect him from bullets.[76] Some of the potions doubled as poisons, although cases of poisoning were uncommon. In any case, the slave "doctor" had to be treated with respect in the quarters.[77]

Some masters respected a quasi "privacy" of valued slaves, allowing them to live in their quarters without much supervision,[78] and in the evenings these quarters became a little bit of Africa. But in the law, the slave had no privacy, for the slave was the master's chattel or real estate, and property has no privacy. The dreaded patrols created by law in the southern colonies might enter all slave dwellings at their discretion. The patrols tried to turn night into day, carrying lanterns with them as they traversed the land, insisting that slaves make light in their homes to aid the patrollers' investigations.[79]

But slaves responded as resourcefully to the patrols as they did to their masters. As they became inarticulate before their masters' anger, so they became invisible to the patrols. The darkness of a moonless night was their ally, just as dark skin was their nemesis in daylight. Men and women made regular trips at night to visit other slaves. In 1688, Governor Francis Nicholson of Maryland was struck by the distance slaves traveled at night "to go and see another tho' at 30 or 40 miles distance." Sometimes the night travelers walked alone, but Nicholson met six or seven at a time during the holidays.[80] Any slave away from the plantation at night was to have a pass, but slaves who could disappear did not need passes. Some turned to African magic for ways to cloak themselves. There was a healthy trade in charms and potions for a variety of purposes, and conjurors in the quarters offered roots, herbs, and potions to cause temporary invisibility. Not content with magic, to foil the patrols wily slaves laid trip wires across roads and detoured through swamps, or rubbed manure or turpentine on themselves to put tracking dogs off the scent. When patrols followed the sounds of slaves singing to break up late-night prayer sessions and social gatherings, slaves countered by setting sentries.[81]

Another form of virtual invisibility was running away. Slavery was first and foremost a labor system, and the runaway could not contribute his or her labor to the owners' or leasees' enterprise.[82] Running away was so common that the law developed a category for the habitual runaway—the "redhibitory slave." Such slaves were not to be sold without a warning to the buyer, and buyers could seek recission of the sale if the slave absconded.[83] Slave runaways often hid in plain sight. Many of the advertisements noted that the slave was "well known in the area." The "molatto named Franke . . . is known by most people in Charlestown, and without doubt harbored by some free Negroes or slaves." She had probably crossed paths with Minos, "now supposed to be lurking in or about the town."[84] Typically, South Carolina forbade slaves and free blacks from "harboring or concealing" a runaway,[85] which implies that many runaways were concealed and harbored in this fashion. On plantations, this was easy; slaves used the outbuildings and these might be viewed by overseers or masters only a few times a year, during planting and harvesting seasons. Landon Carter's slave Simon was a master of disappearing when work was hardest; he merely moved in with nearby slave kin.[86] Runaways ran into one another, spreading gossip from plantation to plantation or making plans for more serious crimes.[87] Runaways might also become aggressors, using invisibility to defend themselves against their would-be recaptors. The governor of Dutch Surinam warned of the powers of runaways there, "an invisible enemy, who shoots you down like ducks in the swamp."[88]

Punishment for all forms of self-sought invisibility was itself highly visible; no punishment more so than whipping. The act of whipping a slave was part of a public ritual whose impact on other slaves derived, in large measure, from its visibility. The master required other slaves to witness the whipping of one of their number—"to let them know" who had the power.[89] The message was received. Former slave Margaret Hughes recalled: "Once I saw my poor old daddy in chains, they chained his feet together, and his hands too, and carry him off to whip him." Nearly seventy-five years after the event, the image was still fresh in her mind. Jerry Hill similarly recalled how the whites had reacted to "various slaves whipped that day for various things, and there were several men around standing and watching . . . one laughed."[90] The sensory impact of whipping outlasted the pain and shame; the slave with many visible marks on his or her back was branded a malcontent, a malingerer, or worse.[91]

Whipping and other forms of corporal punishment of slaves were at one end of a long spectrum of sensory encounters between masters and bondsmen and women; at the other end were the ways in which slaves could demonstrate their independence of mind and body. Masters could see and hear that slaves had wills of their own. Slaves could slow down the pace of work, lose or break tools, constructively mishear instructions, or simply vanish for a time in the endless tug of war over space and time. Masters needed the willing compliance of slaves for the slave labor system to be profitable, and slave resistance that came from a too-ready use of the whip or cane undermined that compliance.[92]

Slave violence against masters or others of the master class was not as common as one might imagine from the conditions of slavery, and actual uprisings were few and far between, but fear of such "petty treason" was never far from the minds of whites. Why? Why, one asks, did the law strain to prohibit the assembly of slaves, when on plantations one saw gangs of slaves working all the time—indeed, when the work gang was the norm? What made slave gatherings seem dangerous to the white viewer familiar with slave gangs working on the plantation?[93] What so concerned northern city magistrates when groups of slaves gathered together on the wharves or in the streets?[94] What frightened masters contemplating the operation of the very system of labor they deployed?

The answer lies again in the realm of the senses. The language of the colonial black codes suggests that from the inception of slavery whites believed that there was a vast subterranean culture of criminal conversations and conspiracies among slaves. The first English-language "black codes," from Barbados, demonstrated that same fear, for gatherings of slaves in excess of a fixed number, without supervision by whites or passes from their masters, were in themselves illegal and subject to the most stringent punishments.[95] The Virginia colony laws in 1680 made meetings of slaves without the consent of the master an offense, for gatherings might have "dangerous consequences."[96] As the Maryland assemblymen concluded in 1717, "it too often happens that Negro slaves and etc. commit many heinous and capital crimes, which are endeavored to be smothered and concealed."[97] Nearly half of all recorded slave crimes in the colonial South involved more than one slave perpetrator. But the figures for prosecutions were not so much a measure of the frequency of gangs of slaves acting as criminals as an expression of the concern white authorities had about reports of multiple perpetrators.[98]

So, again, why the fear among whites of what they could not see and could not hear? Why the belief that what was hidden was dangerous, a belief that turned congregations of slaves into potential packs of bestial rebels in the master's imagination? The asymmetry of the relationship surely created its own tensions, but the whites' immediate response to assemblages of slaves was not the product of guilt, a struggle over the means of production, or fresh experiences with large-scale slave uprisings. Anticipated conflict between slave and master was first and foremost a sensory event. As the few surviving epistolatory accounts of earlier rebellions hint, fear rose in direct proportion to sensuous stimulants, a thesis that an exploration of the Stono, South Carolina, slave rebellion of 1739 and the New York City slave conspiracy of 1741 confirms.[99]

The Stono Rebellion, South Carolina, 1739

The economic and social historian may argue that color distinctions grew out of a labor system and were maintained by a legal system, but in everyday contact between slaves and masters, perceptions of skin color and accent triggered an instantaneous sequence of responses far removed from abstract calculations of labor or law. Is this person of color dangerous to me or docile? the white asked. Is this white person hostile or friendly? the person of color wondered. Meeting the other was first visceral, and in South Carolina, with its black majority, that meeting was inescapable for both peoples.

Ironically, without the highly visible cooperation of whites and blacks, the English colonization of South Carolina would have been stillborn. Slaves turned the tidal lowlands between the Ashley and the Cooper Rivers into Charlestown. Slaves served as "pioneers," clearing land and watching over herds of cattle.[100] Africans who had experience with rice culture in their homelands helped transform the coastal areas into rice plantations, some of which were as wealthy as any agricultural complex in the Western world.[101] But the development of plantation rice culture left whites increasingly isolated in a sea of imported African slaves. By 1740, the colony's population ratio was 2.6 slaves to 1 free person.[102]

Faced with a steadily increasing African population, the planters imposed the brutal practices of Caribbean slave society. The "Negro Laws," augmented from 1702 to 1740, forbid slaves from growing their own crops, owning their own livestock (lest they use horses to ride about the countryside raising rebellion), or selling their own time without their master's permission. All these laws were broken, some when whites connived with blacks to get the profits of illicit black business or unlicenced black entrepreneurship, but such laxity only frightened the white lawgivers the more.[103] The only solution seemed to be complete segregation of the races, but the slave system required that whites live among and supervise blacks. The government responded to the deepening fears among the masters by ordering whites to serve in the patrols and by organizing watches in the city.[104]

As the noose tightened about their necks, slaves grew restive. Some simply ran away to nearby marshes and upland scrub.[105] Sometimes they made it to all the way to the Spanish colony of Florida, a haven for slaves because the Spanish would not return them to their English masters or require bond labor of them. In 1738, seventy slaves fled South Carolina and reached Florida.[106] Other slaves plotted rebellion, although they were invariably betrayed.[107]

The contest of slave and master was sensory warfare with a vengeance. Owners marked their slaves so that possession was visible to any other owner. In the spring of 1738, Thomas Wright lost Paul, who in his year's stay in the colony had learned no English; Charles, an elderly man with the initials *TW* branded on his shoulder; and two new arrivals, who had already been branded with the owner's initials on their shoulders. Benjamin Godin had taken the precaution of branding his new Angolans with the initials *BG* on their chests, but Harry, Cyrus, and Chatham had taken off nonetheless. They joined Sam and Gambia in flight from his plantation. By the summer, Wright had lost five more men, two in Charlestown, two from his Silk-Hope plantation, and one "near Stono Church." The last, "a Negro boy named Bellfast, pretty tall, had on a blue coat, the sleeves turned up with black." Bellfast had with him one of Wright's mounts, a "young grey horse, branded upon the buttock," unlike Bellfast, who was seared with a *TW* on the shoulder.[108]

Advertisements for runaways demonstrate the importance of skin color and language skills in the sensory vocabulary of slavery. The advertisers always noted the shade of skin color of the runaways. Some were mustee, others ebony. But color also homogenized the runaways in the whites' eyes, making one slave indistinguishable from another. Names given by masters meant nothing, for the slaves did not answer to them. Indeed, the runaway's inner life, his or her individuality, experience, or past, did not matter. Instead, what the advertisements tell us is what the master saw (and expected the reader to see) and what the master gave the slave—a brand, a whipping, a suit of clothes.

Masters described the clothing runaways wore in detail, by color, fabric, and style, right down to the buttons, ironically providing the evidence that modern historians have relied on to recover the Africans' delight in vivid colors and striking clothing combinations. To the masters, the slave's African color sense seemed merely whimsical. The important distinction was the difference between "Negro cloth," which they distributed to the slaves once or twice a year, and better-quality woolens or other fabrics. For the master, the garment, like the runaway, was an object rather than a unique expression of personhood.[109]

If running away removed the slave from the line of sight, insurrection made him or her highly visible.[110] There were always hints of rebellion in the air, as slaves' muttering passed from the quarters to the ears of house servants or overseers to the masters. Sometimes slaves boasted about what they would do—if they could, when the could—to their masters. "Fierce talk . . . talking of freedom" floated on the air when slaves had grievances.[111] What plots and threats the whites did not uncover, they imagined. Fears of slave uprisings bred a gun culture in the slaveholding South. Before it adjourned in March 1739, the South Carolina Commons House of Assembly debated how many pistols the law should require planters and Charleston homeowners to carry with them to church. Two seemed adequate.[112]

Throughout the spring and early summer of 1739, rumors of plots continued to reach the ears of the magistrates, and documented cases of slave rage and violence occurred periodically, but there was no large-scale, organized rebellion until the late summer of 1739. Perhaps the news that a war had begun between the English and the Spanish (the "War of Jenkins' Ear") triggered the revolt. As important as seeing the slaves was to the masters, they frequently acted as if the slaves around them were invisible, speaking incautiously about the impact war might have on South Carolina. The coast was long and open to Spanish naval depredations; Spanish Florida might be made a base for invasion of the Carolina low country. Authorities in neighboring Georgia would later complain that slaves who reached Florida would "have arms put in their hands, and become part of their army to fight against us."[113] The slaves listened carefully to what the whites were saying. Word spread within the slave community from house servants, cooks, and carriage hands to the quarters. For the whites, Spanish Florida was a peril. For the slaves, it was a haven—distant, but envisioned as just over the horizon. Undoubtedly some knew about the runaway slave town of Mose, in Spanish Florida, where men of color were free to carry arms and had their own fort.[114]

The rebellion began on the evening of September 8, 1739, with a drainage crew working at a crossing on the Stono River, twenty miles west as the crow flies from Charleston.[115] The law required masters on adjacent parcels of land to supply slaves for "laying out, cutting, sinking, and maintaining" drains and water passages in rivers.[116] The work was tiring, dirty, and sometimes dangerous (snakes occupied the same watercourses). Indeed, in the murderously hot and humid summer, cutting drains was so debilitating that some masters refused to supply their slaves and were consequently fined 12s. 6p. for every day the slave did not appear. Masters rarely sent their skilled workers to the drainage crews, and the men at the drainage ditch knew that the skilled slaves were busy selling their labor for food or clothing while the crew was sweating profusely.[117] In addition, the next day was a Sunday, and the law required that slaves be given the day off, unless the work was urgent.[118] But that determination was left to the commissioners appointed by the colony to finish the work, and they were driving this crew hard. Landowners along the Stono were pressing the Commons House of Assembly for repair of the drainage system.[119]

That evening the drainage crew was upset for a variety of reasons: the difficulty of the work itself; having been singled out to labor while other slaves could use the time to barter or sell their services; and the loss of a day off.[120] Most of the work gang hailed from Angola, so they spoke dialects of Bantu—close enough that they understood one another.[121] Some also knew Spanish or Portuguese, for the Portuguese ran the Angolan slave trade, and Portuguese missionaries had converted some of the human cargo to Christianity.[122] And some must have served in the myriad local militias that contested Angola's endless rounds of civil war.[123] If any of these slaves dreamed of freedom, or of returning to Africa, the dream seemed closer now than at any time since they had been herded into the pens at Luanda on the central West African coast for the "middle passage" to Carolina. The work crew could not miss the implications of the preparations for defense or the conversations among masters about the Spanish danger; bold and determined men could perhaps join the earlier runaways who had reached the haven of Florida.[124] The group decided to steal off and flee to Florida, and then, who knew, perhaps home. They swore a blood oath to stand, march, and fight as one.[125] "Courage! Look out, beyond, and see / The far horizon's beckoning span! / Faith in your God-known destiny! / We are part of some great plan."[126]

First they must have firearms.[127] Angolan soldiers used firearms and at least some of these men saw themselves as soldiers, for they regarded their band as a military one.[128] Early on the morning of the ninth, they broke into a cross-roads storehouse, killed the two watchmen when they resisted the robbery, and stole arms and ammunition. Going out on the road, at night, without passes or white overseers was a serious breach of discipline, for which they could expect corporal punishment; theft of arms and murder were felonies punishable by death, crimes from which there was no turning back. They knew this—or must have guessed it—and to demonstrate their resolve as well as to prevent any of the faint-hearted among them from backsliding, they severed the heads of their victims and set them up on the stairs to the store. Their flight now turned into a martial procession down country lanes, as they destroyed farmhouses and set upon any whites in their way. The slaves probably chanted martial airs and fired their weapons; no need to be silent and submissive now. They had obtained or brought with them drums; they tied a bit of cloth to a pole as a banner and called upon all the slaves in the neighborhood to join their march. They had embraced otherness with a fierce passion, which no onlooker could ignore. At the same time, they had asserted pride in their African origins, pride in their boldness, and pride in their color.

A mass escape had become an armed rebellion, led by men who had seen such rebellions in Africa. Twenty became fifty, and fifty swelled to nearly a hundred by mid-morning. Most were men, as befit an army rather than some motley multitude of refugees. True, their recruiting efforts had largely failed. In a countryside swarming with slaves, they garnered few enlistees. Their otherness was too extreme, too dangerous. The leaders were Angolans, and slaves from other African nations, including the many Gold Coast and Slave Coast bondsmen, either just watched or actively helped their masters flee the advancing troop. One slave, July, helped his master, Thomas Elliot, and his master's family to escape, while another persuaded the African troop not to look for his master, whom he had hidden.[129] When the rebellion was over, the colonial assembly rewarded thirty-one such slaves, most of them probably native-born or long in the colony.[130] But even without significant reinforcements from plantation slaves, the road-crew-turned-rebel-band left its mark upon the land and its owners, killing some two dozen whites and burning half a dozen plantation houses along the way.[131]

The rebels' progress was marked by the smoke of the houses they had destroyed. It was easy to understand why they killed all the whites they met, save those hidden by bondsmen or those whose lives loyal slaves begged for: African armies caused terror by leaving the land wasted. Revenge was surely another motive. And yet why burn the houses? The answer is that burning was the most visible way to announce their martial intentions and strike back at the institution of slavery. Assassination was a hidden crime, which targeted individuals; arson was seen by all and targeted the system of slavery itself. Burning destroyed what the master most valued: his habiliments and the chattel within them. Thus the slave, in law a species of property, turned that legal category on its head by wantonly destroying the assets multiplied by slave labor.[132]

What did the whites see? One of them, colonial Governor William Bull, returning on horseback to Charlestown from the Granville District with four companions, came upon the rebel forces at about eleven in the morning. At first the governor and his companions mistook the approaching armed band for a work gang, but the smoke of burning buildings in the wake of the troop warned them that something was amiss.[133] Surely the rebel band fired its muskets, and the sight and sound of firearms confirmed Bull's alarm, for the law barred slaves from owning or bearing arms.[134] He and his men scattered to warn the countryside and rouse the militia. Bull and his companions had glimpsed the face of the devil—the monstrous reality of their worst nightmares, "so many hellish fiends in the shape of African-slaves."[135] They rode like fury itself, fortunate that the rebels were not mounted, for African armies had large cavalry contingents, and some Africans were able horsemen.[136] Consternation spurred the governor's company on, fear that they had seen only the vanguard of an army ten times the size, gathering itself from every plantation, wherein the color of a person one saw approaching from a distance would signal safety or peril.[137]

Late that day, having marched ten miles from the Stono River to the Edisto River, plundering along the way, the African company stopped to celebrate the day's events. They danced, sang, beat drums, and drank confiscated spirits. Maroon military leaders in Jamaica during the rebellion there, in February 1739, "blew their horns, and some singing" demonstrated their willingness to come to battle "or to make peace if they chose."[138] While some disparaging later accounts tweaked the Stono slaves for celebrating too soon or chastised them for letting the rum they took undo their enterprise, in fact the African troop was preparing for battle and waiting for the reinforcements from the countryside they expected to join them.[139] Many no doubt had "countrymen," fellow Angolans as well as shipmates from the middle passage, whose assistance the leaders of the troop would need to turn the rebellion into a full-scale civil war.[140] In addition, numbers of their original band were still straggling in, arms loaded with spoils from abandoned plantation houses and barns.

At four in the afternoon the first company of mounted militia arrived in the field where the rebels reposed and engaged them in musketry. How did the militia know who was a rebel and who a hanger-on? It did not matter. The "other" was the black man. The lines were drawn by color, not by guilt or innocence. Sensory warfare. The enemy was whoever looked different. Used to the skirmish warfare that characterized the beginning of an Angolan combat, the rebels fell back to fight individually, using cover, abandoning the wounded, and allowing the advancing South Carolina forces to capture those who had tried to hide themselves in the field. But the militiamen left in control of the battlefield did not spare the wounded or the captured, as armies would have in an African war. They questioned the captives and then executed every rebel on the spot.[141]

There is an incident recorded in one first-hand account of these final moments of the battle that captured the intense sensuousness of the rebellion. It may be apocryphal, but it could have occurred when the militia was rounding up stragglers immediately after the battle. "As soon as they saw their masters [in the militia company] they all made off as fast as they could to a thicket of woods excepting one Negro fellow who came up to his master[.] His master asked him if he wanted to kill him[,] the Negro answered he did at the same time snapping a pistol at him but it misfired and his master shot him through the head."[142]

The slave had done something truly revolutionary before he cocked and aimed the pistol—he looked straight at his master. Eye-to-eye contact of this sort was relatively rare; ordinarily the slave did not look directly at the master, but down and to the side.[143] Even John Stedman's much-loved mulatto mistress, Joana, looked away when she rejected his offer of marriage.[144] African-American and African bondsmen and women questioned about their activities, particularly when they were suspected of running away, characteristically had "down cast" eyes, and when owners looked slaves in the eye, they had trouble making eye contact. Thus Ben, a "light skinned mulatto" who had fled his Virginia master in 1745, had "a down look," a characteristic he shared with other runaways and captured felons.[145] Masters also recorded that slaves refused to look at the whip when it was brandished in front of them.[146] In fact, one modern social scientist, interviewing in Senegal, recalled that descendants of slaves had trouble looking him in the eye when they described their ancestors. Others, who had never had a slave forebear, remarked that they could recognize someone shamed by ancestral bondage "by their bearing."[147]

In pairings of unequals, the subordinate or the defeated breaks eye contact first; continued eye-to-eye contact in such cases is a challenge or a threat.[148] Staring at the other is always an invasion of private space. As John Adams' daughter wrote from London to her brother, in 1785, "the English may call the French starers, but I never saw so little civility and politeness in a stare in France as I have here."[149] A stare forces some kind of reply. For us, there are conventions to disarm the impact of the staring eye—a tip of the hat, a nod, a word of apology or explanation. "Don't I know you? Haven't we met before? I love your hat." Other peoples have other customs—the amount of staring allowed without some sort of mitigating or ingratiating gesture or speech varies, but "the license to stare is a function of power."[150] Thus, prolonged eye contact challenges existing power relationships. It may be as fleeting as a glance or as determined as a loving, longing look. The early modern English believed that love came out of the eyes. As John Donne wrote in *Ecstacy,* "sat we two . . . our eye-beams twisted, and did thread, our eyes upon one double string," and in *The Good-Morrow,* "My face in thine eye, thine in mine appears, and true plain hearts do in the faces rest."

Many a flirtatious stare was exchanged between men and women of different colors, an eye contact that violated the taboo of miscegenation but was common nonetheless. In 1790 the English transcriber of Slave Dick's autobiography recorded his own impression that "for as the arrow of a strong archer cannot be turned aside, so the glance of a lively negro girl cannot be resisted."[151] Certainly there was prolonged eye contact between male masters and female slaves purchased as "fancy girls." Like the saucy Maria recalled in Solomon Northrup's autobiographical tale of slavery, some "had no doubt some wealthy single gentleman of good taste would purchase her at once."[152]

The slave rebel who looked his master in the eye issued a sensate demand to be treated as an equal. There were other gestures with eyes—averting them to the side, closing them, rolling them, squinting—which in African customs were a form of disagreement or disapproval but which were read by white masters as evidence of slave insolence.[153] Moreover, the rebel slave probably glared—a malevolent stare that contained all the reasons for animosity that slavery engendered.[154] Even if the episode never took place, it contained a world of information, for the slaves who rose up at Stono stared at their masters long after they should have averted their eyes and accepted their subordinate status. Staring into the eyes of the other was sensory combat of the most intimate kind.

Head up, eyes straight ahead, facing the enemy—the slave rebels issued a sensory challenge to their masters. As Governor Bull later wrote to his Whitehall masters, "they [the rebels] calling out liberty, marched on with colors displayed, and two drums beating, pursuing all the white people they met with."[155] Generations later the grandchildren of the rebels understood exactly what Bull had meant about the rebels' willingness to be seen. Oral traditions retold the glories of the revolt; for the slaves "they take what they want," like a marauding army, and when they faced the militia, they "stand their ground."[156]

If the forms of that sensory assertion were largely borrowed from the Angolans' African heritage, the expression of resistance had an especially strong visual impact because of the colonial setting. The rebels marched as an African army and fought as an African army, not just because it was what they knew, but because they wanted the South Carolinians to see and hear them. For the same reason, the Angolans had made a flag. It gave them courage when they marched behind it; it announced that they were an army, not a ragtag band of deserters or runaways, and it served as a rallying point in battle. What color was the Stono rebels' flag? It was not black; black was the mark of the bondage imposed on them, and in any case, there is no evidence that black clothing or linen was available for such a banner.[157] Slaves' dress exhibited a myriad of colors, but in the 1730s the master class made a concerted effort to standardize slave clothing, issuing "white negro cloth" to the bondsmen and women.[158] When Baron led the Surinam slave rebels, he "planted a white flag within [the Dutch troops'] view, which he meant as a token of defiance and independence."[159] White flags were signals of truce among Europeans, not Africans. Ironically, the Stono rebels probably chose a white banner to symbolize their yearning for freedom.

The Stono Rebellion did not end with the last musket shot. Many of the Africans who fled the fight at the meadow returned to their home plantations and tried to act as if they had never been away. Some of these, particularly those who could be identified by any white person as leaders of the revolt, were summarily executed, but others convinced masters and authorities that they had been coerced or frightened into joining the march. All slaves suspected of complicity or sympathy with the uprising were closely examined. With downcast eyes and gestures of submission, the slaves explained why they had been absent. They may have made their bodies seem smaller, hunched their shoulders, or even cringed. Shaking, stuttering, and agitated hand motions revealed inner emotions. Experienced masters and magistrates believed that slaves' looks invariably gave them away, by the "odd knack . . . or way of turning their eyes inwards," but some no doubt carried off their dissimulation.[160] Some won and some lost the sensory contests.[161]

A week after the battle, some thirty to forty rebels were caught trying to reach Florida. They, like their counterparts captured immediately after the fray, were executed, and their heads were displayed on pikes and poles along the road. The purpose of the display, in one sense like the Africans' placement of the storekeepers' heads on the steps of the warehouse, was mimetic; it was intended to warn potential rebels and sympathizers what would happen to them.[162] So, in 1730, when the Dutch militia raided maroon villages in Surinam, the twelve maroons captured were mutilated and displayed. "The head shall then be severed and displayed on a stake by the riverbank . . . the Negro girls . . . will be tied to a cross, to be broken alive, and then their heads severed, to be exposed by the riverbank on stakes."[163] For the same reason—to make the masters' absolute dominion visible for miles around—the justices of the peace in colonial Alexandria Virginia used the courthouse chimney as the display case for the severed heads of four slaves executed for "petty treason" in 1767.[164]

There was an irony in the whites' grim determination to teach a lesson by dismembering and displaying slaves' corpses. The authorities assumed that the fear of dismemberment among criminals common in English culture would similarly dissuade West Africans who viewed the severed heads from daring to duplicate the victims' crimes. After all, if the head stayed on the chimney, how could the spirit travel back to Africa? But the Africans did not share the fears of the English felon, much less the sanguinary assumptions of the English magistrates or their colonial imitators. The heads on stakes might chill the white passerby with recollections of the horrors of slave insurrection, but the slaves saw the heads differently. The magical beliefs of the Africans taught that the body did not matter. What mattered was the lingering spirit of the deceased. The spirit still had power, could harm or help, could be summoned. Thus, the display did not frighten the slaves who passed it by; quite the reverse. They tried to communicate with the spirit that lingered nearby, knowingly nodded to it, brought fetishes and potions to appease it, recognizing that the fierce courage of the soon-to-die could, after death, give strength to others.[165]

One may posit another purpose to the whites' grisly display of the slaves' corpses, one that had nothing to do with retribution or deterrence and less with irony; these do not require such spectacle. None of the records of the Stono rebellion mentions this purpose, but we have abundant evidence of it from other times and places. Think of the crowds gathered to watch the last spasms of a young black man lynched in the turn-of-the-century South. Look at their faces (postcards were made from photographs of the scenes).[166] The lynch mob gapes with undisguised pleasure at the dying body. The brutal execution of the rebels of Stono was entertainment. "There are images we can't hide from or avoid . . . an evil aspect . . . gapers surrounded where niggers were burned. Being tied to a stake and exterminated seemed common, gory, routine . . . stinging stinking bleeding, draining aching piecing truths."[167] Captured slaves' bodies were appropriated as a gory circus by the white settlers, the lurid made alluring because of the grotesquerie of the captives' otherness in the eyes of the captors.

Visual and auditory avowals of their martial ardor was the core of the rebels' action, not its incidental byproduct, and they were right—the visual and the auditory was what white reporters remembered. South Carolinians had no trouble visualizing the fruits of a successful uprising. How the little army had looked and sounded and what it had left in its wake lingered long in the minds of the master class. Years later, those who had seen the carnage or had lost kin still slept with loaded weapons nearby. The Commons House of Assembly took stock of the affair in 1741, recalling that "on this occasion every breast was filled with concern. Evil brought home to us within our very doors awakened the attention oft he most unthinking . . . at such danger daily hanging over their heads."[168] A year after the battle, South Carolina law banned groups of more than seven slaves "on the high road" when no white was present. An especially loud slave party in Charlestown so unnerved the authorities that they arrested more than fifty slaves and executed many of them for conspiracy.[169] The assembly enacted a law designed to deny slaves the sounds of rebellion: "Absolutely necessary to the safety of this province, that all due care be taken to restrain the wanderings and meetings of Negroes at all times . . . and their using of drums, horns, or other loud instruments, which may call together or give signs or notice to one another of their wicked designs and purposes."[170]

The "Great Negro Conspiracy," New York City, 1741

The Stono rebels were country people in origin and their rebellion occurred in the countryside. Though they worked on land, they were not of it. They were expected to be docile and obedient beasts of burden; "a herd of unpaid laborers under absolute and permanent control" was the ideal.[171] City slaves, by contrast, made a point of demanding their share of the streets, sometimes wore visually striking outfits, and hawked their wares in a distinctive argot that could be heard above the din of traffic.[172] For the colonial city, newly born and growing willy-nilly in all directions, was never possessed by any one person in the way the plantation was owned by an individual. The city was everyone's and no one's, which meant that slaves would move about more freely and work side by side with free persons of color and whites.[173]

All this was true of New York City in the early eighteenth century. Surely there, in the polyglot mixing of peoples from many lands, diversity would dilute the discriminatory sensory messages of otherness. At one time, the door seemed open to this prospect. In New Amsterdam the Dutch had allowed easy manumission of slaves and permitted former slaves to own property and begin businesses. But the English, who became masters of the New Netherland colony, had other ideas. There were seven hundred slaves in the Anglicized city of New York by 1698, over twice as many as had lived in New Amsterdam, a result of the vested interest the English had in the slave trade. The demand for slaves as labor within the city precincts induced slave traders to bring more than a thousand of their human cargo to the colony each year during the first decades of the eighteenth century. Slave auctions occurred weekly at a variety of venues.[174] By 1731, there were almost sixteen hundred slaves resident full time in the city and nearly five thousand in the New York–New Jersey area. Slaves constituted 18 percent of the total population of the city by

1731.[175] By 1738, when Lieutenant Governor George Clarke reported the state of the colony to the Board of Trade in England, there were 8,945 free persons in the city and 1,719 slaves.[176]

As ubiquitous and ambitious for freedom as the city's slaves proved themselves to be, New York law placed increasingly onerous restraints on slaves and free persons of color.[177] Slaves were forbidden to engage in certain businesses, such as selling food and clothing on the streets, lest these become a pretext for disposing of the spoils of pilfering. The law tightened still further in 1730, when innkeepers were forbidden to sell alcohol to slaves, which might incline them to commit crimes, or to entertain them on the premises after dark, which might allow them to plot further mischief.[178] Repression fueled the anxiety of the whites as it did the anger of the slaves. As Governor Robert Hunter, a relative liberal on the matter of race, put it in 1713, "that sort of men" were given to crime.[179]

One of those crimes, arson, particularly frightened the leaders of the colony. Although the better sort had houses of brick and stone, most of the warehouses, all of the barns, and the dwellings of the poor in New York City were constructed of wood. With tar, turpentine, firewood, and straw in the barns and gunpowder in the some of the warehouses, the city was a tinderbox. Even Fort George, the largest royal military enclosure in the region, was prey to arson, for within its wall were stores of explosives, and the walls themselves were wood, not stone. Were the wind to turn on the city when a fire raged, all property might go up in the flames.[180] The authorities conceded that arson could be a form of slave resistance.[181] The city could mount only a feeble defense against fires set by slaves, for there was no trained patrol force (urban police forces lay a century in the future), and the watch consisted of a small number of constables and the freeholders (voting men) of the city themselves. The fire companies were all volunteer and their methods rudimentary.[182]

The slave arsonist was not just a figment of a fevered white imagination. An arson and murder plot that came to fruition on April 1, 1712, gave proof of the whites' vision of slaves as "hellish." A conspiracy of two dozen slaves set fire to an outbuilding and slaughtered the men who arrived to put it out. Twenty-one slaves were indicted by grand juries and convicted by trial juries; eighteen of them were executed in what authorities came to believe was a plot to destroy the city.[183] One correspondent reporting on the cases to his superiors in London noted that "a free Negro who pretends sorcery gave them a powder to rub on their clothes which made them so confident"—no doubt some sort of magical potion designed to make the user invisible. He went on to say that the conspirators had taken a blood oath not to reveal their plan to anyone else.[184]

Blood oaths of secrecy, a nighttime plot, potions that insured invisibility—all these pointed to the city magistrates' central fear: Slaves conspired where they could not be seen. Using whispered jargon and relying on darkness to hide themselves, slaves might at any time be plotting the destruction of the city and the murder of their masters.[185] Such conspiracies were especially hard to uncover (ironically, because the laws that mandated nonintercourse with whites) and at the same time seemed to be brewing everywhere. The invisible, as at Salem in 1692, was more frightening than what could be seen and heard. The dissembling house servant, the ungrateful shop laborer, and the treacherous co-worker were all stock figures of the slave in the white imagination. As one judge of the New York Surpeme Court harrangued a slave convicted of conspiracy: "Thou vile wretch! How much does thy ingratitude enhance your guilt! And your hypocritical canting behavior upon your trial, your protestations of innocence, your dissimulation before God and man, will be no small article against you at the day of judgement."[186]

What made the imagined crime more terrifying was that whites assumed the purpose of slave conspiracies was violence against whites "in a most barbarous manner."[187] New York City newspaper accounts of uprisings in the West Indies always stressed the slaves' intent to blow up buildings full of whites and butcher entire families.[188] New York papers also gave space to the violence of the Stono Rebellion.[189] The morbid fascination with slave uprisings that caused the papers to cover the episodes went beyond mere fear that slaves, "enemies of their own household," would rise in New York City.[190]

If the authorities could hold the color line, convincing all whites to report any suspicious activity among the slaves, then the danger of slave rebellion could be minimized; but many whites continued to consort with slaves. In the gin mills near the docks, whites openly violated the laws against selling alcohol to slaves and allowing slaves to congregate at night, without passes. And these were the least of the criminal activities that occurred in these dens. During the nighttime, criminal activities could be openly discussed and criminal escapades celebrated. One of the most notorious of these gin mills was John Hughson's.[191] Some of the slaves gathered there were malcontents and others were criminals. A few knew about the 1712 conspiracy and the slave uprisings in the Caribbean and South Carolina. The same tremors of war between England and Spain that had set off the Stono rebellion were rocking New York City, and with the port vulnerable to the enemy, a few of Hughson's regulars fantasized aloud about an uprising of slaves.[192]

The regulars at Hughson's knew they had no business consorting together, but the laws did not deter them. They were safe—invisible, cloaked by their anonymity, by the darkness, and by their oaths to one another never to reveal the contents of their conversations to the authorities. These oaths sometimes took the form of African secret society initiations. Other conspirators swore their fidelity on the Bible.[193] And despite the injunction against slave gatherings, the habitués of Hughson's and the other gin mills knew that there was strength in numbers.[194]

In the end, the "conspiracy" amounted to little more than two or three meetings of two dozen slaves boasting of how they would liberate themselves and overcome their masters. It was not all talk, for a few of the slaves belonged to gangs of thieves. Out of the plot came a plan to set fires and steal from houses left unguarded in the tumult. Some nights, the talk went beyond theft to boasts of fighting ability and thence to threats of rape and murder. All talk, though under the law such talk was a capital offense. Word of the conspiracy was widely spread throughout the slave community, and when Caesar and Prince, two of the burglars, were jailed, word began to leak out to the magistrates. Hughson, whose trust the thieves had taken for granted, betrayed them to the aldermen. As city recorder and judge Daniel Horsmanden noted without any conscious irony, Hughson was "blackening" the character of everyone around him in an effort to avoid jail himself.[195]

Although two of the gang members were out of circulation, the plot moved forward. Drunken boasts and idle threats that slaves had shared at Hughson's tavern all winter flared into an epidemic of arson. Behind it Judge Horsmanden and the other colonial leaders saw a horrid plot to overthrow the government. As plots go, this one was mostly drunken swagger. "Will you burn some houses?" deponents recalled being asked, then told that if they related the request to someone not part of the conspiracy the deponent would have his or her head cut off. Soon every male slave who worked in the city was at risk of being seen, or heard, or suspected of attending one of these "frolicks." Certainly the black defendants dreamed of social and political inversion; they would be on top, their masters on the bottom. If one believes some of the slaves' more outrageous testimony, the ringleaders proposed to set their own masters' houses on fire "and have the white women for their wives."[196]

Word of the investigation roused the town and rumor became panic. The "Negroes are rising," rang the cry in the streets. The soldiers at the fort were mustered out and joined the night watch. The City Council met and offered a reward of £100 for anyone bringing information about a suspected arson conspiracy.[197] The spread of so many fires in so many different locales seemed to suggest a plot as easy to effectuate as dropping hot coals on tinder.[198] At the beginning of May, across the Hudson River from Manhattan, in Hackensack,

New Jersey, two slaves were apprehended for setting seven barns aflame. One confessed to three of the fires; the other stood mute. Both were speedily tried and convicted, then burned at the stake.[199]

Publishing his version of the events three years after the fact in response to critics of the trials, Horsmanden insisted that "they could not be judges of such matters, [though] they declared with no small assurance (notwithstanding what we *saw* with our eyes and *heard* with our ears) . . . those who had not the opportunity of *seeing* and *hearing*" could not understand how terrifying the events were and how they taught that "for every one who has negroes, to keep a very watchful eye over them."[200] He was, after all, the eyewitness to all of the examinations, and he took some of the testimony himself, including that from men in jail already condemned to death.[201]

Horsmanden's sensory labor was the opposite of the slave ringleaders'— they concealed and dissimulated; he peered and probed. The justice believed that for every criminal act whose consequences were visible there were a hundred hidden criminal conversations. He had, therefore, to recover the inaudible and uncover the hidden by forcing slaves to confess to their role in planning crimes. The task was a daunting one, for "their unintelligible jargon stands them in great stead, to conceal their meaning," and they seldom told the same story twice. The hearings and trials became a staccato conversation among the justice and the defendants, punctuated by the introduction of new characters and new lines of narrative as more and more slaves were arrested and interrogated.[202]

In the give and take of these examinations, confessions, and denials, the jurors and judges plainly heard and saw what they wanted to see and hear. The whites' anticipation, abetted by confessions from slaves hoping for pardons if they informed on one another and conforming what they said to what was expected of them, revealed a vast insurrection nipped in the bud. Throughout the events, Horsmanden never doubted his ability to discern truth and penetrate falsity.[203] When Sarah Hughson testified against a suspected conspirator, late in the proceedings, "what came from her was delivered with all the visible marks or semblance of sincerity and truth." Against the slave Patrick's "fictitious hyporcitical grin" and his "turning his eyes inward, as it were . . . their looks, at the same time, discovering all the symptoms of the most inveterate malice and resentment," Horsmanden placed the slave Cork's "cheerful, open, honest smile." Though [Cork] had the inherited defect of "of a countenance somewhat ill-favored, naturally of a suspicious look," Horsmanden and the other justices had confidence in Cork's denial of complicity. For the judges, slaves' countenances betrayed their malice or their innocence in plain sight. Defendants in the dock could no more control the tales their bodies told than could witnesses in the cells. The suspects might roll their eyes and throw up their hands, but their faces always betrayed them.[204]

The penetration of the dissimulation of the slaves in the dock was a microcosm of the entire investigatory process. Horsmanden boasted that the plot "would have remained a secret till they had done much more damage" had not the "magistrates" brought "their deeds of darkness . . . to a full light."[205] Light and darkness here were not just metaphors for good and evil but also a shorthand for a sensory campaign waged and won by the authorities. The court literally saw into and overheard what the slaves had tried to conceal. As Horsmanden wrote to Cadwallader Colden on August 17, 1741, "we have been so successful in prying into this scene of darkness and horror as to bring to light near 90 Negroes . . . engaged to be actors in this black tragedy." The counterpoint of light and darkness was for Horsmanden both metaphor and material, just like the blackness of the "Negroes" and the blackness of the tragedy.[206]

One last remarkable providence confirmed Horsmanden's sensory program: Hughson's rotting corpse, hung in chains, had turned black—as black as his heart, as black as the evil he conspired to do. For Horsmanden, an educated English barrister, no less than for his more superstitious readers, the verdict of the senses was plain. Hughson's worst offense was that he was "privy to and promoter of so unparalleled a villainy."[207] Horsmanden recalled that "the beholders were amazed at these appearances; the report of them engaged the attention of many, and drew numbers of all ranks, who had curiosity, to the gibbets, for several days running, in order to be convinced by their own eyes, of the reality of . . . wondrous phenomenons." Hughson's body burst at the seams, and discharged "full pails of corruption."[208]

The Sensory Underpinnings of Jim Crow

By the end of August, four months after the trials of conspirators had begun, the furor quieted. John Hughson and his wife, Sarah; a prostitute named Maragaret Kerry; and John Ury, a schoolmaster fallen on hard times and named as an abettor of the conspiracy, were hanged. Others suspected of attending the meetings of the slaves or at least of knowing about the conspiracy and keeping silent were warned and released. Caesar and Prince were executed for the burglaries, and a total of eighteen slaves were hanged for their part in the conspiracy. Thirteen slaves were burned at the stake, including the first of the incendiaries, one Cuffee, and over seventy slaves were sold away, most to the West Indies. Seven slaves named in the confessions could not be found, most likely having been spirited away by their masters.[209]

Even the highly visible punishment of the conspirators did not defuse Horsmanden's fears. The sensory cues had been so overpowering that he saw plots everywhere. "The city and the people were not yet out of danger from this hellish confederacy." Not all the conspirators had been taken up, and the ones still at large "impiously looked upon [their secret] oath to be so sacred, that they thought . . . the eternal welfare of their souls depended upon the strict observance and execution of it." There was "agitation" in Queens and Nassau counties, on Long Island, where the slaves had mustered themselves into a company of militia, and marched about "by way of play or diversion," so they said. Horsmanden knew different. Horsmanden repeated rumors about slave uprisings in Charleston, whereas in New York captured Spanish slaves muttered darkly about liberation coming at the hands of a Spanish fleet. Then there was the case of Tom, caught trying to start a fire, who confessed that there was a new conspiracy and named names. But none of the men he named confessed, and all had alibis, so Tom was executed alone in the winter of 1742. But Horsmanden was not quite finished. Lest anyone think his construction of the events was "a dream," there was always the stark reality of the fires, "a daily evidence . . . still before our eyes."[210]

Horsmanden argued that the slave confessions demonstrated the moral authority of the court, but in fact the slaves had simply learned how to save themselves. They must confess in contrite and fulsome manner, in words the judges could understand, and they must abandon all pretense of loyalty to one another; only then would their sentences be commuted and their lives spared. Horsmanden suspected that this was simply a different kind of performance by the slaves, and he was right. The confessions were mirrors slaves held up to white culture rather than windows into the hearts of the slaves, mirrors that simultaneously threw back at their prosecutors the image of their own culture and hid the slaves' culture from sight.

By pursuing the conspiracy so closely, the justices had made the slaves too visible, had pushed them in front of the courts and the crowds, had spent too much time listening to them. Henceforth all conversation among slaves would be suspect; all slaves seen after hours in the streets would be regarded as conspirators; and all slaves lurking on street corners would be presumed to be contemplating the butchery of passersby. As the editor of the *New-York Weekly Journal* solemnly warned, "we have learned that this most horrible and wicked conspiracy has been a long time in agitation and almost general among the

Negroes."[211] Horsmanden's perception of events had triumphed, and he inveighed against the negligence of the masters in watching their bondsmen and everywhere found "the daring insolence of Negroes." One people should never trust the other again. If a "veil of . . . mystery" still shrouded some of the details, one stood out: Dark skin color, heretofore the badge of inferiority, was to become the badge of insurrection. No people of color could henceforth be trusted.[212] The masters were now listening a little more closely to the murmurs of the slaves, so that when three slaves in their cups revealed a plot to burn down the town of Schnectady, in 1761, the authorities moved swiftly; the three supposed conspirators were arrested and thirteen other slaves fled to Canada, one step ahead of a posse.[213]

Religious Awakenings

The New York authorities had no shortage of scapegoats to blame for the conspiracy of 1741, but one of the most unusual on its face was the revivalist preacher George Whitefield. In 1739, during his first trip to the colonies, this charismatic Anglican divine addressed crowds of thousands in the city. The *New-York Weekly Journal* reported on November 26, 1739, that "his discourses were pathetic and tinctured with charity. He had audiences more numerous than is seen on such occasions, for it has been observed that there were more on the outside of the meeting house wall than within."[214] His message was one of self-examination and confession of sin. Those who attended his sermons most often came away deeply moved. "With what a flow of words, what a ready profusion of language . . . he looked as if he was clothed with authority from the Great God."[215] No one was exempt from his admonitions—not those who thought themselves righteous by their acts or their church membership, no less those who bore the stigmata of their corruption and sinfulness. All who witnessed his meetings saw a new kind of preaching. Even scoffers joked, "What, Mr. Whitefield could not make people cry this afternoon?"[216] His listeners, believers and scoffers alike, recognized the sensory impact of his message.[217]

In a letter to planters through whose colonies he had passed, Whitefield warned that the Stono uprising of 1739 was a visitation from an angry God. God did not sit placidly by while masters abused their bondsmen and bondswomen. "Think you, your children are in any way better by nature than the poor negroes? No! In no wise! Blacks are just as much, and no more, conceived and born in sin, as white men are; and both if born and bred up here, I am persuaded, are naturally capable of the same improvement." Whitefield did not call for the abolition of slavery, but he demanded that slaves be treated decently. He went further: "Although I pray God the slaves may never be permitted to get the upper hand, yet should such a thing be permitted by Providence, all good men must acknowledge the judgment would be just."[218]

Other Anglican ministers in the South saw how revolutionary Whitefield's preaching might sound to slaves. One of these, Alexander Garden, whose pulpit lay in the center of Charlestown, worried that Whitefield's enthusiasm would be translated by gullible slaves into "something else still worse." They would take his metaphorical "trances, dreams, visitations and revelations" for literal truth. They would mimic the crowds gathered about him with their own gatherings, armed not with visions of heaven but with the weapons of the devil. After the New York City upheaval, Ury, accused of taking part in the arson plot, also blamed Whitefield: "It was through the great encouragement the Negroes had from Mr. Whitefield we had all the disturbance." Even Daniel Horsmanden, whose list of culprits already spanned three continents, was eager to add Whitefield. The minister's enthusiasm, added to the equally inciting notions of "suspicious vagrant strolling preachers," convinced the slaves that their crimes were righteous acts and would be rewarded in the next world. Whitefield's call for the amelioration of slavery in the city was a program that "raised up a bitter spirit in the Negroes against their masters."[219]

This much was true: Slaves came from miles around to hear Whitefield preach, and they believed his message of salvation was for them.[220] Masters had good reason to be worried by the slaves' outpouring of emotion in earshot of evangelical itinerants. In later years, the author of the foremost catechism for slaves would remind every minister who preached to bondsmen and women that "public worship of God should be conducted with reverence and stillness on the part of the congregation . . . [no] exclamations, or responses, or noises, or outcries of any kind during the progress of divine worship; nor boisterous singing immediately at its close."[221] The South Carolina statute against slaves using musical instruments had said as much, and the white power structure of New York City concurred. But what did the revivalists actually say and do?

The Evangelists Seen and Heard

Whitefield, who had gone to America as an Anglican missionary in 1738, found there a fertile field for revival. During his second revival tour, from October 30, 1739, to January 24, 1741, covering the Middle Colonies, then the deep South, then New England, he became the focal point of an evangelical religiosity that was sweeping through the colonies.[222] Still a young man in 1739, he had loved the theater and thought about a career as an actor, and when he had a conversion experience and entered the ministry, he became a preacher with an ecumenical bent. His calling was to sow the seeds of conversion; others would reap them. He needed no notes, had a booming voice, and was willing to preach anywhere to the multitudes. Indeed, he was more at home in the fields and streets than in the meetinghouse. Although his sermons appeared extemporaneous, he kept detailed journals and notebooks, and printers like Benjamin Franklin published extensive accounts of Whitefield's travels, that the word might spread even further. After all, Whitefield was news, and news was good business for a newspaper publisher like Franklin.[223]

At the time Whitefield's preaching was thought to be the beginning of the "a great and general awakening," but its roots lay a generation earlier. Then, as one minister put it, the first step in any effective ministry should be to "awaken" the sleeping sinner.[224] In the 1720s, in both the British Isles and the American colonies, church membership in the dissenting sects was on the decline. Ministers like Solomon Stoddard, of Northampton, Massachusetts, had seen such declines before, but this time he saw an answer in a new ministerial pose. Henceforth, the minister must be a preacher, revitalizing piety from the pulpit.[225] The movement that followed was not really a single event, but a congeries of local revivals, tied together by pulpit-sharing of like-minded ministers, the tours of a handful of galvanizing preachers, and a communications network based on published sermons and narratives of conversions, personal letters, and itinerant preachers. Its most visible leaders, some of them itinerants (Horsmanden's "vagrant strolling preachers"), tutored an entire generation in the transforming power of the word and the emotional effect of the revival meeting.[226]

At the core of the Awakening as the revivalists preached it was a powerful answer to the perceptual conundrum of Christ's church on earth. As Jonathan Edwards put it, near the end of his career, "whether, according to the rule of Christ, any ought to be admitted to the communion and privileges of members of the visible church of Christ in complete standing, but such as are in profession, and in the eye of the church's Christian judgment, godly or gracious persons?"[227] The visible church was composed of willing congregants admitted to the sacraments of the church. One's demeanor, adoption, and understanding of Christian precepts, and for some churches, one's confession of faith and observance acceptable to the congregation and the minister, gained one full membership.[228] The invisible church was the gathering of saints. God knew who they were. Grace bound them together. Introspection's revealing faith reassured them of their salvation. The disjoint between the two churches posed both a sensory and a perceptual dilemma. Calvinism insisted and American churchmen agreed that no one could really know the state of another person's soul. How, then, should the congregation and the minister react when persons approached seeking membership?

Early in Puritanism's career, William Perkins, Richard Rodgers, and others offered a life raft to "weak Christians" who doubted their fate: Look to sanctification, to a practical divinity of study, worship, self-examination, and piety.[229] The outward signs of that sanctification should comfort the doubter, and these signs would be visible to the other members of the church. But later ministers, including respected interpreters of doctrine like John Cotton, insisted that the sign must be internal—whether an overwhelming sense of God's love, of perfect faith, or of the seal of the Holy Spirit upon one's heart various theologians debated endlessly and hotly. A hundred years later, the question remained: What visible or "real" signs of Christian belief and behavior in an applicant for church membership could be trusted? Or, put in other terms, whose perceptions of such signs could be trusted?

The Awakening made this question more immediately sensate, for in time *visible* ceased to be a metaphorical modifier and came to mean the natural process of seeing. The visible and audible signs of grace that the congregation recognized in the minister moved it to tears and sighs. Signs of grace or conversion in the heart of the seeker of salvation in turn became visible and audible expressions that the minister and everyone else could perceive. As one observer of Whitefield in New York versified in 1739,

> See! See! He comes, the heavenly sounds
> Flew from his charming tongue,
> Rebellious men are seized with fear
> With deep conviction stung.
> Listening we stand with vast surprize
> While rapture chains our powers,
> Charmed with the music of his voice
> Nor know the passing hours.[230]

The crediting of such external signs pit doubters against believers, one side regarding the sensate signs as evidence of hypocrisy, the other as proof that conversion had begun. The attempts of ministers to conform their preaching to the new sensory paradigm, the visible and auditory characteristics of the revival meeting, and the somatic impact of the preaching and the gathering on the seeker put the senses at the center of the Awakening even as the perception of otherness divided congregations, ministerial fellowships, and whole towns. The "religious other" was a danger that must be silenced or driven away.

Words of Warning and Comfort

A revival in minister Jonathan Edwards' Northampton, Massachusetts, congregation was the first generally noticed sign of a widespread Awakening in the northern colonies, in large measure because Edwards was the first to develop the communications network that would support the Awakening. Edwards had more or less inherited the congregation of his minister grandfather, Solomon Stoddard. Stoddard, in his later years, had adopted the credo that the minister must "awaken" the sinner before the word of God would penetrate. He and his counterparts in the Connecticut River Valley took to "preaching Christ" by using vivid language and compelling metaphors. As Stoddard's ally Eliphalet Adams wrote in 1725, "we must show [sinners] the destruction and misery that is before them."[231] Across the ocean, Isaac Watts concurred; ministers must "contrive all lively, forcible, and penetrating forms of speech . . . try all methods to raise and awaken the cold, the stupid, the sleepy race of sinners."[232]

Edwards' own father was a clergyman, and young Jonathan graduated from Yale intending to follow in his father's footsteps. He had a mystical bent, a brilliant mind, and a strong love of nature. As a youth of seventeen, he had a conversion experience, though like any good Puritan, he wondered all the time if he had merely fooled himself. He was tall, good-looking, methodical in his preaching, and well aware of the apparent decline in piety throughout the region—until the revival began.

In 1732, young people in Northampton began to attend services more regularly, and a number of young women confessed their spiritual crises to Edwards. By 1734, the behavior of the young had begun to change as well. They seemed more conscious of the need to act in decorous ways, more eager for guidance. "And then, a concern about the great things of religion began," Edwards wrote to another minister in that year, "among old and young, and from the highest to the lowest; all seemed to be seized with a deep concern about their eternal salvation . . . Persons seized with concern are brought to forsake their vices, and ill practices . . . this town never was so full of love, nor so full of joy, nor so full of distress as it has lately been."[233]

News of the revival in Northampton spread through Edwards' moving *Faithful Narrative of the Surprizing Work of God,* which he shared widely. Edwards thought the conversions genuine. His congregants had learned to open their hearts and seek grace. "The engagedness of their hearts in this great concern could not be hid." As the word spread and the people gathered to hear him in church and at weekly lectures, "remarkable tokens of God's presence" appeared in every household. Throughout Northampton, and then the rest of the Connecticut River Valley, there were thousands of "instances of sinners brought out of darkness into marvelous light."[234] The tokens, like the darkness and light, were metaphors, but the revival was real.

While Edwards' text traveled the New England circuit, Whitefield was touring the colonies with his own message, delivered with a whirlwind of sound and gesture. Influential ministers opened their churches to him, and astute advance publicity gained him reputation and following. Whitefield was no theorist, and his doctrinal contribution was negligible. His message was simple: Be born again in Christ.[235] The rest followed naturally. As one of his ministerial supporters, Jonathan Dickinson, wrote in 1742, the essence of this preaching was affective—seen and felt on the spot. The goal was "feeling sensible impression" in the auditory. Indeed, in Dickinson's own essay, an imagined dialogue between an evangelist and an elderly churchgoer somewhat antipathetic to Whitefield, the congregant was so moved by the minister's defense of affective preaching that he suddenly became apprehensive that he was "unsafe . . . It was observed that upon this discourse the gentleman changed countenance, fetched a deep sigh, and sat some time silent in a musing posture." Dickinson, like the ministers who preached to the multitude, took these visual signs—or on this occasion, invented these signs—to say that one could trust the visual evidence of the beginnings of "sanctifying change."[236]

Those who heard Whitefield often began conversion experiences on the spot, moaning and crying out in despair, figuratively and literally wrestling with their sinfulness as they rolled on the ground, all the while seeking release from doubt and shame in a renewal of faith.[237] As different as Whitefield was from Edwards (who always preached from extensive notes "in a low and moderate" tone and followed the traditional division of sermons into doctrine, explication, and application), both men had the same effect on their listeners— they were abject sinners, but everlasting life could still be found if they would pledge themselves to seek the Lord and do his bidding.[238]

Edwards, Whitefield, and others—so-called New Light clergymen—had adopted not only an innovative style of preaching but an evocative language of worship.[239] Their sermons were not just sensuous in a metaphorical way— though they were filled with metaphors. For the preacher must both touch the intellect of the congregant and "win the affections" of sinners. Only then could he find "some signs of the effects of his preaching," the empirical evidence of a congregation agonizing over its sinfulness.[240]

It was a heady message in a turbulent time. Young ministers visited one another's churches recasting old Calvinist ideas of predestination and of the Christian's utter dependency on God in an innovative lexicon. The new, emotionally rich and compelling vocabulary implied that by seeking grace one could find it. As Whitefield told a Philadelphia meeting in 1742, "Faith is the only wedding garment Christ required; he does not call you because you are already, but because he intends to *make you saints* . . . Remember then this day I have invited all, even the worst of sinners . . . to the Lord Jesus. If you perish remember you do not perish for lack of invitation."[241] Even Benjamin Franklin, who wore religion lightly, was impressed. "From being thoughtless or indifferent about religion, it seemed as if all the world were growing religious, so that one could not walk through the town in an evening without hearing psalms sung in different families of every street."[242]

Edwards, Whitefield, and their allies should have anticipated that the excitement would precipitate cleavages in congregations and arguments within the ministry, for some revivalists proposed that adherence to the new style of ministry be a test of fitness for holding a pulpit. Against this test they measured the more traditional ("Old Light") of their colleagues and found them wanting. "Look into the congregations of unconverted ministers," as evangelist Gilbert Tennent wrote in 1740, "and see what a sad security reigns there; not a soul convinced that can be heard of, for many years together, and yet the ministers are easy; for they say they do their duty." Such ministers were "stone-blind . . . as blind as moles."[243] Tennent meant his remarks metaphorically, just as he derided the unconverted minister's prayers as "cold." But Tennent did more than warn of blind ministers; he crossed over congregational lines to preach in other minister's parishes. Such itinerancy led to boundary disputes as well as ideological ones, or more properly (for the ideological controversy precipitated the jurisdictional one), led critics of the itinerants to complain that they destroyed good order, harmony within the ministerial profession, and the faith that congregations had in their home pastors.[244]

At the same time, many ministers decided that the new revivalism was no more than a fad. They were appalled by the sight of people crying out, writhing in pain, and collapsing alongside the pews in church or by the benches at outdoor meetings. As one Virginia Anglican minister complained in 1747, "these [evangelical] itinerants . . . make it their study to screw up people to the greatest heights of religious frenzy, and then leave them in that wild state, for perhaps ten or twelve months, till another enthusiast comes among them, to repeat the same thing."[245]

In the hubbub of ministers' raucous accusations, how could one tell who were the converted ministers and who not? Who was the other, fooling him- or herself with legalisms only, a conterfeit of true grace, secretly living in sin, or hypocrisy, or false hope? Carpers would warn of false prophets, but Edwards and others like him knew that one way to tell the true minister from the huckster was to see how the minister's preaching affected the congregation.[246] For example, Whitefield's slightest gestures transformed those who heard him. In 1742, one Scottish convert recalled that in watching Whitefield preach, "I fell under a great terror . . . hell was represented to my mind, as a pit at the foot of a hill, and a great drove of people marching into it, and I along with them, and when I got very near it, I thought I looked over my shoulder, and saw a very beautiful man, who smiled on me and made a motion to me with his hand to come back."[247] Typically, as Jonathan Parsons preached, he noted that his congregation began to "weep, sigh, and sob."[248]

The evangelical preachers excelled at using inflection and gesture. They could be heard, and what is more, their gestures and choice of words appealed to both the eye and the ear—though not to those who reviled "new methods of speech, tone, and gesture."[249] As Franklin wrote with admiration of Whitefield: "He had a loud and clear voice, and articulated his words so perfectly that he might be heard and understood at a great distance."[250] North Carolina's Herman Husband heard Whitefield preach in 1740, and a decade later vividly remembered others who had come asking one another "What does this man preach? Anything that is news? Who answered, no nothing but what you may read every day in your Bible: for what is this great cry then ? Who was answered after this manner, stay, you will hear him by and by, you never heard the likes before." Another itinerant made an equally indelible impression on young Husband when he "thundered out against sin, and pronounced death and damnation to sinners."[251] As one witness among the thousands who came to hear Gilbert Tennent on Boston Common waxed eloquent in poetry,

> We bless the man sent by the spirit of grace
> To turn poor sinners into wisdom's ways;
> To plow the barr'n and break the fallow ground,
> Dissect the heart and shew the mortal wound.

He wield's GOD's law—the Holy Spirit's sword,
And wound the heart at almost every word.

. . . .

So skillful surgeons first rip up the wound,
Then ply their medicines 'till the patient's sound."[252]

Some revivalists added additional visual and auditory aids to their performance. For example, James Davenport, whose pulpit was on Long Island and
whose preaching included bursts of song and shouts of joy (he and his followers marched through the streets of Boston in the summer of 1742 singing
hymns at the top of their voices), gesture and tonality were essential parts of
preaching. Davenport's "song," published in 1742, had the senses at its heart.
"I see thy face, I hear thy voice" he sang, "such hidden manna . . . as world-
lings do not know, eye hath not seen, near ear hath heard."[253] This was no
metaphor of sensation, but the immediate report of his eyes and ears. When
he visited New London in March 1743, he enjoined his audience to throw
their gaudy clothes and wigs into a bonfire and follow the raiment with un-
godly books. According to one less-than-complimentary eyewitness account,
he shouted over the blazing fire, "thus the souls of the authors of those book,
those of them that are dead, are roasting in the flames of hell." When, the next
night, the bonfire was relit, Davenport called for an end to the idolatry of
things—clothing in particular. That which was "worn for ornament" must be
sacrificed in the cleansing flames. Davenport contributed his britches, saying
"go you with the rest."[254] One skeptical eyewitness described Davenport's visit
to New London as "scarcely worth the hearing. The Praying was without form
or comeliness. It was difficult to distinguish between his praying and preaching for it was all mere confused medley."[255] What Davenport's critics surely
did not miss was the character of his performance. While it struck them as bi-
zarre, it could not be ignored, an admittedly extreme and perhaps even psy-
chotic example of the "affective homiletic style" of preaching that many advocates of the Awakening embraced.[256]

Davenport's gestures were uncharacteristic of most revivalists, but his songs
and facial expressions translated the promptings of the spirit into the actions
of the body. In this sense, his preaching was naturalistic. "Affective preaching"
was a legitimate form of religious communication, though it reached the passions rather than the reasoning faculties.[257] It was not unrestrained so much as
avowedly sensate, and that in two ways: The preaching itself attracted the audience because of its observable qualities, and the impact of the preaching
could easily be measured.

Jonathan Edwards' 1739 sermon series on the work of redemption is a case in point. Edwards was a Calvinist in his theology, and as such the perception of one's own salvation was to him internally rather than externally evident. Better put, one could not entirely trust the external signs of conversion. But his language was filled with external perceptual referrants.[258] These were not mere rhetoric, meant as flourish, but attempts to connect the divine with the natural order, to help his listeners (some of whom surely were not converted) awaken to their dire state, and see and hear the divine. In crude terms, external awakening of the senses had to come before internal perception of divinity. He believed that the works of providence, including salvation, "show us the consistency, order, and beauty" of God's plan. Though seen with human eyes, which cannot comprehend the whole at once, events "will look as though" they are the "tossing of the waves of the sea," but that is a misperception. "In the light," providence is "full of eyes round about," seeing all and directing all. The parts of a single life were "just as the several parts of one building; there are many stones, many pieces of timber, but all are so joined, and fitly framed together, that they make but one building." The course of a human life "may not unfitly be compared to a large and long river, having innumerable branches, beginning in different regions," and may appear disjointed, for a man who "sees but one or two streams at a time, cannot tell what their course tends to."[259]

Critics of the Awakening among the ministry were opposed to the animated and sensate language of the Whitefields and Edwardses as much as to the gyrations of Davenport. As Garden, shunned by Whitefield in Charlestown, wrote after Whitefield had left, enthusiasts might speak of "*impulses, motions,* and *impressions* inwardly as on our hearts and minds, as plainly and distinctly felt and known, as those of the wind, or other material things, outwardly on our bodies are." But this was mere "manner of address" rather than the matter of religion. The "moral" should not be confused with the "physical."[260] But to the ministers who favored the revival, the "marks" of salvation were visible to all, beginning with the quickening of the spirit. Those who watched Whitefield preach admired "how that did burn and boil within him, when he spake of the things" of God. His "his zeal and fire, the passion and flame of his expressions" won over many who might doubt some point of his argument.[261]

Gatherings of Penitants

Whitefield recorded in his journals estimates of the size of the crowds who came to hear him. His Boston tour was a sell-out. On September 20, 1740, he "preached in the morning to about six thousand hearers, in the Reverend Dr.

Sewall's meeting house," then went on to the Common the next day to address "fifteen thousand," many of whom followed him to his lodgings, where he again spoke. On Monday the 22, he preached to "six thousand hearers in the house" of the Reverend Mr. Webb. "Many wept for a considerable time."[262] Surely Whitefield exaggerated—if his numbers were even close to correct, the assemblage would have burst the meetinghouses at the seams and emptied homes and fields throughout the entire county of Suffolk and its neighbors. But other observers confirmed that the crowds he drew were immense. As one report on his 1739 New York tour marveled, "I went to hear him in the evening at the Presbyterian church, where he expounded to above 2000 people within and without doors. I never in my life saw so attentive an audience . . . on Sunday morning at eight o'clock, his congregation consisted of about 1500 people, but at night several thousands came together to hear him."[263]

Following in Whitefield's footsteps was not easy—so great was the Englishman's reputation—but other itinerants boasted of their reception. In 1741, Eleazer Wheelock traveled the circuit outside Boston and at the end of October, in Norton, he "preached in the forenoon to a full assembly. One cried out, many affected." At Taunton, he said, "I was forced to break off my sermon before I had done, the outcry was so great." Wherever he went, "much affection and sobbing throughout the whole assembly" followed him. When James Davenport journeyed from his pulpit, "people flocked in great crowds" to hear him preach the word.[264]

From the pulpit, Wheelock noted a common phenomenon: One of the auditory would cry out and then others would follow. The same occurred when a member of the audience overcome with emotion began to sob, or fell. "Praying, hearing, singing" together, the congregation shared the sensory experience. At a revival meeting in Middleborough, in the Massachusetts county of Plymouth, minister Peter Thacher reported that "one cried out" and the rest of the assembly was soon awash in tears. The sound that in a private bedroom would have meant the last throes of illness, or in forest lane might signal a physical injury, in the context of evangelical listening became a wounded heart. The gathering reverberated with religious noise, a swelling chorus of yearning as the cry of one voice moving through the whole.[265]

Ministers could observe the changes that their preaching worked. James Park, preaching to a multitude at Westerly, in Rhode Island, wrote to the *Christian History* that "the wonderful power of god was said to be visibly manifested . . . several were pricked to the heart, crying out," and then the contagion spread through the throng. At revival meetings in Newark, New Jersey, and Elizabethtown, piety wore this "new face," a face that any observer could see and hear, according to pastor Jonathan Dickinson. "By their tears, and by an audible sobbing and sighing in almost all parts of the assembly . . . there appeared such tokens of a solemn and deep concern, as I never before saw in any congregation whatsoever," Dickinson recalled. Such crying out was not new—that had been recorded from the beginnings of American Puritan worship. What was new was that the crying out and the sobbing were now central to the religious experience of the congregants, distinguishing them from others in their own sight and hearing.[266]

Such sensory evidence could be trusted; it was a sign of the process of conversion, making a seeker into a saint. This was hardly Calvinistic soteriology—the elect were the elect, and they knew themselves by their perfect faith, which could not be seen or heard by the unaided human senses. Indeed, such external signs might just as easily conceal hypocrisy or complacency. But as Jonathan Parsons wrote to the *Christian History*, the revival at East Lyme, Connecticut, provided "many instances" of a sensory nature that were proof of "divine influence."[267] One could see their honesty on "on the very countenances" of those seeking relief from the burden of their sinfulness.[268]

The sensate emanations of conversion flowed out from the assembly of seekers into the lanes and streets beyond the meetinghouse. Within a town, and from town to town, the tide of Awakening swelled on a sea of words. "Talk of religion" replaced the everyday, the licentious, and the dull among worldly concerns.[269] For the assembled seekers, scale, space, and time were all altered. The traditional site of preaching was the meetinghouse, now it was the fields. The scale of preaching had exploded, from the congregation to the crowd, sometimes numbering in the thousands. For the churched, it must have been an overwhelming experience. Rank dissolved, for there were no pews and hence no seating privileges. Family name and contributions meant little, as worshipers simply stood side by side.[270] Dress still denoted one's place in society, but all eyes were directed to the preacher, not to one's neighbor. The time frame of the traditional sermon, Sunday morning and afternoon, was reconfigured; one gathered when the preacher came and stayed until he left. The days of the week might be graced by one of more of these gatherings. The Lord's time was all the time now.

To those assembled, the meeting itself became an overwhelming sensory experience. Most Americans lived in small communities, and rarely did many persons assemble for any reason. But the crowds that arrived to hear the preachers created and noted a new kind of mass sensory experience. As one pilgrim, Nathan Cole, wrote in 1740 of a revival meeting in Connecticut, "there was a great multitude . . . assembled together . . . I turned and looked towards the great river and saw the ferry boats running swift backward and forward bringing over loads of people, and the oars rowed nimble and quick. Everything, men, horses, and boats seemed to be struggling for life. The land and banks over the river looked black with people and horses."[271] The blackness was the collective, not the individual, and the profusion of the masses inspired this observer, a farmer from Middletown, Connecticut. As much as hearing the preaching, the sight of so many worshipers coming together awakened him from his impious slumber.

The multitude in the church and the field included large numbers of women. They were always welcomed among the dissenting congregations, but the Awakening gave them a new voice and made them far more visible than they had been. Women came in unusually large numbers to study with Edwards in the 1730s, and he took the opportunity to make one of these women, Abigail Hutchinson, a focal point of his ruminations on the revival in Northampton. Under his tutelage, she stared into her own sinfulness, in which "she saw nothing but blackness of darkness before her."[272] This was no metaphor. She had gone blind, unable to read the Bible. Light saved her—the light that came from within, from a new understanding of Scripture. But what she saw was not invisible to her, it was real—as real as the truth of God's creation of the world and the hope of eternal life.[273] Women gathered to hear Davenport in New London and followed his call to throw their fancy clothing into the fire and be reborn, changing the way they looked to fit their new feeling of sanctity.[274] Critics of the Awakening were particularly struck by the sight of women among the penitents. One Boston observer upbraided Tennent for "setting the women a gadding about the streets." Instead of chasing after the exhorters, women ought to remain in their places.[275]

Signs of Sin and Salvation

The impact of these words and gatherings on the penitents was overwhelming. Cynical observers might sneer that Whitefield's followers had a "particular down hanging look," but they had to admit that the multitudes had nothing but praise for the revival and its visible outpouring of the spirit.[276] New Light ministers insisted that the eyes of sinners were closed, for they had "corrupt affections," but the repentant were watchful, and saw everything.[277] And those who opposed the revival from their pulpits were blind, for they "could not see it," that is, they literally could not see Whitefield and his cohorts as they were, but took refuge instead in hidebound and dead readings of texts.[278]

The continuing debate between the proponents and the opponents of the

Awakening over who was "other" and who orthodox was, at one level, simple: What did seeing mean? Did one perceive the truths of the Bible through ordinary sight? Could the same sight tell his brethren whether Whitefield's path was the righteous one? Was religious seeing different from everyday seeing? When Old Lights used the verb *to see* they meant *to understand*; when New Lights used *see* they meant *perceive in the flesh*. As Samuel Blair, one of the most vocal proponents of the revival, said to its critics, "What's the matter, is Mr. Whitefield such an inaccessible man?" Did his opponents close their eyes when they were "furiously pressing through a vast crowded multitude to debate with him before so many thousands, by that time he was well got down off the stage, about something he had said, or rather, which he charged him with having said in his sermon?" Did such scoffers not see the consequences of their acts, that "there was a very great tumult and confusion, people pressing exceedingly upon one another to see and hear, so that some weak persons had like to have been crushed down . . . in a sad fright."[279] Not so, replied Whitefield's detractors—if the "mob" that came to hear him suffered, it was on their own head. Its own "bodily convulsions" were like the trances of those possessed by the devil. It was the "wandering spirit" that "hates rules and good order, or bounds and limits."[280]

In such cases, psychology was just as important as theology, for the revival meetings added little to formal theology but much to the lived experience of Christianity. Edwards, no mean lay psychologist himself, noted how visible the agonies of those who sought comfort from him were. They were not "feigning or affecting such manifestations," and neither their reasoning powers nor the old reasons of religion eased their minds. Instead, fear for their souls' state deprived them of their reason. Then, for some, the teaching and comforts of the ministry brought a different, though just as visible, psychological state, in which "a light has appeared." They make a joyous noise, which signals a change of heart. True, Edwards admitted, "a work of the spirit is not to be judged of by any effects on the bodies of men; such as tears, trembling, groans, loud outcries, agonies of bodies," but the laws of nature and common sense tell us that "if there [is] anybody so foolish as from hence to argue, that in whomsoever these things appear, their convictions are not from the spirit of God."

In the first blush of the Awakening, Edwards did not regard the visible transformations of his listeners as signs alone—they were things, which other listeners and observers had to recognize. "The subjects of these uncommon appearances [of extreme emotional or physical agitation], have been of two sorts; either those who have been in great distress from an apprehension of their sin and misery; or those who have been overcome with a sweet sense of the greatness, wonderfulness, and excellency of divine things. Of the multitude of those of the former sort, that I have had opportunity to observe, there have been very few, but their distress has arisen apparently from real proper conviction, and being in a degree sensible of that which was the truth. And though I do not suppose, when such things were observed to be common, that persons have laid themselves under those violent restraints to avoid outward manifestations of their distress, that perhaps they otherwise would have done; yet there have been very few in whom there has been any appearance of feigning or affecting such manifestations, and very many for whom it would have been undoubtedly utterly impossible for them to avoid them."[281]

Edwards knew that the contagion of religious feeling depended upon the sensate display—one could not pass it by without being moved to consider the state of one's own soul. Other so-called New Lights, like Samuel Findley, gloried in that sensuous commotion, the "great religious commotion in the world in our present day." The more visible it was, the more a proof that "God is with us." The "midnight darkness" had lifted, though "dry formalists" did not "see the change."[282] The formalist was blind not just because he was unregenerate, an unfit preacher, but because he did not lift up his eyes from the text to see the faces and the hearts of his congregants. Such men had a "blind obedience" to the law—the letter of Christianity—but did not perceive the workings of its spirit.[283]

To this credulous reception of the report of the senses, opponents of the Awakening replied that the revival movement was merely a "disturbed imagination," an untoward psychological state rather than an enhanced perceptual ability. Critics turned the revivalists' commitment to the visible signs of spirituality back upon them, giving a different diagnosis and prognosis for the enthusiast's demeanor. The enthusiast imagined that he saw and heard something, consumed by "his own passions." Such passionate imaginings were "properly a disease, a sort of madness." Symptoms of the melancholia could be found in the countenance of the afflicted: "A certain wildness is discernable in their general look and air, especially when their imaginations are moved and fired." The disease "loosens their tongues" and "affects their bodies, throws them into convulsions and distortions, into quakings and tremblings." To the eye of the healthy observer, the conduct of the religious enthusiast is "freakish and furious," much like a person "in a frenzy." In the throes of the disease, the enthusiasts "are sure reason has nothing to do with what they see and feel." Their commitment to a sensate faith betrayed them.[284]

Charles Chauncy, the author of these latter cautions and one of the leading

Old Lights in Massachusetts, addressed his remarks to Davenport, whose evangelical contortions in the pulpit and whose denunciations of what he called the unconverted ministry had made him a target of every critic of the Awakening. Yet for many who came to hear him, as well as the other revivalists, conversion (or freshening of the cold spirit) took remarkable somatic and physiological forms. In the congregation there was "plentiful weeping, sighs, and sobs . . . and many crying out in a very great bitterness of soul, as it seemed then by the sound of voices . . . Alas! I am undone . . . O my sins! How they prey upon my vitals."[285] The most noteworthy was the falling experience, which occurred when the sense of sin and the longing for grace took control of the body of the witness: "He generally sinks down in the place where he stood, and is for a few minutes overwhelmed in tears. He then makes a weeping noise . . . he shrieks aloud . . . every tear now leaves his eye, and he shouts aloud for about twenty minutes more. By this time he is speechless and motionless, and lies quiet perhaps an hour . . . Speech and motion return in the same gradual manner; the features become more full than before. Pleasure paints the countenance as peace comes to the soul, and when faith is obtained, the person rises up, and with the most heavenly countenance shouts—'Glory to God."[286] Others fell as if dead, groaned piteously, ran back and forth, or experienced sudden spasms of the limbs or the entire body.[287]

The Awakening Subsides

Which came first, the array of new and striking sights and sounds or the new way of seeing and hearing? Which was cause and which effect? Did the shift to a more materialistic world view, and the consequent emphasis on seeing as a physiological process, induce the ministerial fraternity to view the faces and bodies of their congregants in a new light, or did the contorted postures and outcries of the congregants force the pastors to rethink how they saw and heard the world? Like the puzzle of the chicken and the egg, it seems impossible that the theory and the practice of seeing and hearing can ever be separated. This much is certain, without sensory input, there was no Awakening. The report of the senses made the event what it was.[288]

Then, almost as suddenly as it had sprung into the public imagination, the Awakening subsided. It did not die. Fresh outpourings of the spirit, accompanied by highly visible rites of adult baptism and circuit riding, moved south and west and would return to the Northeast at the end of the century. But for now, war had come again to the northern frontier, the enemy the old deluder and his minions in the familiar form of the French Canadians and their Indian allies. New England was "gripped" by the prospect of renewed conflict, and ministers of all sectarian persuasions threw themselves into fervent preaching against the menace of Roman Catholicism and French arms.[289] In the meantime, some of the leading evangelicals shifted course. Edwards denied that he had "fallen in with these wild people."[290] That was probably fair; he had always argued that his congregation must err on the side of charity toward those who professed to be true Christians and sought membership upon a simple avowal of their faith. After 1742, he had kept Northampton out of the maelstrom of extreme revivalism, even though its decline into its old love of frolics and reels had saddened and disgusted him.[291]

Gilbert Tennent, whose call to arms against the unconverted ministry may be regarded as the beginning of the separatist movement, in 1744 was reconciled to "a meek and peaceable temper and behavior," lest "hard speeches" and "hard thoughts" against his brethren in the pulpit be termed "back-biting." He now declared for a ministry of "discretion and judgment."[292] At the height of the Awakening, Tennet had taken to wearing a "John the Baptist" style great coat, bound with a leather strap, in the pulpit. Now he returned to conventional clothing.[293]

Even Davenport adopted a learned, restrained style of preaching, confessing the error of excessive enthusiasm. In July 1744, as the revival movement ebbed, he published a short retraction and concession that showed, by indirection, how important the report of the senses had been to the revival. His zeal had been "misguided"; he should not have condemned his brethren, or urged their congregations to denounce their pastors, or departed so far from the letter of scripture; but the worst was his "singing with others in the streets." Now his passion had cooled, and his mistaken "impressions" seemed to him an erroneous method. He should, he confessed, have stuck to the "analogy of scripture." He was revived from the blackness of his recent spiritual infirmities, however, and he recognized, belatedly, that blackness was only a metaphor.[294]

In later years there would be other revivals, in which large numbers of sinners gathered to seek salvation. In the southern colonies, echoes of the Great Awakening continued for decades. But for now, the fields where the multitudes had gathered and the preachers held forth on stage returned to the hum of insects and the chatter of birds. Perhaps the fervor could not have been maintained in any case, but the slumber of the Awakening imposed a silence on ecstatic speech just as the end of the itinerants' crusade emptied the roads and lanes of crowds of seekers. Soundscape and landscape returned to normal.[295]

In their pleading, the manner of their coming together with their congregants, and the signs of spirituality in their audiences, the evangelicals and their congregants in the Great Awakening had changed the relation between the report of the senses and the practice of piety. Not only had the visible and auditory signs been important and striking, they meant something in and of themselves; they could be taken at face value, read in a way that Scripture and treatise could not. In sum, the senses could be trusted as never before, or after, as the means by which the aspirant and the congregation could distinguish those who truly acknowledged their sinfulness and the awesome sovereignty of God from those who were artful, willful, ignorant, or dead to religion. As Edwards reported in 1741, "it can't be but that these things should be apparent to people in general through the land; for these things be not done in a corner . . . there has been a great deal of opportunity to observe the manner of the work. And all such as have been much in the way of observing the work, and have been very conversant with those that have been the subjects of it, do see . . . clearly and certainly . . . it to be the work of God."[296]

When Davenport, Edwards, Tennent, and others reinvented their ministries after 1742 and recanted their excesses, they renounced the richly evocative visible and auditory sacramentalism of the Awakening. They continued to use words like *visible* and *auditory, light* and *darkness,* but these became, as they always had been for the critics of the movement, metaphorical rather than experiential. It was ironic, then, that the last sensory battle of the Awakening would be fought not in the fields, in plain sight, but in two immense and learned tomes; not in cries of agonized souls, but in arcane soteriological argument. The controversy over who were saved and how to tell, over who could be full members of the church and take the sacrament of communion, was as old as the Puritan movement, but in the hands of Jonathan Edwards and Ebenezer Frothingham, separatist minister at Wethersfield, Connecticut, the debate became a test of the trustworthiness of the senses, or, more precisely, over whose senses should be trusted.

The question that the penitents raised at the start of the Awakening formed the core of the dispute at its close: What must I do to be saved? As Edwards had put it in the height of the enthusiasm, who are the "visibly real saints?"[297] Despite the season of overflowing passionate seeking, the uncertainty of salvation remained a central maxim of all Calvinist churches. In its waning days, moderate supporters of the Awakening restated that core belief: "And here we think it not amiss to declare, that in dealing with these persons we have been careful to inform them, that the nature of conversion does not consist in these passionate feelings; and to warn them not to look upon their state safe, because they have passed out of deep distress into high joys . . . nor have we gone into such an opinion of the bodily effects with which they work has been attended in some of its subjects, as to judge them any sighs that persons who have been so affected, were then under a saving work of the spirit of God."[298] This immovable central tenet of Calvinism undercut any easy connection between natural vision and proof of assurance. One could not know "to any certainty" if one was safe.[299] During the Awakening the revivalists did not forget this tenet, but neither did they stress it. As the fervor abated, the tenet reappeared where it had always been, at the center of the test for salvation. One simply could not trust one's senses to truly know who was safe.

Edwards had, if not the last word in the retreat from the use of the senses, at least the most imposing.[300] In 1749, disgusted with the backsliding of his congregation and convinced that some he had admitted to the Lord's Supper as saints were in fact not-so-secret hypocrites, he prepared a tract entitled *An Humble Inquiry into the Rules of the Word of God, Concerning the Qualification Requisite to a Complete Standing and Full Communion in the Visible Christian Church.*[301] Its thesis was simple and hardly novel, and the prose was no doubt as agonizing for him to write as it is for us to read. No one could truly know who was a "real" saint, for "it was a common thing . . . for such . . . that are received as eminent saints, among the saints [other full members] to fall away and come to nothing." Churches could accept new members based on sincere profession, evidence of proper conduct, and the candidates' understanding of doctrine, but appearances—the report of the senses—did not touch divine reality.[302] The "eye of Christian judgment" could be trusted, but this was an optical instrument that faced inward, into the heart, and no one but God could read its true meaning. In fine, this eye was a metaphor only. External signs, visible to the naked or natural eye, like acts of righteousness and audible professions of faith, were only probable indications of safety at the judgment day.[303]

Filled with double negatives, qualifications piled one upon another, and near contradictions, the *Humble Inquiry* fully satisfied neither Edwards' friends nor his enemies. While it did not fully reverse his earlier generous view of who might be admitted to communion, it so seriously amended that view as to cast all his earlier writing on the visible church into confusion. "Some positive appearance, or visibility, some outward manifestations" were necessary, but these only "ordinarily render the thing [regeneration in the candidate] probable." That was enough to admit the candidate to the Lord's Supper, but never to be sure of his or her true sainthood.[304]

But this straightforward statement was still not a sufficient guide, for Edwards was already doubling back to warn, "This not my design, in holding the negative of the foregoing question, to affirm, that all who are regularly admitted as members of the visible church in complete standing, ought to be believed to be Godly or gracious [that is, having grace] persons." Visible saints were not necessarily real saints, for "visibility is a relative thing, and has relation to any eye that views or beholds."[305] Edwards was a devotee of John Locke's theories of natural seeing, and he agreed with Locke that our knowledge of the real world is gained through our everyday experiences.[306] But godliness could not be seen by the naked eye. "No man is a saint any more in the eye of a man than he is in the eye of a beast."[307]

What motivated Edwards to conclude, in the end, that "it is needless here to dispute about the nature of visibility," will always be a matter of debate, but the way he phrased his concern for genuine professions of conversion experience suggested that he would only be comfortable when he was the one who decided who belonged in the visible church.[308] In his "Narrative" of the controversy written at the height of his quarrel with his congregation, he had concluded that no one could take visible and audible appearance at its face value. The proof of this proposition lay in his congregation's treatment of him: "Besides the reproaches of my people by word of mouth . . . the whole series of their conduct has this language, uttered too with a loud voice, that I am most insufferably criminal. . . . It has this look, that I am a scandalous person, this is the language of it; it has this appearance to the world." Anyone coming upon these scenes would think that he was at fault; whereas the truth was opposite, and lay beneath the surface of appearances.[309]

Reading the *Humble Inquiry,* Frothingham was furious. He agreed with Edwards that the true Christian church should be a sanctuary for saints, but he disputed Edwards' claim that true saints' powers of sensory discernment did not exceed those of ordinary men. In Frothingham's church, those who pretended to be visible saints when they presented themselves to the congregation would be rejected, for "if the apple is presented, it is visibly seen and known, and more especially if it be tasted of; therefore to have something visible that is requested, amounts to a certain knowledge of the thing thus presented." After all, what was "visibility good for, that will not shut out counterfeit professors or hypocrites?" The "visible evidence of gracious sincerity, or real saintship" was true and could be trusted, though ever so few had it. But a saint of God having divine light shining into the understanding . . . is also to know certainly that such and such persons are true converts, or the saints of God."[310]

One of the tenets of the separatists and the itinerants was that visible conversion was a partial proof of inward assurance.[311] Thus James Davenport could join hands with those who came to him in doubt and assure them that Christ had taken them under his wing. In effect, such assurances did away with the boilerplate incantations of never truly knowing about the state of one's soul that were the essence of traditional Puritanism and were repeated by moderate supporters of the Awakening like Edwards.[312]

But Frothingham's argument was, in a more subtle way, a more crushing blow to the sensory radicalism of the Awakening than was Edwards' direct attack. For Frothingham had limited the power of sight and hearing to a select few—saints who knew one another. This rarefied the report of the senses, for no one who was unregenerate could see what the saints could see. If only saints could see the work of God, then no one but a saint could trust his or her vision; but only the saints knew who were saints, and they contested who fit this category among themselves as well as with the nonseparatists. In the end, no one could be sure whose vision could be credited.

In the holy fervor of Great Awakening gatherings, people trusted their sense impressions to tell them who was saved and who not yet ready. Ordinary people, viewing ordinary people, discerned in one another something extraordinary—signs of grace. They believed what they saw, and so did their ministers. The visible church ceased to be a metaphor; the invisible church ceased to be a dream. Then confidence in the senses faded, the assault on the Awakening won over all but the separatists, and they, driven from the center of the field to its margins, insisted that only they could see—all the rest were blind. In the process, the sensory and auditory display of penitents genuinely seeking grace was confined to the margins of religious experience. A world of disturbing, moving, ecstatic, unnerving sight and sound had to be muted or marginalized, lest its fever pitch again inflame whole regions.

•

Insofar as the outward sign of diversity was otherness, hysterical fear of the other required segregation by color and sect. The sensory cost to the community as a whole from the wanton prosecution of slaves and the fiery division of believers into saved and damned was segregation and sectarianism. Instead of a place where many dialects, styles, and colors could not only coexist but also fertilize one another, the colonies would be congeries of hostile camps sorted by race and church adherence.

When abolition of slavery made its way onto the agenda of the New York State assembly, in the 1780s, the majority wanted to mandate the separation of the races. A draft bill would have forbidden African Americans from marrying whites, giving testimony against whites in court, voting, and holding public office. When gradual emancipation finally came, in 1799, even its advocates assumed that segregation would be the rule.³¹³ In future, blacks would not be allowed to buy tickets to ride in the cabins of the Hudson River steamboats, or to walk along the lanes in Vauxhall gardens, or to take a seat on the new "omnibuses" that ran up and down the city's avenues. They could find jobs as waiters, coachmen, and servants, but not as merchants or salespersons in the new department stores. Free, they were invisible, part of a segregated society with their own houses of worship, amusements, and mutual-aid societies. Even the public almshouse was segregated.³¹⁴ In the meantime, New York City people of color had to bury their dead in the old "Negro Burying Ground" next to the remains of generations of slaves. The races remained separated in death as in life.³¹⁵

Those still enslaved in the South were complicit—they had to be complicit—in their own isolation. Wise heads decided to "put on ol' massa," concealing the powerful antislavery message of African ways. Artifice, the art of the trickster, the power of the slave to reach into the spirit world, all these were African survivals that had to hidden from masters.³¹⁶ Whites came to recognize the impenetrability of the slaves' world. Old hands in the quarters would always initiate newcomers into "the secrets of the group," and no slave was expected, according to one Tennessee judge writing in the antebellum period, to "betray black folks to white people."³¹⁷ When the veil was lifted, even sympathetic whites were struck with the Africans' powers of concealment. Prepared to defend the runaway slave Anthony Burns, Boston lawyer and author Richard Henry Dana found his client "a piteous object, rather weak in mind and body . . . completely cowed and dispirited." After Burns' black supporters assured him that Dana was trustworthy, Burns revealed himself to his lawyer as "self possessed and intelligent," a reality that he had hidden from the white world.³¹⁸

Just so, the self-segregation of those who thought that they alone could see God's will divided colonial religion into permanently warring religious orders. The "other" was the unconverted, the apostate, the damned, the one who did not belong to "our" church. While denominationalism did not need the Great Awakening to develop—indeed, predated it—the sensory crisis of the Awakening, followed by its renunciation, left many of its adherents outside of established churches. Separatist ministers and congregations drifted to the Baptist or Methodist orders, and enthusiasts took their anxiety on the road to the west and south, preaching as much against the established churches as against

Satan. Issues of infant baptism and admission to churches, once handled within doors by compromise, factionalized congregations and formalized sects. In their "alien and exclusionary . . . ritual practices" the evangelical movement denied the experience of true grace to the eyes and ears of the unregenerate, just as the older churches closed ranks against the "nonsense" of the sectarians.[319]

Still, even as the rebel leader and the revival preacher moved to the periphery of the colonial sensory field, they left a sensate heritage that a new generation would draw upon. The slave plotter and the revival minister had dared to call aloud to people and mobilize them in highly visible fashion. Those gatherings implicitly rejected the rank-ordered society that provincial elites labored so assiduously to construct. However strained one might find the ideological linkage, the protest mob of the 1760s and 1770s was the sensory heir of the slave army and the awakened congregation, and those who perceived the dangers of revolution were quick to make the comparison.

CHAPTER FOUR

A World of Difference

The Revolution of the Senses

H O W D O we know our place in the "perceptual field"—the visible and audible array of people and things—in social situations? How are we supposed to treat the people we meet in these situations?[1] Etiquette is a system of words and gestures designed to answer these questions. Its purveyors are serene in their faith that good manners will save the world.[2] As Margaret Wade wrote in her 1924 best-selling book of etiquette, "good manners are just as important as good morals, good education, or good looks." For the students of etiquette, words like *please* and *thank you* never go out of favor, and "scrupulous" politeness is the mark of gentility.[3] In books of manners, we are taught to respect others and treat them as we would like to be treated, for in our modern democracy everyone is equal. But etiquette restrains as well as empowers, some gestures and verbal usages are to be avoided lest they give offense. "The role of manners, then, was and is to help Americans live with the contradictions in their culture. Social rituals did (and still do) this by quietly creating, communicating, and controlling status."[4] As Amy Vanderbilt asked in 1952, "Who needs a book of etiquette? Everyone does . . . Courtesy and friendly knowledge about your neighbor will help prevent tensions."[5]

Good manners is all about sensation and perception. When we say *sir* and *ma'am* we are conveying respect with voice. When we rise at the approach of a newcomer to our circle, we want the stranger to see that he or she is welcome. We use words and gestures to demonstrate our appreciation for other people's space and possessions.[6] Etiquette shows itself and is seen, speaks and is heard. Without the sensation of the gesture and the perception of its polite intent, good manners would have no effect.

The older idea of good manners as a form of respect for others is no longer prominent in our society, not when our motto is fulfill yourself. Usages of deference to parents and elders and of formality with teachers and other professionals have eroded, gone the way of dress codes. Even a hierarchical institutions like the United States Army, where military courtesy requires saluting and rank still has its privileges, recruits by urging inductees to be "an army of one" and promising that the service will help men and women "be all that you can be."

Elsewhere in the world, and earlier in time, manners reflected a more immediate and encompassing sense of rank, status, and privilege. Histories of etiquette in America demonstrate the shift from hierarchical to egalitarian values. Indeed, the eighteenth century invented modern good manners, in part by introducing popular manuals on etiquette. Written for the aspiring young man and the polite young woman, books of manners urged self-control and grace. These were manifested in erect posture, steady eye contact, modulated voice, respectful but not fawning comportment before superiors, and easy but reserved conversation with equals.[7] Even hand gestures mattered. As John Adams, watching Connecticut's Roger Sherman rise to speak in the Second Continental Congress, noted, "Sherman's air is the reverse of grace. There cannot be a more striking contrast to beautiful action, than the motions of his hands. Generally, he stands upright with his hands before him. The fingers of his left hand clenched into a fist, and the wrist of it, grasped with his right hand . . . when he moves a hand, in any thing like action, [the English illustrator William] Hogarth's genius could not have invented as motion more opposite to grace. It is stiffness, and awkwardness, itself. Rigid as starched linen or buckram."[8]

Adams had no doubt read in his youth Eleazar Moody's *The School of Good Manners.* The supposed author was a Boston schoolmaster who taught children that terms and gestures of respect for elders and superiors not only garnered praise but were essential to a well-regulated society.[9] The young were instructed: "Hold up your head; look the person you speak to in the face. Speak in a distinct and elevated tone of voice."[10] As one mid-century broadside reminded youths, ill manners included "omitting to pay proper respect to Company, on entering or leaving a room; putting fingers in nose or ears; contempt in looks, words, or actions; surliness of all kinds; vulgarism in expression; and too much attention to the faults of others."[11]

Refinement was a discipline that gentlemen and ladies imposed on themselves. It could be calibrated with precision precisely because it was sensate.

Politeness, delicacy, sensibility, and taste required the lady or the gentleman not to shout, to eliminate the overly passionate gesture, and to treat inferiors with formal courtesy.[12] George Washington was a model for those who wanted to behave like gentlemen. He looked a visitor in the eye when he spoke, listened politely, and refused to say anything that was not "deliberate, deferential, and engaging."[13] (Washington was too refined for one young Harvard College wag, who made General Washington the target of a verse of "Yankee Doodle": too gaudy by half, both proud and foppish).[14] Nevertheless, being accepted in any polite company required being seen to have good manners. The English aristocrat Philip Stanhope, Lord Chesterfield, reminded his son in the most famous correspondence about etiquette in the eighteenth century: "One of the most important points of life is decency; which is to do what is proper, and where it is proper . . . by which you will see how necessary decency is, to gain the approbation of mankind."[15] Performance mattered above all. The way one performed was the measure of one's virtue, and performance had to be seen and heard. Abstract virtue, valuing the inner life, was not so important, precisely because it could not be so easily seen and heard.

If the eighteenth century opened in the celebration of polite manners, it closed with mobs and revolution—the height of bad manners. Mobs did not respect persons or property and ignored all the rules of etiquette. They abused the refined senses with "unpitying laughter" and "the mimicking of obscenities." The mob was ugly because it looked and sounded ugly, its numbers sometimes throwing garbage or even feces, and always noisy. It let no one ignore its presence.[16] Rebellion was even worse manners. The mob came and went. Rebellion overturned refined polite usages, undermining the very basis of genteel living. Rebellion was "madness and fury," according to Lord William Campbell, royal governor of South Carolina for a year before his colony became independent.[17]

There was a world of sensory difference between the conduct of the gentleman and the behavior of the rebel. In the distance between those poles of perception, a nation was conceived. The revolution in politics was also a revolution of the senses. The leaders of the movement made good use of the unmistakably bad manners of the mob to undo provincial America's dependence on England, then they faced the consequences of the sensory crisis the mob had precipitated. Framers of state and confederation governments had to find a way to preserve revolutionary republicanism based on the sovereignty of the people while curbing the sensate extremities of popular demonstrations.[18]

A Sensory Revolution

I do not mean to argue that the American Revolution of 1776 was fought in a dispute over etiquette, any more than it was fought over human equality.[19] The overriding concern of the revolutionary generation was the establishment of an alternative political system to that of the British Empire.[20] Yet to concede that its primary purpose was a restructuring of public life and constitutional precept should not obscure the vast changes in the way a revolutionary public weal was supposed to look and sound. Before the crisis, politics (if not everyone in the streets, all the time) deferred to the elites, and the elites made themselves known by visible and auditory means.[21] Public appearance was an ongoing theater of contrivance. One dressed, acted, and spoke so that others would know who one was—and not "inquire too deeply" into the person behind the mask. Such masks saved cognitive effort; they announced who one wished to be, and no one need inquire further. The public social performance also protected the inner person against unwanted intrusion.[22] No one could mistake the gentleman whose rank and status were embodied in pose and diction, signaled by dress and medallions and reinforced by a thousand cues as minute as the crook of an elbow or the angle of a chin. The great man left nothing to chance; everyone must know his status at first glance. In portraits of the mandarins, like Allan Ramsay's depiction of John Stuart, Lord Bute, King George III's tutor and advisor, even the background carpets, columns, and verdure suggested that visual elegance and social eminence were inseparable.

By the end of the Revolution, depictions of republican virtue had supplanted displays of aristocratic breeding in American iconography. Samuel Adams swiped at the open display of "luxury" among well-to-do Bostonians who, by 1785, seemed to him to have forgotten the most basic of republican virtues, namely, that one had to look virtuous.[23] The most visible of revolutionary leaders looked the part. "Doctor" Franklin's self-portrait as the

---

Allan Ramsay, *John Stuart, Third Earl of Bute,* 1758

Ramsay's patron was the Scottish noble, who served the Hanoverian kings as Lord Treasurer and tutor to young George (in 1760, George III) of England. Note the ermined robes, lace at wrist and neck, and badges of office. The pose is one of an elegant gentleman fully aware of his high status, erect but at ease. The background of classical pillars and the legend at the foot of the column, painted at Kew Palace, reminds the viewer that the subject holds high office. (The National Trust for Scotland.)

simple Quaker, Washington's displays of public gravitas, and John Adams' quirky homespun integrity were all embodied in easy to grasp visual and auditory means. The ideal republican leader was austere but not unapproachable; his plain-styled determination dictated his dress and lighted his face. Franklin's "good country garb" and beaver hat made him an icon of revolutionary simplicity during his ambassadorial days in France.[24] Portraits of George Washington, many of them copies of Charles Willson Peale's 1772 effort, depicted republican virtue in wartime, a character that lit the man from within. His uniform needed no ostentatious badges or medals, for the background of the painting, entirely the artist's conception, with its waterfall and mountains, suggested that American nature conferred an innate nobility on Americans. Though he had all the power of a king, he "must be a plain republican."[25] That is, he had to appear to be a plain republican. When Adams was inaugurated as president of the United States, in 1797, he arrived in Congress Hall wearing a grey broadcloth suit without fancy buttons or buckles and rode through the streets in a simple carriage drawn by only two horses. He wrote to a correspondent about his countrymen, "they shall have a republican President in earnest." What he meant was, appearances were all important.[26]

Finery and Refinement

At the end of the French and Indian War, the British Empire was the greatest extended sovereignty of its day, a successor to the Roman Empire of ancient times. Even the provincials who dwelt in its far reaches gloried in its wealth and power. By the final third of the century, the embodiment of the American provincial was the Philadelphia businessman, scientist, educator, and politician Benjamin Franklin, and in the summer of 1771, Franklin was a happy man. Not that he ever appeared, in public, to be anything more than what James Boswell had observed, "all jollity and pleasantry."[27] But now he was ensconced in the country home of Jonathan Shipley, the Bishop of St. Asaph, near Winchester, in the south of England. The bishop was a warm supporter of the American protests against parliamentary exactions, which for the past eight years had roiled English and American politics, and a kindly host.[28]

Franklin represented the colony of Massachusetts in England, a paid agent-lobbyist who counseled caution to his hot-headed American correspondents, such as the avid agitator Samuel Adams, and then turned and warmly advocated the rights of the colonies to all in George III's government and Parliament who would listen. But these days were slack times for partisanship. The controversy over the Stamp Act was over, if not forgotten, the Townshend du-

Charles Willson Peale, *George Washington in the Uniform of a Colonel of the Virginia Militia,* **1772**

Peale traveled to Mount Vernon to paint Washington, already a major figure in the American protests. Though posed by the artist as a gentleman of standing in Virginia, Washington wore no badges or medals; in the many portraits for which he sat or stood, he never adorned himself in any way. The fictional background—Washington posed at his home—captured the ideal of American nature. The waterfall and the Indian wigwams, the mountains and even the lighting of clouds and sky suggest that authority comes not from dress but from nature. For example, a tree has replaced the classical pillars in Ramsay's *John Stuart.* The light that seems to originate in Washington's face reminds the viewer that internal character and virtue rather than external rank make a man worthy. (Washington and Lee University.)

ties on lead, paper, and other colonial imports had been rescinded, and even Samuel Adams had to look hard to find reasons to rouse his allies in Boston.[29]

Franklin had the leisure to record the first part of an autobiography. From youth, self-taught, he had always been a swift writer, jocular and plain of speech, pointed in observation, and strong in his opinions. Above all, as the modern editor of the "Autobiography" has noted, "Franklin makes you see."[30] He revealed the origins of his highly sensory style of writing in the earliest portion of the "Autobiography": "I met with an old volume of the *Spectator* [a journal of essays principally by Joseph Addison and Richard Steele, published in London from 1711 to 1712] . . . I had never before seen any of them. I bought it, read it over and over, and was much delighted with it. I thought the writing excellent, and wished if possible to imitate it." He did—copying large portions and memorizing them. He then tried to reproduce the original from memory.[31]

Thus the young, ambitious colonist made himself into a provincial, accepting as the canon of grace and style an English model, copying it, and then using it as a template for his own essays. He made himself over by acting a role. He became a provincial when his audience approved his performance. The most important members of that audience were the patrons Franklin attracted from the provincial elite.[32] When Lieutenant Governor William Keith of Pennsylvania complimented him on his writing with a show of "condescension and politeness I had been quite unused to," the young Franklin was delighted. At this point in his life, he still naively believed that appearance was reality. "This was spoken with such an appearance of cordiality, that I had not the least doubt of his meaning what he said." Though Keith's demeanor, like his support, was a mask (and in time Franklin realized that Keith's promises of support were a chimera), the provincial sensory paradigm required that such masks be worn. It was the surface that mattered. William Burnet, the governor of New York, whom Franklin visited while still in his teens, treated Franklin with "great civility," and, knowing Franklin's love affair with books, showed him his library, "which was a very large one."[33] Burnet did not discuss the content of the books with his young visitor. Content was less important than show.

By 1771, Franklin was himself the consummate provincial, and he understood that his effectiveness as an agent in England rested on the same mastery of appearance and display that he had gained in Pennsylvania, the thousand signals of deference and patronage every day seen and heard, each a tiny square on the bright whirling dance-hall mirror ball that reflected the relationship of the metropolitan center to the colonial peripheries. The ideal of elegance was imperial.[34] The colonial mansion aped the London town home and country seat. Imitation reaffirmed the colonial elite's connection to the imperial center.[35] From Britain came the furniture and fabrics, the books and the rules of taste and fashion within.[36]

Provincials could not compete, but how they tried. Franklin's great adversary in the later stages of the revolutionary crisis, Thomas Hutchinson of Massachusetts, a wealthy merchant, chief justice of the Superior Court of Judicature, lieutenant governor, and finally governor, dressed conservatively (the Puritan strain of his ancestors demanded that he eschew satin and lace) but would not submit to the "indignity" of appearing in public dressed improperly in old and borrowed clothing. He expected those below him to defer to his rank and status, and in turn he served as an overseer of the poor and a charitable donor.[37] The reciprocity of service the elite took upon itself might govern the public conduct of men like Hutchinson, but the mark of their elite status was proper manners, dress, speech, deportment—an amour-proper manifested in visible display.[38]

The provincial sensory model applied as well to the American upper class traveling in Europe. Ralph Izard inherited a South Carolina rice and indigo plantation fortune, was educated in England (the mark of the planter elite abroad), and married Alice DeLancey, niece of the chief justice of New York and one of its wealthiest merchants. The Izards could afford to take the grand tour of Europe in the early 1770s. In Italy they met John Singleton Copley, an American artist, himself a provincial on tour, and had a portrait done. Ralph and Alice were simply but elegantly attired (no badges or gold braid—that was for the real nobility of the blood) and seated at an antique table surrounded by artifacts of European and ancient art. Appearing to be studying a drawing of the statute behind them, they fit their surroundings—a pastorale of classical good manners, ease, and natural virtue.[39] They displayed, performed, and embodied the provincial elite, although they were an ocean across from their homes in America.[40]

Copley was performing as well. He needed the commissions, but that was not why he was traveling abroad. He was already one of the most famous of American-born portrait painters. An acknowledged master of realism, he got the features of the face and the drape of clothing perfect; indeed, his best work was almost photographic in its accuracy. But he feared that all his portraits of Americans were just that, rooted in the everyday life of the upper-class Americans who had commissioned the portraits. He wanted more for his art. He wanted to see and be seen in England, recognized by the Royal Academy, regarded as more than a Boston journeyman whose work never rose above what

John Singleton Copley, *Mr. And Mrs. Ralph Izard,* 1775
In Rome (the Coliseum is in the background), framed by Greek figured vases and Roman statuary, the wealthy planter and his wife on the grand tour seem perfectly at ease. Copley exhibited the portrait at the Royal Academy as *The Conversation,* though no one's lips are moving. The two young people are presumably discussing the drawing in front of them. (Museum of Fine Arts, Boston.)

any able observer would have seen with the naked eye. In 1774, he left Boston to study, paint, and live in London.[41]

As in the Copley portrait of the Izards, things complemented persons in the sensory hierarchy of provincial display. Copley's market bazaar of classical objects was a somewhat obvious demonstration of how important objects of art, particularly objects with ancient pedigree, were to the American provincial arriviste. Everyone recognized the clues that things gave of status. The gentleman rode; the yeoman walked and tugged his cap when the gentleman passed; slaves stepped off the road when a free person approached. Clothing also made the man—a wig was a sign of rank, as was lace, finery, and braid. The poor farmer wore rougher fabrics; the slaves, Negro cloth.[42]

The civic scenery reflected these easily scanned messages when provincial elites carved their imprint on the land. Williamsburg, named after the king and planned as Virginia's new capital by its governor, Francis Nicholson, demonstrated the visual elements of the baroque imperial city writ small. Private spaces receded before the demands of public vistas, for the purpose of the design was to impose on the eye a map of the political and social hierarchy in the province. The streets' width, the rules for setbacks of homes on the avenue, the placement of the public buildings, reminded everyone, at all times, where they stood in the provincial pecking order.[43]

A market square, with courthouse, church, and open-air stalls, was a concession to the needs of year-round residents, but Nicholson, himself an experienced imperial placeman in the colonies, was not particularly concerned with the everyday sights and sounds of a James River town. Instead, the viewer's attention was to be drawn down the long street from Christopher Wren's College of William and Mary, an imposing, four-story brick-building complex, at one end, to the brick-and-mortar capitol, which housed the House of Burgesses and the council in its two wings and central portico, at the other. At right angles to the mid-point of the thoroughfare a wide, short avenue led to the Governor's Palace. This three-story residence, office, and conference center was roofed by 1710, occupied by 1715, and gained a park and formal gardens five years later. Its symmetrical "wings" served as meeting rooms.[44]

In all, the city was a public space in which the pre-existing rules of rank and privilege were visibly reinforced. The public buildings were red brick, expensive and impressive at a time when wood was the standard housing material. Placed so that the eye fell naturally upon them, their symmetry, size, and ornamentation immediately conveyed their grandness. The entire city, like the out-buildings leading up to the planter's big house, served to magnify the palace and the capitol. Interiors performed the same sensory functions. In the palace, formal sitting rooms flanked the central hall, into the back of which flowed a huge, curved staircase, which led to the formal reception room and bedrooms above. No one who entered could fail to be impressed. Within, the meeting rooms were elegantly furnished and richly paneled, as befit the social status as well as the political authority of the governor and his appointees.

Highly visible and audible ceremonies at the palace and the assembly reminded people of the importance of rank in the provincial system. On holidays and the anniversaries of royal births and accessions, the governor led a procession of grandees. Footmen bearing the seals of Britain and the colony preceded him. Rank determined the order of the rest of the cavalcade. Even mealtimes at the palace had set rituals, which reminded onlookers and participants of the difference between high and low status. Seating in the Bruton Parish church also followed this pattern; the governor and the council of the colony sat in the best pews, in the front of church, while those of lesser rank sat in lesser seats.

As private space served public functions, so public functions restated private privileges. The council, when sitting as the highest court in the colony, met on the second floor of the capitol building in a room decorated to impress the onlooker with the awesome authority of the court. The judges' bench was elevated, and the walls, dark polished woods, reflected beams of light from high octagonal windows behind the bench. The judges sat in high-backed, richly cushioned chairs, the governor in the center. The law, like provincial politics, was never abstract or distant; one could see its power and authority, as everyone was expected to know and accept.[45]

In every colonial capital public ceremonies offered a similar array of visual and auditory etiquette. The more fashionable the gathering, the more elaborate the performance. Among the elite congregants, everyone looked at everyone else, and being seen was being. At formal dinners, during the toasts, in the procession into the ballroom—just as at the opening of the colonial legislature or the supreme court—the order of seating and speech were all were scripted. Such scripts told the performers how to perceive what they saw and how to appear to others. In one typical "grand entertainment" held in Williamsburg in 1746 to celebrate the defeat of the Scottish rebels at Culloden, "a very numerous company of gentlemen and ladies appeared at the capital," and after dancing and supper, "the healths of the king, the prince and princess of Wales, the duke, and the rest of the royal family, the governor, success to his majesty's arms, prosperity to this colony, and many other loyal healths were cheerfully drank, and a round of the cannon . . . were discharged at each health, to the number of 18 or 20 rounds, which lasted til near 2 o'clock."[46] The cannons' roar, which once had frightened the Powhatan Indians not far from this very place, now signaled that the provincial elite shared in the triumphs of the empire.

At the ball, men and women displayed their grace, while other men and women observed and rated the dancers. Whispered private conversations merged into the hubbub of music and footfall, and even these conversations were graded for their "elegance and ease."[47] The men's and women's bodies were American, but the dances, the music, and even the dancing masters and

The governor's palace, Colonial Williamsburg

Completed in the first quarter of the eighteenth century and restored in the first half of the twentieth, from an image on a plate at the Bodleian Library, Oxford, the palace was the centerpiece of the capital. Its spacious rooms, grand staircase, and elegant dining hall were meant to impress visitors. From the outside, its design, size, and placement reminded everyone of the governor's place in the hierarchy of empire. (Photograph by author.)

the musicians came from across the sea. Those men who quit the dance floor could retire to gaming rooms, where the most recent varieties of card games, direct from London's clubs, occupied their attention.

The provincial sensory model also manifested itself in the cultural preoccupations of the elite—what today we would call "high-brow" culture. This culture was marked by refinement of manners, elegance in dress and speech, and the display of erudition—more sensate performance. The provincial elite did not talk, they conversed. Polite discourse had to be elevated, but not abstruse or arrogant; flirtatious, but not offensive; intimate, but not familiar. Benjamin Franklin humorously proposed accurate rules for "making oneself a disagreeable companion" in polite conversation: "When other matter fails, talk much of your-self, your education, your knowledge, your circumstances, your successes in business, [and] your victories in disputes."[48]

A man with an astute ear could tell the station of others from conversation, for elegant conversation was the mark of rank. At planter Robert Carter's table after dinner, everyone was expected to engage in conversation. As Christmas 1773 approached, Philip Fithian, the young man Carter had hired to tutor his children, was not impressed by the topics: "Nothing is now to be heard of in conversation, but the balls, the fox-hunts, the fine entertainments, and the good fellowship" of the coming holidays; but he had learned how conversation marked the station and breeding of men and women.[49] As Dr. Alexander Hamilton of Annapolis, Maryland, traveled about the colonies for his health in 1743, he took careful and often caustic note of the speech of his traveling companions. At the outset of his journey, a Mr. Hart took Hamilton to his abode, where they "drank some punch and conversed like a couple of virtuosos." On the road Mr. Dean, a minister, only offered "rambling conversation." Hamilton's landlord's contribution was "so very lumpish and heavy that it disposed me mightily to sleep." Fortunately for the doctor, not all the innkeepers droned on; in Newtown, Maryland, "a deal of comical discourse passed in which the landlord, a man of particular talent at telling comic stories, bore the chief part." Hamilton's exchange with a New Light zealot named, inappropriately, Thomas Quiet, ended in an argument. "He told me flatly that I was damned without redemption."

From their manner of speech Hamilton could tell (or thought he could) his traveling companions' learning, background, and refinement, though some fooled him. William Morrison, whose speech proclaimed him a "plain, homely fellow" had "good linen in his bags, [with] a pair of silver buckles, silver clasps, and gold sleeve buttons." Hamilton's assumption that speech made the man was shared by the many who could tell "a person of more than ordinary rank" by their "polite conversation." Before a man who presented himself in a well-spoken manner, the lower sort "know as well as others how to fawn and cringe."[50]

The provincial gentry learned all these highly sensory distinctions from the cradle. The constant rounds of visiting, seeing and being seen, mediated by the manners that the popular courtesy books taught to the well-brought-up youth, structured the visual and auditory world of the second half of the century. Young Elizabeth Sandwich, though an orphan, acted out good manners by visiting and taking tea, itself a ritualized ceremony in which polite conversation was mandatory. Her diary for the years 1758–61 is a round of "went out;

stayed home; took tea." Behind the terse entries was a world in which seeing people and listening to people was the essential social bond. So, on May 5, 1759, "M. Parr spent part of the morning with us, and drank tea in the afternoon, W. Parr called. Betsy Moode drank tea, and spent part of the evening, went part of the way home with her; had a long discourse with B Moode upstairs." What was important to the twenty-four-year old Quaker—important enough to be recorded in her diary—was whom she met and talked to. She did not describe the substance of the conversations, but we can surmise their content—social rounds were occasions for discussion of people and events, part of the art of conversation itself and of visiting and being visited.[51]

According to the rules of civility, what one did in public—when one could be seen—mattered most of all. One honored visible differences in rank with the courtesy of walking slightly behind, taking off the hat, and speaking when spoken to. Not everyone followed these guidelines to the letter (my argument is not about how much deference there was in the mid-century colonies), but the rules all depended upon the senses. One must give to others the proper space, refrain from leaning too close to another when speaking, and guard one's words, lest they give offense. Anyone could act well bred—the injunctions of these books was not for the elite alone, for what were commonly called the "ornaments" of breeding were worn on the outside of the person, where anyone could see them and anyone could duplicate them.[52]

Houses of Repute

Sandwich not only visited people, she visited houses. Houses signaled their owners' place in society, forming visible cues that everyone understood. In Virginia, for example, the poorest free farmers dwelt in two-to four-room single-story cabins, with no glass for their one or two windows, a floor of pounded dirt, and a weatherboard roof. The better-off had glass windows, a raised wooden floor, and a shingled roof over an attic room. The wealthiest farmers were still not planters, but they had a two-story house whose upstairs and downstairs rooms were divided by interior walls.[53]

Not everyone could afford the most imposing statement of provincial rank—the mansion. In the early part of the century, the Georgian style, with its formal precision and uniformity, its repetition of design elements in symmetrical geometric proportions, and above all, its emphasis on light and airy facades, had made its way to America. Such exactitude required brick instead of wood for large houses, and even though wood framing remained the norm, the elegance of brick soon appeared on all mansion fronts. Improved paint and plaster remade the interiors and exteriors of houses, bringing an appearance of openness and cleanliness. With their pilasters and other carvings, the symmetrical and imposing Georgian facades added depth and individuality to homes.[54] Doorways beckoned with fans of light and plasters resembling classical columns.[55] It said, "Look at me." As Eliza Lucas Pinckney of Charleston recorded of Crowfield mansion on the Cooper River, "the house stands a mile from, but in sight of the road, and makes a very handsome appearance; as you draw nearer new beauties discover themselves."[56] Nomini Hall, the seat of Robert Carter's many estates, "stands on a high piece of land it may be seen a considerable distance: I have seen it as the distance of six miles," Fithian recorded, in 1774.[57] Garden walls, pathways, gates, and facades were contrived to capture the visitor's eye and delight the imagination.

Inside the Georgian home, the signs of refinement were even more striking. Older houses had low ceilings, small casement windows, and were dark, clammy, and reeked of mildew. Their central fireplaces barely heated their rooms. By contrast, the mid-century mansion had high ceilings of gleaming plaster and wainscoted walls, often decorated with wallpaper. Windows were large, double-hung sashes, framed by draperies.[58] As one Newport merchant wrote approvingly, "sash windows are the newest fashion."[59] The sash window mandated the high ceiling, because, unlike the casement window, sash windows were higher than they were wide. The more light in the room, the higher its denizen's status. Expensive candles of spermaceti whale oil gave off a perfumed and uniform light (animal-fat candles, all the poor could afford, burned poorly and stank). With chimneys at either end of the house, which allowed for a fireplace in every room. The well-to-do stayed warm; they could feel their affluence. The fireplace itself was a thing of beauty, often framed by imported Dutch painted tiles and surmounted by a rich wooden mantle. These elegant fireplaces and mantles mattered so much to refined people that they would rather, in Franklin's words, "submit to have damaged furniture, sore eyes, and skins almost smok'd to bacon" than surrender them.[60]

Houses made a series of points about sensory refinement that went beyond mere size, lightness, and expense. The entire effect was calculated to impress the senses and lift up the spirit. Walking through the doorway, the visitor found herself in a light and airy antechamber, the central hallway. Softly cushioned long benches lined the walls so that the visitor might wait in comfort and style for the family to greet her. On either side of the hallway were large doorways opening to the rooms for receiving and entertaining company. At the back of the hall stood the stairway to the next floor, with its wide, smoothly polished hardwood risers and its ornate bannisters, reminding the visitor that there were elegant rooms above.

In sitting rooms and dining rooms, guests could repose in comfort. The hard benches and straight spindle-back chairs of earlier days were moved to servants quarters, replaced in saloons by imported plush, fabric-covered sofas and arm chairs, whose gracefully curved lines suggested elegance and ease. As John Adams marveled after dinner at wealthy merchant Nicholas Boylston's home: "An elegant dinner indeed! Went over the house to view the furniture, which alone coast a thousand pounds sterling. A seat it is for a noble man, a prince. The turkey [Turkish] carpets, the painted hangings, the marble tables, the rich beds with crimson damask curtains and counterpins, the beautiful chimney clock, the spacious garden, are the most magnificent of any thing I have every seen."[61] Evening meals were additional occasions for sumptuary display. As Fithian recalled one such dinner at his employer's mansion, "Half after eight we were run in to supper; the room looked luminous and splendid, four very large candles burning on the table where we supped, three others in different parts of the room, a gay sociable assembly, and four well instructed waiters."[62] Seeing was believing that a provincial planter, living thousands of miles away from the center of empire, was nevertheless an important person in that empire; thus the candles, the room, the food, the waiters together were intended to create a sensory field, a genteel gestalt.

Philip Fithian wrote about Sabine Hall in the twilight of the provincial era. He knew well that his native New Jersey was up in arms about Parliament's exactions on the colonies, and at Carter's table, he heard the great planters warn one another that parliamentary intransigence would lead to colonial resistance on a grand scale. In the soft glow of the candlelight in Carter's mansion, a revolution seemed far away, but it had already begun. Ten years before, one of the most important provincial figures in the colonies, Thomas Hutchinson of Boston, had seen at arm's length the face of rebellion, the visual and aural tumult that preceded political separation by a decade but prepared the way for Independence.

The End of Sensory Provincialism

In 1765, one of the most elegant town houses in Boston belonged to Thomas Hutchinson. It was completed in 1692 for his grandfather, John Foster. A neo-Palladian structure, it demonstrated the regularity and stature that an aspiring leader of the merchant community needed. Surrounded by a fence and gardens, it was a little mansion house within the city. It also served as an office for Foster, as their town homes did for most of the merchants.[63] Hutchinson inherited it in 1743 and moved in with his new bride. The stately mansion house performed more subtle functions than sheltering Hutchinson's growing

family and enabling him to entertain his political patrons in style; it reinforced his view of himself as a provincial leader. From the cupola on the top of
the house, he could see the wharves of the port through which his business
flowed. Perhaps he could imagine, squinting into the eastern horizon at sunrise, the already-bustling business of mid-day at the seaports of Bristol, Plymouth, and London across the ocean. He was part of a great Atlantic commercial empire, its agent and its beneficiary. Clothing, demeanor, and home
sent the same message, and Hutchinson was proud of what he saw in the
mirror.

But for the men and women of the lower orders who cleaned his chimneys,
carted his wines up the hill from the harbor, and cared for his carriage horses,
the man and the house wore a different aspect. Boston in 1765 was no longer
a small Puritan town with a relatively short distance from the top to the bot-

Thomas Hutchinson's mansion, Garden Court Street, Boston.
The construction was begun in 1686 for Hutchinson's father. The house was finally
razed in 1834. One can see how it dwarfed the visitor. (Drawing in the *American Magazine of
Useful and Entertaining Knowledge*, 1836.)

tom of society. The nearly one hundred fifty merchant leaders of the town had a "pervasive" influence on its growth, but many artisans and laborers could no longer afford to own homes or pay rent in Boston's inflated precincts. They had to move out to make way for the warehouses and the bourses, the wide streets and spacious homes of their betters. The French and Indian War was a great burden on the town, and its fell most heavily upon the poor. Hutchinson, with his cool and aloof personality, his apparent indifference to popularity, and his concern for correct appearances sent a different message to the ordinary Bostonian from the one he wanted to send and believed he was sending. Where he saw substance, they saw a facade, and it fed their animosity against him.[64]

A more perceptive man might have gleaned some of his unpopularity from the faces and the tones of the draymen and porters, but Hutchinson was oblivious to it. He saw his duty as an officer of the crown and he saw his opportunities for advancement. Given his place in the government in 1765, as chief justice of the Massachusetts Superior Court of Judicature and Lieutenant Governor of the colony, it was his duty to support the new imposts that George Grenville and his ministry in England had shepherded through Parliament. Hutchinson personally opposed the plan to print all legal documents, newspapers, college degrees, and a host of other writings on prestamped paper. The embossed tax stamp would have made the authority of Parliament too visible, though Hutchinson did not couch his concern in sensory terms. Nevertheless, he knew a patronage opportunity when he saw it, and he urged Andrew Oliver, brother of Peter Oliver, Hutchinson's brother-in-law, to take advantage of the fees that would come to the stamp distributor in the colony.[65]

While Massachusetts' General Court drafted petitions against the act, the "loyal nine," a group of Boston merchants led by Samuel Adams—none of them friends to the Hutchinson-Oliver political machine—roused the South Boston gang led by Ebenezer McIntosh, a cobbler by trade and a bone crusher by avocation, to pressure the new stamp collector to resign his commission. Together these men, later calling themselves "Sons of Liberty," engaged in public demonstrations against the hated act even before its details were known in the colony.[66]

Their methods were visually and audibly striking—another performance, but this one deliberately assaulting the provincial sensibility. Governor Francis Bernard, ordinarily a fairly insensitive example of the political placeman sent to govern the colonies by the imperial government, recognized the sensate nature of the mob's attack. From Castle William, whose safety he sought in the midst of the disturbance, he wrote on August 15: "Murmurs were continually heard" in the spring, which gave way to "libels . . . urged with such vehemence" that the mob grew bold.[67]

The leaders of the mob promoted what Bernard saw as improper boldness in the lower orders. Crowds were not disorganized masses of mindless anima; they had a structure, a purpose, and they used symbolic language as well as acts to get a message across. Adopting his classification scheme, we are not here concerned with casual crowds, like sightseers, audiences (like the Great Awakening gatherings in Chapter 3), crowds escaping from some danger, or food rioters and other economically motivated crowds, although in some cases economic want or perceived peculation by a particular group provided the motivation for some in the crowd.[68]

A new kind of sensate warfare had begun. On the night of August 13, the ringleaders stuffed a cloth effigy of Oliver with rags and hanged it on a "liberty tree" (the celebrated name came later), a giant elm under whose high leafy arms hundreds could gather, at the corner of modern Washington and Essex Streets. Pinned to the effigy were notes denouncing those who subverted liberty and various doggerel rhymes, such as "What greater pleasure can there be then to see a stamp-man hanging on a tree."[69] Next to Oliver swung a giant boot with a picture of the devil peeking out, a play on words for Lord Bute, an early ally of Grenville. The sole of the boot was "green vile"—another pun, this one on the name of Grenville himself. The liberty tree stood at the narrow neck of land over which working people and farmers with their produce passed to enter Boston. When the effigies were discovered on the morning of the fourteenth, thousands stopped to gawk and gossip—though soon almost everyone knew whose work the effigies had been.[70]

Effigies were identifiable by some symbol; a play on a name, like the boot for Lord Bute, or a message pinned to the life-sized rag doll, like those adorning the Oliver effigy.[71] The Stamp Act scarecrows were mordant satire; elsewhere, at other times, effigies were reverential icons (e.g. those in Westminister abbey), closer in design to memorial statuary.[72] But English political cartoons of the era adapted the effigy style to reduce well-known political figures to caricatures. (One of the most famous of these cartoons was a procession in which George Grenville carried the "dead" Stamp Act in a miniature coffin after Parliament had repealed the law.) There is no accurate depiction or description of the Oliver effigy, but a year later the *Boston Gazette* printed silhouettes of effigies of Grenville and Lord Bute, the two men most responsible for the hated legislation.

Governor Bernard ordered the sheriff to take down the effigies, but he was cowed by the growing number of raucous protestors, and the governor found

After Benjamin Wilson, *The Repeal; or, The Funeral of Miss Americ Stamp*, 1766.

The cartoon, published in England, is an attack on Grenville's ministry. Grenville is carrying the effigy of the coffin, followed by a tearful Lord Bute. Every major politician in the ministry walked in the procession. The little dog shows his disrespect for Dr. Scott, chaplain to Lord Sandwich (who walks just ahead of the two bishops). Scott had written public defenses of the Stamp Act. The cartoon satirized state funerals as well as the imposture of Grenville's allies. (John Carter Brown Library, Brown University.)

that his council, sitting in the state house a dozen blocks away from the liberty tree, was just as hesitant to act. In whispered tones (so as not to be overheard) they insisted that "it was a trifling business, which, if let alone, would subside of itself, but, if taken notice of would become a serious affair." The marchers staged a mock funeral for the effigies in the early evening. The protestors cut down the figures, paraded them past the councilors in the state house, then burned and buried them. In case the governor's men had not heard the procession, the mourners gave "three hazzahs," a triumphant cry. Furthermore, each stage of the interment had a meaning in the rituals of "Pope's Day," the

Anon. Lord Bute and George Grenville.

Like the effigies in the streets, the two-dimensional engraving is full of visual puns and symbols. Bute wears highland Scottish garb and stands beneath a gibbet, chained, like Grenville, to the devil. He passes a paper, no doubt the hated prestamped paper, to the two men. Note the religious motif that connects the political sins of the two ministers of state to the language Puritan ministers used, in the 1600s, to condemn the Pequots and King Philip. *(Boston Gazette, 1766)*

anti–Roman Catholic frolics of the mob in the early fall, when effigies, banners born aloft on poles, masquerades, and contests of strength between various local gangs (often ending in knock-down brawls) spilled out over the entire city. In these, the artisans and laborers engaged in a kind of charivari (carnival), or upside-down celebration, common in early modern societies throughout the Western world, in which the lower classes openly and noisily satirized the entire social caste system. On such occasions, the often-disguised poor people thumbed their noses at those in authority, and the latter turned a blind eye to the insults. When the governor's council advised him to ignore what was happening in the streets below, they were likening the Stamp Act protests to the seasonal carnivals.[73]

Tradesmen and craft masters like Paul Revere led the satirical services for the unlamented dead, and then the crowd dispersed.[74] Other merchants and shopkeepers who hated the Stamp Act and had incited the protest returned to their homes, assuming that their work was done. When the sun disappeared, apprentices, rope workers from the shipyards, unemployed sailors, and day laborers reassembled, some fresh from a few drinks in the many taverns along King Street and its abutting alleys. Tavern keepers like John Marston joined them in the streets, in part because they were his patrons. His Golden Ball tavern welcomed thirsty Sons of Liberty like those who planned to continue the protest that night.[75]

The mob, now led by Ebenezer McIntosh in person, shifted from parading with symbolic figurines to breaking and entering houses along King Street, to ripping the boards off the partially completed Oliver warehouse and carrying them to his home, were they were burned. They pulled down his garden fence, and hearing what they thought were insults or threats from within, where Oliver's friends had gathered (he had wisely fled, hearing rumors that the real object of the mob was his person), the pillagers entered the house, broke the windows, opened casks of wine, and toasted his health. When Lieutenant Governor Hutchinson and the sheriff arrived to assess the damage (and urge whoever was still on the premises to disperse), they were met with shouts of "To your arms, my boys," followed by a shower of stones, which scattered the officials. The governor asked the colonel of the militia to "beat an alarm," but he replied, "as soon as the drum is heard, the drummer would be knocked down, and the drum broke, and . . . probably all of the drummers of the regiment were in the mob."[76]

Hutchinson, not an especially vivid writer himself, was moved by the daily spectacle of marches and mock funerals to adopt highly depictive language in reporting his own travails. As he wrote to the colony's agent in London, Richard Jackson, on the evening of August 26, while at supper with his children, a well-wisher ran up to the house and warned that the mob was on its way. Pulled away from the defense of his home by his daughter's plea that he depart, he was not there to see the vanguard of the mob break down his door with axes. The rest of the mob surged through the house and the cellar, and rushed back out into the street in search of Hutchinson.

He returned at four in the morning to find that "one of the best finished houses in the province had nothing remaining but the bare walls and floors. Not contented with tearing off all the wainscot and hangings and splitting the doors to pieces they beat down the partition [interior] walls and although that alone cost them near two hours they cut down the cupola or lanthern and they began to take the slate and boards from the roof." They carried off his tableware, family pictures, furniture, clothing, and about £900 sterling. They also destroyed his books and papers, including "manuscripts . . . I had been collecting for 30 years besides a great number of public papers in my custody." Hutchinson was left with the clothes on his back and the kindness of his neighbors to provide for him and his family.[77]

Historians have argued that the destruction of Hutchinson's and Oliver's houses, and other structures of stamp tax collectors and government officials, grew out of the anti–Stamp Act agitation.[78] Hutchinson himself judged that "such is the resentment of the people against the stamp duty that there can be no dependence upon the general court to take any steps to enforce or rather advise the payment of it."[79] This kind of explanation shifts our angle of vision up and out—from the mob at work to the leaders of the "Whig opposition" and from Boston to the imperial connection itself. When Hutchinson looked into what Bernard Bailyn called "the face of revolution," he saw an entire world gone mad, not just a bunch of drunken boys.[80]

But the mob was not simply the sharp end of a very long spear that hidden and powerful partisan manipulators wielded against imperial power. The mob had a mind of its own, with a sensory message it wanted to deliver that did not simply mirror the ideological propositions of Whig protest organizers. We can begin to fathom that mind and explain the sensory warfare by asking a simple question: Why didn't the mob burn the houses of the miscreant officials? Burning (see Chapter Three) was a highly effective way to frighten an elite. The Stamp Act mobs burned effigies of Oliver and others. They set bonfires.[81] Put in other terms, why go to immense labor—Hutchinson reported that they took hours to tear down the interior walls and cupola—rather than set fires and sit back and watch?

Perhaps the mob feared that a fire would spread? Boston's dock area had been gutted by a fire in 1760, and some of those in the mob had lost their homes, tools, and clothing. In his deeply moving sermon after the devastating Boston fire of 1760, Jonathan Mayhew told his parishioners that fire was a natural danger but should always be regarded as God's warning to his chosen people to repent. No one would set a fire lightly, even a divine fire to scourge one of Satan's abettors, like Hutchinson.[82] But Hutchinson's house was surrounded by a garden, and a carefully set fire could have been controlled. Moreover, Hutchinson had chaired the committee that denied recompense for damages which many of these men claimed after the 1760 fire. What better payback than to set his home ablaze?[83]

If their purpose was merely to destroy, fire would have served. But the nighttime mob had another purpose. The leading historian of these events argues that the house itself, with its impersonal geometrical facade and its haughty design, was the target of the mob.[84] This is true but is only part of the answer to the question. Bernard's and Hutchinson's reports hint at additional motives for the pillagers. When the mob arrived at Oliver's house, they "searched about for Mr. Oliver, declaring that they would kill him." So, too, when they burst into Hutchinson's mansion, they ran up the stairs and through all the rooms looking for him. His son, remaining behind the fleeing lieutenant governor, heard the mob cry, "Damn him he is upstairs, we will have him."[85] They were not attacking the houses at first, but demanding that the homeowners make public announcement of their opposition to the Stamp Act. Thus Oliver was not allowed to resign his distributorship of stamps in private or at the government house. He had to walk behind McIntosh to the liberty tree and in front of it swear his compliance with the mob's wishes. The submission had to be as visible as the protests. Only when officials refused to play their part in this street theater did the mob turn into what appeared to be a band of looters who "plundered and sacked" the residence.[86]

But this answer is still incomplete. When the mob tore down a house, they tore down the next most visible symbol of provincial authority after the man of the house himself. The relationship of the house to its owner made the house a target, and that relationship was not conveyed in a deed stored in a courthouse. The daytime parade, with its hanging of the effigy and later dismemberment and burning, had sent a message of dire portent—comply or die. When the mob reformed in the night, it adopted the tactic of pulling down houses to heighten the terror. At Oliver's and Hutchinson's, the leaders of the mob assumed (with good reason) that the two miscreants were either hiding in the house or lurking nearby, where they could see and hear the destruction of their prized possessions.[87] Years later, Peter Oliver, chief justice of the colony, Hutchinson's brother-in-law and Andrew's brother, recalled that "one of the rioters declared, the next morning, that the first places which they looked into were the beds, in order to murder the children."[88] One suspects this story is panicky hyperbole, but it demonstrates that the Hutchinson clan knew perfectly well that they, rather than the house, were the first target of the mob's wrath.[89]

Attacks on stamp collectors and their allies in other venues had the same sensate aim—to frighten, to gain public confessions, to insure that the elite bowed to the "people"—and thus took the same form. In Newport, Rhode Island, the mob erected and mutilated effigies of Martin Howard (a lawyer supporting the tax), Dr. Thomas Moffat, and stamp distributor Augustus Johnson, then got drunk and donned disguises in preparation for a night of looting. According to Moffat, the mob broke into Howard's house, "destroying and demolishing all his furniture, instantly dashing into pieces all his china, [and] looking glasses and then stripping and plundering every apartment of every article, carrying off all his wearing apparel, [and] bed and table linen in the most open daring and unrestrained manner." After a similarly destructive visit to Moffat's abode, it returned to Howard's ruined dwelling and tore up the floor. Then back to Moffat's house, which it stripped to its timbers. Johnson's house was spared when he swore to give up the patronage plum that he had incautiously accepted.[90]

When they could not force the human objects of their anger to recant, members of the mob turned to the visible signs of elite status, the things that the ruling class prized, and tore them apart. Martin and Moffat had fled to the king's ship *Cygnet* in the harbor, forfeiting their homes. In the process, a protest against an imperial policy became an assault on a domestic ruling class. Seen in other terms, the visible connection between the provincial elite and the imperial center the provincial elite so prized made them a target. The illogic of this transference of aggression (illogical because many in the colonial elite did not favor the Stamp Act and had little to do with its passage) was paralleled by a physical illogic—to get at the elite, the mob had to destroy what most mattered to it: its homes, clothing, furniture, books, papers—all the signs of provincial status. But demolishing and looting the homes of the rich did not improve the situation of the poor or change imperial policies.

The same intensely sensate performance was the centerpiece of the New York City riot of November 1, 1765. Learning that the hated stamps had arrived at Fort George, protest marchers first lit candles by the hundreds, then, bearing a sea of lights aloft, flowed down Broadway toward the fort. At their head was an old seaman who carried on his shoulders an effigy of acting Lieutenant Governor Cadwallader Colden. For his perfidy in promising to enforce the Stamp Act, his effigy was labeled "Chief murderer of their rights and privileges." When the aldermen of the city arrived and told the crowd to disperse, its leaders offered them safety if they would surrender the streets. The aldermen prudently fled to Fort George, where they joined an increasingly agitated Colden.[91]

Colden had received a note similar to the one pinned on the effigy. A smaller crowd was already at work in the commons (where City Hall stands today), erecting gallows from which to hang Colden's effigy and a devil with a boot in his hand. A third throng, composed mainly of seamen and young men, set off for Bowling Green, at the tip of Manhattan island, and there set a bonfire into which Colden's carriage and the effigies were flung. Next was Major Thomas James's house, gutted. He was a merchant rightly suspected of supporting Colden and disliked for his arrogance. To the sound of the city's church bells and in the grotesque shadows of the bonfire, the mob cut his featherbeds open and burned some three hundred books, as well as official papers and manuscripts. James's Vaux-Hall mansion became a shell. Although the various crowds seemed to move about in a kind of Brownian motion, randomly appearing and dissolving, the motion had a focus: All marches led to the foot of the walls of Fort George. There, in plain sight of the terrified garrison and refugees within, the mob gathered.[92]

If the mob was an actor and its march a performance, the audience was not amused. The day after the New York City riot of November 1, Isaac Sears, a sea captain, wartime privateer, and son-in-law of the tavern owner whose doors were always open to the crowd, addressed it, bidding them tell Colden to bring out the stamps. To underline the message, Sears' comrades threw together another Colden effigy, attached it to a pole (so that those on the walls of the fort could see it better), and marched from the commons down Broadway toward the fort.[93] The next week, papers, broadsides, and placards nailed to doors warned that if the stamps were distributed, the mob would assault Fort George.[94] Such intimidation worked only when it inflamed the senses of the officials.

During demonstrations against the Stamp Act in New Haven, Connecticut, one "Cato" (seditious libel was a serious crime still, even when the libeler had the support of the mob, and leaders of the protests invariably used pseudonyms when they published) addressed Parliament: "Will the cries of your despairing, dying brethren be music pleasing to your ears?"[95] Not if the protesters could help it. They gathered before the home of collector of stamps designate Jared Ingersoll and demanded that he resign or they would pull his house down around him. In West Haven, a mob led a horse-borne giant effigy of Ingersoll through the streets. Evil eyes peered out from its internally lit head. The mob pelted the giant with stones, led it to Mount Misery, and tried it for traducing the colony's freedoms. Then it was burned. No one could have missed the show.[96]

In Albany, New York, suspected Stamp Act sympathizer (and future loyalist) Henry Van Schaack became the object of the mob's derision. On January 4 and 5, 1766, a gathering of two to three hundred men twice called him to account for his views and demanded that he take an oath against the act. When he demurred and fled, the mob forced entry to his home and hurled his belongings through the windows. The Sons of Liberty were only satisfied when, wet, cold, and frightened, he publically pledged his obedience to the will of the multitude.[97]

The officials were not the only audience; the mob also performed for its own entertainment. The papers the mob pinned to the effigies were never seen by the men named in them. Instead, they were meant to incite the mob. Take, for example, the end of the verse pinned to the left arm of Andrew Oliver's rag double: "Then to *see* a stamp man hanging on a tree." Beneath the gallows from which Howard's effigy drooped in the Newport riots the protesters had tacked a poem: "He who for a pot of base sordid pelf [money] his country betrays, makes a rope for himself. Of this an example, before you we bring in these infamous rouges, who in effigy swing." Over and over, the demonstrators told one another, "Behold," this is the fate of the traitor to his country's interests.[98]

But the first, most striking point of all their actions was to help the government envision the power of the mob, to mount a cavalcade of sensory terrors that no one could avoid seeing and hearing, with each act as sensuously compelling as it could be made. It was not the messages pinned to the breast and arms of the effigies, or the ideological content of the mob's demands, but the auditory and visual impact of their acts that mattered most to them and their victims.[99] They even warned officials not to attempt to use sensory means to re-establish their authority. As the note that "Benevolus" nailed to the door of Fort George on the morning of November 3, 1765, told Colden, "I well know the guides of the people would only show you that they may dare also, but don't incense them, for God's sake, by an impolitical contempt."[100]

The objects of mob violence got the sensory message. In fact, the mob's victims appealed to the same first-hand sensory, "autotopic" authority by which the first English explorers of North America had validated their accounts of the Indians. As Jonathan Sewall, a Boston loyalist, wrote (using the pseudonym *Massachusettensis*) in 1775, "Perhaps by this time some of you may inquire who it is that suffers his pen to run so freely. I will tell you, it is a native of this province, that knew it before many that are now basking in the rays of political sunshine, had a being . . . he could see distinctly all the political maneuvers of the province . . . saw the small seed of sedition, when it was implanted . . . [and] watched the plant until it has become a great tree."[101] His authority as an opponent of the mob derived from his first-hand experience of it. Governor Sir Henry Moore (who replaced Colden) wrote to the ministry in January 1766 that the Sons of Liberty boys had "children nightly trampouze the streets with lanthorns [lanterns] upon poles and hallowing."[102] Moore's ears were assaulted, and that assault gave his report its potency.

To the eighteenth-century gentleman trained to modulate his tones and beware of giving insult by his utterances, raucous street noise must have been both offensive and frightening.[103] Colonial cultural elites, even opponents of the Stamp Act like Massachusetts attorney James Otis Jr., agreed that emotions should be conveyed by "proper variations in tone . . . without much parade or pomp."[104] What Charlestown, South Carolina, merchant Henry Laurens remembered, after a Stamp Act mob had entered his house and searched it for stamps in October 1765, was that they "menaced very loudly."[105] Worse, perhaps, for those who opposed the demonstrations, the people "had been deluded by sound only." Gentlemen might once have tried to cool the mob by "talking in the measured language of a courtier, but when such a weight of vengeance is suspended over our heads . . . delicacy itself would be ill timed."[106] Instead of the measured dictions prescribed for polite conversation, lawful authority would have to speak with "a loud voice, to command silence" while the Riot Act was read—assuming of course that the authorities could get within hailing distance of the malicious revelers.[107]

The World Turned Upside Down

The violence of the anti–Stamp Act mobs seemed "infectious," a "contagion" spreading from colony to colony in a tidal wave that bore down the warehouses, homes, and offices of the collectors.[108] Who could miss the scenes of carnage? For their part, men like Hutchinson, Laurens, and Sewall recognized the primacy of the sensate and catalogued the acts of pillage and plunder with a horrified precision that would have done justice to the novels of the day. Men who were restrained in their manner of speaking and writing in other circumstances abandoned all punctuation and other niceties of eighteenth-century genteel prose style when they compiled the inventory of their sensory ordeal.

The mob mocked provincial standards of authority and ceremony by inverting them. The processions of crowds, the shouting of slogans, the candle lighting, the bonfires, even the effigies of the devil were effective performances because they were so familiar to the governing classes from their own celebrations. The elite marched to the sessions of the legislature and court; they dressed up, sometimes in masks, for formal balls; their toasts had the character of choral chanting. Indeed, before the populace had adopted the devil effigy for the stamp collectors, the elite had used it to symbolize the evil pact between Satan and the Roman Catholics in the Pope's Day festivities.[109]

The mob had turned the provincial sensory paradigm upside down. In the abuse of customs officials in coastal New England, in 1768, and in New York, in 1769, the mob was giving back to the elite a topsy-turvy version of its own sensory world.[110] Peter Oliver, who thought these episodes were "first invented at a pandemonium of [John Milton's] devils," provided a satirical "recipe" for the tarring and feathering ceremony: "First, strip a person naked, then heat the tar until it is thin, and pour it upon the naked flesh, or rub it over with a tar brush . . . after which, sprinkle decently upon the tar, whilst it is yet warm, as many feathers as well stick to it."[111] Crowned with goose feathers instead of fine hats, their imported jackets and vests stripped off and replaced with a coat of tar, the victims became the opposite of what they saw themselves to be.[112]

The same tactics of visible and auditory terrorism were employed by mobs in succeeding years, with similar responses from the victims. The leaders of the mob violence that swept through the colonies between 1765 and 1773 took lessons from the Stamp Act riots, though not the political lessons the Sons of Liberty claimed to be teaching. These occasions had little to do with the repeal of the Stamp Act or the issue of parliamentary taxation of the colonies and everything to do with the sensate performance of topsy-turvy. Consider one example drawn from rural North Carolina, about as far away as one can travel in setting from Boston and New York. The cast of characters in these rural demonstrations was different from the antitax mobs of the cities, and the issues did not involve imperial governance—at least not directly—but the sensory structure was strikingly similar to the pulling down of the Hutchinson home.

Tenants and freeholders in central and northern North Carolina were inspired by the Sons of Liberty to "regulate public grievances and abuses of power."[113] In 1766, Herman Husband, a farmer, Quaker reformer, and political visionary began a campaign to make local government more responsive to the economic needs of the farmers and to curb the excesses of absentee landlords and their agents. He had come to the region as the agent of Maryland investors, liked what he saw, and stayed. But many of his neighbors were illiterate, some were squatters without title, and some had obtained title to the land from unscrupulous promoters and speculators. The farmers had promised to repay loans for the land, for tools, for seed and livestock, leaving behind a trail of paper whose words were unfamiliar and distant but whose import, in court, was potentially catastrophic for the debtor.

The farmer could see and touch the land, the tools, the livestock, a house and its furnishings. These were the fruit of his labors and the materials of his world. But he could not see or touch the law, with its imposing and foreign idiom and its rituals. Perhaps this gap between the sensate landscape of farms and the impenetrable texts of authority would not have mattered had the farmer known the judges and the judges known the farmers, face to face; then some allowance might have been made for the impersonality of the legal process. But central North Carolina had experienced rapid, almost uncontrolled population growth in the post–French and Indian War period, and merchants from the coast, aided by squadrons of lawyers descending on the county, were both gouging the farmers and using the courts to press for payment. Worse for the farmers, the weather played havoc with their crops, making it harder for them to pay their mounting debts.[114]

Husband and other Quakers had formed the Sandy Creek Association to promote their reform project, fusing the ideals of the Great Awakening with the organizing tactics of the Sons of Liberty.[115] In 1768, Husband's movement gave way to a more violent form of protest, called the "Regulation." In the spring of 1768, the Regulators were intercepted outside of Hillsborough, in the center of the colony, by the sheriff and other offices. What should have been a grievance session became a small riot, in which some Regulators fired shots into the home of Edmund Fanning, a lawyer and clerk of the county court, which sat in the town. Fanning, colonel of the local militia, called out the troops (who turned out to be sympathetic to the Regulators) and obtained from his own court arrest warrants for the ringleaders. Husband agreed to attempt to negotiate a settlement and found himself under arrest. Seven hundred men marched into Hillsborough the next day, and the authorities prudently released Husband and other prisoners to the custody of the mob. Governor William Tryon raised a small force from the eastern counties to enforce the warrants, but this only incited the Regulators to recruit a larger force. In the meantime, a jury acquitted Husband, but other Regulators were fined. Fanning was also found guilty of misconduct and fined five pennies. No one was satisfied with the outcome, in part because nothing was done about the abusive fashion in which taxes were collected.[116]

It was difficult to resolve the dispute, in part, because it revolved around competing visual performances, and these in turn entailed widely disparate ideals of how authority should present itself. Tryon needed the taxes, among other reasons, to pay for a new "palace" in New Bern, on the Neuse River a few miles north and west of Pamlico Sound. He had brought housewright John Hawks to New Bern in 1765 to begin construction. Hawks' plan for the palace would have made it, in the words of one visitor to the colony shortly after the plans were publicized, "exceed for magnificence and architecture any edifice in the continent." That is what Tryon wanted—to impress those who came to view the building. The assembly voted an initial fund of £5,000 in late 1766 and provided the rest of the £10,000 two years later.

The completed palace boasted russet-colored brick walls, rubbed brick window arches, and a thirty-foot pediment with a white marble sconce of the royal arms. Plastered within and stuccoed without, with a multitude of sash windows, skylights, cellars, and drains, the palace would cover twelve lots of land—to a total of £10,665 by Hawks' estimate. The two wings of the house would have cost over £4,000 more. The interior was magnificent. Visitors to the palace, when Tryon and his family took up residence at the start of 1771, stood first in a grand entry hall, facing two mahogany staircases. The interior was "gay with color." Tryon delighted in "this much admired structure."[117]

Tryon was not the only gentleman posturing. When William McPherson visited Hillsborough in the fall of 1768 he found Fanning "viewing this part of the army[,] they being in an exercising form, the drums baiting and the colors flying."[118] Fanning, the target of much of the rioting in days to come, was as much the model provincial leader as Tryon was the model imperial placeman. Fanning, a Long Islander of well-to-do parents, had been educated at Yale and read law in North Carolina in the office of the attorney general. On close personal terms with Tryon's predecessor, Governor Arthur Dobbs, Fanning accumulated official posts in Orange County and ran a successful law practice. He looked the part, as one local wag complained in verse: "When Fanning first to Orange came / He looked both pale and wan. / An old patched coat upon his back / An old mare he rode on. / . . . But by his civil robberies / He's laced his coat with gold."[119]

The Regulators had not missed the show or misunderstood its significance. Tryon, Fanning, and others were making the same sensory argument that Hutchinson had thought his richly appointed home supported: Legitimate provincial authority was underwritten and sustained by visual display. To be somebody was to be seen to be somebody. The Regulators, like the Sons of Liberty in Boston, demurred. Indeed, as Husband was later to write, explaining why the riots had been confined to Orange County and Hillsborough, "No other county was blessed with a Fanning, whose rigid vice could not brook a detection, and whose despotism would not suffer him to think the men that chose him their [assembly] representative his equals."[120]

Husband told his followers to keep their eyes open for all such provincial gentlemens' displays of arrogance and corruption: "You may easily find out

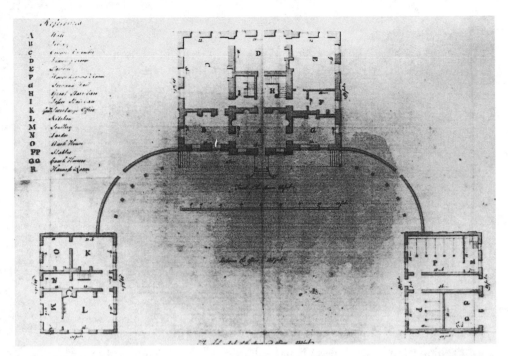

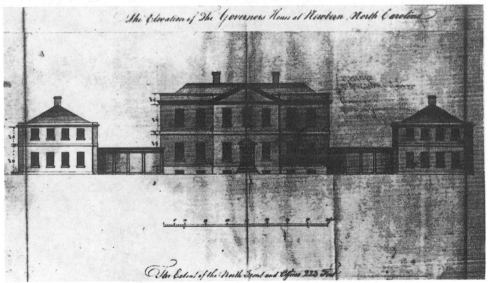

John Hawks, First Floor Plan (*top*) **and Elevation** (*bottom*),
Tryon's Palace, New Bern, North Carolina, 1767

This elegant building with flankers resembles the palace at Williamsburg. Like that building and Hutchinson's home, it both delighted and demeaned the visitor. (Public Record Office, London.)

who was tools to the governor, and who concurred in past assemblies to lay burdens on us, the edifice [Tryon's palace], paying the troops . . . let them stand as beacons, set a mark on them, that ages to come may hold their memories in abhorrence."[121] Other Regulators knew exactly what Husband meant, sneered at "this famous house," and groused, "we want no such house."[122]

Ill will came to a head at the September 1770 session of the Hillsborough court. When Judge Richard Henderson convened the proceedings, more than one hundred fifty Regulators, led by Husband, entered his courtroom and forced him to leave the bench. What started as a demonstration soon became a riot. Henderson's report to Tryon on September 29, 1770, provided a firsthand, albeit somewhat overexcited account of the event. No sooner had Henderson opened court than the courthouse "filled as close as one man could stand by another, some with clubs, others with whips and switches." A spokesman for the Regulators in attendance addressed Henderson, saying that they wanted the cases against the Regulators, as well as those against people who were late in their payment of taxes, dropped. Henderson trod water, and for half an hour the standoff continued, until the crowd lost patience, drove Fanning from the bench, and chased him into a back room. Others on the

Governor's Mansion (Tryon's "Palace"), New Bern, North Carolina
This mansion was the perfect embodiment of imperial power in the provinces of empire. (Benson John Lossing, *The Pictorial Field-Book of the Revolution* [New York, 1852], vol. 2.)

bench and at the bar were either beaten or beat a prudent retreat. Fanning was recaptured, beaten, then allowed to return home under house arrest. Henderson slipped away.

The next day Fanning departed in haste, bearing the bruises of the rioters' switches, abandoning his home to the not-so-tender mercies of the Regulators. According to Henderson, they "broke and entered his mansion house, destroyed every article of furniture . . . his papers were carried into the streets by armfuls and destroyed, his wearing apparel shared the same fate."[123] The gold-laced jacket was ripped to shreds and tied to a pole, then paraded about the streets.[124] In short, everything that made Fanning look like a provincial gentleman—his house, his cloths, his papers—had to be destroyed in plain sight. By killing the house and its contents, the mob was not only defacing the man but also denying the legitimacy of the provincial sensory. As a Regulator jingle later depicted the events, "With hat in hand, at our command / To salute us every one, sir," the rioters had forced the elite to show their respect to the Regulation.[125]

After the Hillsborough riot, in the process of calling for troops to suppress the regulators, Tryon made a speech to the assembly. Promising to look into the charges of financial malfeasance and punish the corrupt officials, he reminded the delegates that when mobs strike, "social liberty" yields to "brutal licentiousness." But the government of the colony had already "shown itself able to control them." If they did not submit to its authority, the armed force he would lead would "wipe away the stain thrown by these deluded people and their seditious ringleaders."[126] In other words, the combat to come, like the rioting recently passed, was all about verbal and visible posturing. Before he put down the Regulators at the battle of Alamance, on May 16, 1771, he offered them pardon if they would accept his authority. After the battle, he pardoned all but six.[127]

To his own troops, Tryon was gracious and deferential. He wore the mask of the eighteenth-century gentleman: "The Governor impressed with the most affectionate sense of gratitude gives thanks to both officers and soldiers of the army for the vigorous and generous support they afford him yesterday in the battle near Alamance."[128] From beginning to end, he played the patrician for all to see, trumping the Regulators' disorder (indeed, had they not run at the battle they might have won the day) with his own discipline and magnanimity, a pose readily caricatured by Husband. "The governor is a well bred gentleman, for he calls the Regulators one while Gentlemen, and at another time, banditti, insurgents, rebels, etc . . . therefore Gov. Tryon is a gentleman."[129] That is, a "gentleman's" words could never be trusted.

The Search for a Revolutionary Sensory Model

Looking back at the long season of riots in New England, New York, and North Carolina, one could easily mistake them for the sort of ad hoc, rough-and-ready violence that townsmen practiced when they chased Royal Navy press gangs and shut down local houses of ill repute. The Stamp Act and Regulator demonstrations were somewhat more organized, aimed at royal rather than local abuses, and they had a political ideology.[130] Were we to stress the political and ideological side of the story, however, we would miss the sensory warfare. The mob destroyed the visible signs of provincial authority. Still embedded in the discarded finery and refinement, in the torn gold brocades and fine wainscoting, sensory provincialism could no longer command. The very symbols that had once told the onlooker and listener that a man had arrived in the imperial world now told against him. The people would no longer wait at his door, hat in hand, or pace his spacious entry hall, waiting for an audience.

Indeed, as popular party spokesmen like Samuel Adams averred in 1769, the Whigs would no longer tolerate the way that placemen like Governor Bernard and provincial politicians like Lieutenant Governor Hutchinson "practiced the art of political appearance." Their depictions of the riots to their superiors in Whitehall had been "masterly invention." Either they could not see or they were masters of deception, hoping that their lies "would never have seen the light of day." By contrast, the Sons of Liberty met in the open and openly debated their course of action. Anyone could see and hear them.[131] Yale wit John Trumbull put Adams' sensory insight to satirical verse in the fall of 1775. His fictional Tory "Squire M'Fingal" could not see what was in front of his nose. "For any man with half an eye / What stands before him may espy; / But optics sharp it needs I ween / To see what is not to be seen." M'Fingal saw ogres where men stood and envisioned horrors that were not so.[132]

Whether Adams' and Trumbull's condemnation of Bernard and Hutchinson was truthful or self-serving, it demonstrated that during the revolutionary crisis, the sensory world of provincialism, which once rested firmly upon a visible hierarchy of orders stretching across an ocean, had been shaken to its core by the "plain language of freemen."[133]

Liberty Seen and Heard

But what visible and audible signs of authority could replace the provincial ones? Surely some were needed to prove that the mob was in actuality the "people" aroused for liberty. As John Adams wrote in defense of the Boston crowd in his 1775 *Novanglus* essays, "Now *the people* see and feel, that the horrible calamities [of the past] are come upon them, and they now sufficiently execrate the men who have brought these things upon them . . . The love of liberty" [italics added] spurred the people on, no longer a mob but men who resented the injury done to their honor.[134] Angry loyalists sneered back that the protestors should adopt monstrous icons to fit their disordered view of the world. Peter Oliver proposed the Hydra, the ancient Greek mythical demon whose snakelike mane represented the insinuating cleverness of Whig leaders. Oliver offered in addition the image of a "black regiment" of congregationalist ministers whose self-importance seemed to grow with their role in promoting rebellion.[135]

By contrast, Whig defenders of the protests insisted that the success of the demonstrations ultimately depended upon the development of a new visual and auditory legitimacy, plainly depicted and widely circulated. The fabrication of a systemic revolutionary semiotic was not easy, however. Too much of the practice of resistance to authority displayed bad manners. Burning effigies and breaking windows might attract attention and display power, but such acts were not constitutive in any way. What the Whigs needed were pictures and sounds of ordered liberty.

The leaders of the Sons of Liberty first tackled this problem when Boston was occupied by British regulars in 1768. Smarting from the free rein the Sons of Liberty seemed to have in the city, Governor Bernard had pressed the home government to send regular troops. In October 1768, almost two thousand British soldiers arrived under the command of Major General Thomas Gage. Whig leaders decried the imposition of the troops but worked out an arrangement with Gage and his officers that allowed civil magistrates to try soldiers accused of crimes, while restraining mob demonstrations. In the meantime, the troops and their officers faced a continuing stream of insults and abuse from the townspeople, a problem off-duty soldiers made worse by competing with local laborers for jobs and picking fights with young toughs in the dock area.

British forbearance and Whig elite mediation were successful until the cold and cloudy night of March 5, 1770. After a week of fistfights between off-duty soldiers and young townsmen, a mob congregated in front of the customshouse sentry box. The sentry on duty, private Hugh White, a brawler himself, called out for assistance, and Captain Thomas Preston led seven other soldiers to the rescue. Confronted by an angry mob a bayonet's length away, Preston tried to reason his way out of trouble. Unfortunately, one of his relief party was knocked down and rose up firing his musket. A ragged volley followed. When the smoke cleared, the mob fled, leaving three men dead, a fourth dying, and a fifth, a boy who had come to see the hubbub, fatally wounded. Soon thousands of angry city dwellers arrived, to face the better part of two regiments ordered out of barracks and into battle formation. Only the timely intervention of Governor Hutchinson sent the crowd home and the troops back to their quarters.

Wishing to avoid reprisals and hoping that a conviction was inevitable, resistance leaders prevailed upon two of their number, John Adams and Josiah Quincy Jr., to represent the British soldiers. They took the job seriously, for at the first trial, of Preston, Adams insisted, "Whatever effect [the outcome of the trials] may have on politics" the rules "of common law, the law of the land" must be honored.[136] Adams, himself always uncomfortable with noisy gatherings of the plebs, appealed to the senses of the jury (knowing that the sheriff had selected as jurors only those men whose loyalty to the crown was certain) in his defense of Preston: "We have been entertained with a great variety of phrases, to avoid calling this sort of people a mob . . . The plain English is, gentlemen, most probably a motley rabble of saucy boys, Negroes and mulattos, Irish teagues and outlandish jack tars; and why we should scruple to call such a set of people a mob, I can't conceive, unless the name is too respectable for them."[137] Hard-pressed to make his case, Adams reverted to prerevolutionary imagery.

During the course of his opening address to the jury in the trial of the soldiers, Quincy took a different tack. He used visual imagery to denounce the military occupation of Boston and offer a visualization of a world of legally protected rights. "I say, Gentlemen, and appeal to you for the truth of what I say, that many on this continent *viewed* their chains as already forged, they *saw* fetters as prepared, they *beheld* the soldiers as fastening and riveting for ages, the shackles of their bondage" [italics added]. Indignation was warranted; perceptions warned of enslavement, but Boston's Whigs were not incendiaries. "With the justice of these apprehensions, you and I have nothing to do in this place. Disquisitions of this sort are for the Senate . . . they are for statesmen and politicians . . . but we, gentlemen, are confined in our excursions, by the rigid rules of law." Law suits and trials afforded the opportunity to show the misuse of power without throwing bricks through windows. "Upon the *real, actual* existence of these apprehensions, in the community, we may judge— they are *facts* falling properly within our cognizance . . . but you are to determine on the facts coming to your knowledge [at this trial]—you are to think, judge, and act, as jurymen, and not as statesmen."[138] To see the law at work— that was Quincy's proposed sensory model for the Whig protest.

Quincy groped toward a revolutionary semiotics resting on legal concepts, but the law was all words, too dry and arcane, too easily manipulated by a handful of lawyers, to appeal to the imagination of the protestors. Funerals worked far better than courtroom argument. Funerals brought together the Whig elite and the masses, providing the occasion for orations while the etiquette of burial constrained the mob from disorderly conduct. The Boston Massacre had given the resistance movement its first true martyrs, and their interments brought out the entire city in solemn, silent procession.

But how to capture the ephemeral moment in a permanent medium—how to keep the emotions of the procession and burial alive—that was the Whigs' problem. Five days after the shooting, the publishers of the Whig *Boston Gazette* asked Paul Revere to engrave a picture of the victims' coffins for an issue on the massacre. Revere, already a veteran Son of Liberty, was trying to make ends meet as an engraver, tooth puller, and silversmith. He had come from the working poor and moved up to the artisan class, but these were hard times for craftsmen in the North End of Boston, and the crisis had not made it easy for him to support his wife and children.[139] He leapt at the chance to put his craft at the service of the city.

Paul Revere, *The Four Coffins*

Rude but effective, this engraving is entirely different from Wilson's complex satire of the funeral of the Stamp Act. The coffins bear the initials of the dead. (*Boston Gazette*, 1770.)

No sooner had he finished this work than there fell into his hands, some-how, a drawing of the shooting itself by a rival printer, young Harry Pelham. Revere plagiarized Pelham's work and from it produced one of the most fa-mous pieces of artistic propaganda in American history. Indeed, Revere was in such a hurry to sell the print that he got the names of the victims wrong and left out one of the soldiers. Still, copies of engraving, hand-tinted, soon adorned the rooms of thousands of New England homes.

Pelham had drawn upon and Revere had elaborated familiar kinds of visual symbolism to highlight the evil of the British occupation of Boston. First, the customshouse, visible on the left of the picture, is mockingly mislabeled "Butcher's Hall," a jibe every Bostonian who purchased the print would have understood. Second, both engravers manipulated the facts to show the troops in the worst light. In the print there is no snow or ice, certainly no evidence of the ice balls that the crowd threw at the guard. The moon appears, when in fact cloud had obscured the sky and thus the vision of both sides. Pelham and Revere had depicted the British as malevolent and inhumane and the mob as innocent. So malevolent did the guard's purpose seem that Quincy had to re-mind the jurors at the Preston trial to disregard the engraving.

The poem that Revere added reinforced the visual messages. "Unhappy Boston, See Thy sons deplore, / Thy hallowed Walks besmeared with guiltless gore," the verses begin, in a fashion typical of the oratorical style favored by the Whig protestors. Such oratory (whether in verse or prose) was meant to persuade by repeating core values (e.g. Boston's religious origins are recalled in the phrase "hallowed walks") in a language that was natural and easy to un-derstand and yet still expressed the passions of the moment—a "language of the heart." In this case, poem and picture together effectively conveyed moral outrage.[140]

Through imaginative depiction, Revere had transformed a riot into a sacred monument of liberty. But the iconography of the piece was still traditional. In no way did it suggest that the rebels were trying to create a new kind of pub-lic mise en scène. This was the sensory dilemma of the revolutionaries in a nutshell. They could deface, in all senses of the word, the provincial sensory world, they could provide dumb shows of virtue and sacrifice, but they had not yet agreed upon how a distinctly republican public sphere would look or sound.

Appropriate visual and auditory display should have combined simplicity, virtue, and the promise of progress. At first, the liberty tree served this pur-pose. Beneath its crown of leaves, the people could gather to hear Whig ora-

Paul Revere, *The Bloody Massacre,* **1770**

Much copied and admired as *The Boston Massacre,* Revere's hasty work omitted one of the British soldiers, turned dark night to brightly lit evening, moved Preston from the front of his men to the rear, ignored the snow and ice, and added the sign "Butcher's Hall" over the royal customshouse. The engraving came complete with incendiary verses and names for all the fallen. (Clarence S. Brigham, *Paul Revere's Engravings* [New York, 1969].)

tors. On its limbs the crowd could display effigies. As a living thing, it could symbolize the organic necessity of resistance. Moreover, its location on the neck of land where the city connected to the hinterland made it accessible to the many artisans and laborers who lived outside the city and traveled past the site.[141] But the liberty tree had three defects as a symbol of revolutionary aims: There was hardly enough space around it for all the demonstrators to gather; it was not replaceable; and it was immobile. In fact, in 1774 the old elm disappeared, victim of the malice of British troops in Boston.[142]

The leaders of the crowd turned to a more austere and mobile cousin of the liberty tree, the liberty pole. Its placement, on the commons, a hill, or at a prominent street crossing, ensured that it would be easily accessible. Poles were erected in relatively open spaces so that crowds could gather around them. The protestors did not invent the pole, which was an adaptation of the flagpole; the New York City liberty pole was the flagpole in front of the barracks of the Sixteenth Regiment of Foot garrisoned in the city. A more distant relative may have been the maypole, around which English people gathered to celebrate the coming of spring. Under the maypole, as one disgruntled Puritan observer complained, "the drum is struck up, the pieces [of ordnance] discharged, the musicians play, and the rout fall a dancing till the evening." The English Puritans tried unsuccessfully to suppress the practice, and in the Restoration period, after 1660, maypoles graced town commons throughout the land. The London maypole on Cornhill was visible for miles.[143] Like maypoles, liberty poles could be erected easily (or re-erected when knocked down) and banners could be flown from them. Even when British troops tried to blow up the liberty pole in New York City, it proved nearly impossible to destroy.[144]

The liberty pole would remain a visible symbol of resistance to Parliament throughout the crisis, but its relative immobility and fragility made it vulnerable. Borrowing from the wardrobe of disguises that they employed in earlier mob actions, in 1773 the Boston Sons of Liberty unveiled a mobile yet equally visible (and far more audible) symbol of protest: the American Indian. After the Pontiac Rebellion in the Great Lakes Region, most New Englanders viewed Indians as dangerously violent. Still, many New England Indians had fought on the English side in the French and Indian War, and just about every New England coastal town in the early 1770s had Indians working as domestics, laborers, and carters.[145] There must have been Algonquians among the mob that pulled down Hutchinson's house. A mob dressed as Indians assaulted a government informant in Gloucester, in March 1770.[146] Whatever the prevailing attitude toward Native Americans, Samuel Adams and the Sons of Liberty re-enacted an Indian raid at the destruction of the tea in December 1773.

The customs duties on tea were part of a parliamentary effort to aid the ailing East India Company, but Boston's Sons of Liberty regarded the duty as a tax passed by Parliament without the consent of the colonists. Whig leaders in the other port cities concurred, and Samuel Adams' committee of correspondence coordinated a nonimportation of tea agreement up and down the coast. Some colonial merchants, including Thomas Hutchinson (by now governor of the colony), nevertheless arranged to import the tea. But when the ships carrying the casks of tea arrived in Boston harbor, in November 1773, the captains refused to land the tea unless the duty was paid. The importers, knowing that the tea would be destroyed, refused to pay the duty, and the Royal Navy in the harbor refused to allow the ships to depart without the colonial governor's sanction. This left Hutchinson in a no-win situation.

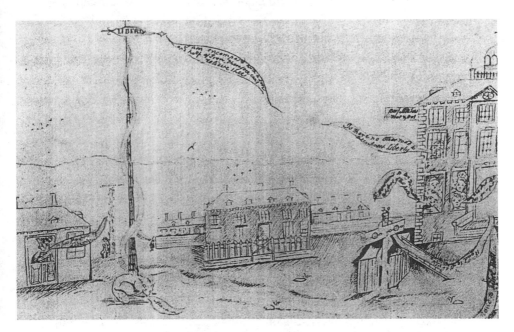

Pierre Eugène Du Simitière, *New York Liberty Pole*
The pole was the flagstaff outside the barracks of the British troops quartered in the city. The banner was visible and the insult palpable to the troops, one of whom, *at the lower left*, is not pleased by the prospect of "liberty." (Library Company of Philadelphia.)

In the meantime, more and more people gathered around Griffin's wharf, where the ships carrying the tea were berthed. When the failure of negotiations was reported to the town meeting at the Old South Church late in the afternoon of December 16, Samuel Adams stood up and announced that the "people" had done all they could to compromise. A "war whoop" sounded from the back of the room, some among the thousands gathered shouted "the Mohawks are here," and the meeting dissolved in a bustle of motion and noise.[147]

According to Peter Oliver, the "the mob had, partly, Indians dresses procured for them," and whiled away their time that afternoon "hissing and clapping, cursing and swearing until it grew near to darkness."[148] Their disguises, combined with their whooping and howling, recaptured New England folk memories of terrifying raids not fifty years before. Indeed, Governor Hutchinson's attempt to guard the ships still holding consignments of tea berthed with two dozen armed men inadvertently made the prospect of an Indian "raid" seem even more authentic, although the planning for the destruction of the tea chests had started on the last two days of November 1773 and continued throughout the first two weeks of December.

When the mob of perhaps a hundred and fifty men rushed onto the ships and started hacking open the casks and throwing the tea overboard, the water in the harbor turned murky and brown. The complexion of the protest had grown darker and at the same time more visible to every vessel in the port. John Andrews, no friend to the mob, and "still not crediting it without ocular demonstration," went to watch and later reported, "they say the actors were Indians from Narragansett. Whether they were or not, to a transient observer they appeared as such, being clothed in blankets with the heads muffled, and copper colored countenances, being each armed with a hatchet or axe, and pair pistols, nor was their dialect different from what I conceive these geniuses to speak, as their jargon was unintelligible to all but themselves."[149] Peter Oliver reported that many said "it was done by a crew of Mohawk Indians," but he knew otherwise.[150]

No one familiar with the past decade's troubles could have mistaken for Indians the crowd that burst onto the wharf, for many of the ringleaders were already well known from previous mob actions.[151] One, George Hewes, a shoemaker by trade who had taken part in many of the demonstrations, recalled in his old age that he had "got himself up as an Indian and daubed his 'face and hands with coal dust in the shop of [a] blacksmith . . . I fell in with many who were dressed, equipped, and painted as I was, and who fell in with me and marched in order to the place of our destination.'"[152]

If the raiders' disguises fooled no one among the thousands of onlookers—
why then bother? The answer was easy for Oliver and other soon-to-be loyalists—Indians and devils shared the same vivid color and choleric amorality.
Eighty years before, Cotton Mather had said as much. The loyalists were
echoing the same line as the witch hunters. But the leaders of the protest did
not see themselves as the devils' agents. It was the evil ministry of Lord North
in England and his collaborators in the colonies who were demonic. As the
Sons of Liberty in New York remonstrated the day before the events in Boston
took place, the parliamentary tax on tea was a "diabolic project" to "enslave"
Americans.[153] In their speeches against the act during the afternoon of the disturbance, the leaders of the Boston Sons of Liberty made the same point. By
insisting that Americans purchase East India Company Tea and by taxing that
tea, Parliament had made the most visible demonstration it could that its
power over the colonists was absolute. In this sense, the issue was not the tax
at all. It was a contest of visible power. By the same token, the dumping of the
tea in the harbor could not be overlooked by Parliament. As John Adams
wrote on the day after the events, "The question is whether the destruction of
this tea was necessary. I apprehend it was absolutely and indispensably so. To
let it be landed, would be giving up the principle of taxation by parliamentary
authority, against which the continent have struggled for ten years." But
again, the confrontation was not about ideas or words; it was more about being seen. As Adams continued in his diary, "this is the most magnificent
movement of all. There is a dignity, a majesty, a sublimity, in this last effort of
the patriot that I greatly admire. The people should never rise, without doing
something to be remembered."[154]

Thus the "Mohawks" of Boston did not care if Oliver or others saw
through their disguises. The costumes were meant not to hide but to send a
message. And if not a message of wild Indians' aversion to tea, then of what?
Of American liberty, surely, for who were the paradigmatic symbols of liberty in the New World? British cartoonists had long depicted America as an
Indian.

At Griffin's wharf that night, the Indian was transformed in an instant from
the savage to the natural American, although the process would take another
hundred years to complete.[155] Thus James Warren was aware of no irony when
fellow Whig John Adams reported to him that "all things were conducted
with great order, decency, and perfect submission to government."[156] The
American Indian was the perfect visual anodyne to the foppish, corrupt British placeman, and would continue to be so for the rest of the crisis. Paul Revere adopted the symbolism in 1774. When Virginia's Burgesses gathered in

Anon. [English], *The Deplorable State of America,* 1765.
America is an Indian maiden. (British Museum.)

June 1775 to defend the colony's rights, some came dressed as though it were a costume party, with an Indian tomahawk at their hips.[157]

Indian blankets, hatchets, and paint, like liberty poles and funeral processions, would do for an image of the American rebel, but these could not depict republican gravity. Indeed, when English political cartoonists used the Indian to represent Americans, they intended to satirize as much as lionize. When they could, colonial Whig publicists lauded the mob for its "decency and good order," but Indians and mobs were still the antithesis of good manners.[158]

George Washington, isolated from much of the violence of the mobs throughout the crisis and still very much a provincial in outlook, if no longer in loyalties (after the Stamp Act he declined his customary seat at the table of Virginia's royal governor, Lord Dunmore), was one of the first of the revolutionaries to think about the problem of creating an orderly and respectable Whig image. As early as 1765, he wrote to a London merchant that Americans might have to do without some of the finery of dress if they were to be seen from England as an independent-minded people.[159] Homespun, Washington knew, sent a visual message of virtue and simplicity, the opposite of corrupt luxury. The Whig gentleman could as easily don locally produced garments as imported silks and lace. When the Whig leaders declared for a policy of non-importation of fabrics from England, patriotic women vied with one another in spinning competitions and displays. These were well attended and much admired by local Whig leaders. The women were, one observer was reassured to discover, "of good fashion and unexceptionable reputation."[160] They looked like models of sobriety. Massachusetts revolutionary Timothy Pickering wrote to his wife from Philadelphia in 1775 that his own "greyish coat and brown hat" and unpowdered hair attained "a becoming simplicity." Homespun dress captured the virtue of protest, just as imported brocade had captured the elegance of the empire.[161]

When Washington arrived at the Continental Congress's second session, in May 1775, he wore the plain buff and blue uniform of a colonel in the Virginia militia. Though he said almost nothing as he sat with the Virginia delegation, his solution to the political problem of defining resistance was sensuous rather than intellectual. He would embody the answer in his posture, his

Paul Revere, copy of Anon., *America Swallowing the Bitter Draught,* 1774.
America is still an Indian maiden. (Clarence S. Brigham, *Paul Revere's Engravings* [New York, 1969].)

dress, and his tone. John Adams, already hot for independence and given to minute descriptions of people and places, noted that Washington "appears at Congress in uniform."[162] Washington instinctively understood the need to project an image of virtuous, manly gentility. Indeed, throughout the crisis years he was lionized in the British press, even as it excoriated the other revolutionaries as rabble, precisely because he seemed to be "a man of sense and great integrity . . . polite . . . reserved."[163]

Washington's sensory contribution to the invention of a revolutionary sensory model went beyond his own dignity, bearing, and clothes sense. In time, he would turn the militia, a mob in arms, into a disciplined army. The British would recognize that feat when they saw his troops in battle, and so, too, after a time, would the men under his command. His example and their own discipline kept men in line in the face of the enemy and allowed them to load and fire their weapons in unison and attack and retreat in order. The Continentals credited their victories in battle to the virtue of their cause, the aid of Providence, and their natural, innate courage—to what could not be seen. Washington knew better, and early on concluded that only a regular army that was well drilled and willing to present itself in the face of the enemy could defeat the British in America.[164] But he was not above allowing others to manipulate his image against this backdrop of American native virtue. At his death, he was still seen as Cincinnatus, the simple republican leaving his field to serve his country and returning to them when his task was done.[165]

Words for a Revolution

The revolutionaries turned to words to celebrate what arms strove to gain. "Where freedom holds the sacred standard high," Trumbull promised, "in mighty pomp America shall rise / . . . this land her Steele and Addison shall view, / the former glories equally by the new / Some future Shakespeare charm the rising age / And hold in magic chains the listning stage."[166] But in what cadences and pauses, what words and sounds, would the revolutionaries explain themselves? Could they piece together a revolutionary tone whose sensate qualities matched its visionary fervor?

Historians have long noticed that some revolutionary proponents' aural performance rivaled the ardor of the Great Awakening preacher. The visceral power of the revival sermon was resuscitated in the "civil millennialism" of New England ministers during the trying days of the French and Indian War. In the clergymen's eyes, the New Englanders went off to holy war against the papist French Canadians and their Indian allies.[167] When the revival generation of preachers had grown older, in the 1760s, they reckoned that their mes-

John James Barralet, *General Washington's Resignation,* **1799**

The republic, symbolized not by an Indian but by Liberty, is grateful, and Mount Vernon, at center right rear, beckons. Washington still abjures adornment. (Metropolitan
Museum of Art, New York City.)

sage was still good "for the common people." For those who were godly, a "clear sight" revealed the perfections of God and his works.[168] Such thoughts were revolutionary in an ironic way. The revivalists believed neither in religious toleration nor in political liberty. Certainly they did not see themselves as the harbingers of a movement to protect American liberty from British corruption. But the logic of their vision lent itself to that cause, and their performance—the visible and auditory side of their preaching—gave impetus to that movement. The leveling cast of their language, their willingness to preach to large crowds out of doors, the anti-authoritarian pose they adopted—all could be absorbed by anti-imperial agitators. Even the anti-revival ministers joined in the association of providence, independence, and piety—patriotism uniting what sectarianism had severed.[169]

No one better anticipated the new revolutionary religious diction than Boston's Jonathan Mayhew, whose ties to radical ministers and booksellers in England brought to the colonies the classics of eighteenth-century English reform writing.[170] In 1748, Mayhew linked perception to political action in a way that paralleled the writings of the first revivalists. He proclaimed his belief that all men had the ability to see with their own eyes what was good and what was evil. He espoused a kind of sensory egalitarianism. Some had greater acuity, others saw more dimly, and circumstances of perception might vary, but "study and improvement" enabled all to see. In 1750, he tied this sensory ability to religious liberty and by 1766 had connected it to resistance to tyranny. His sermon in honor of the repeal of the Stamp Act catalogued the "dismal mixed scene of murmuring, despondence, tumult, and outrage" that the act had occasioned. Its impress was upon the faces of the people, either "melancholy" and "lethargic"; or frenzied, as if assaulted by "a raging fever"; or "determined" to run "all risks." Compared to these "dreadful scenes," repeal of the act brought order, beauty, and happiness. One could trust one's eyes and ears, which told the story of the vindication of liberty, just as they told the story of true conversions. God would not deceive the senses of his chosen people.[171]

The invocation of the almighty was a regular feature of the "Massacre Day Orations," which took place in Boston each March 5 after 1770. Patriotic orators fashioned a new kind of rhetoric—plain on its outside, fueled by righteous indignation within, and adorned with references to rights and liberties. The Massacre Day speeches roused their audiences because they allowed them to see as well as hear. The speakers painted word pictures of the horror of that day, the corruption of the British army that perpetrated the horrors, and the punishment that followed their guilt. Joseph Warren's 1775 speech was typical in its impact and especially visual in its language. "Approach we then the melancholy walk of death, hither let me call the gay companion; here let him drop a farewell tear upon that body which so late he saw vigorous and warm with social mirth—hither let me lead the tender mother to weep over her beloved son . . . take heed, ye orphan babe, lest, whilst your streaming eyes are fixed upon the ghastly corpse, your feet slide on the stones bespattered with your father's brains."[172] Not so sanguinary as Warren, who would himself fall at the Battle of Bunker Hill, William Tudor nevertheless captured the look of the enemy in his 1779 address: "We . . . saw our harbor crowded with hostile ships; our streets with soldiers . . . vain of the splendid pomp attendant on regular armies, they contemptuously looked down on our peaceful order of citizens . . . Hence that arrogance in the carriage of the officers, hence that licentiousness and brutality in the common soldiers."[173]

In the first iteration of the new canon revolutionary speech was to be bold, direct, and emotional. It must move people to action. Above all, it was speech that must be seen to be truly heard. As one correspondent to the *Pennsylvania Gazette* wrote in April 1779, "O that God would raise up, and send on the American stage . . . some Whitefield, or rather, someone in the spirit and power of an Elijah."[174] Who else but Patrick Henry would serve in this role? He did not write his speeches or publish them; no need—his impact was immediate, seizing the emotions of his hearers. One listener admitted that he "involuntarily felt his wrists to assure himself that the fetters were not already pressing his flesh"after hearing Henry speak of the chains of slavery.[175] He could mobilize his audience, motivate them, and give them a reason for fighting. As he was recalled to say in his March 23, 1775, "Give me liberty or give me death" speech to the Burgesses, it was "no time for ceremony."[176]

Henry's language was a composite of evangelical prophecy, fustian vernacular, and Whig commonplaces, but the precise words were never so important as the way in which the oration was delivered. Sound and fury mattered more than logic. As one old preacher remembered Henry's March 23 oration: "His voice rose louder and louder, until the walls of the building and all within them seemed to shake and rock in its tremendous vibrations. Finally his pale face and glaring eyes became terrible to look upon."[177] Years later Edmund Randolph, representative of the younger generation of Virginia's political elite, recalled hearing Henry speak on March 23. Randolph could summon little of the content, but he still heard the cadences, for Henry had "a pronunciation which might disgust in a drawing room [but] yet may find access to the hearts of a popular assembly." Henry's pauses, his vehemence, and his flashing countenance "alarmed" the listener to the danger at hand.[178] Such

warnings were common at revival meetings, and comparison to the evangelicals was warranted, for Henry had long admired the revivalists' style.[179] In
short sentences and with allusions to the Bible and to everyday life, Henry
thundered: "We have prostrated ourselves before the throne . . . and we have
been spurned with contempt."[180] Would the House of Burgesses, would any
assembly of free Americans, stand still for parliamentary exactions? Never.

Henry's hyperbole reflected the growing fierceness of the controversy. It was
the era of the first American loyalty oaths, when suspected loyalists were harassed by revolutionary "committees of safety" and the Whigs themselves were
coming to realize that they must answer the question debated at the Second
Continental Congress: "Do we aim at independency?" In the weeks after news
of Lexington and Concord had arrived in Philadelphia, the delegates were
choosing sides. When George III issued a proclamation, in the autumn of
1775, that Americans had "proceeded to open and avowed rebellion," he stated
a fact that all the protestations of America's friends in Parliament could not
gainsay. In December, the king unleashed the Royal Navy to prey on rebel
American shipping and American ports. Governor Lord Dunmore had already offered freedom to those slaves willing to turn upon their masters in
Virginia, and many flocked to his standard, causing consternation among the
patriot party there.[181]

In plain-spoken and forthright language, suitable for reading aloud, Thomas Paine offered an answer to the question of independency.[182] Paine was
English—indeed, he had only arrived in the colonies in 1774. He was not particularly familiar with the colonial politics behind the dispute with Britain,
and he had taken no part in the transatlantic conversation that had shaped the
content of the American protests.[183] But he grasped, as few did, the need for a
sensate revolutionary vocabulary and style of protest writing, "words that address every citizen directly and without mediation of any kind."[184] Paine was
no gentleman, no lover of hierarchy—crowned or medaled—and he believed
what he saw. As editor of the *Pennsylvania Magazine,* a post Franklin's letters
of introduction had opened to him, Paine gave hints of his belief in the equal
rights of all peoples. He opposed slavery, titles of nobility, and excesses of display. "Dignities and high sounding names have different effects on different
beholders. The luster of the star and the title of my lord over-awe the superstitious vulgar, and forbid them to inquire into the character of the possessor."
The fine-sounding title, like the elegant garment and the refined home, were
the sensory counterfeits of true character. "But the reasonable freeman sees
through the magic of a title, and examines the man before he approves him."

The eye and the ear of the free-born man worked together to pierce the surface of imposture and penetrate to the reality of things.[185]

Thomas Paine's January 1776 series of newspaper essays, called, after the author's pseudonym, *Common Sense,* was full of visualizations and tactile representations. At its center stood "the people," not some abstract political entity, the subject of a polite discourse, but a palpable mass—the mob reconfigured as the citizenry. "Some convenient tree will afford them a state-house, under the branches of which, the whole colony may assembly to deliberate on public matters." Under the liberty tree, government was visible to all. When governments had to become representative, they could and should still be visible. "However our eyes may be dazzled with show, or our ears deceived by sound . . . the more simple a thing is, the less liable it is to be disordered."

England's government operated on a different principle, a principle of hidden power, conspiracy, and false fronts. Law in such a system concealed rather than revealed the mainsprings of power. "The constitution of England is so exceedingly complex, that the nation may suffer for years together without being able to discover in which part the fault lies." One could not even tell where the power to rule came from, much less see it fully in its workings. Paine suspected that "could we take off the dark covering of antiquity, and trace them to their first rise, that we should find the first [kings] nothing better than the principal ruffian of some restless gang." Against this darkened screen, the bright sunlight of the American cause shined. Those who rejected this depiction of affairs must be "weak men, who cannot see [and] prejudiced men, who will not see." His prose, as he admitted, was the very opposite of elegant Georgian style—"nothing more than simple facts, plain arguments, and common sense."[186] Above all, his approach appealed to the senses. Thus, the words *Common Sense* had a second meaning: the report of the ordinary man's eyes and ears.

Of course, such disclaimers were hardly new and read somewhat disingenuously. Paine was self-taught, but he was well aware of literary fashions in Britain, where he had schoolmastered for a time.[187] Paine's style adopted the fad for "natural speech," which Thomas Reid had promoted in his popular *Inquiry into the Human Mind* (1771). He called for a diction that "every man understands by the principles of his nature."[188] On the stage, in elocution manuals, and in essays on politics, English commentators praised conversation that allowed the natural sentiments to show themselves. For the Whigs in America, the artful speech of placemen and aristocrats in the pay of the crown was thus doubly suspect. Not only was its politics misguided, its rhetoric and tone were misleading. General Gage might "speak with art and finesse," Trumbull warned, but honied words were poison in the ears of the unwary.[189]

The elocution of gentlemen was to be replaced, then, by the genuineness and candor of honest speech. The essence of the latter was common sense discourse reduced to writing. Paine was rumored to have read sections of his first draft of *Common Sense* aloud to Philadelphia doctor Benjamin Rush, a strong supporter of the resistance. Fair enough, for Paine expected that the work would be read aloud and heard more often than simply read.[190] More important, Paine and Rush assumed that natural speech theory—and practice—empowered Paine to avoid all artifice.[191]

Another argument against the elegant provincial tongue was that it invoked the senses metaphorically—like the references to light and darkness that ministers had used before and after the Great Awakening. Instead, Paine believed that revolutionary sensory expression must be genuine; it must convey the reality of parliamentary exactions and colonial exertions. "These proceedings may at first appear strange and difficult; but like all other steps which we have already passed over, will in a little time become familiar and agreeable."[192] As one broadside that circulated in Virginia during the crisis proclaimed, the words of the patriot must "strip every measure of that disguise under cover of which it may be artfully obtruded on his mind, and penetrate through all the sinister designs and secret machinations of the enemies of freedom."[193]

No flights of elegant dissimulation would suffice in the speeches of the delegates to the Continental Congress. As James Duane told his fellow delegates on September 8, 1774, the debate must be "above the reach of cunning and the arts of oppression."[194] Plainly, Duane, a careful lawyer, understood Reid's admonition, but he need not have urged his fellow delegates to speak their hearts. Everyone at the Congress had his own view of what needed saying to Britain, the other colonists, and one another. One would have to look hard to find a wordier crew. We have no record of their speeches, but we have letters, notes on debates, and drafts for speeches, and these show that the precise wording of petitions, remonstrances, and letters meant a great deal to the delegates.

The delegates' personal letters are full of sensory detail. Many of the delegates had never spent any time in Philadelphia, and they savored the new sights and sounds. John Adams, in particular, recorded the dimensions, look, and smell of every street and building he entered. On September 5, 1774, he and a comrade "walked to Carpenter's hall, where they took a view of the room, and of the chamber where is an excellent library, there is also a long entry, where gentlemen may walk, and a convenient chamber opposite . . . the general cry was, that this was a good room, and question was put, whether we were satisfied with this room, and it passed."[195] John Adams' private correspondence bristled with keen-edged portraits of the "sharpers, gamblers, and horse jockeys" who trimmed their politics to the moment. But true defenders of liberty had "drawn a line by the banks of the ocean."[196] Close the eyes, and one could see the trimmers and the true blues.

Silas Deane of Wethersfield, Connecticut, who arrived the same day, wrote to his wife Elizabeth that "the tavern appeared tolerable . . . but to our surprise here was no fruit, bad rum, and nothing of the meat kind but salt pork . . . I called for bread cheese and porter. . . . but I could not taste them . . . We set out . . . for this city at five o'clock and arrived at six. Not a garden, nor the appearance of one, in the neighborhood of this city, equal to ours."[197] Deane's correspondence with his wife remained richly evocative of sounds and sights, part travelogue, part ceremonial procession, part review of the troops that hastily gathered to cheer the New England delegations on their way. On his return to Congress's second session, in May 1775, he met the Newark (New Jersey) "grenadiers," a troop of horsemen, a "genteel company" that paraded in the "most polite manner." Rough men in arms from Woodbridge appeared next, "but they meant well," as did the college students with their swords who turned out in Princeton, and the Trenton militia colonel in his phaeton, convoyed by ten men on horseback "with bayonets fixed." As the delegates approached Philadelphia, "the air rent with shout and huzzas. My little bay horses were put in such a fright that I was in fear of killing several of the spectators."[198]

Privately, Adams longed for a way to depict Massachusetts' agony so that everyone could see. As he wrote to William Tudor a month later, "I wish that you and all the rest of our friends had been more explicit, in your private, confidential letters to us."[199] All the world's eyes were on Philadelphia and Boston, as John's fellow delegate Samuel Adams was prepared to inform Thomas Gage in another private missive.[200] But one looks in vain in the delegates' drafts of public speeches and published petitions for sensory remarks.

Where had the striking depictive imagery of the earlier protests gone?

In the course of conversations at the Continental Congress from May 1774 to June 1776, the revolutionaries concluded that sensory language did not work. The plain speech that had moved the colonists to call the Congress did not sit well in grand declarations of rights. It was too rooted in immediate experience, too local—in a word, too tangible. In tiny steps the revolutionaries abandoned the sensate modes they had recently explored. In the late summer of 1774, delegates agreed with James Duane that the "rights of the colonies" were "derived" from "the common law of England," "our charters," and "our several codes of provincial laws."[201] A month later, as the delegates were wrestling with the inherent difficulties of asking Parliament to renounce its own sovereignty over the colonies, Richard Henry Lee of Virginia rested the Whigs' cause on "liberty and ancient rights."[202] Samuel Ward of Rhode Island concurred: "All good government is founded in compact."[203] Ward had cited as authority John Locke's theory of the contractual origin of government in a state of nature.[204] Inexorably, the debaters veered away from the rich context of actual events they had seen and heard toward a metaphorical origin story. In the latter, "nature" was a concept, not a collection of describable things, and man in a state of nature was an abstraction, not a person experiencing a sensory event, like Harriot at Roanoke, Mary Rowlandson in captivity, or Daniel Horsmanden during the New York City arson scare. Only in this intentionally denatured setting of "just principles" did the colonists have rights that Parliament and the crown could not rescind.[205]

Not all the delegates turned to natural rights arguments immediately—some held out for more detailed, historically grounded disquisitions. John Dickinson cleaved to the "detail of facts herein before recited," but in his drafts he scratched out colorful and evocative phrases like "inflamed" in favor of the nonsensory "artfully provoked."[206] Dickinson knew that to appeal to those beyond the ambit of Congress he would have to recur to "the invaluable rights that form a considerable part of that mild system of government."[207] By the winter of 1774/45, even Duane conceded that "colonization is a new case unprovided for by the constitution, and it is therefore necessary to remedy the defect by a new system founded on *general principles* of liberty" [italics added].[208] Natural rights traveled over the ocean better than depictive language, having less baggage, as Silas Deane wrote to Samuel Adams when the delegates returned home in 1774 and as Richard Henry Lee reminded Patrick Henry in April 1776.[209] Phrased in lofty and universal eloquence, "a very few simple principles, principles that would invariably operate," the case for American rights would not seem to rest upon the sufferings of any particular person or region.[210]

Patrick Henry remained the exception. His oratory had always been sensuous, and so was his contribution to the first Congress. At the outset, he warned the delegates that they were surveying new ground in pictorial terms. "Where are your land marks? Your boundaries of colonies?"[211] Rereading one of the very few examples of Henry's actual phrasing, one is reminded how sensuous his oratory must have been. On October 22, 1774, he drafted an address to the king against the Coercive Acts that reduced the quarrel to human terms. One of the acts provided for trial in Nova Scotia of purported crimes in Massachusetts. "How deplorable must be the condition of that man who is seized and shackled in America, must bid adieu to his native country and embark for a distant one when the pains and sufferings of a tedious imprisonment will not be alleviated by the assistance of friends or the hope that innocence will be acquitted. On the contrary the unhappy sufferer far removed from the possibility of proving his innocence and from all that can minister to his necessities or soften his distresses must sink under the accumulated misery and find no asylum but in death."[212] One can picture the scene. But Henry's vivid word pictures were lost in the welter of lofty and principled disquisition, and he went home.

From May of 1775, when the Second Congress convened, to June 7, 1776, when Richard Henry Lee, a Virginia delegate, returned from the Virginia Convention with instructions to introduce a resolution, "that these united colonies are, and of right ought to be, free and independent states," the swirl of events outran the imagination and astounded the eye and ear. But inside the Congress, the language of protest and official proclamation betrayed little of the sensory detail of these events. Not that the delegates were insensible of the sights and sounds of war; they were not. After the victories at Concord and Bunker Hill, John Dickinson warned Congress, "We have not yet tasted deeply of that bitter cup called the fortunes of war. A bloody battle lost—that peculiar distress of the brave defenders of American liberties in the Massachusetts Bay—the multitude thrown out of employ by the loss of their fisheries and the stoppage of their other trade—disease breaking out among their troops . . . the danger of insurrection by Negroes in southern colonies—incursions of Canadians and Indians upon the northern colonies"—real enough concerns, but depicted in the abstract. It would have been easy enough to make any one of them strikingly sensate, but Dickinson preferred "every method to avoid extremities" in language, just as he urged restraint in policy.[213]

Out of doors, New England had gone to war with Britain; a massive British army and fleet were descending upon New York City, a Congressional Army had invaded Canada and been driven back into New York, and groups of determined assemblymen had reconstituted themselves provincial governments and met in churches, taverns, and local halls to plan new kinds of government. Privy to all this, Congress became a busy, buzzing news service, mail-sorting room, and gossip factory of first-hand reports and hearsay. Everyone conceded the sensory overload—but only privately. Everyone acknowledged the disheartening effect of the Canadian military fiasco. "Congress hears with great regret" and "it has given us much concern" became the litany of outgoing correspondence.[214]

Such details—the sensory side of the conflict—were almost too much to bear, raising constant anxiety. Delegates feared that the "war and bloodshed" would cause some at home to lose their resolve. "I pray God we may not be taken in the snare," Josiah Bartlett worried.[215] For this reason alone, Congress might have averted its eyes and covered its ears to the sensory report of war, but that was not the only reason it fabricated an official jargon that coded and categorized events without reference to their sensory impact. The aim was to elevate the American cause above a mere partisan squabble and place it on the highest ground of principled resistance to tyranny. Principled language was both refuge from the torrent of the senses and a staging ground for the oratorical offensive.

The foremost example of this desensitization of discourse was the Declaration of Independence. On June 11, 1776, Congress selected a committee to draft a declaration stating the causes and confirming the meaning of Lee's resolution. Jefferson, John Adams, Franklin, Roger Sherman of Connecticut, and Robert R. Livingston of New York agreed to serve. Conventional wisdom has given Jefferson pride of place in the drafting process, but Jefferson had help. The committee laid out the principal sections of the document, and Jefferson, accepting the charge of writing a first draft, listened to the committee's suggestions.[216] He had at hand his own earlier essays, including his *Declaration of the Causes of Taking Up Arms* (1774), as well as a wealth of earlier declarations of rights and grievances. And he was a lawyer, highly practiced in drawing up bills in plain English to gain his clients "equity" in the courts of Virginia.[217]

The resulting Declaration of Independence was many things: a legal document, a piece of revolutionary propaganda, a rhetorical exercise, an explication of political necessity, and a rationale for armed insurrection. A marvelous piece of work, justly celebrated. The language, read throughout the former colonies, now independent states, echoed and gave finality to the petitions, declarations, and remonstrances the Whig opposition had composed throughout the previous decade. "The history of the present king of Great Britain is a history of repeated injuries and usurpations, all having in direct object the establishment of an absolute tyranny over these states." The litany of injuries, infringements, and usurpations that followed proved that George

III had violated his own laws as well as the settled usages of the colonies. He refused to assent to colonial legislation or delayed that assent; harassed, dissolved, and delayed re-election of the legislatures; prevented migrants from coming to the colonies; obstructed the courts and suborned the judges; and "sent hither swarms of officers." When harassment failed to produce subservience, the king dispatched armed forces to the colonies, quartered them upon private citizens, cut off trade, imposed taxes, denied trial by jury, and curtailed chartered privileges—all without the consent of the colonists. Finally, he had "abdicated government" by declaring war on his own subjects, exciting domestic insurrection among the colonists and their servants and slaves, and raising armies of foreign mercenaries to bring the people under his heel. Against these impositions the colonists had petitioned for redress, to no avail. The colonists then turned to their fellow Britons. "Nor have we been wanting in our attentions to our British brethren," Jefferson continued. "We have warned them, from time to time, of attempts by their legislature to extend an unwarrantable jurisdiction over us. We have reminded them of the circumstances of our emigration and settlement here." But the British people "have been deaf to the voice of justice and consanguinity." There was no recourse but independence.[218]

But not one tear, not one shout, not one sensate evidence of pain or anger did the draft confess. Though the streets of Boston, Philadelphia, and New York City were filled with the marching sounds of armed men and General Washington's increasingly morbid reports to the Congress from New York City limned out the prospective destruction of the Continental Army by the approaching British, the Declaration envisioned nothing of the gritty texture of a nation at war. Even the enemy was blandly portrayed—George III was evil, but a denatured, abstract evil. Jefferson had penned a marvel of cold reason and occasional hyperbole, a perfect example of the sterility of natural rights reasoning. Natural rights gains its power by divorcing itself from setting and particularity. One cannot smell or touch or taste natural rights. One can "see" them, but only metaphorically, and hear them, but only as words in an argument. Close one's eyes and listen to the sonorous tones of the Declaration—and there is nothing for the imagination—no color or motion. By turning to natural rights philosophy to justify rebellion the revolutionaries abjured the world of the senses in favor of logic and law.

For all its analytical symmetry, the Declaration discounted the sensuous complexity of the struggle, its ironies and contradictions. In this, the declaration resembled the early portraiture of Washington and the depiction of the virtuous victims in the engravings of the Boston Massacre and the Battle of Lexington. Republican virtue was representation without disconcerting detail. No warts.

Jefferson's litany of abuses was as much rhetorical device as were the effigies that the Sons of Liberty bore on poles, but it did not imperil the republican cause the way that the mob's behavior did. For the sensory enterprise of the mob was to make the plight of Everyman visible, to give Everyman the power to shout at authority, to let Everyman carry the effigy and light the bonfire. But what Jefferson proposed and the Congress adopted was the outline of a republican etiquette that diminished the inherent egalitarianism of the mob by reducing the role that the senses would play in the new nation's politics.

Republican Etiquette

After independence had been voted in Congress, John Adams wrote that it "ought to be commemorated, as the day of deliverance, by solemn acts of devotion to God almighty. It ought to be solemnized with pomp and parade, with shows, games, sports, guns, bells, bonfires and illuminations, from one end of this continent to the other, from this time forward forever more."[219] But the profusion of patriotic republican parades and fetes, speeches and toasts, that celebrated the sacred day in years to come had a uniformity and flatness that denied rather than opened up the senses. Even in the midst of war, the celebration of the Fourth in Philadelphia was "conducted with the greatest order and decorum."[220] Moderation—"sedateness"—was the hallmark of these celebrations, a proof that American republicanism would never descend into the very mob anarchy that the provincial officials had decried.[221] Women, Indians, and African Americans were systematically and pointedly excluded from these public displays of republican sentiment—just as they were from the political life of the new republic. To borrow the telling words of historian Simon Newman, the managed street performances of the last decade of the century "sanitized and de-radicalized many of the most popular rites and symbols . . . turning others into an everyday part of the political activity and identity of white male American citizens, shorn of much of their revolutionary significance."[222]

Truly republican sensate expressions must educate the eye and elevate the ear. Its images and sounds were demonstrations of loyalty to a new regime, all the more necessary to sustain the latter's fragile condition. For the monitors of this true republicanism, proper dress, including women's hairdos, should be simple and austere. When the British Army retreated from its year-long occupation of Philadelphia, in June of 1778, the revolutionary leadership encouraged the public scourging of British sympathizers. Their excess in personal adornment affronted the republicans. Women who had consorted with the British or went back and forth between the British in the city and the revolutionary army encamped at Valley Forge to the northwest of the city were condemned not as political backsliders but as whores. Beneath of windows of the City Tavern, where the revolutionaries feasted their return to power, a crowd paraded a young female volunteer, her hair pomaded in rude parody of aristocratic high style.[223] Like the scapegoat in the Bible, she represented the dangers of allowing too much decorative liberty to women, and by implication, to all those who deviated from the norm of republican simplicity.

In matters of visible personal performance once so freely expressed as dancing, the new sensory canons of republicanism dictated exclusion of someone "who has not taken a decisive part in favor of American Independence," according to the Dancing Assembly of Philadelphia. Even the old wild dances were to be replaced by ordered footwork with names like "Burgoyne's Defeat."[224] Public spaces were policed by revolutionary eyes and ears to prevent unorthodox sensory displays. Private spaces were manufactured so that the public need not be bothered by uncouth excess. At inns, "booths," whose high seat backs kept conversations from prying ears, stole space from the traditional long tables, where everyone could hear everyone else's words. Homespun was still honored, although it need no longer be rude; domestic textile factories could now duplicate the rich fabrics of English and Continental origin.[225] Republican discourse was not the same as provincial discourse, but its tone was as civil and polite.[226]

The tavern, once the source of the mob's energy and its headquarters, now a source of embarrassment to the revolutionary leadership, came under particular scrutiny in the effort to fashion a republican sensory etiquette. Philadelphia's Benjamin Rush, whose radical credentials were unimpeachable, condemned the rowdy fellowship that spilled from the tavern into the streets. Too-liberal laws had fostered unsightly licentiousness.[227] Such loud and coarse crowds undermined the legitimacy of the new republic; they had to be curbed, denounced, or avoided. As Thomas Tucker opined in 1784, "tumultuous proceedings are as unnecessary as they would be improper and ineffectual. Other means are in our hands, as much preferable as good order is to confusion, as peace to discord, as efficacy and security to disappointment and ruin."[228]

Even the Boston Massacre Oration changed its tone. As Dr. Thomas Welsh told a gathering on the Commons in 1783, "in prosecution of the subject, I presume I shall not offend a respectable part of my audience," the men who fought. They, like the men who battled tyranny in the English civil wars of the 1640s, like the Romans who defeated Hannibal, had labored through "a long and bloody war. " But now republicans had "to maintain [America's] dignity and importance among the kingdoms of the earth." In aid of this, "nature" had secured America's frontiers from European incursions. "Henceforth shall the American wilderness blossom as the rose, and every man shall sit under his vine and under his fig tree."[229]

Literary and philosophical metaphors, allusions, and references replaced the searing sensuousness of the first orations. To school the revolutionary mob to perform its solemn duties as a republican electorate, political leaders agreed that the voice of the people must be well modulated and their gatherings ordered and planned. Banners and badges that had once betokened a spontaneous and encompassing image of a revolutionary people became campaign miscellanea.[230]

In the 1790s, the opposing Democratic-Republican and Federalist partisans' antipathy was real, and rival demonstrators took to the streets, but the tricolor and white ribbons donned by opposing sides were conventions with little innovative or spontaneous sensory content. Civility had triumphed over sensory excess. When radical William Keteltas was paraded through the New York City streets in 1794 to embarrass the ruling Federalists, his supporters wore liberty caps and carried banners. That was the extent of their sensory assault.[231] The Democratic-Republican leadership had little use for mobs, and the Federalists wanted celebrations of order without "excess and indecency . . . rude mirth and hilarity."[232] Holdovers from the sensory wars of the 1760s, like the fiery Herman Husband, continued to engage in "apocalyptic imagery," but his was a voice, literally, in the wilderness.[233] Democrats like the farmer William Manning might claim autotopic authority for their political expressions, but their prose showed no inclination to sensuousness. Manning wrote in his *Key of Liberty* (1797), "I am not a man of learning . . . but I always thought it my duty to search into and see for myself in all matters. I was in the Concord fight and saw the first blood shed." But not even his "illustrations" were depictive.[234] Political wars there would be, but fought under the republican rules of etiquette.

•

By the end of the revolutionary era, republican sensory etiquette impressed conformity on the good citizen and enumerated a long list of people who were not to be seen or heard. Not everyone could march in the parade or give the address on the Fourth of July. Not everyone was fit to vote or hold office.

Women were supposed to retire to the domestic scene and watch the patriotic parade go by from the sitting-room window. African Americans fared worse. The young white female volunteer who played the harlot at the July Fourth 1778 Philadelphia mock parade became, in popular memory, a black woman, whose crime was no longer aristocratic pretension but disgusting and disfiguring sexuality. As Susan Klepp said of the altered local memory of the event, "blackness was becoming a permanent, racialized sign of exclusion and sexual threat," requiring and justifying the segregation of the many free blacks in Philadelphia.[235]

The answer to the question of how to attach people to one another and to the state lay in political good manners. In 1788, Timothy Dwight, one of the revolutionary era Yale graduates who found a calling in the pulpit and a penchant for poetry, delighted that "order shines, where blest confusion lay." Only Satan, one of the villains of his mock epic *The Triumph of Infidelity* (1788), assayed to "hurl round all realms" the old sensory chaos of the mob. Public virtue must show itself in polite sympathy and impartiality.[236] Only certain people were capable of exhibiting such republican qualities, and the exhibition must be orderly and disciplined. As the broadside advertising President Washington's visit to Boston in 1789 reminded the people of the town, "As this town is shortly to be honoured with a visit from the PRESIDENT of the United States: In order that we may pay our respects to him, in a manner whereby every inhabitant may see so illustrious and amiable a character, and to prevent the disorder and danger which must ensue from a great assembly of people without order, a Committee appointed by a respectable number of inhabitants, met for the purpose" of arranging the following parade route: each order of artisans, tradesmen, manufacturers to march behind its own flag, with the selectmen marching first, then the overseers of the poor, the treasurer and clerk, the magistrates, and so on, to the end of the procession, where the wheelwrights and seamen marched.[237] The seamen, so visible and audible in the revolutionary mob, made up the rear of the republican procession, where their shabby dress and uncouth manner would not be noticed. In 1790, Washington began to host weekly "levées," at which he greeted guests with a stately and distant bow instead of a republican handshake. Critics of his manners exploded that "the noblesse and courtiers" were making a comeback. The aristocratic pretensions of such gatherings were decried as a "deviation from the principles and spirit of our political institutions."[238] But even Washington's critics had adopted the denatured language of the new etiquette. They had no choice.

Coda

EARLY American history is enshrined in our nation's capitol, whose rotunda is graced by eight larger than life historical murals. They depict the landing of Columbus at the Island of Guanahani, West Indies, October 12, 1492; the discovery of the Mississippi by De Soto, 1541; the baptism of Pocahontas at Jamestown, Virginia, 1613; the embarkation of the Pilgrims at Delft Haven, Holland, July 22, 1620; the Declaration of Independence in Congress, at the Independence Hall, Philadelphia, July 4, 1776; the surrender of General Burgoyne at Saratoga, New York, October 17, 1777; the surrender of Lord Cornwallis at Yorktown, Virginia, October 19, 1781; and General George Washington resigning his commission to Congress as Commander in Chief of the Army at Annapolis, Maryland, December 23, 1783.[1]

All of the figures in these grand assemblages wear solemn faces. No one is smiling; no one seems angry—not even when they are surrendering an army. They seem to know, as do those who view the paintings, that they are part of history. Great events in history require a grand serenity of feature. The bodies are heroically proportioned. Their dramatic poses, even when we realize that the artist has invented the scene, almost compel our belief in the accuracy of the depiction. Our senses consent to the proposition; this is how history should look.

We have performed the same act of willing sensory illusion for the words of our founding fathers. Their addresses have become undying texts of universal principles, applicable at all times and in all places. Turning to their works with reverence, we worry, "Is the standard of reflection and conduct set by the founders too high?"[2] The surviving documentary evidence of their debates, the originals of the Declaration and the Constitution, endure under yellow glass, like paté in aspic in the foyer of the National Archives. Who could sense, from the reverential silence of the visitors to this tomblike hall, the clamor that had brought the nation into being? Should the history of past words sound like this?

I think not. If there is a lesson in the episodes I have traced in the preceding chapters, it is that history is always a lively and contested sensate process. Indeed, the story of these four sensory worlds is one of competition among groups for the primacy of their version of sensation and their vision of the world. The museum and the archive may house the evidence of the past, but it is up to the historians and the readers of history to breathe sensuous life into the sources. Then the original events again become a plenum, in which possibilities that time and mischance foreclosed present themselves. When we reject the too-easy history of the rotunda murals and the archival displays, we opt for a livelier past. We recover the warring sensory worlds of early America and open ourselves to the realization that the same sensory cues that motivate us to make decisions every day also influenced figures in our history.

That project grows more important each day. In our world, the repetition of uniform and bland stimuli—the strip mall, the office tower, the ramps on the interstate—pose a challenge to any history or historian of the senses.[3] Our sensate past is disappearing faster than we can recall it. Returning to the sites described in this book a visitor has to feel loss and sadness. One example suffices to make the point. Driving along NC 12 on the outer banks at Nags Head, North Carolina, opposite Roanoke Island, once an unspoiled vista of dunes, sea grasses, and ocean, you can no longer see the water; there are too many three-story condominiums perched on stilts above the sand dunes.

Perhaps this verdict is too apocalyptic, too final, too dyspeptic. Doing history will always require imagination, and imaginative history will always reveal contesting visions. By engaging in sensory history we can stimulate our powers of imagination to their fullest extent. The engaged imagination can then demand the rescue of historical sites from "wastelands . . . jetsammed with litter."[4] Such histories of the senses would fulfill the highest purpose of historical scholarship: to make the past live again.

Notes

Introduction

1. To be fair, the contest isn't simply between naive realism and deconstruction, even within literary theory. The aftermath of one of the most hilarious academic episodes in modern fiction, the presentation of Vita Leonne's paper "The Lesbian Phallus of Dorian Gray," has a sober side: "The argument at the [English department] seminar luncheon . . . was between two people who no longer spoke the same language. Weissmann, *pace* Cleanth Brooks, still believed in beauty and truth and all ye need know. Vita believed that the ode, the urn, and even the Greeks whose representations were posed around it all had the same ontological value, that they were all nodes of a vast, sticky web of signifiers, none of them any more important or 'real' than any other." James Hynes, *The Lecturer's Tale* (New York, 2001), 99.

2. Immediate sensate experience profoundly affects our lives-and always has. See e.g. Diane Ackerman, *A Natural History of the Senses* (New York, 1990).

3. A distinction that will reappear throughout the book: Sensation is the immediate encounter with sensory stimuli; the secondary processing I call *perception*.

4. John Updike and Charles Frazier, novelists commenting on history, in Mark C. Carnes, ed., *Novel/History: Historians and Novelists Confront America's Past (and Each Other)* (New York, 2001), 58 and 315, respectively. Novelists take liberties with what they find in archives or scholarly books, but historians take liberties, too. Novelists probe the human heart, but so do the best historians. It's the purpose that distinguishes the two enterprises. Bruce K. Smith, "How Sound Is Sound History?: A Reply to Mark Smith," *Journal of the Historical Society* 2 (2002), 313, argues for the importance of actual sound recovered from documents and the causal connection between such recovered sound and the actions of historical figures.

5. Susan Sontag, "About Hodgkin" [1995], in *Where the Stress Falls: Essays* (New York, 2001), 160.

6. See T. K. Johansen, *Aristotle on the Sense Organs* (Cambridge, 1998), 27 and after.

7. John Locke, *An Essay Concerning Human Understanding* [1690], ed. Russell Kirk (Chicago, 1960), 17, 57. On the history of the idea of the senses, see Constance Classen,

Worlds of Sense: Exploring the Senses in History and across Cultures (London, 1993), 3–10, 79–105.

8. See, generally, Nicholas Humphrey, *A History of the Mind* (New York, 1992). Reid thus anticipated by a hundred years the study of signs and systems of signs. On semiotics and communication of sense messages, see Thomas A. Sebeok, *A Sign Is Just a Sign* (Bloomington, Ind., 1991), 25–29.

9. James Boswell, *Life of Johnson* [1799], ed. R. W. Chapman (New York, 1998), 333. For the philosophical idealist's response that "this beauty . . . the sublimity of the sky . . . exists only for the appreciative observer," see Josiah Royce, *The Spirit of Modern Philosophy* (Boston, 1892), 354–55.

10. David Park, *The Fire within the Eye: A Historical Essay on the Nature and Meaning of Light* (Princeton, 1997), 230–69.

11. John Berger, *Ways of Seeing* (New York, 1973), 7.

12. Colin G. Calloway, *The World Turned Upside Down: Indian Voices from Early America* (Boston, 1994), 34.

13. *The Voyages of Jacques Cartier,* trans. Henry Percival Biggar, with an introduction by Ramsay Cook (Toronto, 1993), 20–21.

14. Mark Smith, *Listening to Nineteenth-Century America* (Chapel Hill, N.C., 2001), 262, 265. A similar point enfuses Richard Cullen Rath, "Worlds Chanted into Being: Soundways in Early America" (Ph.D. diss., Brandeis University, 2001), 7–9, 30–36, and after.

15. Winthrop D. Jordan, *Tumult and Silence at Second Creek: An Inquiry into a Civil War Slave Conspiracy,* rev. ed. (Baton Rouge, La., 1995), 167.

16. Classen, *Worlds of Sense,* 20.

17. Ibid., 20–36; Classen, *Aroma: The Cultural History of Smell* (London, 1994), 149; Georges Vigarello, *Concepts of Cleanliness: Changing Attitudes in France since the Middle Ages,* trans. Jean Birrell (Cambridge, 1988), 144–51; Alain Corbin, *The Foul and the Fragrant: Odor and the French Social Imagination* (Cambridge, Mass., 1986), 48–49; Gabrielle J. Dorland, *Scents Appeal: The Silent Persuasion of Aromatic Encounters* (Mendham, N.J., 1993), 116–17.

18. Alvar Núñez Cabeza de Vaca, *Relación* [1542], translated as *The Narrative of Cabeza de Vaca,* in John Franklin Jamison, ed., *Original Narratives of Early American History* (New York, 1907), 82. Eighty percent of all germs pass from individual to individual by touching. Philip M. Tierno, *The Secret Life of Germs* (New York, 2001), 10. Touching per se was not necessary to catch European airborne diseases; close proximity to a cough or sneeze would do.

19. Pedro de Castañeda de Nárjeda was the secretary for Francisco Coronado. See "The Narrative of the Expedition of Coronado," ed. Frederick W. Hodge, in idem, ed., *Spanish Explorers in the Southern United States, 1528–1543* (Austin, Tex., 1984).

20. Cabeza de Vaca, *Relación,* 99, 102; Philips Ball, *Bright Earth: Art and the Invention of Color* (New York, 2001), 130–31, 134.

21. Adam Smith, "Of the External Senses," in Adam Smith, *Essays on Philosophical*

Subjects [1790], ed. W. P. D. Wightman and J. C. Bryce (Oxford, 1980), 156–61. On touching, my source is Bob Klein, a certified practitioner of neuromuscular and craniosacral therapy.

22. The aroma and taste "wine wheel," created by Ann Noble in the Viniculture Department at the University of California, Davis, has more than a hundred words to describe the "nose" and the taste of wine, from metallic to floral.

23. *From the Earth to the Moon*, an HBO series (1999), episode 9.

24. Sabine MacCormack, "Limits of Understanding: Perceptions of Greco-Roman and Amerindian Paganism in Early Modern Europe," in Karen Ordahl Kupperman, ed., *America in European Consciousness, 1493–1750* (Chapel Hill, N.C., 1995), 79.

25. De Acosta quoted in Anthony Pagden, *European Encounters with the New World: From Renaissance to Romanticism* (New Haven, Conn., 1993), 53.

26. Pagden, *Encounters*, 51, 57, 60.

27. From the "humanistic geographer," the distinction between "scenery"—what we see—and "landscape"—what is—has become essential. Kenneth R. Olwig, "Landscape as a Contested Topos," in Paul C. Adams, Steven Hoelscher, and Karen E. Till, eds., *Textures of Place: Exploring Human Geographies* (Minneapolis, 2001), 94. Yi-Fu Tuan, *Topophilia: A Study of Environmental Perception, Attitudes, and Values* (Englewood Cliffs, N.J., 1974), 79, 132–33, argues that places are not just spaces but have human textures, that is, perceptual aspects as well as topographical ones.

28. See e.g. Don Gifford, *The Farther Shore: A Natural History of Perception, 1798–1984* (New York, 1990), 22–34.

29. Jonathan Hale, *The Old Way of Seeing: How Architecture Lost Its Magic (and How to Get It Back)* (Boston, 1994), 1–44, 148–73.

30. Burns does not think he is doing history: "The historical documentarian's vocation, whether in a film series or a book of this kind, is not precisely the same as the historian's . . . the documentary delights in recording and conveying . . . that there was once a time when people looked like this, or sounded like this." Burns, Jacket Notes, *Original Soundtrack Recording: The Civil War* (1990). I disagree; the historian of the senses is awfully close to the "documentarian."

31. I am not subscribing to the naive perceptual realism of the sort that biographer Catherine Drinker Bowen indulged during her trip to Leningrad to gather background material for her Tchaikovsky biography: "I think that I have never found my material so quickly nor made so direct a transition from the present to the past. Actually it was not I who accomplished this magic. Simply the scenes were before me and spoke in terms of their own authority." *Adventures of a Biographer* (Boston, 1946), 30–31.

32. George Humphrey Yetter, *Williamsburg Before and After: The Rebirth of Virginia's Colonial Capital* (Williamsburg, Va., 1988), 49–71.

33. Related to the author by one of the curators during a visit to the Indian wigwam outside the rebuilt settlement. On the general problem of recovering colonial dialects, see Jacob Bennett, "The Folk Speech of Maine: Clues to Colonial English," in Peter Benes and Jane M. Benes, eds., *American Speech: 1600 to the Present* (Boston, 1985), 27–34.

34. Joseph Conforti, *Imagining New England: Explorations of Regional Identity from the Pilgrims to the Mid-Twentieth Century* (Chapel Hill, N.C., 2001), 234–248.

35. These issues are in Richard Handler and Eric Gable, *The New History in an Old Museum: Creating the Past at Colonial Williamsburg* (Durham, N.C., 1997), esp. 78–101.

36. Karen E. Sutton, "Confronting Slavery Face to Face: A Twenty-first-Century Interpreter's Perspective on Eighteenth-Century Slavery," *Common-Place* 1, no. 4 (July 2001). (www.commonplace.org)

37. Howard Mansfield, *The Same Ax, Twice: Restoration and Renewal in a Throwaway Age* (Hanover, N.H., 2000), 32.

38. *Hagerstown (Maryland) Herald-Mail,* July 5, 1998.

39. John Tierney, "Going Where a Lot of Other Dudes with Really Great Equipment Have Gone Before," *New York Times Sunday Magazine,* July 26, 1998, 20.

40. Earl J. Hess, *The Union Soldier in Battle: Enduring the Ordeal of Combat* (Lawrence, Kans., 1997),15–19.

41. Peter Charles Hoffer, *The Devil's Disciples: Makers of the Salem Witchcraft Trials* (Baltimore, 1996). We are warned to beware the confessions of the "barefoot historians" in Karen Halttunen, "Self, Subject, and the 'Barefoot Historian,'" *Journal of American History* 89 (2002), 20–24. Claims to personal authority, she fears, too easily escape the confines of prefaces and cross over a "fine line" into textual narcissism. She notes that the term was coined by John Stilgoe to explain his own approach to historical eyewitnessing; see his *Alongshore* (New Haven, Conn., 1994), 8. On balance, I find Stilgoe's personal ruminations immensely attractive. Indeed, they started me on my journey (though I do not recall going barefoot).

42. Laurel Thatcher Ulrich, "A Pail of Cream," *Journal of American History* 89 (2002), 46.

43. Idem, *A Midwife's Tale: The Life of Martha Ballard, Based on Her Diary, 1785–1812* (New York, 1990), 33.

44. *Henry David Thoreau, An American Landscape: Selected Writings from His Journals,* ed. Robert L. Rothwell (New York, 1991), entry for June, 1845, 16–17.

45. Ibid., entry for March 5, 1858, 156–57.

46. See e.g. John Demos, "In Search of Reasons for Historians to Read Novels," *American Historical Review* 103 (1998), 1526–29, and the reply in Jonathan D. Spence, "Margaret Atwood and the Edges of History," ibid., 1522–25. Demos's prize-winning *The Unredeemed Captive: A Family Story from Early America* (New York, 1994) imagined what a young woman might be thinking as a representative of her family tried to ransom her, against her will, from the Indians who had taken her captive years before. Demos is not the only historian to invent conversations and interior dialogues. Stephen B. Oates, *The Approaching Fury: Voices of the Storm, 1820–1861* (New York, 1998), has done it wholesale.

47. Wilbur R. Jacobs, *Francis Parkman, Historian as Hero* (Austin, Tex., 1991), 89.

48. On Parkman and his notebook, see ibid., 5, 35–36, 92, 123.

49. Cf. Ian Steele, *Betrayals: Fort William Henry and the Massacre* (New York, 1990), 169 and after.

50. Francis Parkman, July 17, 1842, *The Journals of Francis Parkman,* ed. Mason Wade (New York, 1947), 1:47.

51. Francis Parkman, *Montcalm and Wolfe* [1884] (New York, 1995), 286. The fort has reappeared, restored by the Fort William Henry Corporation in 1956. David R. Starbuck, *The Great Warpath: British Military Sites from Albany to Crown Point* (Hanover, N.H., 1999), 89.

52. Samuel Eliot Morison, *The European Discovery of America: The Southern Voyages, A.D. 1492–1616* (New York, 1974), ix–x.

53. Authors of "microhistories" in particular aspire to a rich evocation of place and time. But there are obstacles here, too. Jill Lapore, "Historians Who Love Too Much: Reflections on Microhistory and Biography," *Journal of American History* 88 (2001), 129–44.

54. Lee Miller, *Roanoke: Solving the Mystery of the Lost Colony* (New York, 2000), 117.

55. Imagination is what makes historical writing possible: "This act of rudimentary interpretation—bordering indeed upon those instinctive mental reactions without which no sensation would become a perception." Marc Bloch, *The Historian's Craft* [1942], trans. Peter Putnam (New York, 1953), 52–53. We then become what Denis Donoghue called "epireaders" of texts—we hear the voices of the historical protagonists speak the words on the page. See *Ferocious Alphabets* (Boston, 1981), 146–47.

56. David McCally, *The Everglades: An Environmental History* (Gainesville, Fla., 1999), 176–81.

57. Simon Schama, *Dead Certainties (Unwarranted Speculations)* (New York, 1991), 322.

58. Sebeok, *A Sign Is Just a Sign,* 12–13. Semiotics is an academic black hole, sucking in all other disciplines, including the sciences. See e.g. Umberto Eco, *A Theory of Semiotics* (Bloomington, Ind., 1976), 9–14. On semiotics and historical documents, see Brian Stock, *Listening for the Text: On the Uses of the Past* (Baltimore, 1990), 95–112, and, generally, Robert Blair St. George, *Conversing by Signs: Poetics of Implication in Colonial New England Culture* (Chapel Hill, N.C., 1998).

59. Frederick Jackson Turner, "The Significance of the Frontier in American History" (1893), in George Rogers Taylor, ed., *The Turner Thesis,* 3d ed. (Lexington, Mass., 1972), 8.

60. Ray Allen Billington, *Frederick Jackson Turner: Historian, Scholar, Teacher* (New York, 1973), 449–71.

61. The plan laid out in Alain Corbin, *Time, Desire, and Horror: Towards a History of the Senses,* trans. Jean Birrell (Cambridge, 1995), 181–95.

62. Alain Corbin, *Village Bells: Sound and Meaning in the Nineteenth-Century French Countryside* (New York, 1998), 3–44. David Cressy likens the tolling of the bells in early modern England to a "vocabulary" of celebration whose "timing, duration, volume, intensity, and panache" varied with the occasion and the bell ringer. *Bonfires and Bells: National Memory and the Protestant Calendar in Elizabethan and Stuart England* (London, 1989), 68.

63. Later published as "American Businessmen and the Japan Trade, 1931–1939, A Case Study of Attitude Formation," *Pacific Historical Review* 41 (1972), 189–205.

Chapter 1 · Brave New Worlds

1. See e.g. Leslie Brothers, *Friday's Footprint: How Society Shapes the Human Mind* (New York, 1997), and Howard Gardiner, *The Mind's New Science: A History of the Cognitive Revolution* (New York, 1987).

2. There is a good discussion in Robert Jervis, *Perception and Misperception in International Politics* (Princeton, 1976), 117 202.

3. Peter Gould and Rodney White, *Mental Maps*, rev. ed. (Boston, 1986), 3–30.

4. One of the reasons for the explosion of travel anthologies in England in the 1580s was that the works of the Spanish and French were not trusted and that England's rivals kept much of what they found secret. The English publications were part of a propaganda war against Spain. David Beers Quinn, ed., *The Roanoke Voyages, 1584–1590* (New York, 1991), 1:5–9, 2:718–25.

5. See e.g. Anthony Grafton, *New Worlds, Ancient Texts: The Power of Tradition and the Shock of Discovery* (Cambridge, Mass., 1992); John F. Moffit and Santiago Sebastián, *O Brave New People: The European Invention of the American Indian* (Albuquerque, 1996), 266–336; Jack P. Greene, *The Intellectual Construction of America: Exceptionalism and Identity from 1492 to 1800* (Chapel Hill, N.C., 1992); the essays in Karen Ordahl Kupperman, ed., *America in European Consciousness, 1493–1750* (Chapel Hill, N.C., 1995).

6. Anthony Pagden, *The Fall of Natural Man: The American Indian and the Origins of Comparative Ethnology* (Cambridge, 1982); 12: analogy, description, samples, classification—all depend on what "could be seen."

7. Grafton, *New Worlds, Ancient Texts;* Stephen Greenblatt, *Marvelous Possessions: The Wonder of the New World* (Chicago, 1991); Tvestan Todorov, *The Conquest of America: The Question of the Other* (New York, 1984); Eric R. Wolf, *Europe and the People without History* (Berkeley, 1982).

8. Yi-Fu Tuan, *Topophilia: A Study of Environmental Perception, Attitudes, and Values* (Englewood Cliffs, N.J., 1974), 66.

9. Charles Hudson, "The Hernando de Soto Expedition," in Hudson and Carmen Chavez Tesser, eds., *The Forgotten Centuries: Indians and Europeans in the American South, 1521–1704* (Athens, Ga., 1993), 74–103; David Ewing Duncan, *Hernando De Soto: A Savage Quest in the Americas* (New York, 1995).

10. Neal Salisbury, *Manitou and Providence: Indians, Europeans, and the Making of New England* (New York, 1982), 34–39; Daniel Richter, *Facing East from the Indian Country: A Native History of Early America* (Cambridge, Mass., 2001), 14. By convention, in lower-case letters, manitou is spiritual power; every living being has it. In upper case, Manitou is a demigod, the visible embodiment of power.

11. James H. Merrell, *The Indians' New World: Catawbas and Their Neighbors from European Contact through the Era of Removal* (Chapel Hill, N.C., 1989), 12.

12. See e.g. Alden T. Vaughan, "Early English Paradigms for New World Natives," in Vaughan, *Roots of American Racism: Essays on the Colonial Experience* (New York, 1995), 34–54. Some of these cognitive reorderings were more favorable than others. Later, when

time, contact, and circumstance had changed, the English would redeploy words to justify altered political interests. E.g. Peter Hulme, *Colonial Encounters: Europe and the Native Caribbean, 1492–1797* (London, 1986), 172. But Hulme mistakes the effect for the cause—the murderous wordplay came at the end of the story.

13. With all due respect to three magnificent essays, I do not agree with the late dating of mutual mistrust in Joyce Chaplin, *Subject Matter: Technology, the Body, and Science on the Anglo-American Frontier, 1500–1676* (Cambridge, Mass., 2001), Karen Ordahl Kupperman, *Indians and English: Facing Off in Early America* ((Ithaca, N.Y., 2000), and Michael Leroy Oberg, *Dominion and Civility: English Imperialism and Native America, 1585–1685* (Ithaca, N.Y., 2001). It did not take generations for the process of sensory degradation and perceptual derogation to begin. I do not, however, subscribe to the extermination-from-the-outset thesis of Richard Drinnon, *Facing West: The Metaphysics of Indian Hating and Empire Building* (Minneapolis, 1980) or Francis Jennings, *The Invasion of America: Indians, Colonialism, and the Cant of Conquest* (New York, 1975). There was a time of genuine wonder at sensory novelties.

14. See e.g. John Smith, *Generall History of Virginia* [1624], in Philip L. Barbour, ed., *The Complete Works of Captain John Smith* (Chapel Hill, N.C., 1986), 2:296.

15. Even when, for a time, the relative weakness of the Europeans permitted a "middle ground" on which native and newcomer had to listen to one another's voices and respect one another's customs, neither side truly saw the world as the other did. On the middle ground, see Richard White, *The Middle Ground: Indians, Empires, and Republics in the Great Lakes Region, 1650–1815* (Cambridge, 1991), 52–55 and after.

16. John Heckwelder, *An Account of the History, Manners, and Customs of the Indian Nations, Who Once Inhabited Pennsylvania and the Neighboring States* (Philadelphia, 1819), 54–59; reprinted as "An Indian Tradition of the first Arrival of the Dutch on Manhatten [sic] Island," *Collections of the New-York Historical Society* (1841) 1:69–74. Karen Ordahl Kupperman excerpted a portion of the latter in the second edition of her *Major Problems in American Colonial History* (Boston, 2000), 30–32.

17. Peter Charles Hoffer, *The Brave New World: A History of Early America* (Boston, 2000), 110–14, 131–35, 215–16.

18. Indian oral culture was basic to all Indian social life. Colin Calloway, *New Worlds for All: Indians, Europeans, and the Remaking of Early America* (Baltimore, 1997), 132; idem, ed., *The World Turned Upside Down: Indian Voices from Early America* (Boston, 1994), 12.

19. Leslie Marmon Silko, *Storyteller* (New York, 1981), 247.

20. The Indians used piles of rocks, post holes, belts of shells, deerskin pictographs, and other aids to memory when telling historical stories. See e.g. Kupperman, *Indians and English*, 91.

21. James Axtell, *Natives and Newcomers: The Cultural Origins of North America* (New York, 2001), 164–67; Daniel Richter, *The Ordeal of the Longhouse: The Peoples of the Iroquois League in the Era of European Colonization* (Chapel Hill, N.C.,1992), 24–29; Salisbury, *Manitou and Providence*, 34–39.

22. Silko, *Storyteller,* 38.

23. Axtell, *Beyond 1492: Encounters in Colonial North America* (New York, 1992), 63–70.

24. James H. Merrell, *Catawba* (New York, 1999), 40–41. The closing up of space and time between scholarly narrator and historical subject is a perceptual as well as a literary endeavor. So, "Read over the shoulder of Edward Dromgoole a letter . . . Eavesdrop as James Finley urges a younger itinerant to preach . . . Listen as John Brooks sulks" are stage directions for readers so that they can join the historian as she goes back to the past. Christine Leigh Heyrman, *Southern Cross: The Beginnings of the Bible Belt* (New York, 1997), 234.

25. Roger Williams, paraphrased in Laurel Thatcher Ulrich, *The Age of Homespun* (New York, 2001), 54.

26. Josephine Paterek, *Encyclopedia of American Indian Costume* (New York, 1904), 49–51.

27. William Wood, *New England's Prospect* [1634], ed. Alden T. Vaughan (Amherst, Mass., 1977), 85.

28. Kupperman, *Indians and English,* 64.

29. George Percy, "Observations, in Philip Barbour, ed., *The Jamestown Voyages under the First Charter, 1606–1609* (Cambridge, 1969), 1:136.

30. Ulrich, *Homespun,* 55.

31. George Chicken, "Journal of the March of the Carolinians into the Cherokee Mountains, in the Yemassee Indian War, 1715–1716," *Yearbook of the City of Charleston* (1894), 330, 332; Laurier Turgeon, "Beads, Bodies, and Regimes of Value in France and North America, ca. 1500–1650," MacNeil Center for Early American Studies, February 9, 2001, used with permission.

32. Ferdinando Gorges, "A Brief Narration," in David B. Quinn and Alison M. Quinn, eds., *The English New England Voyages, 1602–1608* (London, 1983), 350. Black was the universal color of mourning among northeastern Indians. Erik R. Seeman, "Reading Indians' Deathbed Scenes: Ethnohistorical and Representational Approaches," *Journal of American History* 88 (2001), 35.

33. Merrell, *Into the American Woods,* 169.

34. [Edward Winslow], *A Relation or Journal of the Beginning and Proceeding of the English Plantation settled at Plymouth* [London, 1622], ed. Dwight B. Heath (New York, 1963), 56.

35. James Adair, *History of the American Indians* [1775] (New York, 1960), 408.

36. Nancy Shoemaker, "How Indians Got to Be Red," *American Historical Review* 102 (1997), 625–44; Alden T. Vaughan, "From White Man to Redskin: Changing Anglo-American Perceptions of the American Indian," *American Historical Review* 87 (1982), 917–53; Chaplin, *Subject Matter,* 138–39.

37. "A Relation of Maryland"[1635], in Clayton Colman Hall, ed., *Original Narratives of Early American History: Narratives of Early Maryland* (New York, 1910), 88. Father John White, ministering to the Indians in early Maryland, found their blue and red face paint ghastly. Kupperman, *Indians and English,* 62.

38. Percy, "Observations," in Barbour, ed., *Jamestown Voyages*, 1:137.

39. Gabriel Archer, "Account of Captain Bartholomew Gosnold's Voyage to 'North Virginia'" [1602], in Quinn and Quinn, eds., *The New England Voyages*, 1:103; Kupperman, *Indians and English*, 58–69.

40. Calvin Martin, *Keepers of the Game: Indian-Animal Relations and the Fur Trade* (Berkeley, 1978); Richard Cullen Rath, "Worlds Chanted into Being: Soundways in Early America" (Ph.D. diss., Brandeis University, 2001),115–18.

41. "With Indians insisting that formal talks be in their tongue, that chore [of overcoming the language barrier] usually fell to the colonists." Merrell, *Into the American Woods*, 182–83. But at first, signs would be enough.

42. On giving, taking, and the social meanings of exchanges, see Axtell, *Natives and Newcomers*, 22, 39–41; Merrell, *The Indians' New World*, 31, 149–53; White, *Middle Ground*, 112–19.

43. "The formation of sacred circles of spectators" was a common feature in the creation of ritual space. Kathleen J. Bragdon, *Native People of Southern New England, 1500–1650* (Norman, Okla., 1996), 219. Surviving native depictions and visitors' accounts of ceremonial group dancing shows a circular movement, sometimes the entire group joining, sometimes an individual dancing surrounded by a circle of villagers. Other ceremonies around the council or sacred fire took the circular shape.

44. White, *Middle Ground*, 20–23.

45. In a 1633 Montagnais story the French priests offered the Indians the Host and the sacramental wine. The Indians thought they were tasting blocks of wood and human blood. Richter, *Facing East from the Indian Country*, 12.

46. On Indian cannibalism in wartime, see Ian Steele, *Warpaths: Invasions of North America* (New York, 1994), 183; Kupperman, *Indians and English*, 47–48; 113–14.

47. Formal oratory had its own rules. Merrell, *Into the American Woods*, 212–14. Speeches could last for hours, and listeners were respectful, taking turns and murmuring assent.

48. Edmond Atkin, "Report and Plan" [1755], in Wilbur R. Jacobs, ed., *The Appalachian Indian Frontier: The Edmond Atkin Report and Plan of 1755* (Lincoln, Nebr., 1967), 10.

49. Bragdon, *Native People*, 173–74; James Axtell, *The Invasion Within: The Contest of Cultures in Colonial North America* (New York, 1985), 87–88; Sandra M. Gustafson, *Eloquence Is Power: Oratory and Performance in Early America* (Chapel Hill, N.C., 2000), 34–35.

50. Smith, *Generall History of Virginia*, in Barbour, ed., *Works of Smith*, 2: 149–50.

51. Percy, "Observations," in Barbour, ed., *Jamestown Voyages* 1:143.

52. John Hays and Benjamin Franklin, respectively, quoted in Merrell, *Into the American Woods*, 103, 258.

53. "Taste was always a trial or a test." Diane Ackerman, *A Natural History of the Senses* (New York, 1990),128.

54. Peter Mancall, *Deadly Medicine: Indians and Alcohol in Early America* (Ithaca,

N.Y., 1995), notes that the Indians fitted the drinking of alcohol into other customs and rarely got drunker than their white companions.

55. Bruce G. Trigger, "Early Native American Responses to European Contact: Romantic versus Rationalistic Interpretations," *Journal of American History* 77 (1991), 1195–1215; Turgeon, "French Fishers, Fur Traders, and Amerindians during the Sixteenth Century: History and Archeology," *William and Mary Quarterly,* 3d ser. 50 (1998), 585–610; Richter, *Facing East from Indian Country,* 44 45.

56. Turgeon, "Beads."

57. Smith, "A True Relation," in Barbour, ed., *Works of Smith,* 1:263. Glass-making, including beads, was one of the crafts practiced at Jamestown, although the beads Smith had on hand probably came from England, Venice, or Portugal. William M. Kelso, *Jamestown Rediscovery, I: Search for the 1607 Fort* (Jamestown, Va., 1995), 18.

58. [Winslow], *Relation,* 56.

59. John White, "Narrative of the Voyage [1587]," in David Beers Quinn, ed., *The Roanoke Voyages, 1584–1590* (New York, 1991), 2:526–27.

60. Roger Williams to John Winthrop, June 2, 1637, in *The Correspondence of Roger Williams,* ed. Glenn LaFantasie (Hanover, N.H., 1988), 1:83–84.

61. William Bradford, [Journal] *Of Plymouth Plantation (1620–1647),* ed. Samuel Eliot Morison (New York, 1966), 96.

62. See e.g. Merrell, *Into the American Woods,* 187–89, 195, 206–7.

63. Percy, "Discourse," in Barbour, ed., *Jamestown Voyages,* 135.

64. Archer, "Account," in Quinn and Quinn, eds., *The New England Voyages,* 133–34.

65. James Axtell, "Babel of Tongues," in Edward G. Gray and Norman Fiering, eds., *The Language Encounter in the Americas, 1492–1800* (New York, 2000), 20–21.

66. Each society, each culture, has its own way of making sense of its world. Marshall Sahlins, *Islands of History* (Chicago, 1985), 34.

67. Thomas Morton, *New English Canaan* [1637], ed. Jack Dempsey (Scituate, Mass., 2000), 40, 41.

68. John Lawson, *A New Voyage to Carolina* (London, 1709), 26. The English were convinced that the natives could even sense changes in the weather before it occurred. Hulme, *Colonial Encounters,* 100; Rath, "Worlds Chanted into Being," 81–82.

69. Frederic W. Gleach, *Powhatan's World and Colonial Virginia: A Conflict of Cultures* (Lincoln, Nebr., 1997), 33.

70. Quinn, ed., *Roanoke Voyages,* 2:895; Plymouth Hall Historical Museum, native inhabitants display; Richter, *Ordeal of the Longhouse,* 1.

71. Neal Salisbury, *Manitou and Providence,* 37–39.

72. Colin M. Turnbull, *The Human Cycle* (New York, 1983), 50–51 and after; Paul Rodaway, *Sensuous Geographies: Body, Sense, and Place* (London, 1994), 108–13.

73. Smith, "A True Relation," in Barbour, ed., *Works of Smith,* 1:188. On the difference between English and Indian maps of the world, see Cynthia Jean Van Zandt, "Negotiating Settlement: Colonialism, Cultural Exchange, and Conflict in Early Colonial Atlantic North America, 1580–1660" (Ph.D. diss., University of Connecticut, 1998).

74. William Wood, *New England Prospect* [1634], ed. Alden T. Vaughan (Amherst, Mass., 1977), 101.

75. Bobby Lake-Thom, *Spirits of the Earth: A Guide to Native American Nature Symbols, Stories, and Ceremonies* (New York, 1997), 198.

76. Such consciousness of history verged on historylessness. Sahlins, *Islands,* 51. But local histories (or recent memories) were more precise. That is, a particular village elder would know exactly how many years earlier the village had failed in the hunt or the crops had failed.

77. Åke Hultkrantz, *Belief and Worship in Native North America* (Syracuse, N.Y., 1981), 120, 123, 139; Timothy Silver, *A New Face on the Countryside: Indians, Colonists, and Slaves in South Atlantic Forests, 1500–1800* (New York, 1990), 41.

78. F. Scott Momaday, *House Made of Dawn* (New York, 1968),12.

79. Ibid., 33.

80. Simon Ortiz, quoted in Peter Matthiessen, *Indian Country* (New York, 1984), 10–11.

81. Lake-Thom, *Spirits of the Earth,* 15. "But there is still another dimension to the limitation of our own system of thought suggested by the contrasts of a pensée sauvage: not only the relativity of our notion of 'objectivity' but the absolute sense of a world-in-itself that lies behind it. The evident difference between common average Western empirical judgments and Hawaiians' or New Guineans' is that ours suppose a world from which spirit and subjectivity were long ago evacuated." Sahlins, *How 'Natives' Think: About Captain Cook, for Example* (Chicago, 1995), 163.

82. Bragdon, *Native People,* 190–91.

83. John Demos, *The Unredeemed Captive: A Family Story from Early America* (New York, 1994), 240.

84. Quoted in Kupperman, *Indians and English,* 129.

85. Morton, *New English Canaan,* 107.

86. Thomas Shepard, *The Clear Sun-Shine of the Gospel Breaking Forth Upon the Indians of New-England* (London, 1647), 10. *Black coat* was a "disparaging term for a minister." Richard M. Lederer Jr., *Colonial American English* (Essex, Conn., 1985), 31. It is entirely possible that the Indian relating the dream to the black-coated ministers is subtly teasing them.

87. Gleach, *Powhatan's World,* 38.

88. Miantonomi's statement appears in Lyon Gardiner's *Relation, Massachusetts Historical Society Collections,* 3d ser. (1833) 3:154.

89. Robert Fox, ed., *Thomas Harriot: An Elizabethan Man of Science* (Aldershot, Eng., 2000).

90. Oberg, *Dominion and Civility,* 9.

91. Thomas Harriot, *A Brief and True Report,* in Quinn, ed., *Roanoke Voyages,* 1:318.

92. Ibid., 321, 323, 324.

93. Ibid., 333–41, 372–73.

94. Ibid., 345. The strange attracted the eye, but Harriot had no illusions. England was better. For a parallel, see Clifford Geetz, *Works and Lives: The Anthropologist as Au-*

thor (Stanford, Calif., 1988), 71. The Elizabethan English elite was especially ethnocentric. Howard Mumford Jones, *O Strange New World: American Culture, the Formative Years* (New York, 1967), 162–93.

95. Sidney Perkowitz, *The Empire of Light: A History of Discovery in Science and Art* (Washington, D.C., 1996), 126–28.

96. David Park, *The Fire within the Eye: A Historical Essay on the Nature and Meaning of Light* (Princeton, 1997), 172–73.

97. Bacon also wanted "sound houses" and "perfume houses." Quoted in Leigh Eric Schmidt, *Hearing Things: Religion, Illusion, and the American Enlightenment* (Cambridge, Mass., 2000), 22; on Bacon and the general project of using the New World as an laboratory for investigation of nature, see Chaplin, *Subject Matter,* 40–41.

98. Percy, "Discourse," in Barbour, ed., *Jamestown Voyages,* 1:129. On the meaning of events in the heavens for the English, see Keith Thomas, *Religion and the Decline of Magic* (New York, 1971), 298–300.

99. John Witthoft, "Archeology as a Key to the Colonial Fur Trade," *Minnesota History* 40 (1966), 203–9.

100. Percy, "Discourse," in Barbour, ed., *Jamestown Voyages,* 1:130.

101. Quoted in Van Zandt, "Negotiating Settlement," 49.

102. Percy, "Discourse," in Barbour, ed., *Jamestown Voyages,* 1:130.

103. Alfred W. Crosby, *The Measurement of Reality: Quantification and Western Society, 1250–1600* (Cambridge, 1997), 227–40.

104. Harriot, *Report* in Quinn, ed., *Roanoke Voyages,* 1:321.

105. Smith, "A True Relation," in Barbour, ed., *Jamestown Voyages* 1:181. Without realizing it, Smith had adopted the postures and role of the Indian orator, using gestures and mien to convey the importance of his words. Recognizing that he (inadvertently) adopted the correct postures and intonations for the orator, the Pamunky responded favorably to his performance, as he recalled, and "with kind speeches and bread [Opechancanough] requited me." (ibid.)

106. Harriot, *Report,* in Quinn, ed., *Roanoke Voyages,* 1:323.

107. Ibid., 319.

108. Pagden, *European Encounters,* 51–87.

109. Bradford, *Of Plymouth Plantation,* ed. Samuel Eliot Morison (New York, 1952), 62. Bradford feared what he could not see.

110. Walter Raleigh quoted in Simon Schama, *Landscape and Memory* (New York, 1995), 314.

111. Arthur Barlow, "Discourse of the First Voyage to Virginia" [1584], in Quinn, ed., *Roanoke Voyages,*1:94.

112. Harriot, *Report,* in Quinn, ed., *Roanoke Voyages,* 1:371.

113. Percy, "Discourse," in Barbour, ed., *Jamestown Voyages,* 1:131.

114. On bows and arrows, see Chaplin, *Subject Matter,* 102.

115. Ralph Lane to Sir Francis Walsingham, August 12, 1585, in Quinn, ed., *Roanoke Voyages* 2:199.

116. Harriot, *Report,* in Quinn, ed., *Roanoke Voyages,* 1:317–18, 325, 327.

117. Smith, *Generall History of Virginia,* in Barbour, ed., *Works of Smith,* 2:101.

118. [Winslow], *Relation,* 16.

119. Smith, "Prospectus for the Generall History" [1623], in Barbour, ed., *Works of Smith,* 2:16.

120. Harriot was no soldier, but many of the men Raleigh sent with Harriot were veterans of the Irish wars. They saw the colony as an outpost against Spanish expansion in the as yet undeclared war for American empire. Quinn, ed., *Roanoke Voyages,* 2:717–23, 772–78.

121. The action of the wind, waves, and rain caused the dunes to migrate, moving landward, leaving treacherous low tides at the edges of the barrier beaches. Bill Perry, *A Sierra Club Naturalist's Guide to the Middle Atlantic Coast* (San Francisco, 1985), 77–91.

122. Barlow, "Discourse," in Quinn, ed., *Roanoke Voyages,* 1:95.

123. Hakluyt's *Principal Navigations, Voyages, Traffiques, and Discoveries of the English Nation,* the first volume of which was published in London in 1589 and followed by two more volumes in 1598 and 1600, became the bible of the explorers, their backers, and the general reading public. Much in the collected journals, letters, and reports is typically sensory. "In this island" off the Coast of Sierra Leone, the diarist of the first John Hawkins voyage to Africa and the Caribbean reported, "we sojourned unto the one and twentieth of December [1564] where having taken certain Negroes, and as much of their fruits, rice, and millet, as we could well carry away . . . we departed." "Voyage Made by Master John Hawkins . . . to the Coast of Guinea, and the Indies of Nova Hispania," in Irwin R. Blacker, ed., *Hakluyt's Voyages* (New York, 1965), 125.

124. Richard Hakluyt (the younger), *Discourse of Western Planting* [1584], in Peter C. Mancall, ed., *Envisioning America: English Plans for the Colonization of North America, 1580–1640* (Boston, 1995), 46–47.

125. The Indians practiced controlled burning of brush, "cool" fires that cleared forests for planting, while replenishing the nutrients in the soil. William Cronon, *Changes in the Land: Indians, Colonists and the Ecology of New England* (New York, 1983), 47–51.

126. Giles Milton, *Big Chief Elizabeth: How England's Adventurers Gambled and Won the New World* (London, 2000), 112.

127. Quoted in Merrell, *Into the American Woods,* 25.

128. Smith, *The Acoustic World of Early Modern England,* 40–95.

129. Schama, *Landscape and Memory,* 142–58. The trial of the witches of Peddle Forest, in Lancashire in 1612, was perhaps the most noteworthy single English witchcraft case. In it, the forest itself was a leading character—people in the village were afraid to go into the woods.

130. [Winslow], *Relation,* 46.

131. William Stacey, "A True Repertory," in Louis B. Wright, ed., *A Voyage to Virginia in 1609* (Charlottesville, Va., 1964), 4.

132. Quinn, ed., *Roanoke Voyages,* 2:585.

133. White, "Narrative of the 1590 Voyage," in Quinn, ed., *Roanoke Voyages,* 2:613.

134. Drake, "A Summary and True Discourse of Sire Frances Drake West Indian Voyage," in Quinn, ed., *Roanoke Voyages,* 1:297. On trumpets and other devices to warn of danger and signal position, see Rath, "Worlds Chanted into Being," 112–13.

135. David Cressy, *Bonfires and Bells* (London, 1989), 80–81.

136. White, "Voyage," 1590, in Quinn, ed., *Roanoke Voyages,* 2:585.

137. See e.g. [Winslow], *Relation,* 33, 43, 23.

138. Drake, "Summary and True Discourse," in Quinn, ed., *Roanoke Voyages,* 1:300.

139. The 1580s ushered in the age of the "estate map" in England. It showed precise boundaries and holdings. Andrew McRae, *God Speed the Plow: the Representation of Agrarian England, 1500–1660* (New York, 1996), 189–92.

140. Van Zandt, "Negotiating Settlement," 32, 35; John Noble Wilford, *The Mapmakers* (New York, 1981), 56–88. The Indians had maps. These used pictographs and other designs to indicate the relation of features of nature to villages and people's territories. But precise measurement of distance was not a characteristic of Indian maps.

141. Sara Stidstone Gronim, "Geography and Persuasion," *William and Mary Quarterly,* 3d ser. 58 (2001), 374–75.

142. In fact, the monstrous Indian seems to resemble the engraver Theodore de Bry's version of John White's drawing of a Roanoke warrior. As far as the English were concerned, images of Indians were interchangeable. Had the Powhatans seen the map illustration they would have identified the tattooing, the decoration, and the hair style as belonging to a coastal Roanoke instead of a Powhatan. Indian diplomacy and warfare required visual identification of friends and enemies from a safe distance.

143. Van Zandt, "Negotiating Settlement," 61.

144. Chaplin, *Subject Matter,* 150.

145. Smith, *Acoustic World,* 313, 328.

146. Axtell, "Bable of Tongues," 19.

147. Oberg, *Dominion and Civility,* 17, 22.

148. Roger Williams, "A Key into the Language of America," ed. J. Hammond Trumbull, in *The Complete Writings of Roger Williams* (New York, 1963), 1:23.

149. The best modern account of what went wrong at Roanoke is David Beers Quinn, *Set Fair for Roanoke: Voyages and Colonies, 1584–1606* (Chapel Hill, N.C.,1986).

150. On pidgins and creoles, see Mark Sebba, *Contact Languages: Pidgins and Creoles* (New York, 1997), 37–56, 70–133.

151. Ira Berlin, *Many Thousands Gone: The First Two Centuries of Slavery in North America* (Cambridge, Mass., 1998), 29–46.

152. Samuel Eliot Morison, *The European Discovery of America: The Southern Voyages, A.D. 1942–1616* (New York, 1974), 67, 94.

153. Frances Karttunen, "Interpreters Snatched from the Shore: The Successful and the Others," in Gray and Fiering, eds., *Language Encounter,* 215–29.

154. Daniel H. Usner Jr., *Indians, Settlers, and Slaves in a Frontier Exchange Economy: The Lower Mississippi Valley before 1783* (Chapel Hill, 1992), 258–59.

155. Ives Goddard, "The Use of Pidgins and Jargons on the East Coast of North America," in Gray and Fiering, eds., *Language Encounter,* 61–75.

156. Axtell, "Babel of Tongues," in ibid., 36; Mark Catesby, *The Natural History of Carolina, Florida, and the Bahama Islands . . . ,* 2 vols., (London, 1731–43), 1:xvi.

157. Edward G. Gray, *New World Babel: Languages and Nations in Early America* (Princeton, 1999), 3–27; Gray, "Introduction," in Gray and Fiering, eds., *The Language Encounter* 9; Axtell, "Babel of Tongues," in ibid., 16.

158. On Manteo's role, Alden T. Vaughan, "Sir Walter Ralegh's Indian Interpreters, 1584–1618," *William and Mary Quarterly,* 3d ser. 59 (2002), 343–57.

159. Axtell, "Babel of Tongues," 36; Merrell, *Into the American Woods,* 184–85.

160. George Horse Capture, quoted in Gleach, *Powhatan's World,* 106.

161. Pagden, *European Encounters with the New World,* 17–23.

162. Patricia Seed, *Ceremonial Processions in Europe's Conquest of the New World, 1492–1640* (New York, 1995), 69–98.

163. Todorov, *Conquest,* 27 and after.

164. Axtell, *The Invasion Within,* 132.

165. Lane, "Letter to Raleigh," in Quinn, ed., *Roanoke Voyages,* 1:277

166. Edward G. Gray, *New World Babel,* 43–84.

167. Vaughan, "Ralegh's Indian Interpreters," 355–56.

168. Gray, *New World Babel,* 42, 51. Neal Salisbury, "Squanto: Last of the Patuxets," in David Sweet and Gary Nash, eds., *Struggle and Survival in Colonial America* (Berkeley, 1981), 228–44.

169. Smith, *Acoustic World,* 292. For the ethnocentrism, see Winthrop Jordan, *White over Black: American Attitudes towards the Negro, 1550–1812* (Chapel Hill, N.C., 1968), 41–43.

170. Smith, *Acoustic World,* 310; Lane, "Discourse," in Quinn, ed., *Roanoke Voyages,* 1:278.

171. [Winslow], *Relation,* 55.

172. Smith, *Generall History of Virginia,* in Barbour, ed., *Works of Smith,* 2:149.

173. Gordon M. Sayre, *Le Sauvage Américains: Representations of Native Americans in French and English Colonial Literature* (Chapel Hill, N.C., 1997), 190–216.

174. Samuel Purchas, *Hakluytus Postumus; or, Purchas His Pilgrimes* [1625], 20 vols. (reprint ed., New York, 1965), 1:486.

175. Kelso, *Jamestown Rediscovery I,* 16–17.

176. Morton, *New England Canaan,* 43.

177. Williams, "A Key into the Language of America," in Trumbull, ed., *The Complete Writings of Roger Williams,* 1:160.

178. A useful guide to English heraldry is Stephen Friar and John Ferguson, *Basic Heraldry* (London, 1993).

179. White, "Voyage of 1587," in Quinn, ed., *Roanoke Voyages,* 2:511.

180. Ibid., 2:525–26.

181. Peter Charles Hoffer, *Law and People in Colonial America,* 2d ed. (Baltimore, 1998), 52–53.

182. On Hakluyt, see David Armitage, *The Ideological Origins of the British Empire* (Cambridge, 2000), 72–81.

183. From 1580 to 1583, Ireland writhed in the grip of civil war. See Nicholas P. Canny, "Identity formation in Ireland: The Emergence of the Anglo-Irish," in Canny and Anthony Pagden, ed., *Colonial Identity in the Atlantic World, 1500–1800* (Princeton, 1987), 159–212; Canny, "The Marginal Kingdom: Ireland as a Problem in the First English Empire" in Bernard Bailyn and Philip D. Morgan, eds., *Strangers within the Realm: Cultural Margins of the First British Empire* (Chapel Hill, N.C., 1991), 35–66; and John McGurk, *The Elizabethan Conquest of Ireland* (Manchester, Eng., 1997).

184. Harriot, *Report,* in Quinn, ed., *Roanoke Voyages,* 1:381.

185. Lane, "Discourse," in Quinn, ed., *Roanoke Voyages,* 1:271. The same grievance was lodged against the Irish during the war they waged from 1579 against the English. The Irish attacked from ambush and then vanished. Lane had seen the results first hand when he served in Ireland.

186. Waymouth, "The Jewel of Artes," in Quinn and Quinn, eds., *New England Voyages,* 233.

187. "A Relation of Maryland," in Hall, ed., *Narratives of Early Maryland,* 76.

188. Lane, "Discourse," in Quinn, ed., *Roanoke Voyages,* 1:263, 262.

189. Ibid., 271, 2.

190. Indeed, some archeologists now believe that the mounds at the water's edge in Roanoke National Park are the remains of Confederate Civil War bastions.

191. Ivor Noel Hume, *The Virginia Adventure: Roanoke to James Towne. An Archeological and Historical Odyssey* (New York, 1994), 32–79.

192. Lane, "Report to Walsingham, September 3, 1585, in Quinn, ed., *Roanoke Voyages,* 1:210.

193. Quinn, ed., *Roanoke Voyages* 2:903–10.

194. Hume, *Virginia Adventure,* 60–63.

195. Richter, *Ordeal of the Longhouse,* 17–18; Malone, *Skulking Way of War,* 14–17; Craig S. Keener, "An Ethnohistorical Analysis of Iroquois Assault Tactics Used against Fortified Settlements of the Northeast in the Seventeenth Century," *Ethnohistory* 46 (1999), 777–807.

196. Claudia Gellman Mink, *Cahokia, City of the Sun* (Collinsville, Ill., 1999), 26.

197. At the Warren-Wilson site. See Roy S. Dickens Jr., *Cherokee Prehistory: The Pisgah Phase in the Appalachian Summit Region* (Knoxville, 1976), 30–31, 46–51. The estimate of the spacing comes from military historian Wayne E. Lee.

198. Philip Vincent, "True Relation," in Charles Orr, ed., *History of the Pequot War* (Cleveland, 1897), 104.

199. Pequot Museum, Mashantucket Pequot Reservation. The author took the measurements.

200. John B. Jackson, "In Search of a Proto-Landscape," in George F. Thompson, ed., *Landscape in America* (Austin, Tex., 1995), 48.

201. Gleach, *Powhatan's World,* 36–37.

202. Kupperman, *Indians and English,* 141.

203. Although reconstructions of eastern woodlands Indian fortifications involve much speculation, it is possible that some Indian forts had no spaces between the verti-

cals of the palisade and the warriors instead used wall walks, from which they could fire arrows down upon attackers. For example, the excavations at the Tuscarora fort at Neoheroka, in North Carolina, suggest this defense structure. State Archeological Office of North Carolina, courtesy of Wayne E. Lee.

204. Some English observers assumed that the Indians were especially susceptible to disease—in other words, it was the Indians' own fault. Joyce E. Chaplin, "Natural Philosophy and an Early Racial Idiom in North America: Comparing English and Indian Bodies," *William and Mary Quarterly,* 3d ser. 54 (1997), 244–49.

205. Harriot, *Report,* in Quinn, ed., *Roanoke Voyages,* 1:378–79, 380.

206. On witchcraft and Indians, see Alfred W. Cave, "Indian Shamans and English Witches in Seventeenth-Century New England," *Essex Institute Historical Collections* 128 (1992), 239–54; Harold E. Driver, *Indians of North America* (Chicago, 1961), 517, 523, 540.

207. The fortress was an artificial contrivance and an obvious proof that the Europeans were a people who understood, approved, and pursued warfare on a large scale. Willard B. Robinson, *American Forts: Architectural Form and Function* (Urbana, Ill., 1977), 7–12; Marguerita Z. Herman, *Ramparts: Fortification from the Renaissance to West Point* (Garden City, N.Y., 1992), 19–38.

208. The debate over how modern the English war machine was rages on unabated. See the summary in Wayne E. Lee, "State of the Art: Seventeenth-Century American Military History," paper presented to the Organization of American Historians, April 13, 2002, cited by permission.

209. Quinn, ed., *Roanoke Voyages,* 1:22, 120, 149, 179.

210. Reproduced in Hume, *Virginia Adventure,* 31, 33.

211. Merrell, *Into the American Woods,* 309.

212. Helen Roundtree, *Pocahontas's People: The Potomac Indians of Virginia through Four Centuries* (Norman, Okla., 1990), 12.

213. Bragdon, *Native People,* 170; Driver, *Indians of North America,* 373; Roundtree, *Pocahontas's People,* 73. Deeds in war and preparations for war were both occasions to change a personal name.

214. Quinn, ed., *Roanoke Voyages,* 2:899, 893–94.

215. Merrell, *Into the American Woods,* 20, 49. We do know what name the Pilgrims Indian neighbors gave these Englishmen in 1620: *wotowequenage.* It meant, roughly translated, cutthroats. Morton, *New English Canaan,* 111.

216. Lane, "Discourse," in Quinn, ed., *Roanoke Voyages,* 1:286.

217. As did the English at Jamestown. Percy, "Discourse," in Barbour, ed., *Jamestown Voyages,* 1:131.

218. Chaplin, *Subject Matter,* 99–100.

219. Oberg, *Dominion and Civility,* 44.

220. Lane, "Discourse," in Quinn, ed., *Roanoke Voyages,* 1:265, 278, 286. This was the reason why the Indians ambushed Howe the next year.

221. Oberg, *Dominion and Civility,* 45: "For Lane, Roanoke must in many ways have seemed Ireland all over again."

222. A vivid account of these first days is Philip L. Barbour, *The Three Worlds of John Smith* (Boston, 1964).

223. On the Jamestown fort, see Kelso, *Jamestown Rediscovery* (Jamestown, Va., 1997), 3:27–39, 4:29–42; Hume, *Virginia Adventure*, 143–89. The reconstructed fort is at Jamestown Settlement, on the mainland about a mile up river from the actual site.

224. Archer, "Relation," in Barbour, ed., *Jamestown Voyages*, 1:99, 100, 101, 82.

225. Ibid., 83, 84, 85, 86.

226. White, *Middle Ground*, 50–53. Edmund S. Morgan, *American Slavery, American Freedom* (New York, 1978), 48, and Oberg, *Dominion and Civility*, 51 and after, argue that founders of Virginia hoped for a multiracial society, with the Indians providing contented laborers.

227. Oberg, *Dominion and Civility*, 55, estimates that fourteen thousand of the twenty thousand Indians in the region were under Powhatan's dominion.

228. On the Indian fascination with European weapons, see e.g. Merrell, *Indians' New World*, 38. On Jamestown's founding, see the introduction by Barbour, in *Works of Smith*, 1:5–10; Alden T. Vaughan, *American Genesis: Captain John Smith and the Founding of Virginia* (Boston, 1976), 29–33; Carville Earle, "Ecological Causes of the Virginia Mortality Crisis, 1607–1624," in Earle, *Geographical Inquiry and American Historical Problems* (Stanford, Calif., 1992), 25–58; Roundtree, *Pocahontas's People*, 11, 30–31, 34. The colonists were armed to the teeth. Ivor Noël Hume, *Martin's Hundred* (New York, 1982), 201–6.

229. Percy, "Discourse," in Barbour, ed., *Jamestown Voyages* 1:139–40.

230. See e.g. French Canadian descriptions of the traditional Huron-Iroquois battles that they witnessed in 1609. Mark Lescarbot, "The Voyage of Monsieur de Monts into New France, [1603–1611], in Purchas, *Hakluytus Posthumus; or, Purchas His Pilgrimes* [1625], 18:292–93; Sayre, *Les Sauvages Américaines*, 74–77, 249–58. The Paspahegh retreated not because they had lost but because they had delivered their message and were suffering dead and wounded at an unacceptably high rate.

231. Archer, "Relation," in Barbour, ed., *Jamestown Voyages*, 1:95, 97–98. The English noted more than once the Indians' wailing at the death of any of their number.

232. Percy, "Discourse," in Barbour, ed., *Jamestown Voyages*, 1:142

233. Percy, Smith, and other members of the Jamestown council fought in the Low Countries before they signed on for Virginia. Kelso, *Jamestown Rediscovery II* (Jamestown, Va., 1996), 28, 15, 31, 33. In Jamestown, housing was primitive—but the "English wigwam" of waddle and daub walls, thatched roof, and clay chimney was not much different from the poor English cottager's abode. See David Freeman Hawke, *Everyday Life in Early America* (New York, 1988), 48–50; Hugh Morrison, *Early American Architecture* (New York, 1952), 8–12.

234. Smith plays Lane's role in Oberg's account of Jamestown—the fierce frontier leader who has no truck with Indians' side of the story. *Dominion and Civility*, 58 and after.

235. John Smith, "A True Relation" [1608], in Barbour, ed., *Jamestown Voyages*, 1:170, 172.

236. Quotations from Alden T. Vaughan, "'Expulsion of the Salvages': English Policy

and the Virginia Massacre of 1622," *William and Mary Quarterly,* 3d ser. 35 (1978), 60, 61, 63, 65.

237. William Stacey [1611], quoted in ibid., 66 n.29.

238. See e.g. Roundtree, *Pocahontas's People,* 8.

239. Robert Gray, Sermon, 1609, quoted in Vaughan, "Expulsion," 61.

240. Gary B. Nash, "The Image of the Indian in the Southern Colonial Mind," *William and Mary Quarterly,* 3d ser. 29 (1972), 197–230.

241. Or perhaps a little later, when Smith had insulted Opechancanough. J. Frederick Fauz, "Opechancanough: Indian Resistance Leader," in David G. Sweet and Gary B. Nash, eds., *Struggle and Survival in Colonial America* (Berkeley, 1981), 26.

242. Smith, *Generall History of Virginia* [1624], in Barbour, ed., *Works of Smith,* 2:293, 294.

243. Ibid., 2:294.

244. Wood, *New England's Propsect,* 103 ("it being the custom to cut off the heads, hands, and feet [of their enemies in war] to bring home to their wives and children as true tokens of their renowned victory"). The Algonquians believed that the body travels to the afterlife entire; thus, decapitation denied the enemy eternal rest. Jill Lapore, *The Name of War: King Philip's War and the Origins of American Identity* (New York, 1998), 180. The same punishment was practiced on the Indians. Francis West got so frustrated with buying corn from the Potomacs in 1610 that he beheaded two of their warriors. Roundtree, *Pocahontas's People,* 53.

245. Gleach, *Powhatan's World,* 45, 49–51. Axtell, *The Invasion Within,* 86, 312–14, and Richter, *Ordeal of the Longhouse,* 35–36. 65–70, describe Iroquois Indian torture of prisoners.

246. E.g. Roger Williams to John Winthrop, July 3, 1637, in *Correspondence of Roger Williams,* 1:90.

247. Smith, *Generall History of Virginia,* in Barbour, ed., *Works of Smith,* 2:297.

248. Gleach, *Powhatan's World,* 153.

249. Smith to the Treasurer and Council of the Virginia Company, ca. December 1608, in Barbour, ed., *Jamestown Voyages,* 1:244.

250. Smith, *Depiction of New England* [1616], in Barbour, ed., *Works of Smith,* 1:330, 334, 348.

251. McRae, *God Speed the Plow,* 1–2.

252. Vaughan, *American Genesis,* 98–112; Joseph C. Robert, *The Story of Tobacco in America* (Chapel Hill, N.C., 1949), 6–10.

253. Vaughan, *American Genesis,* 99; Morgan, *American Slavery, American Freedom,* 108–30.

254. "Letter of Sir Francis Wyatt, Governor of Virginia, 1621– [1623], *William and Mary Quarterly,* 2d ser. 6 (1926), 116, 117, 118.

255. Cronon, *Changes in the Land,* 19–33; Bragdon, *Native People,* 55–79.

256. Gordon G. Whitney, *From Coastal Wilderness to Fruited Plain: A History of Environmental Change in Temperate North America 1500 to the Present* (Cambridge, 1994), 102–3.

257. Cronon, *Changes in the Land,* 108–56; Rhys Isaac, *The Transformation of Virginia, 1740–1790* (Chapel Hill, N.C., 1982), 18–57.

258. Roundtree, *Pocahontas's People,* 74, 80.

259. Calvin Martin, *Keepers of the Game: Indian-Animal Relationships and the Fur Trade* (Berkeley, 1978); Shepherd Kretch III, ed., *Indians, Animals, and the Fur Trade: A Critique of Keepers of the Game* (Athens, Ga., 1981).

260. Roundtree, *Pocahontas's People,* 81–127.

261. Sylvia Frey, "Rethinking the American Revolution," *William and Mary Quarterly,* 3d ser. 53 (1996), 369.

262. Seed, *Ceremonies of Possession,* 19, argues that the English always left these "fixed objects" on the land to establish possessory rights. See also Isaac, *Transformation of Virginia,* 18–42.

263. Chaplin, *Subject Matter,* 153.

264. Merrell, *Into the American Woods,* 52.

265. Allan Kulikoff, *From British Peasants to Colonial American Farmers* (Chapel Hill, N.C., 2000), 117–18; George Davis, "Topographic Terms in Virginia," *American Speech* 15 (1940), 3–38, 149–79, 262–300, 381–419; Mary R. Miller, "Place Names of the Northern Neck of Virginia," *Names* 24 (1976), 9–23.

266. Richter, *Facing East from Indian Country,* 58–59.

267. James Fenimore Cooper, *The Pioneers, or the Source of the Susquehanna, A Descriptive Tale* [1823], ed. James Franklin Beard (Albany, N.Y., 1980), 239, 242.

268. Alan Taylor, *William's Cooper's Town: Power and Persuasion on the Frontier of the Early American Republic* (New York, 1996), 32.

269. Cooper, *Pioneers,* 235; William Cooper, *A Guide in the Wilderness,* quoted in Taylor, *William Cooper's Town,* 32–33.

Chapter 2 · Invisible Worlds

1. Linda McGraw, "Lab Test for Prions May Yield Diagnostic Tool for TSE Disease," Agriculture Research Service News and Information Report, USDA, October 31, 1999.

2. In quantum theory, location is never more than a probability—there is no "there" there. But the tutorial for "Visual Quantum Mechanics," at the website http://phys. educ.ksu.edu, relies on interactive computer-generated visuals and graphics to teach quantum mechanics to high school students. We need to use visual simulations to teach what we can never see.

3. James Glanz, "Listen Closely: From Tiny Hum Came Big Bang," *New York Times,* April 30, 2001, A1: "The new observations do not see the quantum fluctuations directly."

4. Iona Opie and Moira Tatem, eds., *Oxford Dictionary of Superstitions* (New York, 1989) and David Pickering, *Cassell Dictionary of Superstition* (London, 1995). Both go back into the early modern period of European history.

5. Confabulation is discussed in the context of accusations of witchcraft in Lawrence Wright, *Remembering Satan: A Case of Recovered Memory and the Shattering of an American Family* (New York, 1994), 110–45, and Lucy S. McGough, *Child Witnesses: Fragile Voices in the American Legal System* (New Haven, Conn., 1994), 48–49.

6. John Davenport, a New Haven puritan minister, writing in 1665, quoted in Michael Winship, *Seers of God: Puritan Providentialism in the Restoration and Early Enlightenment* (Baltimore, 1996), 37.

7. Keith Thomas, *Religion and the Decline of Magic* (New York, 1971), 470–71 and after. Winship, *Seers of God,* 36–52, notes that Puritans in England and the colonies were more prone to find illumination in omens and prodigies than were their Anglican ministerial counterparts.

8. Robert Boyle, *Experimenta and Observationes Physic . . . to Which Are Added, a Small Collection of Strange Reports* (London, 1691), pt. 2, 2; Boyle to Joseph Glanvill, September 18, 1678, in *The Correspondence of Robert Boyle,* ed. Michael Hunter, Antonio Clericuzio, and Lawrence M. Principe (London, 2001), 4:456; Increase Mather, *Angelographica* (Boston, 1696), quoted in Richard Godbeer, *The Devil's Dominion: Magic and Religion in Early New England* (Cambridge, 1993), 61.

9. Stuart Clark, *Thinking with Demons: The Idea of Witchcraft in Early Modern Europe* (Oxford, 1997), 80–93.

10. Jeffrey Burton Russell, *The Devil* (Ithaca, N.Y., 1977), 36, 250–60; Richard Baxter, *Certainty of the World of Spirits* (London, 1691), 107; John Hale, *A Modest Inquiry into the Nature of Witchcraft* [1697], in George Lincoln Burr, ed., *Narratives of the Witchcraft Cases, 1648–1706* (New York, 1914), 420; Cotton Mather, *A Brand Pluck'd Out of the Burning* [1693], in Burr, ed., *Narratives,* 261.

11. Thomas, *Religion and the Decline of Magic,* 472, 474.

12. William Perkins, *A Discourse on the Damned Art of Witchcraft* (London, 1610); John Brinley, *A Discovery of the Impostures of Witches and Astrologers* (London, 1680), preface; John Cotta, *The Trial of Witchcraft* (London, 1616); 15 and after. The devil was always behind the witches' dealings. John Bernard, *Guide to Grand Jurymen* (London, 1630), 11–18; John Gaule, *Select Cases of Conscience Touching Witches and Witchcraft* (London, 1646), 60 and after.

13. See the cases in C. L'Estrange Ewen, comp., *Witch Hunting and Witch Trials* (London, 1929).

14. The pact between the witch and the devil was essential to the witches' power. Wayne Shumaker, *The Occult Sciences in the Renaissance* (Berkeley, 1972), 72, 73, 80, 81; Peter Charles Hoffer, *The Devil's Disciples: Makers of the Salem Witchcraft Trials* (Baltimore, 1996), 81.

15. On the general decline of the belief in the supernatural among the elites, see Peter Burke, *Popular Culture in Early Modern Europe* (Cambridge, 1994), 274–81, and Herbert Leventhal, *In the Shadow of the Enlightenment: Occultism and Renaissance Science in Eighteenth-Century America* (New York, 1976), 85–103. On New England, see David D. Hall, *Worlds of Wonder, Days of Judgment: Popular Religious Belief in Early New England* (New York, 1989), 112–15; and Winship, *Seers of God,* 131–43.

16. On New Englanders' taking of the land, see William Cronon, *Changes in the Land: Indians, Colonists and the Ecology of New England* (New York, 1983), 54–81; Gloria L. Main, *Peoples of a Spacious Land: Families and Cultures in Colonial New England* (Cambridge, Mass., 2001), 23, 40, 53, 188.

17. The entire discussion owes much to Alfred A. Cave, *The Pequot War* (Amherst, Mass., 1995).

18. William A. Starna, "The Pequots in the Early Seventeenth Century," in Lawrence M. Hauptman and James D. Wherry, eds., *The Pequots in Southern New England: The Rise and Fall of an American Indian Nation* (Norman, Okla., 1990), 36–37; Laurel Thatcher Ulrich, *The Age of Homespun* (New York, 2001), 45; Jack Campisi, "Pequot History," *Mashantucket Pequot Museum and Research Center Guidebook* (Mashantucket, Conn., 2000), 41.

19. Cave, *Pequot War,* 13–68. The prospect of occupying Pequot lands changed New Englanders' views of the Pequots. When the Pequots lived beyond the pale of English settlements, William Wood regarded them as "a stately, warlike people, of whom [he] never heard any misdemeanor, but that they were just and equal in their dealings, not treacherous either to their countrymen or English, requiters of courtesies, affable towards the English." *New England's Prospect* [1634], ed. Alden T. Vaughan (Amherst, Mass., 1977), 80.

20. Roger Williams, quoted in Cave, *Pequot War,* 45.

21. Cave, *The Pequot War,* 75–76 and after, ascribes the New Englanders' animus against the Pequots to themes in Puritan cosmology.

22. On the Puritanism of the migrants, see Virginia Dejong Anderson, *New England's Generation: The First Migration and the Formation of Society and Culture in the Seventeenth Century* (New York, 1991). But contra, see David Cressy, *Coming Over: Migration and Communication between England and New England in the Seventeenth Century* (New York, 1987).

23. Michael Winship, *Making Heretics: Militant Protestantism and Free Grace in Massachusetts, 1636–1641* (Princeton, 2002), 12–27, includes a review of modern scholarship. On lectures as festival, ibid., 37, 85–86.

24. Charles E. Hambrick-Stowe, *The Practice of Piety: Puritan Devotional Disciplines in Seventeenth-Century New England* (Chapel Hill, N.C.,1982), 116–23, 126–29.

25. On Puritan worship and church organization, see Patrick Collinson, *English Puritanism* (London, 1983), and Stephen Foster, *The Long Argument: English Puritanism and the Shaping of a New England Culture, 1570–1700* (Chapel Hill, N.C., 1991).

26. The English immigrants clung to a univariate definition of proprietorship: If a claimant to land improved it and recorded title in the appropriate deed books, the claimant had legal ownership. All others could be dispossessed. The idea worked an obvious hardship on Native Americans, whose notion of use did not include allodial or absolute dominion by individuals. Peter Charles Hoffer, *Law and People in Colonial America,* 2d ed. (Baltimore, 1998), 54, 69–71.

27. Harriet Chapman Chesebrough, *Glimpses of Saybrook in Colonial Days* (Saybrook, Conn., 1985), 9. At Saybrook Point in Old Saybrook, the outlines of the fort feature illustrated markers on the war and the fort.

28. Ibid., 9–10; Cave, *Pequot War,* 91, 92.

29. See e.g. Roger Williams to Massachusetts Governor John Winthrop, October 24, 1636, referring to Williams' earlier efforts to gain intelligence about Pequot intentions, in

Glenn W. LaFantasie, ed., *The Correspondence of Roger Williams* (Hanover, N.H., 1988), 1:65.

30. Cave, *Pequot War,* 109–13.

31. Lion Gardener, "Relation," in Charles Orr, ed., *History of the Pequot War* (Cleveland, 1897), 129–30, 131, 132.

32. Ibid.; John Underhill, *Newes from America* [1638], in Orr, ed., *History of the Pequot War,* 60, 62.

33. The account, widely reported at the time, appeared in Judge Samuel Sewall's letters, a sermon by Cotton Mather, and in various histories of Maine, including William Williamson's *History of Maine* (1832) and Charles Banks' *History of York* (1931). Information courtesy of Emerson W. Baker, October 27, 1999, and Ann M. Little, October 24, 1999, "Re: Record of Indian Mocking Preacher," Omohundro Institute of Early American History Net (H-OIEAHC@msu.edu).

34. Indians whooped on purpose, to taunt and to signal. The Puritans recognized these purposes and replied in kind, with challenges, cheers, and taunts of their own. See Gilman C. Gates, *Saybrook at the Mouth of the Connecticut: The First One Hundred Years* (Salem, 1935), 45.

35. I am grateful to the staff of the Keeney Memorial Cultural Center in Wethersfield for the tour of the town and the probable site of the raid. After the raid, Wethersfield remained under a malign edict—crop failures and witchcraft accusations in the 1650s, followed by an outbreak of "great fever" and civil disorder.

36. Cave, *Pequot War,* 123–56.

37. Hooker to Winthrop, May 1637, in Massachusetts Historical Society, *Winthrop Papers,* Vol. 3, *1631–1637* (Boston, 1943), 408.

38. Shepard to Winthrop, May 1637, *Winthrop Papers,* 3:408. Winthrop recorded in his journal that the Connecticut troops "slew about one hundred and fifty old men, women, and children." *The Journal of John Winthrop, 1630–1649,* ed. Richard S. Dunn, James Savage, and Laetitita Yeandle (Cambridge, Mass., 1996), 220.

39. Cave, *Pequot War,* 146–51.

40. Underhill put the number of Indian dead at 400. The Pequot Museum provides a number of 600, following Mason. Cave, *Pequot War,* 151, accepts the higher estimate. Underwood, Mason, and their men never went through the burnt reed mats, bark slats, furs, and other debris on the floor of the wigwams they had incinerated to count casualties hidden from view. From evidence at the Pequot Museum on the Mashantucket Reservation and investigation of the site of the fort on the Mystic, we can arrive at an upper limit of our own. At the reconstructed wigwams in the Pequot village at the museum, one can count the sleeping mats. The wigwam, on average, accommodated six or seven people. Each wigwam was separated from its neighbors by ten feet or so. Even assuming that the Mystic village was a refugee camp overflowing with people seeking protection within the walls from the marauding English, 600 Pequots would have needed approximately 100 wigwams to live in any comfort, Pequot-style. Thus, the area of each wigwam and its surrounding space would be 236 sq. ft. (where the diameter of the space is 30 ft.), and if there were 100 wigwams, the area inside the palisade (assuming some

space between wigwams and the palisade) would be 141,600 sq. ft. This would produce a diameter of the circular enclosure of about 425 feet at minimum.

But a fort of such dimensions would not fit where the fort actually stood. There is no longer a monument to mark this spot. The statue of John Mason that once stood at the corner of Pequot and Clift Streets, on the Groton side of the Mystic River, is now gone. But the site makes sense. It is on a plateau about sixty feet above the river bank, at a distance from it of about one half mile. The land slopes down sharply from the site where the statue once stood. No one would build a palisaded village on a slope, so the land available for the village was limited to the flat space, which, paced off, is about three hundred feet in diameter. It would have contained three hundred to four hundred people nicely.

41. John Gabriel Stedman, *Narrative of a Five Years Expedition against the Revolted Negroes of Surinam* [1790], ed. Richard Price and Sally Price (Baltimore, 1988), 406. Cave, *Pequot War,* 151, argues that the massacre "was an act of terrorism intended to break Pequot morale." But if the Pequots' response at the time was any indication, the wanton killing had the opposite effect. They grew almost insanely brave with grief. Ibid., 152–58.

42. We can also put the tragedy of the massacre in a long context of even more tragic events befalling the Pequots. Neal Salisbury, "Indians and Colonists in Southern New England after the Pequot War," in Hauptman and Wherry, eds., *The Pequots,* 85. But the killing of women was not, as Ann Kibbey (*The Interpretation of Material Shapes in Puritanism: A Study of Rhetoric, Prejudice, and Violence* [Cambridge, 1986], 93) suggests, part of Puritanism's hatred of women. The militiamen simply could not tell the difference between men and women in the smoke, darkness, and confusion of the fighting. In addition, Indian women were probably combatants in the final stages of the fighting.

43. Winship, *Making Heretics,* 154–55, 212, 215, 217; Cave, *Pequot War,* 110 and after.

44. Underhill, *Newes,* 57, 64, 66; Neal Salisbury, *Manitou and Providence: Indians, Europeans, and the Making of New England* (New York, 1982), 224, suggests that the New Englanders reacted to the Pequots' posturing.

45. John Mason, "A Brief History of the Pequot War" [1670?], in Orr, ed., *History of the Pequot War,* 15, 26, 27, 28, 29, 30.

46. Ibid., 30–31.

47. Ibid., 16,18,19, 23.

48. Thomas Shepard, *God's Plot: The Paradoxes of Puritan Piety, Being the Autobiography and Journal of Thomas Shepard,* ed. Michael McGiffert (Amherst, Mass., 1971), 67–68.

49. McGiffert, "Introduction," in ibid., 21.

50. Underhill, 84, 81.

51. Ibid., 84, 82, 81. But the English were frustrated as well with the Pequot's style of hit-and-run raids. Ronald Dale Karr, "Why Should You Be So Furious": The Violence of the Pequot War," *Journal of American History* 85 (1998), 886.

52. William Bradford, [Journal] *Of Plymouth Plantation (1620–1647),* ed. Samuel Eliot Morison (New York, 1966), 296.

53. Williams to Winthrop, June 30, 1637, LaFantasie, ed., *Correspondence of Williams,* 1:88–89.

54. Ibid., 94.

55. Philip Vincent, *A True Relation of the Late Battle Fought in New-England Between the English and the Pequet Savages* (London, 1638), 3, 5.

56. Edward Johnson, *Wonder-Working Providence of Sion's Savior in New England* [1654], ed. J. Franklin Jameson (New York, 1910), 168.

57. William Hubbard, *A Supplement Concerning the War with the Pequots* [1677], in Samuel G. Drake, ed., Hubbard, *History of the Indian Wars* (Roxbury, Mass., 1865), 7, 12, 27, 32.

58. *New England's First Fruits* (London, 1643), 20–21. In fact, many Pequots had escaped the wrath of the New Englanders, taken as captives by the Mohegan allies of the English or quietly incorporated into Narragansett towns.

59. John Eliot, *A Late and Further Manifestation of the Progress of the Gospel Amongst the Indians in New-England* . . . (London, 1655), 1, 2, 9, 11. On the project of "reducing" the Indians to "civilization," see James Axtell, *The Invasion Within: The Contest of Cultures in Colonial North America* (New York, 1985), 218–41.

60. Monequassum, quoted in Daniel Richter, *Facing East from the Indian Country: A Native History of Early America* (Cambridge, Mass., 2001), 114. Richter is convinced, and has convinced me, that Eliot did not invent—that he tried to be accurate. Ibid., 118, 123. The Indians' speeches were genuine, that is, they were Indian in origin and character. But it was Puritan rhetorical theory that words could be divinely inspired. Kibbey, *Material Shapes,* 8.

61. Eliot, *A Brief Narrative of the Progress of the Gospel Amonst the Indians in New-England* . . . (London, 1671).

62. Eliot, *Late and Further Manifestation,* 11.

63. Thomas Shepard, *The Clear Sun-Shine of the Gospel Breaking Forth upon the Indians in New-England* (London, 1648), 7.

64. Richter, *Facing East from Indian Country,* 125.

65. For the English missionaries, the "savage" needed "both spiritual and material clothing." Ulrich, *Homespun,* 54.

66. At its head was Robert Boyle, a noteworthy scientist who was himself something of a mystic and, although an Anglican, friendly to the Puritans. Joyce Chaplin, *Subject Matter: Technology, the Body, and Science on the Anglo-American Frontier, 1500–1676* (Cambridge, Mass., 2001), 288–308.

67. John Eliot and Thomas Mayhew Jr., *Tears of Repentance* (London, 1653), 17.

68. Gookin, quoted in Ann M. Little, "'Shoot That Rogue, for He Hath an Englishman's Coat On': Cultural Cross-Dressing on the New England Frontier, 1620–1760," *New England Quarterly* 54 (2001), 251.

69. Alden T. Vaughan, *New England Frontier: Puritans and Indians, 1620–1675* (Boston, 1965), 260–308.

70. *New England's First Fruits,* 15. I am grateful to Laura M. Stevens, "Early Empathy for the Vanishing Indian," in Andrew Burstein and Nancy Isenberg, eds., *Mortal Remains: Death and Mourning in Early America* (Philadelphia, 2002), for pointing out this treatise.

71. Eliot, *Late and Further Manifestation,* preface.

72. Increase Mather, *A Brief History of the War with the Indians in New England* (London, 1676), 1.

73. Samuel G. Drake, *Biography and History of the Indians of North America* (Boston, 1851), 278–79, 286–87, 288–93.

74. Yasuhide Kawashima, *Igniting King Philip's War: The John Sassamon Murder Trial* (Lawrence, Kans., 2001); Daniel R. Mandell, *Behind the Frontier: Indians in Eighteenth Century Massachusetts* (Lincoln, Nebr., 1996), 20–25; Virginia DeJohn Anderson, "King Philip's Herds: Indians, Colonists, and the Problem of Livestock in Early New England," *William and Mary Quarterly,* 3d ser. 51 (1994), 601–4.

75. Surveys of the war include Russell Bourne, *The Red King's Rebellion: Racial Politics in New England, 1675–1678* (New York, 1990), Jill Lapore, *The Name of War: King Philip's War and the Origins of American Identity* (New York, 1998), 71–121; Douglas Leach, *Flintlock and Tomahawk: New England in King Philip's War* (New York, 1958).

76. The note's contents and provenance are disputed, but many think it the work of James Printer, Eliot's apprentice at the Cambridge, Massachusetts, press that turned out the Algonquian versions of the Bible. Lapore, *Name of War,* 283 n.96.

77. It is one of the ironies of this war that the Indians were most effective when they adopted European total-war tactics, like the use of massed firepower, and the New Englanders were most effective when they adopted Indian tactics of ambush. Patrick M. Malone, *The Skulking Way of War: Technology and Tactics among the New England Indians* ([1991], Baltimore, 1993), 106–25.

78. Richard Slotkin, *Regeneration through Violence: The Mythology of the American Frontier, 1600–1860* (Norman, Okla., 1975), 79–80; Lapore, *Name of War,* 50–51.

79. Nathaniel Saltonstall, July 22, 1675, quoted in Lapore, *Name of War,* 71. The lustful heathen is a stock figure. So were the "swamps" to which Indians fled as refuges and in which they hid in ambush and placed their fortified towns. Ibid., 87–89. But some of the refuges were swamps, for example, the Pocasset area east of Narragansett Bay. Ian Steele, *Warpaths: Invasions of North America* (New York, 1994), 101. The whole area was swampy. Leach, *Flintlock and Tomahawk,* 39.

80. Eric B. Schultz and Michael J. Tougias, *King Philip's War: The History and Legacy of America's Forgotten Conflict* (Woodstock, Vt., 1999), have traced most of these village sites and describe them; see ibid., 143–46.

81. Standard tactics called for moving noncombatants to dry areas within swamps while the warriors engaged enemy raiding parties. See e.g. Keith F. Otterbein, "Huron vs. Iroquois: A Case Study in Inter-tribal Warfare," *Ethnohistory* 26 (1979), 141–52.

82. Cf. e.g. Cotton Mather's references, in his *Decennium Luctuosum: An History of Remarkable Occurrences in the Long War Which New-England Hath Had with the Indians Savages, from the year 1688 to the year 1698* (Boston, 1699), to inaccessible swamps to which the Abenaki Indians of Maine had fled during King William's war. These he termed *desarts,* meaning deserted places.

83. Increase Mather, *The History of King Philip's War* [1676], ed. Samuel G. Drake (Boston, 1862), 46.

84. For the argument that the initial shock of seeing the burned and butchered corpses of the victims of Indian raids did not dull with time, see Mary Beth Norton, "Pannick at the Eastward," paper presented to the McNeil Center for Early American Studies, February 8, 2002, 8, cited by permission.

85. James Quannapaquait, "Relation," in Neal Salisbury, ed., *The Sovereignty and Goodness of God, by Mary Rowlandson, with Related Documents* (Boston, 1997), 119–28.

86. Church, cited in Lepore, *Name of War,* 73.

87. Ibid., 173.

88. Mather, cited in ibid., 174.

89. On Increase Mather, see Michael G. Hall, *The Last American Puritan: The Life of Increase Mather, 1639–1723* (Middletown, Conn., 1984), Robert Middlekauf, *The Mathers: Three Generations of Puritan Intellectuals, 1596–1728* (London, 1971) (the witchcraft cases are treated at 149–61, in a chapter aptly entitled "The Invisible World," although Middlekauf is not interested in sensation per se), and Darren Staloff, *The Making of an American Thinking Class: Intellectuals and Intelligentsia in Puritan Massachusetts* (New York, 1998), 169–88.

90. Richard Slotkin and James K. Folsom, eds., *So Dreadfull a Judgment: Puritan Responses to King Philip's War, 1676–1677* (Middletown, Conn., 1978), 57, 69, 72–73.

91. Mather, *King Philip's War,* 46, 36.

92. Ibid., 84, 90, 47. The reference to the devil in black reminded readers that Indians were also called "black men" in New England. Drake, *Biography and History,* 286.

93. Daniel Gookin, *An Historical Account of the Doings and the Sufferings of the Christian Indians in New England* [1677], *Transactions and Collections of the American Antiquarian Society* (Cambridge, Mass., 1836), 2:436–37.

94. Ibid., 454.

95. Mather, *King Philip's War,* 136, 123, 132, 138.

96. Ibid., 48, 61, 63.

97. Thomas Wheeler, *A Thankfull Rememberance of Gods Mercy to Several Persons at Quabaug or Brookfield* [1676], in Slotkin and Folsom, eds., *Dreadfull Judgment,* 241.

98. Samuel Nowell, *Abraham in Arms,* in Slotkin and Folsom, eds., *Dreadfull Judgment,* 276, 280.

99. William Hubbard, *The History of the Indian Wars,* ed. Samuel G. Drake (Roxbury, Mass., 1865), 287, 53, 223.

100. Lapore, *Name of War,* xvii.

101. Somewhat cynically: "So, whenever disaster struck, the preachers and pamphleteers were quick to indicate its direct origin in the moral delinquencies of the people." Thomas, *Religion and the Decline of Magic,* 84.

102. Alden T. Vaughan and Edward W. Clark, *Puritans among the Indians: Accounts of Captivity and Redemption, 1676–1724* (Cambridge, Mass., 1981), 3.

103. Laurel Thatcher Ulrich, *Good Wives: Image and Reality in the Lives of Women in Northern New England, 1650–1750* (New York, 1980), 202–14.

104. Vaughan and Clark, *Puritans among the Indians,* 1.

105. Consider, for example, the excerpts in Frederick Drimmer, ed., *Captured by the*

Indians: Fifteen Firsthand Accounts, 1750–1870 (New York, 1961). Many of the stories have the same basic themes, and the events described are eerily similar to those in the Puritan narratives, but the manner of narration is entirely factual in most of the firsthand accounts in Drimmer. Although many of the narrators were religious, they saw and reported the events in secular fashion.

106. Vaughan and Clark, *Puritans among the Indians,* 23–24; Salisbury, "Introduction," *Sovereignty and Goodness of God,* 40–41.

107. Salisbury, "Introduction," *Sovereignty and Goodness of God,* 15–21; Vaughan, *New England Frontier,* 292–93.

108. Rowlandson, *Sovereignty and Goodness of God,* 69–70.

109. Ibid., 70, 71.

110. Ibid., 71, 74, 75.

111. Ibid., 76, 77.

112. See e.g. Quentin Stockwell's narrative, he taken from Deerfield in the fall of 1677. The narrative was transmitted to Increase Mather and included in his *An Essay for the Recording of Illustrious Providences* (Boston, 1684), 39–58. Stockwell did not notice what anyone was wearing, although he did record with some detail the daily route, victuals, and bickering among the Indians.

113. Rowlandson, *Sovereignty and Goodness of God,* 103, 106. The level of detail is amazing, and Rowlandson has given us one of the finest pictures of the elite Indians' dress. Quinnapin and Weetamoo were wearing all their finery, demonstrating how, even in rebellion, they hybridized European and native ideas of elegance. But note that the beginning and the end of this indelible inventory is the invocation of the invisible world: "I can but stand in admiration to see the wonderful power of God, in providing for such a vast number of our enemies in wilderness, where there was nothing to be seen, but from hand to mouth." Ibid.

114. Ibid., 78, 79, 81, 85, 101. On the "White Indians," see James Axtell, "The White Indians of Colonial America," *William and Mary Quarterly,* 3d ser. 32 (1975), 55–88.

115. John Easton, "A Relacion of the Indian War" [1675], in Salisbury, ed., *Sovereignty and Goodness of God,* 115; Rowlandson, *Sovereignty and Goodness of God,* 78, 82.

116. Ibid., 91.

117. On the son, Kenneth Silverman, *The Life and Times of Cotton Mather* (New York, 1984) and Middlekauf, *The Mathers,* 191–368.

118. Increase Mather, quoted in Salisbury, ed., *Sovereignty and Goodness of God,* 64–65.

119. Thomas, *Religion and the Decline of Magic,* 26–27, 30, 32, 54, 75–76.

120. Slotkin, *Regeneration,* 95, 113–14.

121. Rowlandson, *Sovereignty and Goodness of God,* 112. To be sure, some of this renunciation of the material world is staple Christian theology, but in this context, the immediacy and freshness of her reading of the invisible world implied that she needed no minister to tell her what God wanted.

122. Salisbury, "Introduction," *Sovereignty and Goodness of God,* 44–46.

123. "Cotton's colleagues maintained that graces of sanctification manifested themselves in the regenerate [the saved] in empirically discernable ways." William K. B.

Stoever, *'A Faire and Easie Way to Heaven': Covenant Theology and Antinomianism in Early Massachusetts* (Middletown, Conn., 1978), 46. For the argument that Hutchinson had undermined the conventions of gendered power, see Mary Beth Norton, *Founding Mothers and Fathers: Gendered Power and the Forming of American Society* (New York, 1996), 359–99. On John Winthrop's attempt at spin control, making Hutchinson appear to be central when in fact her trial came at the end of the crisis and she had never been its central figure, see Winship, *Making Heretics*, 184–85. But the unintended consequence of Winthrop's literary sleight-of-hand was that women who appeared to claim the power to see into the unknown and interpret their findings for others were suspected of undermining the authority of men.

124. Mather, in Salisbury, ed., *Sovereignty and Goodness of God*, 67.

125. On the concept of the learned clergy as a hegemonic elite, see Staloff, *Making of an American Thinking Class*.

126. Hoffer, *Devil's Disciples*, 60–81; Godbeer, *Devil's Dominion*, 42.

127. Robert Calef, *More Wonders of the Invisible World* [1700], in Burr, ed., *Narratives*, 297–98.

128. See Thomas, *Religion and the Decline of Magic*, 104 and after, on the project in England, and Winship, *Seers of God*, 63, on the American end. How self-serving was this clerical appropriation of the invisible world? Thomas: "The [Protestant] theologians of the post–Reformation period were thus imposing the doctrine of God's omnipotence upon a populace long accustomed to a variety of other types of [supernatural] explanation." *Religion and the Decline of Magic*, 111. David D. Hall finds that the clergy and the laity still shared basic assumptions about the supernatural; *Worlds of Wonder, Days of Judgment*, 94, but in the 1680s, this "consensus" was breaking down. Ibid., 112–13.

129. Increase Mather, *An Essay for the Recording of Illustrious Providences* (Boston, 1684), preface, 175.

130. Ibid., 127, 176, 179, 202, 213–14, 222. Here Mather may have been influenced by Boyle, for Boyle had warned over and over that all stories of witchcraft must be "warranted with testimonies and authorities" lest the scoffer and the atheist cite the stories as proof of the nonexistence of the entire spirit world. Boyle to Glanville, September 18, 1768, *Correspondence of Boyle*, 4:256; Boyle, unpublished dedicatory to the second edition of *Strange Reports* [1691], quoted in Michael Hunter, *Robert Boyle, 1627–1691: Scrupulosity and Science* (Woodbridge, Eng., 2000), 230–31.

131. Increase Mather was much taken with the scientific method then developing in England. Winship, *Seers of God*, 60–66. He was an amateur scientist and subscribed to the transactions of the English Royal Society, the leading scientific institution of its day. Many members of the Royal Society were believers in astrology, the spirit world, and the power of the devil, in particular Boyle, whose work Mather admired, Hunter, *Boyle*, 102–3. So Increase Mather's acceptance of spectral evidence at this time would not have been seen as untoward.

132. Jane Kamensky, *Governing the Tongue: The Politics of Speech in Early New England* (New York, 1977), 17–42, 127–49.

133. Mather, *Illustrious Providences*, 169–70, 243, 259. The ministers could thus turn

speech into text and thereby prevent speech from undermining ministerial authority. Mather and others were well aware of the dangers of uncontrolled speech. Contrary to Sandra M. Gustafson, *Eloquence Is Power: Oratory and Performance in Early America* (Chapel Hill, N.C., 2000), 42, the testimony of victims of witchcraft had not "posed a verbal challenge to the textual discipline that anchored the patriarchy of puritan New England." It was what the witnesses saw and felt that frightened the ministers and posed a danger to order and safety.

134. Mather, *Illustrious Providences,* 234, 249, 175.

135. Richard Slotkin, *Regeneration through Violence,* 79–83; Lapore, *Name of War,* 35, 49; Gray, *New World Babel,* 62–73; Hall, *Worlds of Wonder, Days of Judgment,* 221–70; Richard D. Brown, *Knowledge Is Power: The Diffusion of Information in Early America* (New York, 1989), 16–41.

136. A number of seventeenth-century scientists wanted to determine whether the powers of the devil were predictable and measurable (Clark, *Thinking with Demons,* 167–77, 294–311), but the project yielded little and was largely abandoned by the next century. Nor was it new. See David Wootton, "Reginald Scot/Abraham Fleming/The Family of Love," in Stuart Clark, ed., *The Languages of Witchcraft: Narrative, Ideology, and Meaning in Early Modern Culture* (New York, 2001), 120.

137. Mather, *Illustrious Providences,* 142 and after; John Putnam Demos, *Entertaining Satan: Witchcraft and the Culture of Early New England* (New York, 1982), 133–37, 148–49.

138. Cotton Mather, *Memorable Providences Relating to Witchcrafts and Possessions* [1689], in Burr, ed., *Narratives,* 94–134.

139. Cotton Mather, *The Wonders of the Invisible World* [1692], in Burr, ed., *Narratives,* 211.

140. Mather, *Memorable Providences,* in Burr, ed., *Narratives,* 102, 107.

141. Ibid., 123, 103, 115. Boyle had written almost a decade before that too-close in-quiry into the operations of the demonic was "spiritually dangerous, in that the knowl-edge obtained by such means could involve entering into a league with the Devil." Boyle quoted in Hunter, *Boyle,* 232. Silverman, *Life and Times,* 91, finds that Cotton was simply wedded to idea that the children were not dissembling and that the devil had di-rected Martha Goodwin's fits of anger and petulance.

142. Silverman, *Life and Times,* 245–54.

143. Cotton Mather, *Memorable Providences,* in Burr, ed., *Narratives,* 115, 133.

144. Cotton Mather, *Wonders of the Invisible World,* in ibid., 246, 247. Silverman, *Life and Times,* 94, suggests that Cotton may have adopted a "scientific pneumatological" theory, where the force exerted itself through air pressure, like thunder (also unseen but felt on the ears).

145. Cotton Mather, *Magnalia Christi Americana, Books I and II* [1702], ed. Kenneth B. Murdock with the assistance of Elizabeth W. Miller (Cambridge, Mass., 1977), 330, 327.

146. The Quakers were the real threat, for no one in Massachusetts would openly de-fend the Catholics or the atheists. Was their shaking and ecstasy not close to possession? Silverman, *Life and Times,* 88. But the danger from the Quakers was deeper, for they

were suspects of witchcraft and critics of the prosecution of witches. Hoffer, *Devil's Disciples,* 100. What is more, the Quakers claimed their own monopoly on religious visions and voices. As George Fox, founder of the movement, wrote of his 1647 conversion experience in his journals, "Oh then I heard a voice which said, 'there is one, even Christ Jesus, that can speak to thy condition [of doubt and yearning], and when I heard it my heart did leap for joy . . . For I had been brought through the very ocean of darkness and death . . . and I saw the honest white, and the seed of God lying thick on the ground." Fox, *Journal,* in Douglas V. Steere, ed., *Quaker Spirituality: Selected Writings* (New York, 1984), 65, 67.

147. John Morrill, "Government and Politics: England and Wales, 1625–1701," in Christopher Haigh, ed. *The Cambridge Historical Encyclopedia of Great Britain and Ireland* (Cambridge, 1985), 203–5; "Secret Letter of Invitation," July 30, 1688, in Paul L. Hughes and Robert F. Fries, eds., *Crown and Parliament in Tudor-Stuart England: A Documentary Constitutional History, 1485–1714* (New York, 1959), 301.

148. Richard Ashcraft, *Revolutionary Politics and Locke's Two Treatises of Government* (Princeton, 1986), 338–466.

149. Nathaniel Byfield, "Account of the Insurrection, April 29, 1689," in Michael G. Hall et al., eds., *the Glorious Revolution in America: Documents on the Colonial Crisis of 1689* (New York, 1964), 47; David S. Lovejoy, *The Glorious Revolution in America* (New York, 1972), 242–46.

150. Steele, *Warpaths,* 137–50.

151. The Indians still had powwows who communed with the spirits, believed in the supernatural powers of animals, saw demigods in wild places, and went on vision quests—which was what made their version of the invisible world so threatening to the New England intellectual elite in the first place. Lapore, *Name of War,* 180.

152. *The Diary of Cotton Mather,* ed. Worthington C. Ford (New York, 1911), 1:144.

153. The connection was direct: Rumors of war coincided with rumors of witchcraft practices among the Indians. See James E. Kences, "Some Unexplored Relationships of Essex County Witchcraft to the Indian Wars of 1675 and 1689," *Essex Institute Historical Collections* 120 (1984), 179–212. But the Indians themselves were petrified of witches, and "a witch discovered among one's own lineage or clan, after all, could be more dangerous than one operating from afar—he or she could tear the heart out of one's family." Matthew Dennis, "Seneca Possessed: Witch-Hunting and the Contest for Power and Authority on the Frontiers of the Early American Republic," paper presented at the New World Orders Conference, McNeil Center for Early American Studies, Philadelphia, October 20, 2001, 14, cited by permission.

154. Cotton Mather, *Memorable Providences,* in Burr, ed., *Narratives,* 99.

155. Ibid., 533.

156. E.g. Cotton Mather, *A Brand Pluck'd Out of the Burning* [1692], in Burr, ed., *Narratives,* 282.

157. Clark, *Thinking with Demons,* 371, 411.

158. See the lists of earlier cases in Demos, *Entertaining Satan,* Godbeer, *Devil's Do-*

minion, Carol Karlsen, *The Devil in the Shape of a Woman: Witchcraft in Colonial New England* (New York, 1987), and Richard Weisman, *Witchcraft, Magic, and Religion in Seventeenth-Century Massachusetts* (Amherst, 1984). David D. Hall, ed., *Witch Hunting in Seventeenth-Century New England* (Boston, 1991), is a documentary collection of earlier cases.

159. The panic was not accidental. One of the tactics of the raiders on the frontier was to exploit panic. See John E. Ferling, *A Wilderness of Miseries: War and Warriors in Early America* (Westport, Conn., 1980), 34–35, 45.

160. Paul Boyer and Stephen Nissenbaum, *Salem Possessed: The Social Origins of Witchcraft* (Cambridge, Mass.,1974), 179–216.

161. Hoffer, *Devil's Disciples,* 102–112.

162. Book-length accounts abound. Bryan F. Le Beau, *The Story of the Salem Witch Trials* (Upper Saddle River, N.J., 1998), Elaine G. Breslaw, *Tituba: Reluctant Witch of Salem* (New York, 1996), David C. Brown, *A Guide to the Salem Witchcraft Hysteria of 1692* (privately printed, 1984), Larry Gragg, *Salem Witchcraft Crisis* (New York, 1992), Francis Hill, *A Delusion of Satan: The Full Story of the Salem Witch Trials* (New York, 1995), Chadwick Hansen, *Witchcraft at Salem* (New York, 1969), Mary Beth Norton, *In the Devil's Snare: The Salem Witchcraft Crisis of 1692* (New York, 2002), Bernard Rosenthal, *Salem Story: Reading the Witch Trials of 1692* (Cambridge, 1993), and Richard B. Trask, *"The Devil Hath Been Raised": A Documentary History of the Salem Village Witchcraft Outbreak of March 1692* (West Kennebunk, Me., 1992), as well as Hoffer, *The Devil's Disciples,* and Hoffer, *The Salem Witchcraft Trials: A Legal History* (Lawrence, Kans., 1997). On the setting, see David Konig, *Law and Society in Puritan Massachusetts: Essex County, 1629–1692* (Chapel Hill, N.C.,1979) and Boyer and Nissenbaum, *Salem Possessed.*

163. Hoffer, *Devil's Disciples,* 131–78.

164. Le Beau, *Witch Trials,* 210; Hoffer, *Devil's Disciples,* 181, 188.

165. The legal issues surrounding spectral evidence are treated in Hoffer, *Devil's Disciples,* 109, 145–50, 168, 170. 180, 191.

166. Paul Boyer and Stephen Nissenbaum, eds., *The Salem Witchcraft Papers: Verbatim Transcripts of the Legal Documents of the Salem Witchcraft Outbreak of 1692,* 3vols. (New York, 1977), 1:184–86 [hereafter *SWP*].

167. On the devil, magic, and witches' voices, see Kamensky, *Governing the Tongue,* 153–79.

168. Deodat Lawson, *A Brief and True Narrative of Some Remarkable Passages Relating to Sundry Persons Afflicted by Witchcraft* [1692], in Burr, ed., *Narratives,* 158, 159.

169. Samuel Sewall's diary recorded many instances when the cry of fire sent people rushing into the streets. In the two volumes of the diary, *The Diary of Samuel Sewall,* ed. M. Halsey Thomas (New York, 1973), there are sixty-three references to fires, most of which expressed Sewall's concern triggered by the cry of fire.

170. *SWP,* 1:80 (In her deposition Sarah Nurse said she saw Sarah Bibber, one of the accusers, pull out pins from her clothing and prick herself at Rebecca Nurse's examination).

171. Foster, *Long Argument,* 261, finds Hathorne the most rigorous and unsympathetic

NOTES TO PAGES 117–122 ❖ 287

of the examiners. But John Winthrop himself had set the pattern; suspects were not allowed to stand mute or to answer evasively. Winthrop, *History of New England,* ed. James Savage (Boston, 1826), 47.

172. Hoffer, *Devil's Disciples,* 122, 165, 166.

173. See Karlsen, *The Devil in the Shape of a Woman,* 11–14, 135–36, 225–41; Demos, *Entertaining Satan,* 97–131.

174. Hoffer, *Devil's Disciples,* 46–50, 91–95; Boyer and Nissenbaum, *Salem Possessed,* 124–30.

175. See e.g. Hansen, *Witchcraft at Salem,* 85–86; Norton, *Devil's Snare,* 124 and after.

176. Words on a page cannot convey shading, volume, or emotion. We cannot duplicate accent and rhythm, either. "It is impossible to replicate exactly the voices and other sounds of the long past. They are gone." Winthrop D. Jordan, *Tumult and Silence at Second Creek: An Inquiry into a Civil War Slave Conspiracy,* rev ed. (Baton Rouge, La., 1995), 22.

177. Despite the "verbatim" in the title of the Boyer and Nissenbaum collection of documents. On the ways that the taking down of notes and the preparation of trial records influenced what was said as well as what was recorded, see Peter Rushton, "Texts of Authority: Witchcraft Accusations and the Demonstration of Truth in Early Modern England," in Clark, ed., *Languages of Witchcraft,* 24–25, 27–30.

178. Even Parris, hardly a disinterested officer of the court, was pressed into service. See e.g. *SWP,* 1:289. Some of the suspects whose words he wrote were his own parishioners.

179. Hoffer, *Devil's Disciples,* xvi–xvii, 59, 64, 106–7, 109.

180. Clark, *Thinking with Demons,* 3, 7. See also Clark, "Introduction," in Clark, ed., *Languages of Witchcraft,* esp. 6, 9, 11, on "reading" witchcraft.

181. *SWP,* 1:49, 59, 65–66, 74.

182. Ibid., 83, 86, 92, 93.

183. So, apparently, did English apparitions. See Malcolm Gaskill, "Witches and Witnesses in Old and New England," in Clark, ed., *Languages of Witchcraft,* 61. Gaskill finds these depositions evidence of mentalities in action and fantasies for the dispossessed.

184. *SWP,* 1:96, 97, 100.

185. Ibid., 102–3, 105–6.

186. Ibid., 104.

187. Ibid., 95, 113.

188. Ibid., 122, 123, 124, 125, 126, 127, 128.

189. Ibid., 135, 139–40. The grand jury found a true bill on the indictment of both women, but at trial in January 1693, the jury acquitted both.

190. Ibid., 145, 163.

191. Ibid., 160–61.

192. Ibid., 164.

193. The French could not prevent their Indians allies from killing women and children in Portland, Maine, after its garrison had surrendered to the French in 1691. Stories

of the massacre spread through New England like wildfire. Norton, *Devil's Snare,* 102–11; Peter Charles Hoffer, *The Brave New World: A History of Early America* (Boston, 2000), 272.

194. *SWP,* 1:166–67.

195. Ibid., 2:342, 500, 514.

196. Ibid., 1:217, 232, 2:412, 421 (the examinations of Abigail and Deliverance Hobbs, whose confessions condemned a number of other women).

197. E.g. ibid., 1:135; 2:406 (terms of two years).

198. Hoffer, *Devil's Disciples,* 89.

199. *SWP,* 2:387, 371, 390, 502, 372 (witches like to dance, an activity the Puritans frowned upon).

200. Lawson, *Brief and True Narrative,* in Burr, ed., *Narratives,* 154.

201. *SWP,* 2:362. By the end of May the yellow bird was all over the country. See e.g. ibid., 528.

202. Ibid., 1:202, 280, 281, 2:528, 545, 387.

203. Thomas, *Religion and the Decline of Magic,* 479–86.

204. *SWP,* 1:245, 168–69.

205. Ibid., 1:227, 280.

206. Ibid., 2:406, 539, 540.

207. Ibid., 520–21; Hoffer, *Devil's Disciples,* 70.

208. *SWP,* 2:526.

209. Compare the homey comforts and rural peace of Henry Beston, *Northern Farm: A Glorious Year on a Small Maine Farm* (New York, 1948), 16–17 and after, with the *SWP* testimony.

210. Rowlandson, *Sovereignty and Goodness of God,* 111.

211. Ibid.

212. *SWP,* 2:558, 3:708.

213. There was great interest in monstrous births in New England, as evidences of individual transgressions and proofs of God's purpose. See Robert Blair St. George, *Conversing by Signs: Poetics of Implication in Colonial New England Culture* (Chapel Hill, N.C., 1998), 169–73. But no monsters added to Salem's agony.

214. Hoffer, *Devil's Disciples,* 62.

215. St. George, *Conversing by Signs,* 120, 123.

216. Foster, *Long Argument,* 259, called Cotton Mather's draft of the "Return of the Ministers" "schizoid."

217. Cotton Mather to John Richards, May 31, in Kenneth Silverman, ed., *Selected Letters of Cotton Mather* (Baton Rouge, La., 1971), 35, 40. Silverman, *Life and Times,* 98–100, argues strongly that Mather was opposed to the use of spectral evidence. But David Levin, "Did the Mathers Disagree about the Salem Witchcraft Trials?" *Proceedings of the American Antiquarian Society* 95 (1985), 19–37, finds that the younger Mather accepted spectral evidence.

218. Silverman, *Life and Times,* 105.

219. Mather to John Cotton, August 5, 1692, in Worthington C. Ford, ed., *Diary of Cotton Mather* (New York, 1911), 142.

220. Willard, *Some Miscellany Observations Respecting Witchcraft in a Dialogue Between S and B* [1692] (reprint ed., Boston, 1869), 8, 16, 21. On Willard's role in earlier cases, see Demos, *Entertaining Satan*, 99–131. On his role in the Salem crisis, see Mark A. Peterson, "'Ordinary' Preaching and the Interpretation of the Salem Witchcraft Crisis by the Boston Clergy," *Essex Institute Historical Collections* 129 (1993), 94–100; David C. Brown, "Salem Witchcraft Trials: Samuel Willard's *Some Miscellany Observations*," *Essex Institute Historical Collections* 128 (1992), 207–36; Stephen L. Robbins, "Samuel Willard and the Specters of God's Wrathful Lion," *New England Quarterly* 60 (1987), 596–603.

221. Increase Mather was torn, given Cotton's well-publicized views, his own attachment to the ruling party that had supported the trials, and his well-honed sense of political caution. Hall, *The Last American Puritan*, 261.

222. Hoffer, *Devil's Disciples*, 144–47.

223. Foster, *Long Argument*, 262; Hoffer, *Devil's Disciples*, 181–82.

224. Hoffer, *Devil's Disciples*, 142–45; Winship, *Seers of God*, 119.

225. Increase Mather, *Illustrious Providences*, 169, 204.

226. Increase Mather, *Cases of Conscience*, preface.

227. Hoffer, *Devil's Disciples*, 137–38.

228. Cotton Mather, *Magnalia Christi Americana*, ed. Murdock, 331; Hoffer, *Devil's Disciples*, 184–85.

229. But in an addendum, Increase denied that he and Cotton disagreed or that he had anything but praise for his son's work. Hall, *The Last American Puritan*, 263.

230. Cotton Mather, *Wonders of the Invisible World*, in Burr, ed., *Narratives*, 214, 217, 247. He may, however, have attended the hearings, for he remarked that he had seen the "children" in agony during testimony. Silverman, *Life and Times*, 105.

231. Cotton Mather, *Brand Pluck'd Out of the Burning*, in Burr, ed., *Narratives*, 282.

232. Hall, *Worlds of Wonder, Days of Judgment*, 84.

233. Calef, *More Wonders of the Invisible World*, in Burr, ed., *Narratives*, 299, 304, 313.

234. Winship, *Seers of God*, 120, 127, 131.

235. Cotton Mather, *Magnalia*, 326.

236. Cotton Mather, *Theopolis Americana* (Boston, 1710), 29.

237. Winship, *Seers of God*, 133; Foster, *Long Argument*, 286.

238. Erik R. Seeman, *Pious Persuasions: Laity and Clergy in Eighteenth-Century New England* (Baltimore, 1999), 67, finds plenty of evidence that the laity continued to believe in quasimagical concepts of baptism, astrology, and other forms of occultism, in the face of ministerial wrath. But these variant ideas would never again be part of mainstream religious practice.

239. Godbeer, *Devil's Dominion*, 227–33.

240. Mark Catesby, *The Natural History of Carolina, Florida, and the Bahama Islands . . .*, 2 vols., (London, 17311–43), 2:xxx; Leventhal, *In the Shadow of the Enlightenment*, 85–103; Schmidt, *Hearing Things*, 3–4.

241. Benjamin Bayley, an Anglican rector, in 1708, quoted in Schmidt, *Hearing Things,* 71.

242. Jonathan Edwards, *Treatise on the Religious Affections* [1746], in John E. Smith, ed., *The Works of Jonathan Edwards* (New Haven, Conn., 1959), 2:149, 173, 206–7, 216; Ann Taves, *Fits, Trances, and Visions: Experiencing Religion and Explaining Experience* (Princeton, 1999), 49.

243. Taves, *Fits,* 56.

244. Ann Kirschner, "Tending to Edify, Astonish, and Instruct: Published Accounts of Dreams and Visions in the Early Republic," paper delivered at the McNeil Center for Early American Studies, March 23, 2001, cited by permission.

245. George Ripley, "Discourses on the Philosophy of Religion" [1836], in Perry Miller, ed., *The Transcendentalists: An Anthology* (Cambridge, Mass., 1967), 133; and see Schmidt, *Hearing Things,* the chapter on ventriloquism.

Chapter 3 · Other Worlds

1. Perry R. Hinton, *Stereotypes, Cognition, and Culture* (Philadelphia, 2000), 40–41, 69, 72, 83–84, 91–92, 158.

2. See e.g. T. W. Adorno et al., *The Authoritarian Personality* [1950] (New York, 1969), 145–50.

3. Irving Goffman, *Stigma: Notes on the Management of Spoiled Identity* (New York, 1963), 5.

4. Henry Louis Gates Jr., "White Like Me," *New Yorker,* June 17, 1996, 66–78; Kimberlyn Leary, "*Passing* Posing, and 'Keeping it Real,'" *Constellation,* March 1999, 86–98; Gayle Wald, *Crossing the Line: Racial Passing in Twentieth-Century U.S. Literature and Culture* (Durham, N.C., 2000); Jon-Christian Sedges, "Lynchings and Passing," *Consolations: Law and Narrative in African American Life* (Ann Arbor, Mich., 2000), 184–201; Patricia J. Williams, *Seeing a Color-Blind Future: The Paradox of Race* (New York, 1997), 3–9.

5. I do not mean to conflate color and race. *Race* is a social and cultural construction, a word that signifies an attitude rather than a thing, and is most often used to rank and demean rather than to describe. See e.g. Barbara Jeanne Fields, "Ideology and Race in American History," in J. Morgan Kousser and James M. McPherson, eds., *Region, Race, and Reconstruction: Essays in Honor of C. Vann Woodward* (New York, 1982), 143–78; Joseph L. Graves Jr., *The Emperor's New Clothes: Biological Theories of Race at the Millennium* (New Brunswick, N.J., 2001).

6. Walter Mosley, *Fearless Jones* (New York, 2000), 11, 37, 45, 82.

7. See e.g. Michael Eric Dyson, *Race Rules: Navigating the Color Line* (Chapel Hill, N.C., 1996).

8. In the course of thinking about affirmative action, a contributor wrote: "What I never told my friend is that when he was hired, his race was considered over and above his experience and competence." "The Ethicist," Randy Cohen, replied, "your friend was not hired only because of his race; he was hired because he could do the job, and

race was also a factor—as it has been for all of us in this country since colonial times." *New York Time Magazine,* May 27, 2001, 18.

9. Benjamin Franklin, "Observations concerning the Increase of Mankind," in Leonard W. Labaree et al., eds., *The Papers of Benjamin Franklin,* 36 vols. (New Haven, Conn., 1959–), 4:234; Olaudah Equiano, "The Interesting Narrative of the Life of Olaudah Equiano" [1789], in Giles Gunn, ed., *Early American Writing* (New York, 1994), 517–18.

10. Christina Smith, *Christian America? What Evangelicals Really Want* (Berkeley, 2000), 21, 22, 47, 56; William Martin, *With God on Our Side: The Rise of the Religious Right in America* (New York, 1996), 3–24.

11. Susan O'Brien, "A Transatlantic Community of Saints: The Great Awakening and the First Evangelical Network, 1735–1755," *American Historical Review* 91 (1986), 811–32.

12. Christopher Grasso, *A Speaking Aristocracy: Transforming Public Discourse in Eighteenth-Century Connecticut* (Chapel Hill, N.C., 1999), 103.

13. Wheelock, quoted in William D. Piersen, *Black Yankees: The Development of an Afro-American Subculture in Eighteenth-Century New England* (Amherst, Mass., 1988), 70.

14. My assumption, based on the words of the minsters who participated in the "Great and General Awakening," is that there really was a Great Awakening. But see Jon Butler, "Enthusiasm Described and Decried: The Great Awakening as Interpretive Fiction," *Journal of American History* 69 (1983), 305–25; Butler, *Awash in a Sea of Faith* (Cambridge, Mass., 1990), 165–66; and Joseph A. Conforti, *Jonathan Edwards, Religious Tradition, and American Culture* (Chapel Hill, N.C., 1995), 12 and after, arguing that the idea of a sweeping first Awakening was invented by early-nineteenth-century advocates of Jonathan Edwards' theology.

15. Charles Woodmason, *The Carolina Backcountry on the Eve of the Revolution: The Journal and Other Writings of Charles Woodmason, Anglican Itinerant,* ed. Richard J. Hooker (Chapel Hill, N.C., 1969), 56.

16. Martin, *With God on Our Side,* 168–90, 191–220; Michael Winship, *Making Heretics: Militant Protestantism and Free Grace in Massachusetts, 1636–1641* (Princeton, 2002), 24.

17. David Eltis, *The Rise of African Slavery in the Americas* (Cambridge, 2000), 7.

18. Orlando Patterson, *Slavery and Social Death: A Comparative Study* (Cambridge, Mass., 1982), 61; David Brion Davis, *The Problem of Slavery in Western Culture* (Ithaca, N.Y., 1966), 51–52.

19. Peter Kolchin, *American Slavery, 1619–1877* (New York, 1993), 4.

20. So, for example, in Spanish slave law as applied in Spain, a slave who married a free person would become free, but under a Spanish imperial rescript published in 1538, an African slave who married a free Indian Christian did not become free. The crown wanted slaves to be exposed to Christianity but did not want to lose their labor. The effect was to make skin color rather than marital status or religious adherence the defining characteristic of slavery. Alan Watson, *Slave Law in the Americas* (Athens, Ga., 1989), 48 and after.

21. Winthrop Jordan, *White over Black*, rev. ed.(Baltimore, 1969), 3–43.

22. Philip D. Morgan, "British Encounters with Africans and African-Americans," in Bernard Bailyn and Philip D. Morgan, eds., *Strangers within the Realm: Cultural Margins of the First British Empire* (Chapel Hill, N.C., 1991), 159. The "white-black" interaction is not a metaphor or a shorthand; it is crucial to understanding all phases of the otherness of slavery. Ibid., 163. Here one must, or rather, should face the problem of homogenization that color and other sensory markers of otherness pose. The "other" defined by skin color or accent, when seen or heard, becomes one rather than many. There are no individuals, only a group, sect, class, race, people, or nation. This is a danger to which all studies of race relations in America are prone. See e.g. James Sidbury, *Ploughshares into Swords: Race, Rebellion, and Identity in Gabriel's Virginia, 1730–1810* (Cambridge, 1997), 2 and after.

23. See Shane White, "Pinkster: Afro-Dutch Syncretization in New York City and the Hudson Valley," *Journal of American Folklore* 102 (1989), 70.

24. Samuel Davies, quoted in Patricia U. Bonomi, *Under the Cope of Heaven: Religion, Society, and Politics in Colonial America* (New York, 1986), 125–26.

25. Quotations from Piersen, *Black Yankees,* 66, 67.

26. In 1870, a young New England teacher named Elizabeth Kilham, traveling in the South, recorded her impressions of the shouting, clapping, dancing, singing, and personal exulting of the African American congregants at "Old Billy's" church on the Georgia Sea Islands: "One of those scenes, which, when read of, seem the exaggerations of a disordered imagination; and when witnessed, leave an impression like the memory of some horrid nightmare—so wild is the torrent of excitement, that, sweeping away reason and sense, tosses men and women upon its waves, mingling the words of religion with the howlings of wild beasts, and the ravings of madmen." Elizabeth Kilham, "Sketches in Color," *Putnam's Magazine,* March 15, 1870, 305. I am grateful to the work of Shane White and Graham White for calling this article to my attention.

27. Jordan, *White over Black,* 4–11; Eltis, *The Rise of African Slavery,* table on 9.

28. John Gabriel Stedman, *Narrative of a Five Years Expedition against the Revolted Negroes of Surinam* [1790], ed. Richard Price and Sally Price (Baltimore, 1988), 43. Edward Shippen Sr. to Joseph Shippen Jr., August 1, 1756, quoted in Peter Rhodes Silver, "Indian Hating and the Rise of Whiteness in Provincial Pennsylvania" (Ph.D. diss., Yale University, 2000), 230. Shippen knew, of course, that Indians painted their faces black when they went to war, whatever side they fought on. The English had remarked on this color preference in the 1630s, as I noted in Chapter 1. The Indians began to see the utility in homogenization of their own color in the wake of Pontiac's Rebellion (1763–65). The Shawnees, attempting to create a pan-Indian coalition to bar colonial incursions into the Ohio Valley, spoke of "all you [natives] who inhabit the same continent, and are of the same colour." Shawnee headman (1769), quoted in Woody Holton, *Forced Founders: Indians, Debtors, Slaves, and the Making of the American Revolution in Virginia* (Chapel Hill, N.C., 1999), 20.

29. Joyce Chaplin, *Subject Matter: Technology, the Body, and Science on the Anglo-American Frontier, 1500–1676* (Cambridge, Mass., 2001), 139–41.

30. William Petty, quoted in Edmund S. Morgan, *American Slavery, American Freedom: The Ordeal of Colonial Virginia* (New York, 1975), 325.

31. Jordan, *White over Black,* 216–59.

32. William M. Wiecek, "The Statutory Law of Slavery and Race in the Thirteen Mainland Colonies of British America," *William and Mary Quarterly,* 3d ser. 34 (1977); 258–80; Watson, *Slave Law in the Americas,* 63–82.

33. Slave law of 1680, quoted in A. Leon Higginbotham, *In the Matter of Color: Race and the American Legal Process, the Colonial Period* (New York, 1978), 39.

34. Morgan Godwyn, quoted in Thomas D. Morris, *Southern Slavery and the Law, 1619–1860* (Chapel Hill, N.C., 1996), 17. Southern state courts always regarded color as a badge of slavery. Ibid., 25.

35. Julius Goebel Jr. and T. Raymond Naughton, *Law Enforcement in Colonial New York: A Study in Criminal Procedure* (New York, 1944), 418.

36. Act of 1740, John F. Grimké, comp., *Public Laws of the State of South Carolina, From Its First Establishment . . .* (Philadelphia, 1790), 1:167. Little had changed in antebellum America, for that matter. In 1835, the Michigan Constitutional convention "came to the remarkable conclusion that Indians ought to be considered white [for the purposes of voting rights] because the word *white* simply meant 'not black': 'the word white was used in contradiction to the black alone, and though the Indian was copper colored, he was not to be classed among the latter.'" Quoted in Alexander Keyssar, *The Right to Vote: The Contested History of Democracy in the United States* (New York, 2000), 59.

37. *Acts Passed by the General Assembly of New York, 1712* (New York, 1712), 159.

38. William Byrd to Lord Egmont, July 12, 1736, *Virginia Magazine of History and Biography* 36 (1928), 222.

39. Herman Husband to Lord Granville, quoted in Marjoleine Kars, *Breaking Loose Together: The Regulator Rebellion in Pre-Revolutionary North Carolina* (Chapel Hill, N.C., 2002), 25.

40. Abigail Adams, quoted in David McCullough, *John Adams* (New York, 2001), 346.

41. Thomas Jefferson, *Notes on the State of Virginia* [1781], ed. William Peden (Chapel Hill, N.C., 1955), 138.

42. Ibid., 139. Jefferson was one in a long line of whites who claimed to be able to read black bodies. Though the black was "other" and often concealed or dissimulated, the experts could penetrate these facades. Ariela J. Gross, *Double Character: Slavery and Mastery in the Antebellum Southern Courtroom* (Princeton, 2000), 123.

43. Morgan, *American Slavery, American Freedom,* 328.

44. Stedman, *Narrative,* 242.

45. Thomas R. R. Cobb, *An Inquiry into the Law of Negro Slavery in the United States of America* [1858], ed. Paul Finkelman (Athens, Ga., 1999), 22–23.

46. David C. Littlefield, *Rice and Slaves: Ethnicity and the Slave Trade in Colonial South Carolina* (Baton Rouge, La., 1981), 8–21, 25, 31, 73.

47. Morgan, "British Encounters," 178–79.

48. Peter Wood, *Black Majority: Negroes In Colonial South Carolina from 1670 through*

the Stono Rebellion (New York, 1974), 179; David Galenson, *Traders, Planters, and Slaves: Market Behavior in Early English America* (Cambridge, 1986), 56.

49. Joseph Holt Ingraham, *The Southwest, by a Yankee* [1835], quoted in Walter Johnson, *Soul by Soul: Life Inside the Antebellum Slave Market* (Cambridge, Mass., 1999), 135, 139. Johnson suggests that color-based distinctions also reduced the "blurred spectrum" of visual bodies to a stable order.

50. Anon., *Great Auction Sale of Slaves at Savannah, Georgia* (New York, 1859), 3.

51. One of the many paradoxes of color in this setting: There is no entry for *color,* or for any of the many colors that Europeans recorded of their African slaves, in the most recent dictionary of African American slavery, Randall M. Miller and John David Smith, eds., *Dictionary of Afro-American Slavery* (New York, 1988); nor is there a subject heading for *color* or for *black* in the index to the many volumes of George P. Rawick, ed., *The American Slave: A Composite Autobiography* [1941], 19 vols. (reprint ed., Westport, Conn., 1972). The word *black* appears only as a modifier of other terms, such as "church, black"; "ministers, black"; "masters, black"; "landownership, black"; and as part of a phrase, as in "free blacks." "Whites," however, is a subject heading. Donald M. Jacobs, assisted by Steven Fershleiser, *Index to the American Slave* (Westport, Conn., 1981). Color was everywhere a definition of status, origin, employment, and habitat but was nowhere recognized—the highly visible vanishing before our eyes.

52. Byrd, "Secret History" [1728], *William Byrd's Histories of the Dividing Line Betwixt Virginia and North Carolina,* ed. William K. Boyd (New York, 1967), 57. But light-skinned women were generally preferred over darker-skinned women, at least as house servants. Johnson, *Soul by Soul,* 151. In the slave market, prices rose proportionately with the perceived "whiteness" of the slave. Ibid., 155.

53. Lathan A. Windley, ed., *Runaway Slave Advertisements: A Documentary History from the 1730s to 1790,* Vol. 3, *South Carolina* (Westport, Conn., 1983), 2, 7, 8.

54. Johnson, *Soul by Soul,* 142.

55. Douglas R. Egerton, *He Shall Go Out Free: The Lives of Denmark Vesey* (Madison, Wis., 1999), 91; Sidbury, *Ploughshares into Swords,* 43.

56. Generally, Mark Smith, *Listening to Nineteenth-Century America* (Chapel Hill, N.C., 2001), 150–71.

57. Quoted in Philip D. Morgan, *Slave Counterpoint: Black Culture in the Eighteenth-Century Chesapeake and Lowcountry* (Chapel Hill, N.C., 1998), 122.

58. Cynthia S. West, "Diane McIntyre," in *African Dance,* ed. Katherine Welsh Asante (Trenton, N.J., 1996), 133; Mechal Sobel, *The World They Made Together: Black and White Values in Eighteenth-Century Virginia* (Princeton, 1987), 141–42; Eugene Genovese, *Roll, Jordan, Roll: The World the Slaves Made* (New York, 1974), 199, 324; Piersen, *Black Yankees,* 121–22.

59. Fannie Berry, recalling the aural celebration of freedom at Appomattox Court House in April 1865, quoted in Grace Elizabeth Hale, *Making Whiteness: The Culture of Segregation in the South, 1890–1940* (New York, 1998), 1.

60. The importance of funeral rites in the African American community survived

slavery. See Karla Holloway, *Passed On: African American Mourning Stories* (Durham, N.C., 2002).

61. Quoted in Michael Mullin, *Africa in America: Slave Acculturation and Resistance in the American South and the British Caribbean, 1736–1831* (Urbana, Ill., 1992), 65, 66. See also Pierson, *Black Yankees,* 76.

62. Wood, *Black Majority,* 172–86; Morgan, *Slave Counterpoint,* 562–80.

63. Maureen Warner Lewis, "The African Impact on Language and Literature in the English-Speaking Caribbean: Continued Existence of African Languages, A Case Study of Yoruba in Trinidad," in Margaret E. Graham and Franklin W. Knight, eds., *Africa and the Caribbean: The Legacies of a Link* (Baltimore, 1979), 104.

64. Wood, *Black Majority,* 172–91, Michael Craton, *Searching for the Invisible Man: Slaves and Plantation Life in Jamaica* (Cambridge, Mass., 1978), 55, 59, 157; Jerome S. Handler and JoAnn Jacoby, "Slave Names and Naming in Barbados, 1650–1830," *William and Mary Quarterly,* 3d ser. 53 (1996), 685–729. Allan Kulikoff told me that few of these names survived the first generation, at least in the Chesapeake. He concedes that his findings are based on slave masters' estate inventories, however, and that this source might underreport the number of African slaves who kept their old names and passed them on without the master's explicit consent. Moreover, in South Carolina, where slaves usually lived among other slaves, African names would have persisted longer than in the Chesapeake, his area of study, where slaves had far more contact with free persons.

65. See e.g. Genovese, *Roll, Jordan, Roll,* 324.

66. Charles Joyner, *Down by the Riverside: A South Carolina Slave Community* (Urbana, Ill., 1984), 152–69.

67. Rhys Isaac, *The Transformation of Virginia, 1740–1790* (Chapel Hill, N.C., 1982), 340–41.

68. Smith, *Listening to Nineteenth-Century America,* 68.

69. Pearl Primus, "African Dance," in Asante, ed., *African Dance,* 3. On slave homes, Mullin, *Africa in America,* 100–126; Morgan, *Slave Counterpoint,* 104–23; Allan Kulikoff, *Tobacco and Slaves: The Development of Southern Cultures in the Chesapeake, 1680–1800* (Chapel Hill, N.C., 1986), 368.

70. John Michael Vlach, "Afro Americans," in Dell Upton, ed., *America's Architectural Roots: Ethnic Groups That Built America* (New York, 1986), 43.

71. Terrence W. Epperson, "'A Separate House for the Christian Slaves, One for the Negro Slaves': The Archeology of Race and Identity in Late Seventeenth-Century Virginia," in Charles E. Orser Jr., ed., *Race and the Archeology of Identity* (Salt Lake City, 2001), 54–67.

72. Nor yet forgotten: "Quaint, outlandish heathen gods / Black men fashion out of rods, / Clay, and brittle bits of stone, / In a likeness like their own . . . Lord forgive me if my need / Sometimes shapes a human creed." Countee Cullen, *Heritage.* For the archeology: Anne Elizabeth Yentsch, *A Cheaspeake Family and Their Slaves: A Study in Historical Archeology* (Cambridge, 1992), 200–208; James Deetz, *In Small Things Forgotten: The Archeology of Early American Life* (New York, 1977), 138–54.

73. Yentsch, *Chesapeake Family,* 192; Brent Staples, "To Be a Slave in Brooklyn," *New York Times Magazine,* June 24, 2001, 35; Anne-Marie Cantwell and Diana diZerega Wall, *Unearthing Gotham: The Archeology of New York City* (New Haven, Conn., 2001), 290. On the return to Africa of the spirits, see Michael A. Gomez, *Exchanging Our Country Marks: The Transformation of African Identities in the Colonial and Antebellum South* (Chapel Hill, N.C., 1998), 114–34; Morgan, *Slave Counterpoint,* 641.

74. Anne Bell recalling the slavery times in George P. Rawick, ed., *The American Slave: A Composite Autobiography* [1941], Vol. 2, *South Carolina Narratives,* pts. 1 and 2 (reprint ed., Westport, Conn., 1971), 53. M. E. Abrams told an interviewer that there were ghosts in the old houses, and "witchery turned black cats to white." Ibid., 4. See also Sobel, *World They Made Together,* 96–97.

75. John Thornton, *Africa and Africans in the Making of the Atlantic World, 1400–1800,* 2d ed. (Cambridge, 1998), 239–47; Charles Joyner, "The World of the Plantation Slaves," in Edward D. C. Campbell Jr. and Kym S. Rice, eds., *Before Freedom Came: African American Life in the Antebellum South* (Charlottesville, Va., 1991), 76. In the civil wars that roiled Sierra Leone in the 1990s, troops on both sides wore amulets prepared by juju men to protect the wearer from harm.

76. Stedman, *Narrative,* 582, 405.

77. Morgan, "Slave Life in Piedmont Virginia, 1720–1800," in Lois Green Carr, Philip Morgan, and Jean Russo, eds., *Colonial Chesapeake Society* (Williamsburg, Va., 1989), 433–84; Morgan, *Slave Counterpoint,* 610–18. Morgan notes that the suspects were often called "Doctor," although their conduct is far closer to that of Thornton's African priests than colonial physicians.

78. Morgan, *Slave Counterpoint,* 113.

79. Sally E. Hadden, *Slave Patrols: Law and Violence in Virginia and the Carolinas* (Cambridge, Mass., 2001), 107.

80. Nicholson, quoted in Sobel, *World They Made Together,* 33.

81. Hadden, *Slave Patrols,* 108–9, 116–17, 132.

82. Sidbury, *Ploughshares into Swords,* 24, and generally, Ira Berlin and Philip D. Morgan, eds., *Cultivation and Culture: Labor and the Shaping of Slave Life in the Americas* (Charlottesville, Va., 1993).

83. Gross, *Double Character,* 34.

84. Windley, ed., *Runaway Slave Advertisements,* 3:9–10.

85. Act of 1740, in Grimké, comp., *Public Laws . . . of South Carolina,* 1:170.

86. Isaac, *Transformation of Virginia,* 335–341.

87. Winthrop D. Jordan, *Tumult and Silence at Second Creek: An Inquiry into a Civil War Slave Conspiracy,* rev ed. (Baton Rouge, La., 1995), 124.

88. J. J. Mauricius, writing in 1751, quoted in Peter Linebaugh and Marcus Rediker, *The Many-Headed Hydra: Sailors, Slaves, Commoners, and the Hidden History of the Revolutionary Atlantic* (Boston, 2000), 4.

89. Stephen Pembroke, a runaway slave, quoted in *New York Tribune,* July 18, 1854, reprinted in John W. Blassingame, ed., *Slave Testimony: Two Centuries of Letters, Speeches, Interviews, and Autobiographies* (Baton Rouge, La., 1977), 139. Whipping was the most

common form of severe corporeal punishment. Herbert G. Gutman, *Power and Culture: Essays on the American Working Class,* ed. Ira Berlin (New York, 1987), 303.

90. Rawick, ed., *The American Slave,* vol. 2, *South Carolina Narratives,* 328, 289.

91. Gross, *Double Character,* 130.

92. See e.g. Ira Berlin and Philip D. Morgan, "Labor and the Shaping of Slave Life in the Americas," in Berlin and Morgan, eds., *Cultivation and Culture,* 1–45; Genovese, *Roll, Jordan, Roll,* 309–24.

93. Genovese, *Roll, Jordan, Roll,* 365–88.

94. Thomas J. Davis, *A Rumor of Revolt: The "Great Negro Plot" in Colonial New York* (New York, 1985), 31, 32.

95. Richard S. Dunn, *Sugar and Slaves: The Rise of the Planter Class in the English West Indies, 1624–1713* (Chapel Hill, N.C., 1972), 239–46; Peter Charles Hoffer, "Introduction," in Hoffer and William S. Scott, eds., *Criminal Proceedings in Colonial Virginia. Volume Ten: American Legal Records* (Athens, Ga., 1985), xlv–lii.

96. Higginbotham, *In the Matter of Color,* 39.

97. *The Laws of the Province of Maryland, Collected into One Volume* (Philadelphia, 1718), 200.

98. Morgan, *Slave Counterpoint,* 473. But the large number here may simply be an artifact of how slaves were caught; the more slaves participated in a crime, the more likely one of them was to talk about it and the more likely the authorities were to learn the identities of the accessories and principals in the crime.

99. Herbert Aptheker, *American Negro Slave Revolts* (New York, 1969), 162–80, reprints letters on these otherwise elusive events. The letters always reported the correspondents visceral response to what they saw and heard.

100. Wood, *Black Majority,* 3–62.

101. Ibid., 95–130; John J. McCusker and Russell R. Menard, *The Economy of British America, 1607–1789,* rev ed. (Chapel Hill, N.C., 1991), 174–85.

102. Wood, *Black Majority,* 131–66.

103. Ibid., 195–217.

104. Hadden, *Slave Patrols,* 9, 20, 21–22, 24; Wood, *Black Majority,* 274–77. The model was the Barbados patrolling system.

105. Ibid., 238–67.

106. Morgan, *Slave Counterpoint,* 450.

107. Aptheker, *Slave Revolts,* 173, 175, 180.

108. Windley, ed., *Runaway Slave Advertisements,* 3:31–34. I have not included the habitual runaways—slaves who had been in the country for years, mastering the language and gaining skill, or who were well known in the region.

109. Shane White and Graham White, *Stylin': African American Expressive Culture from Its Beginnings to the Zoot Suit* (Ithaca, N.Y., 1998), 8–13.

110. Gomez, *Country Marks,* 137.

111. Jordan, *Tumult and Silence,* 117.

112. *Colonial Records of South Carolina: The Journal of the Commons House of Assembly, November 10, 1736–June 7, 1739,* ed. J. H. Easterby (Columbia, S.C., 1951), 673–74.

113. President William Stephens to Benjamin Martyn, December 1, 1742, in *Documents Illustrative of the History of the Slave Trade to America,* ed. Elizabeth Donnan (Washington D.C., 1935), 4:604.

114. On Mose, see Jane Landers, "Garcia Real de Santa Teresa de Mose: A Free Black Town in Spanish Colonial Florida," *American Historical Review* 95 (1990), 9–30.

115. On the place of the revolt in Carolina history, see Wood, *Black Majority,* 308–26; Robert Olwell, *Masters, Slaves, and Subjects: The Culture of Power in the South Carolina Low Country, 1740–1790* (Ithaca, N.Y., 1998), 21–25; and M. Eugene Sirmans, *Colonial South Carolina, A Political History, 1663–1763* (Chapel Hill, N.C., 1966), 208. The documentary evidence is abstracted in Michael Mullin, ed., *American Negro Slavery: A Documentary History* (New York, 1976), 84–88.

116. For example, on the Stono River, Act of 1754, in Grimké, comp., *Public Laws of . . . South Carolina,* 1:229–30.

117. Wood, *Black Majority,* 206–8. I believe the rebellion began on the evening of September 8 and not, as is usually argued, during the wee hours of the next day.

118. Statute of 1740, in Grimké, comp., *Public Laws of . . . South Carolina,* 1:168.

119. *Colonial Records of South Carolina: The Journal of the Commons House of Assembly, November 10, 1736–June 7, 1739,* 690.

120. Morgan, *Slave Counterpoint,* 186, 202. The task system prevalent in South Carolina gave slaves time to themselves when their assigned tasks for the day or week were done. This did not apply to labor on river gangs.

121. The Angolan and Congolese slaves were from different regions, and many dialects of Bantu were spoken, but by that time the slaves could understand one another. Wood, *Black Majority,* 189; Gomez, *Country Marks,* 135.

122. Thus the composition of the work crew violated the unwritten rule that no collection of slaves should be purchased by any one planter or set to any one task composed of men who spoke the same language.

123. John K. Thornton, "African Dimensions of the Stono Rebellion," *American Historical Review* 96 (1991), 1101–13, stresses the Angolan dimension of the revolt. Richard Cullen Rath, "Worlds Chanted into Being: Soundways in Early America" (Ph.D. diss., Brandeis University, 2001), 27–28, 143–44, discusses the rebels' use of drums.

124. The slaves must have known that they could find a safe haven in Florida, for slaves had run there after wounding and killing South Carolinians and Georgians. "An Account of the Negro Insurrection in South Carolina" [n.d.], *Colonial Records of the State of Georgia,* ed. Allan D. Candler et al. (Atlanta, 1913), 22 pt. 2; 232–33.

125. Stedman recalled that the slave rebels in Surinam set great store by blood oaths, never breaking them and requiring the Dutch troops to take them before a peace could be concluded. *Narrative,* 72–73.

126. James Weldon Johnson, *Fifty Years* (wvu.edu/~lawfac/lp-2001/Johnson-j.w.html).

127. Whenever a revolt was rumored, the planters reminded one another to lock up their firearms. Michael Craton, *Testing the Chains: Resistance to Slavery in the British West Indies* (Ithaca, N.Y., 1982), 111. In the New York City slave conspiracy of 1741, whites feared that slaves planned "to seize and carry away the arms" in the fort and "to seize

their masters' arms." One white abettor of the conspiracy was believed to have "bought and procured arms, ammunition, and powder for the purpose." *New-York Weekly Journal,* June 15, 1741. An abortive and smaller- scale Virginia slave revolt in 1751 began with slaves arming themselves with muskets. Morgan, *Slave Counterpoint,* 465. Egerton, *He Shall Go Out Free,* 142, notes that the Charleston arsenal was a target of the rebels in 1822.

128. George Cato, "The Stono Insurrection Described by a Descendant of the Leader," in *The American Slave: A Composite Autobiography,* ed. George P. Rawick (Westport, Conn., 1977), suppl., ser. 1, 11:98–100.

129. Wood, *Black Majority,* 308–26.

130. *Colonial Records of South Carolina: Journal of the Commons House of Assembly, September 12, 1739—March 26, 1741,* ed J. H. Easterby (Columbia, S.C., 1952), 50, 63–65. Morgan, *Slave Counterpoint,* 470, argues that most of these men would probably have been native born.

131. "Account of Negro Insurrection," 233–36; "Letter from South Carolina," September 28, 1739, reprinted in *Boston News-Letter,* November 1–8, 1739.

132. Setting fires and stealing firearms were part of the plan that Gabriel formulated to subdue Richmond and begin his rebellion in 1800. Sidbury, *Ploughshares into Swords,* 67. Kenneth Stampp, *The Peculiar Institution: Slavery in the Ante-bellum South* (New York, 1956), 127–28, argues that arson was the slave's prime weapon against the oppressive master. Michael Meranze, *Laboratories of Virtue: Punishment, Revolution, and Authority in Philadelphia, 1760–1835* (Chapel Hill, N.C., 1996), 31, agrees. Slave arson was a felony punishable by death throughout the colonies. Morris, *Slavery and the Law,* 330–31. Masters in South Carolina particularly feared arson by slaves. Michael Stephen Hindus, *Prison and Plantation: Crimes, Justice, and Authority in Massachusetts and South Carolina, 1767–1878* (Chapel Hill, N.C., 1980), 144. Arson was a time-honored part of all slave rebellions. See e.g. Mullin, *Africa in America,* 255. One further note: Arson was not just a slave crime; people in what the elites dismissed as, variously, the lower orders, the "giddy multitude," and "disgruntled underlings" practiced it regularly. Thus Hittee, an Indian girl, was found guilty of burning her master's house in 1712, undoubtedly as a form of revenge. *Diary of Samuel Sewall,* ed. M. Halsey Thomas (New York, 1973), 2:683.

133. Arson was interpreted as a sign of slave rebellion. When barns and sheds began to go up in smoke, authorities in the town of York, Pennsylvania, immediately assumed that slaves were the culprits. Broadside, "To the Inhabitants of York and Its Vicinity, March 21, 1803." Library Company of Philadelphia. Isaac, a slave, confessed. Ted Stickler, "Into Wickedness: Violence and Motive in the York County, Pennsylvania of the Early Republic," paper presented at the McNeil Center for Early American Studies, July 12, 2001. Cited by permission; *Louis Miller: Sketches and Chronicles,* ed. Robert P. Turner (York, Pa., 1966), 35.

134. In the wake of the growing criticism of the count of guns in probate records reported in Michael Bellesiles, *Arming America* (New York, 2000), a crucial point has been overlooked. Whether 40 percent (Bellesiles) or 60 percent (his critics) of southern colonial estate inventories included working firearms was not as important as who had the

firearms and what they were used for. The firearms were not owned by slaves but by their masters, and their purpose was to deter or put down slave insurrections. On the law, see e.g. Higginbotham, *In the Matter of Color,* 39.

135. The way that Stedman phrased his impression of the rebels as they roasted yams with the faggots that would be used to immolate them later in the day. Stedman, *Narrative,* 102. Compare Landon Carter, who had grown up with slaves and owned hundreds on his Tidewater plantation, writing on August 31, 1778: "Slaves are devils and to make them otherwise than slaves would be to set devils free." *The Diary of Colonel Landon Carter of Sabine Hall, 1752–1778,* ed.. Jack P. Greene (Charlottesville, Va., 1964), 2:1149.

136. William Bull to Board of Trade, October 6, 1739, Letters and Papers from the Governors, March 1739–April 1740, CO 5/367, p. 114, South Carolina Department of Archives and History; Thornton, *Africa and Africans,* 47–48.

137. The reports that reached other colonies had the revolt putting the colony "into the utmost confusion, expecting in it a general plot" by the slaves. *New–York Weekly Journal* November 19, 1739.

138. Mullin, *Africa in America,* 50.

139. "Account of the Negro Insurrection," 223.

140. Thornton, *Africa and Africans,* 324.

141. "Letter from South Carolina"; "A Ranger's Report of Travels with Governor [James] Oglethorpe," September 20, 1739, in Newton Dennison Mereness, ed., *Travels in the American Colonies* (New York, 1916), 222–23.

142. "A Ranger with Oglethorpe," 223.

143. Jonathan Prude, "'To Look upon the "Lower Sort"': Runaway Ads and the Appearance of Unfree Laborers in America, 1750–1800," *Journal of American History* 78 (1991), 141. The "down look" was common enough among slaves but not as common as masters imagined. White and White, *Stylin',* 68–69. The slave might also try on a "roguish down look" or a "sneaking down look."

144. Stedman, *Narrative,* 100.

145. *Virginia Gazette,* November 14–21, 1745; *Virginia Gazette,* October 28–November 4, 1737; *Virginia Gazette,* May 15, 1752. I am grateful to Thomas M. Costa and Harold Gill for calling these references to my attention.

146. *Diary of Colonel Landon Carter,* 2:940. Sometimes the downcast look became a suicidal self-hatred. Gerald W. Mullin, *Flight and Rebellion: Slave Resistance in Eighteenth-Century Virginia* (New York, 1972), 60.

147. Martin A. Klein to the author, July 9, 2001. Klein did his study in Senegal; see Klein, *Islam and Imperialism in Senegal, Sine-Saloum, 1847–1914* (Stanford, Calif., 1968).

148. Desmond Morris, *Manwatching: A Field Guide to Human Behavior* (New York, 1977), 73, 74.

149. Nabby Adams, quoted in McCullough, *Adams,* 343.

150. W. Michael Reisman, *Law in Brief Encounters* (New Haven, Conn., 1999), 35.

151. John Davis, quoted in Sobel, *World They Made Together,* 150.

152. Northrup's tale is quoted in Genovese, *Roll, Jordan, Roll,* 417.

153. White and White, *Stylin',* 70–71.

154. There is an echo—distant to be sure, but still an echo—of the Stono slave's defiant stare in the bitter glare that the black suspect gives the police, in David Simon, *Homicide: A Year on the Killing Streets* (New York, 1991), 489.

155. Bull to Colonial Office, October 5, 1739, CO 5/388, p. 164, South Carolina Department of Archives and History.

156. Cato, "The Stono Insurrection Described by a Descendant of the Leader," 100.

157. The runaway slave advertisements often noted the cut and the color of the runaway's clothing, but mention is almost never made of a runaway wearing black. Mark M. Smith, "Remembering Mary, Shaping Revolt: Reconsidering the Stono Rebellion," *Journal of Southern History* 67 (2001), 513–34, also believes that the flag was white, but for different reasons.

158. Morgan, *Slave Counterpoint*, 130.

159. Stedman, *Narrative*, 84.

160. Daniel Horsmanden, *The New-York Conspiracy* [1744], ed. Thomas J. Davis (Boston, 1971), 63.

161. "Non-verbal leakage"—evidence of lying. Morris, *Manwatching*, 106, 109; Michael Argyle, *Bodily Communication* (London, 1988), 58. Runaways lying to passersby exhibited the same kind of rapid hand motions, as well as stammers. Mullin, *Flight and Rebellion*, 80.

162. The law gave to the freeholder's courts assembled to hear and determine slave felonies the discretion to choose the means of punishment "to deter others from offending in the like kind." Act of 1740, in Grimké, comp., *Public Acts . . . of South Carolina*, 1:167.

163. Richard Price, *Alabi's World* (Baltimore, 1990), 24.

164. A Leon Higginbotham and Anne F. Jacobs, "'The Law Only as an Enemy': The Legitimation of Racial Powerlessness through the Colonial and Antebellum Criminal Laws of Virginia," *North Carolina Law Review* 70 (1992), 1039.

165. The arguments in the paragraph about English ideas of the impact of mutilation on convicts at home, and the counterpoise of Obeah in slave cultures, were inspired by Vincent Brown, "Spectacular Terror and Sacred Authority in Jamaican Slave Society," paper read to the McNeil Center for Early American Studies, February 22, 2002, 14–28, cited by permission. The surmises about how slaves regarded the severed heads are my own.

166. See e.g. Hale, *Making Whiteness*, chap. 5; Bill Sasser, "Strange Fruit," *New York Times,* January 13, 2000, on the James Allen exhibition of the postcards; James Allen, ed., *Without Sanctuary: Lynching Photography in America* (Santa Fe, N.M., 2000).

167. A. J. Verdelle, "The Truth of the Picnic: Writing about American Slavery," *Common-Place* 1 (July 2001) (www.common-place.org).

168. *Journal of the Council and House of Assembly,* Session of July 1, 1741, 84.

169. Aptheker, *Slave Revolts*, 189.

170. Act of 1740, in Grimké, comp., *Public Laws . . . of South Carolina*, 1:174, 172.

171. Craton, *Searching for the Invisible Man*, 11.

172. Olwell, *Slaves and Masters*, 20; Morgan, *Slave Counterpoint*, 466; White and White, *Stylin'*, 23–24.

173. The idea of the city that belongs to no one comes from Richard Sennett, *The Conscience of the Eye: The Design and Social Life of Cities* (New York, 1990), 205.

174. Edgar J. McManus, *A History of Negro Slavery in New York* (Syracuse, 1965), 23–39.

175. Joyce Goodfriend, *Before the Melting Pot: Society and Culture in Colonial New York City, 1664–1730* (Princeton, 1992), 111–31; Graham Russell Hodges, *Root and Branch: African Americans in New York and East Jersey* (Chapel Hill, N.C., 1999), 69–88.

176. "State of the Province of New York, 1738," in E. B. O'Callaghan, ed., *The Documentary History of the State of New-York* (Albany, 1851), 4:186.

177. In 1702, the legislature ordered that no one was to engage in business or trade with slaves without the permission of the slave's owner. Slaves were not to gather in groups of more than three persons without permission. Free persons were not to entertain slaves in a house or place of business without permission of the owner. *The Laws of Her Majesty's Colony of New York* (New York, 1709), 53–54. Those masters who wished to free a slave had to provide two sureties to a bond that the slave would not become a burden on the parish or city authorities. *Acts Passed by the General Assembly of Colony of New York* (New York, 1712), 159.

178. *Acts Passed by the General Assembly of the Colony of New York, in October, 1730* (New York, 1730). In fact, prosecutions for slave offenses against their masters far outnumbered prosecutions of slaves for crimes against property. Douglas Greenberg, *Crime and Law Enforcement in the Colony of New York, 1691–1776* (Ithaca, N.Y., 1974), 73–74.

179. Hodges, *Root and Branch*, 64, 66–67. Technically speaking, the offense was petty treason rather than murder, for a servant or slave killing a master was a worse offense than a simple murder. Punishment for the former was more sanguinary than simple hanging.

180. Edwin G. Burrows and Michael Wallace, *Gotham: A History of New York City to 1898* (New York, 1998), 110, 185.

181. Slave arson had become a standard weapon of revenge for slaves and a regular suspicion for authorities by the 1740s. Horsmanden, *New-York Conspiracy*, 26–27, 29, 31.

182. Burrows and Wallace, *Gotham*, 143.

183. Kenneth Scott, "The Slave Insurrection in New York in 1712," *New-York Historical Society Quarterly* 45 (1961), 43–74.

184. Hodges, *Root and Branch*, 64–65; McManus, *Negro Slavery in New York*, 122–26; Oscar Williams, *African Americans and Colonial Legislation in the Middle Colonies* (New York, 198), 55–56.

185. On the law of conspiracy see Peter Charles Hoffer, *The Great New York Conspiracy: Slavery, Crime, and Colonial Law* (Lawrence, Kans., 2003). Conspiracy was the centerpiece of the authorities' attempt to make the slave plots visible. For example, Maryland colonial law of 1692 mirrored the English definition of the crime of conspiracy (a plot to commit perjury), but by 1717 Maryland legislators had amended the colonial code to include slave conspiracies of any kind, with any outcome. *The Laws of the Province of Maryland*, 2, 119. The New York slave code of 1712, followed by the New Jersey code in 1714, made it a crime for whites to "conspire" with slaves to commit insurrection, but the concern of the lawmakers was obviously the conduct of the slaves, not their free

accessories. *Laws of the Royal Colony of New Jersey, 1703–1745, New Jersey Archives,* 3d ser. (Trenton, N.J.,1977), 2:136–37.

186. Horsmanden, sentencing Ben to death, June 15, 1741, *New-York Conspiracy,* 174.

187. *New-York Weekly Journal,* November 19, 1739.

188. For example, the *New-York Weekly Journal* from March through April 1737 devoted four full issues to the foiled slave conspiracy on Antigua. No gory prospect (the uprising was nipped in the bud) was missed.

189. *New-York Weekly Journal,* November 19, 1739; *New York Gazette,* December 3, 1739.

190. Horsmanden, *New-York Conspiracy,* 11.

191. Linebaugh and Rediker, *Many-Headed Hydra,* 174.

192. Horsmanden, *New-York Conspiracy,* 224 (testimony of Jack, June 26, 1741).

193. Ibid., 216 (testimony of London): "They all agreed to what Hughson said, and did swear and kissed the book."

194. Linebaugh and Rediker, *Many-Headed Hydra,* 183.

195. Horsmanden, *New-York Conspiracy,* 20.

196. E.g. ibid., 120–21, 195. The same inversion of power, over property, women, and government, appeared in the Second Creek conspiracy, in Mississippi, sometime during the summer of 1861. Jordan, *Tumult and Silence,* 167. The taking of the women "as wives," rather than simply raping them, suggests that in the minds of the perpetrators the act was legitimate rather than criminal.

197. Horsmanden, *New-York Conspiracy,* 22–33.

198. In the end, Quaco's arson at the fort avenged him on Lt. Gov. William Clarke, who would not let Quaco visit his wife; Cuffee admitted to setting the fire at Philipse's storehouse, Jack owned up to leaving the coals at Murray's barn, and other slaves came forward (in the shadow of the gallows) with similar admissions. Hoffer, *Conspiracy,* 116–26.

199. Horsmanden, *New-York Conspiracy,* 50. Arson and conspiracy were always assumed to travel together. McManus, *Negro Slavery in New York,* 139.

200. Horsmanden, *New-York Conspiracy,* 10, 11.

201. Hoffer, *Conspiracy,* 7–9. Horsmanden was both an imperial bureaucrat and a local notable, serving as a member of the council appointed by the royal governor and as recorder of the city. His appointment to the high bench was the capstone of his public service.

202. Horsmanden, *New-York Conspiracy,* 7, 11; Hoffer, *Conspiracy,* 70–71, 92–94.

203. It was a time when men of learning believed that the report of the senses penetrated to the heart of things, "a deep belief in knowing by seeing," particularly when the senses belonged to men of breeding and experience and the objects observed were the lower classes. Prude, "To Look upon the 'Lower Sort,'" 128.

204. Horsmanden, *New-York Conspiracy,* 349, 57, 63, 132–33 (the Hughsons, at trial).

205. *New-York Weekly Journal,* June 15, 1741.

206. Horsmanden to Colden, August 7, 1741, *Letters and Papers of Cadwallader Colden, Collections of the New-York Historical Society* (New York, 1918), 2:226.

207. *New-York Weekly Journal,* June 15, 1741.

208. Horsmanden, *New-York Conspiracy,* 273, 274.

209. Ibid., 212–16, 290, 338, 379–81 (on Ury), tables after 465 (on outcomes of trials). The conviction of Ury seems to be as much for his secret Catholicism as for any part he had in the arson plot. Hoffer, *Conspiracy,* 152–64. Ibid., 130–51.

210. Horsmanden, *New-York Conspiracy,* 386–87, 405, 411, 442.

211. *New-York Weekly Journal,* June 15, 1741.

212. Horsmanden, *New-York Conspiracy,* 411, 442.

213. McManus, *Negro Slavery in New York,* 139.

214. *New-York Weekly Journal,* November 26, 1739.

215. Josiah Smith, *The Character, Preaching, etc. of the Reverend Mr. George Whitefield,* quoted in Sandra M. Gustafson, *Eloquence Is Power: Oratory and Performance in Early America* (Chapel Hill, N.C., 2000), 46.

216. Quoted in Nina Reid-Maroney, *Philadelphia's Enlightenment, 1740–1800* (Westport, Conn., 2001), 18.

217. Historians have likened Whitefield's preaching to a kind of public performance. See e.g. Harry S. Stout, *The Divine Dramatist: George Whitefield and the Rise of Modern Evangelism* (Grand Rapids, Mich., 1991); Frank Lambert, *"Pedlar in Divinity": George Whitefield and the Transatlantic Revivals, 1737–1770* (Princeton, 1994).

218. Whitefield quoted in Sobel, *World They Made Together,* 182; David S. Lovejoy, *Religious Enthusiasm in the New World: Heresy to Revolution* (Cambridge, Mass., 1985), 203–4. Thus when Gabriel recruited slaves to his cause in 1800, he turned to the Bible, as did his lieutenants. Sidbury, *Ploughshares into Swords,* 82.

219. Quotations from Linebaugh and Rediker, *Many-Headed Hydra,* 190–93.

220. Piersen, *Black Yankees,* 65–66.

221. Charles Colcock Jones, quoted in Smith, *Listening to Nineteenth-Century America,* 2001), 62.

222. In all, Whitefield made thirteen trips to the colonies from his home in England. Keith J. Hardman, *Seasons of Refreshing: Evangelism and Revivals in America* (Grand Rapids, Mich., 1994), 85–92; Stout, *The Divine Dramatist,* 87–132.

223. Frank Lambert, *Inventing the "Great Awakening"* (Princeton, 1999), 51, 92–134; Lambert, *"Pedlar in Divinity,"* 103–29.

224. Jonathan Marsh, *The Great Care and Concern of Men under Gospel Light* (New London, Conn., 1721), 13.

225. Michael J. Crawford, *Seasons of Grace: Colonial New England's Revival Tradition in Its British Context* (New York, 1991), 65.

226. Crawford, *Seasons of Grace,* 84, 99–104; Lovejoy, *Religious Enthusiasm,* 180.

227. Jonathan Edwards, *An Humble Inquiry into the Rules of the Word of God, Concerning the Qualification Requite to a Complete Standing and Full Communion in the Visible Christian Church* [1750], in David D. Hall, ed., *Ecclesiastical Writings, The Works of Jonathan Edwards* (New Haven, Conn., 1994), 12:174.

228. On the introduction of the test of a profession of faith before the congregation as a qualification for full membership, see Edmund S. Morgan, *Visible Saints: The History of a Puritan Idea* (Ithaca, N.Y., 1963).

229. Winship, *Making Heretics*, 11–24.

230. *New-York Weekly Journal*, November 26, 1739. Prude, "To Look upon the 'Lower Sort,'" 126–28. The Puritan ministry had always used figurative sensory language in its preaching. Kibbey, *Material Shapes*, 11.

231. Eliphalet Adams, *The Work of Ministers* (New London, 1725), 15.

232. Watts, quoted in Crawford, *Seasons of Grace*, 84.

233. Edwards, *A Faithful Narrative* [1737, 1738], in C. C. Goen, ed., *The Great Awakening, The Works of Jonathan Edwards* (New Haven, Conn., 1972), 4:146–47.

234. Ibid., 150, 152.

235. Richard L. Bushman, *The Great Awakening: Documents on the Revival of Religion, 1740–1745* (New York, 1970), 66.

236. Jonathan Dickinson, *A Display of God's Special Grace* (Boston, 1742), 21, 27, 28, 36–37, 70–71.

237. Stout, *The Divine Dramatist*, 113–32.

238. Jonathan Parsons, *Letter to the "The Christian History" for 1744*, reprinted in Alan Heimert and Perry Miller, eds., *The Great Awakening: Documents Illustrating the Crisis and Its Consequences* (Indianapolis, 1967), 1:391.

239. Timothy D. Hall, *Contested Boundaries: Itinerancy and the Reshaping of the Colonial American Religious World* (Durham, N.C., 1994), 71–75

240. Gilbert Tennent, *The Espousals; or, A Passionate Perswasive to a Marriage with the Lamb of God* (Boston, 1741), 8.

241. Whitefield, *The Marriage of Cana* (Philadelphia, 1742), 38, 39.

242. Benjamin Franklin, *The Autobiography of Benjamin Franklin*, ed. Leonard W. Labaree et al. (New Haven, Conn., 1964), 179.

243. Tennent, *The Dangers of an Unconverted Ministry* (Philadelphia, 1741), 13, 18.

244. Hall, *Contested Boundaries*, 36–37, 41–44. Critics of the itinerants turned to natural metaphors to decry the newcomers: They were like comets flying through the heavens, disturbing the natural order of the celestial bodies. Ibid., 45.

245. Quoted in Peter Charles Hoffer, *The Brave New World: A History of Early America* (Boston, 2000), 373.

246. Edwards, *The Distinguishing Marks of a Work of the Spirit of God* [1741], in Goen, ed., *Works of Edwards*, 4:259.

247. Quoted in Harry S. Stout, "George Whitefield in Three Countries," in Mark A. Noll, David W. Bebbington, and George A. Rawlyk, eds., *Evangelism: Comparative Studies of Popular Protestantism in North America, the British Isles, and Beyond, 1700–1900* (New York, 1994), 67.

248. *Christian History*, 2:125.

249. Timothy Walker, *The Way to Try All Pretended Apostles* (Boston, 1743), 5.

250. Franklin, *Autobiography*, 179.

251. Herman Husband, "Some Remarks on Religion," reprinted in Heimert and Miller, eds., *The Great Awakening*, 638, 639.

252. "On the Reverend Mr. Gilbert Tennent's Powerful and Successful Preaching in Boston" [1741], in ibid., 192–93.

253. Davenport, *Reverend Mr. Davenport's Song* (Boston, 1742), 2.

254. *Boston Weekly Post-Boy,* March 28, 1743, quoted in Bushman, *Great Awakening,* 52; *Christian History* 2:406, 408; C. C. Goen, *Revivalism and Separatism in New England, 1740–1800* (New Haven, Conn., 1962), 24–25.

255. Joshua Hempstead, "Diary," March 27, 1743, in J. M. Bumsted, ed., *The Great Awakening* (Waltham, Mass., 1970), 89.

256. Crawford, *Seasons of Grace,* 52.

257. Perry Miller, *Jonathan Edwards* (Toronto, 1949), 52–67; Crawford, *Seasons of Grace,* 87–88.

258. There is (as there was then) controversy over how much, if anything, was new in the theology of the revivalists. Was a strong emphasis on the centrality of Christ and the awfulness of sin new? See e.g. Lovejoy, *Religious Enthusiasm,* 181. Was the New England theology that Edwards developed in his Stockbridge years (1751–58) anything more than an attempt to put the key doctrines of traditional Calvinism out of reach of Arminianism? In any case, much of the fullness of the New England theology came after the Awakening had subsided.

259. Jonathan Edwards, *A History of the Work of Redemption* [1739], in John F. Wilson, ed., *The Works of Jonathan Edwards* (New Haven, Conn., 1989), 9:519, 520.

260. Alexander Garden, *Regeneration and the Testimony of the Spirit* (Charleston, 1740), 3, i, 10.

261. Josiah Smith, "A Sermon, on the Character, Preaching, and etc. of the Rev. Minister Whitefield" [1740], reprinted in Heimert and Miller, eds., *The Great Awakening,* 67.

262. George Whitefield, *Journals,* in Bumsted, ed., *The Great Awakening,* 70, 71.

263. *New England Weekly Journal,* December, 4, 1739.

264. Eleazar Wheelock, *Diary,* in Bumsted, ed., *The Great Awakening,* 85; *Christian History,* 2:116.

265. *Christian History,* 1:415, 2:89, 90.

266. Ibid., 206, 226, 255, 415; 2:253.

267. Ibid., 2:145, 146.

268. Jonathan Edwards, *Faithful Narrative* [1737], in Goen, ed., *Works of Edwards,* 4:150.

269. Ibid., 152, 153.

270. Susan Juster, *Disorderly Women: Sexual Politics and Evangelicism in Revolutionary New England* (Ithaca, N.Y., 1994), 23–24.

271. Nathan Cole, "Autobiography" [1740], reprinted in Heimert and Miller, eds., *The Great Awakening,* 186.

272. Edwards, *A Faithful Narrative* [1737], in Goen, ed., *Works of Edwards,* 4:192.

273. We take this blindness and sight as figurative, but to Hutchinson it was literal. If the divine light was only visible to the inner eye, "not visible to the senses" (Gustafson, *Eloquence Is Power,* 57), then God became a sign, not a real being.

274. Dr. Alexander Hamilton, "Itinerarium," in Wendy Martin, ed., *Colonial American Travel Narratives* (New York, 1994), 296.

275. *Boston Weekly Post-Boy,* July 12, 1742. The correspondent is not identified.

276. Hamilton, "Itinerarium," 296.

277. Jonathan Dickinson, *The Witness of the Spirit* [1740], 2d ed. (Boston, 1743) 9, 30.

278. Samuel Blair, *A Particular Consideration . . .* (Philadelphia, 1741), 3.

279. Ibid., 5–6.

280. "A True and Genuine Account of a Wonderful Wandering Spirit" [1741], reprinted in Heimert and Miller, eds., *The Great Awakening,* 148.

281. Jonathan Edwards, *The Distinguishing Marks of a Work of the Spirit* [1741], in Goen, ed., *Works of Edwards,* 4:232–35, 264.

282. Samuel Findley, "Christ Triumphing" [1741], reprinted in Heimert and Miller, eds., *The Great Awakening,* 154–55, 163, 164.

283. Gilbert Tennent, *Remarks upon a Protestation* (Philadelphia, 1741), 18.

284. Charles Chauncy, *Enthusiasm Described and Cautioned Against* [1742], (Boston, 1743), ii, 3, 4, 6, 27.

285. *Christian History,* 1:190, 198.

286. John Brown, communication to the *New York Missionary Magazine* 3 (1802), 182–3. Brown, the Presbyterian minister in the Waxhaws district of South Carolina, witnessed the great revival meeting there. I am grateful to Peter Moore for this and subsequent references to the falling exercise and other bodily proofs of repentence to appear in his book on the Waxhaws.

287. William Henry Foote, *Sketches of North Carolina* (New York, 1846), 409–12.

288. The importance of the senses—immediate, telling, distinguishing—cannot be subordinated to a study of signs or semiotics, although these, embodied in texts, may have been an influence on the ministers in their libraries. On semiotics and Edwards, see Stephen H. Daniel, *The Philosophy of Jonathan Edwards: A Study in Divine Semiotics* (Bloomington, Ind., 1994).

289. Nathan O. Hatch, *The Sacred Cause of Liberty: Republican Thought and the Millennium in Revolutionary New England* (New Haven, Conn., 1977), 32, 37.

290. Edwards, "Farewell-Sermon," quoted in Grasso, *Speaking Aristocracy,* 125.

291. Goen, *Revivalism and Separation,* 160; Hall, "Introduction," in Hall, ed., *Works of Edwards,* 12:44, 49.

292. Gilbert Tennent, *The Necessity of Studying to Be Quiet and Doing Our Own Business* (Philadelphia, 1744), 4, 7, 9, 11, 21.

293. Milton J. Coalter Jr., *Gilbert Tennent, Son of Thunder* (New York, 1986), 121.

294. Davenport, *The Reverend Mr. Davenport's Confession and Retraction* (Boston, 1744), 5; Davenport, *A Letter from Mr. James Davenport to Mr. Jonathan Barber* (Philadelphia, 1744), 4, 6–7.

295. Not quite. In England, where Whitefield and others continued their evangelism, rowdy mobs assaulted the preachers, abused the auditory, and used the signals of older religion—the bells and bonfires—to call up their minions. In July 1743, Whitefield recorded that no sooner had he entered one town to preach than he "heard the signals, such as the blowing of horns and the ringing of bells, for gathering the mob." Whitefield, quoted in Stout, *The Divine Dramatist,* 179.

296. Jonathan Edwards, *The Distinguishing Marks of a Work of the Spirit of God* (Boston, 1741), 66.

297. Edwards, *Thoughts on . . . Religion in New England,* in Goen, ed., *Works of Edwards,* 3:395.

298. *Testimony and Advice of an Assembly of Pastors of Churches in New-England* (Boston, 1743), 9–10.

299. Dickinson, *Display of God's Special Grace,* 71.

300. One must bear in mind that by this time Edwards had fought the rationalists in the person of Charles Chauncy, the radicals in the person of James Davenport, the separatists, the Moravians, and all non-Calvinists. See e.g. Harry S. Stout, *The New England Soul: Preaching and Religious Culture in Colonial New England* (New York, 1986), 201–11; William Breitenbach, "Religious Affections and Affectations," in Barbara B. Oberg and Harry S. Stout, eds., *Benjamin Franklin, Jonathan Edwards, and the Representation of American Culture* (New York, 1993), 15; Hall, "Introduction," in Hall, ed., *Works of Edwards,* 12:49.

301. Miller, *Jonathan Edwards,* 196–215, suggests that Edwards' low pay had something to do with his disenchantment with his congregation.

302. Edwards, *Religious Affections,* quoted in Hall, "Introduction," in Hall, ed., *Works of Edwards,* 12:58, 49, 50, 63.

303. Edwards, *Humble Inquiry,* in Hall, ed., *Works of Edwards,* 12:177, 190.

304. Ibid., 178.

305. Ibid., 179, 185.

306. In defending *Humble Inquiry* from critics, Edwards twice cited Locke's *Essay on the Human Understanding* to show that words that were not signifiers of things were mere noise and that probability was merely a conjunction of past experiences in our minds. Edwards, *Misrepresentations Corrected* [1752], in Hall, ed., *Works of Edwards,* 12:388 n and 409 n. On Edwards' and Locke's ideas of perception, see Norman Fiering, *Jonathan Edwards's Moral Thought and Its British Context* (Chapel Hill, N.C.,1981), 35–40 (Locke is important but is only one of many philosophical influences somewhat eclectically arrayed in Edwards' thought), and Miller, *Jonathan Edwards,* 52–67 (Locke's essay is the key to understanding Edwards' intellectual world).

307. Edwards, *Humble Inquiry,* in Hall, ed., *Works of Edwards,* 12:185.

308. Ibid., 12:188; Hall, "Introduction," in ibid., 62, 73. Here my reading of Edwards differs sharply from that of Perry Miller, *Jonathan Edwards,* 186–89 (finding that Edwards did not differentiate the inward from the outward eye).

309. Edwards, "Narrative of Communion Controversy," in Hall, ed., *Works of Edwards,* 12:544.

310. Ebenezer Frothingham, *The Articles of Faith and Practice, with the Covenant, that is Confessed by the Separate Churches of Christ in this Land* (Newport, 1750), 25, 28, 32–33, 37, 38, 46, 49. Although he denied any intention of censuring any of his brethren of the cloth, he went after Edwards for stopping short of the separatist position himself and then vilifying and misrepresenting separatist views.

311. Hall, *Contested Boundaries,* 78–79.

312. From the testimony of Nathaniel Shepherd, who "seemed to see Christ's justice" when Davenport, "a wonderful man to search hypocrites," awakened Shepherd. Shepherd's confession, "in his own hand," reprinted in Isaac Backus, *A Discourse, Showing the Nature and Necessity of an Internal Call to Preach the Everlasting Gospel* (Boston, 1754), in William G. McLoughlin, ed., *Isaac Backus on Church, State, and Calvinism, Pamphlets, 1754–1789* (Cambridge, Mass., 1968), 123.

313. McManus, *Negro Slavery in New York,* 166–79; Ira Berlin, *Many Thousands Gone: The First Two Centuries of Slavery in North America* (Cambridge, Mass., 1998), 237–38.

314. Burrows and Wallace, *Gotham,* 546–49.

315. Cantwell and Wall, *Unearthing Gotham,* 282–85.

316. Gilbert Osofsky, "Introduction," in Osofsky, ed., *Puttin' on Ole Massa: The Slave Narratives of Henry Bibb, William Wells Brown, and Solomon Northrup* (New York, 1969), 9–44.

317. Quoted in Stampp, *Peculiar Institution,* 332.

318. White and White, *Stylin',* 63–64.

319. On the troubles that the revival congregants and ministers caused in North Carolina, see Kars, *Breaking Loose Together,* 84–90; on the enthusiasm in Virginia, see Isaac, *Transformation of Virginia,* 161–80. On the rise of the sectaries in the revolutionary South, see Christine Leigh Heyrman, *Southern Cross: The Beginnings of the Bible Belt* (New York, 1997), 20–21. Charles Woodmason (quoted in ibid., 21) was the author of the word "nonsense."

Chapter 4 · A World of Difference

1. A perceptual field is a sensory context—the scenery or setting—that we are able to take in during a particular event. See Kurt Lewin, *Field Theory in Social Science: Selected Theoretical Papers,* ed. Dorwin Cartwright (New York, 1951).

2. Sarah Kortum, *The Hatless Man: An Anthology of Odd and Forgotten Manners* (New York, 1995), xi, xiii.

3. Margaret Wade, *Social Usage in America* (New York, 1924), 5, 95.

4. C. Dallett Hemphill, *Bowing to Necessities: A History of Manners in America, 1620–1860* (New York, 1999), 9.

5. Amy Vanderbilt, *Amy Vanderbilt's Complete Book of Etiquette* (New York, 1952), i, 244.

6. Elizabeth L. Post, *Emily Post's Etiquette,* 14th ed. (New York, 1984), 20, 28, 90.

7. Hemphill, *Bowing to Necessities,* 70, 71, 74.

8. John Adams, September 15, 1775, in *The Diary and Autobiography of John Adams,* ed. Lyman Butterfield et al. (Cambridge, Mass., 1961), 2:173.

9. Arthur Schlesinger, *Learning How to Behave: A Historical Study of American Etiquette Books* (New York, 1947), 4.

10. Benjamin Rush to his daughter Julia, quoted in Hemphill, *Bowing to Necessities,* 104.

11. John Griffith, quoted in Gerald Carson, *The Polite Americans: A Wide-Angle View of Our More or Less Good Manners Over Three Hundred Years* (New York, 1966), 65.

12. Richard L. Bushman, *The Refinement of America: Persons, Houses, Cities* (New York, 1992), 80, 81.

13. George Mercer on Washington, quoted in Carson, *The Polite Americans,* 27.

14. Edward Bangs' version of "Yankee Doodle" in 1775, quoted in William Pencak, "Play as Prelude to Revolution: Boston, 1765–1776," in Matthew Dennis, Simon P. Newman, and William Pencak, eds., *Riot and Revelry in Early America* (University Park, Pa., 2002), 148.

15. Lord Chesterfield to his son, July 24, 1739, in *The Letters of the Earl of Chesterfield to His Son,* ed. Charles Strachey (New York, 1925) 1:39.

16. E. P. Thompson, *Customs in Common: Studies in Traditional Popular Culture* (New York, 1991), 469, 479–80.

17. Quoted in Ted Morgan, *Wilderness at Dawn: The Settling of the North American Continent* (New York, 1993), 377.

18. We do have here a thesis (the provincial sensory paradigm), its antithesis (the mob insists on its ugliness being seen and heard to overthrow imperial rule), and a synthesis (a republican etiquette that looked and sounded stable)—but the sequence did not follow in lock-step. Some of the revolutionaries remained provincials in their distaste for the excessively egalitarian pose of the mob, while others resisted the reimposition of visual and audible hierarchy after 1776.

19. Though there was a "contagion of liberty," whose consequences included the gradual abolition of slavery in much of the North. Ira Berlin, *Many Thousands Gone: The First Two Centuries of Slavery in North America* (Cambridge, Mass., 1998), 228–55; Bernard Bailyn, *Ideological Origins of the American Revolution* (Cambridge, Mass., 1967), 230–71.

20. See e.g. Bailyn, "The Central Themes of the American Revolution," in Bernard Bailyn, *Faces of Revolution: Personalities and Themes in the Struggle for American Independence* (New York, 1990), 200–268.

21. On deference and its travails, see Richard Beeman, "Deference, Republicanism, and the Emergence of Popular Politics in Eighteenth-Century America," *William and Mary Quarterly,* 3d ser. 49 (1992), 401–30; Gordon Wood, *The Radicalism of the American Revolution* (New York, 1991), 43–92. For the argument that deference was never what it seemed or what the elites wanted, see Michael Zuckerman, "Tocqueville, Turner, and Turds: Four Stories of Manners in Early America," *Journal of American History* 85 (1998), 13–42.

22. Richard Sennett, *The Fall of Public Man* (New York, 1977), 68, 79.

23. Kenneth Silverman, *A Cultural History of the American Revolution* (New York, 1987), 558–63.

24. But Franklin's long and sincere attachment to the empire and his many visits to England had made him suspect in the eyes of his more consistently radical countrymen. His patriotism after 1775 thus had an exaggerated character. Gordon Wood, in a talk at the McNeil Center for Early American Studies, March 6, 2002.

25. John Higham, *Hanging Together: Unity and Diversity in American Culture,* ed. Carl J. Guarneri (New Haven, Conn., 2001), 37.

26. Adams, quoted in David McCullough, *John Adams* (New York, 2001), 468.

27. James Boswell, quoted in Esmond Wright, *Franklin of Philadelphia* (Cambridge, Mass., 1986), 216.

28. Eliga H. Gould, *The Persistence of Empire: British Political Culture in the Age of the American Revolution* (Chapel Hill, N.C., 1993), 106–47.

29. Verner W. Crane, *Benjamin Franklin and a Rising People* (Boston, 1954), 122–44. The quiet ended when news of the "Destruction of the Tea," as it was then known, or the "Boston Tea Party," as it was later depicted, arrived in England. Alfred F. Young, *The Shoemaker and the Tea Party: Memory and the American Revolution* (Boston, 1999), 155–56.

30. Leonard W. Labaree et al., "Introduction," in Franklin, *The Autobiography of Benjmain Franklin* (New Haven, Conn., 1964), 7.

31. Franklin, *Autobiography*, 61–62.

32. Despite a strong admonition from my colleague Allan Kulikoff that I stick to the term *ruling class,* I have used the words *elite* and *upper class* as synonyms. They do not mean precisely the same thing, but together the three imply more than "ruling class."

33. Franklin, *Autobiography*, 80, 86, 85.

34. "Whether celebrated as the seat of commerce and the cultivated product of modern civilization, derogated as corrupt, luxurious and disordered, simply viewed with astonishment, London continued to inspire writers and artists. It had become a city of words and images." John Brewer, *The Pleasures of the Imagination: English Culture in the Eighteenth-Century* (New York, 1997), 54.

35. Bernard Bailyn and John Clive, "England's Provinces: Scotland and America," *William and Mary Quarterly*, 3d ser. 11 (1954), 200–213.

36. Brewer, *The Pleasures of the Imagination*, 493–98; David Shields, *Civil Tongues and Polite Letters in British America* (Chapel Hill, N.C.,1997), 54. Ian K. Steele, *The English Atlantic, 1675–1740: An Exploration of Communication and Community* (New York, 1986), provides the prologue to this Atlantic transit of manners and information.

37. Hutchinson, quoted in Bernard Bailyn, *The Ordeal of Thomas Hutchinson* (New York, 1974), 20; Hutchinson, quoted in Josiah Quincy, ed., *Reports of Cases Argued and Adjudged in the Superior Court of Judicature of the Province of Massachusetts Bay between 1762 and 1771* (Boston, 1865), 173.

38. Kenneth Lockridge, *The Diary, and Life, of William Byrd II of Virginia, 1674–1744* (New York, 1987), 70.

39. The pastorale had a multiplicity of meanings. Andrew McRae, *God Speed the Plow, The Representation of Agrarian England, 1500–1600* (New York, 1966), 273–74; Laurel Thatcher Ulrich, *The Age of Homespun* (New York, 2001), 150.

40. Richard H. Saunders and Ellen G. Miles, *American Colonial Portraits, 1700–1776* (Washington, D.C., 1987), 244–46. The artist and the subject "collude" to create an image rather than simply replicate reality. Sometimes they play tricks on the viewer, or introduce a kind of visual intertextuality in which they borrow from older conventions of portraiture. Peter Burke, *Eyewitnessing: The Uses of Images as Historical Evidence* (Ithaca, N.Y., 2001), 26.

41. E. P. Richardson, *Painting in America: From 1502 to the Present* (New York, 1965), 71–76, 93–94; R. Peter Mooz, "Colonial Art," in John Wilmerdung, ed., *The Genius of American Painting* (New York, 1973), 68–71.

42. See e.g. Rhys Isaac, *The Transformation of Virginia, 1740–1790* (Chapel Hill, N.C., 1982), 70–80.

43. Bushman, *Refinement of America,* 151–53; John W. Reps, *Town Planning in Frontier America* (Princeton, 1965), 137–44.

44. For a pictorial tour and visual treat, see George Humphrey Yetter, *Williamsburg Before and After: The Rebirth of Virginia's Colonial Capital* (Williamsburg, Va., 1988), 14–27, 73–155.

45. This and the preceding descriptions of Colonial Williamsburg buildings are personal impressions of visits to the restored palace and capitol in November 1996 and March 2001. I am grateful to Colonial Williamsburg for the courtesies extended to me.

46. Quoted in Shields, *Civil Tongues,* 146–47.

47. Joseph Shippen, "Lines Written in an Assembly Room," quoted in Shields, *Civil Tongues,* 150.

48. Franklin, "Rules for Making Oneself a Disagreeable Companion," in *The Papers of Benjamin Franklin,* ed. Leonard W. Labaree et al., 36 vols. (New Haven, Conn., 1959–), 4:73.

49. Hunter Dickinson Farish, ed., *Journal and Letters of Philip Vickers Fithian, 1773–1774: A Plantation Tutor of the Old Dominion* (Charlottesville, Va., 1968), 34; Brown, *Knowledge Is Power,* 61.

50. Hamilton, "Itinerarium," 178, 179, 181, 184, 182, 186, 197.

51. *The Diary of Elizabeth Drinker,* ed., Elaine Forman Crane (Boston, 1994), 4–20. A social historian with the right ear and eye for Philadelphia life in the closing decades of the eighteenth century could do with the silences and taciturnity of Elizabeth Sandwich Drinker's diary what Laurel Thatcher Ulrich did for midwife Martha Ballard's equally terse journal entries in *A Midwife's Tale.*

52. Bushman, *Refinement of America,* 30–46.

53. Lois Green Carr, Russell R. Menard, and Lorena Walsh, *Robert Cole's World: Agriculture and Society in Early Maryland* (Chapel Hill, N.C., 1991), 90–94, 102–10; Isaac, *Transformation of Virginia,* 65–68; John E. Crowley, *The Invention of Comfort: Sensibilities and Design in Early Modern Britain and Early America* (Baltimore, 2001), 82–87; Darrett B. and Anita H. Rutman, *A Place in Time: Middlesex County, Virginia, 1650–1750* (New York, 1984), 67–69.

54. Hugh Morrison, *Early American Architecture: From the First Colonial Settlements to the National Period* (New York, 1952), 271–317.

55. Bushman, *Refinement of America,* 103–22.

56. Pinckney, quoted in ibid., 132–33.

57. *Journal and Letters of . . . . Fithian,* 80.

58. These and the following are impressions from visits to Whitfield House (1639) and Hyland House (1660), Guilford, Conn.; Hart House (1767), Old Saybrook, Conn.; Nichols-Hunter House (1748), Newport, R.I.; Governor Yates House (1760), Schnec-

tady, N.Y.; Sparrow House (1640) and Howland House (1667), Plymouth, Mass.; Vassall-Adams Mansion (ca. 1730), Quincy, Mass.; Moffatt-Ladd House (1763), Portsmouth, N.H.; Ashley House (ca. 1730), Deerfield, Mass.; and Carter's Grove (1750s), Williamsburg, Va. For tours of the houses, my thanks to the Henry Whitfield Museum, in Guildford, the Old Saybrook Historical Society, the Preservation Society of Newport County, H. G. Harlow of Schnectady, the Pilgrim John Howland Society, the National Park Service, the Colonial Dames of America in the State of New Hampshire, Colonial Deerfield, and Colonial Williamsburg.

59. Bushman, *Refinement of America,* 124; Crowley, *Invention of Comfort,* 68–69, 100.

60. Franklin, quoted in Crowley, *Invention of Comfort,* 173.

61. John Adams, *Diary and Autobiography of John Adams,* 1:294–95.

62. *Journal and Letters of . . . Fithian,* 34.

63. Thomas M. Doerflinger, *A Vigorous Spirit of Enterprise: Merchants and Economic Development in Revolutionary Philadelphia* (Chapel Hill, N.C., 1986), 23, 26, 36, 40.

64. James A. Henretta, "Economic Development and Social Structure in Colonial Boston," *William and Mary Quarterly,* 3d ser. 22 (1965), 89 (the growing gap in actual wealth). "The inhabitants of the grand Georgian houses, with their elegantly appointed rooms filled with fashionably dressed friends, could not, despite wealth and sophistication, disregard the ordinary people." Richard L. Bushman, *King and People in Provincial Massachusetts* (Chapel Hill, N.C.,1985), 85. On Boston's travail in the French and Indian War and the Depression of 1763, see Gary B. Nash, *The Urban Crucible: Social Change, Political Consciousness, and the Origins of the American Revolution* (Cambridge, Mass., 1979), 241–43; St. George, *Conversing by Signs,* 240–42.

65. The best single volume on the Stamp Act controversy is still Edmund S. Morgan and Helen M. Morgan, *The Stamp Act Crisis: Prologue to Revolution,* rev. ed. (New York, 1962). But see Bailyn, *Hutchinson,* 66.

66. Pauline Maier, *From Resistance to Revolution: Colonial Radicals and the Development of American Opposition to Britain, 1765–1776* (New York, 1972), 77–100, argues that the actual organization arose out of the demonstrations rather than the planning of them.

67. Francis Bernard to Lord Halifax, August 14, 1765, reprinted in Edmund S. Morgan, ed., *Prologue to Revolution: Sources and Documents on the Stamp Act Crisis, 1764–1766* (New York, 1959), 106. Words like *mob* and *crowd, gathering,* and *assemblage* had specific connotations to those who used them in the eighteenth century. The use of the word also depended upon the situation of the speaker or writer.

68. George Rudé, *The Crowd in History: A Study of Popular Disturbances in France and England, 1730–1848,* rev ed. (London, 1981), 4–10.

69. *Newport Mercury,* August 26, 1765.

70. Esther Forbes, *Paul Revere and the World He Lived In* (Boston, 1942), 101–2.

71. On reputation of Bute, see J. Steven Watson, *The Reign of George III, 1760–1815* (Oxford, 1960), 98–99; Louis Kronenberger, *The Extraordinary Mr. Wilkes: His Life and Times* (New York, 1974), 27–66.

72. St. George, *Conversing by Signs,* 250–51.

73. Bernard to Halifax, August 15, 1765, in Morgan, ed., *Prologue,* 107. On the carnival

and the "rough music," or quasipolitical violence, that sometimes ensued, see Thomas Humphrey, "Crowd and Court: Rough Music and Popular Justice in Colonial New York," in Dennis, Newman, and Pencak, eds., *Riot and Revelry in Early America,* 107–24; Alfred F. Young, "English Plebeian Culture and Eighteenth-Century American Radicalism," in Margaret Jacob and James Jacob, eds., *Origins of Anglo-American Radicalism* (London, 1984), 184–212.

74. Forbes, *Revere,* 102.

75. David W. Conroy, *In Public Houses: Drink and the Revolution of Authority in Colonial Massachusetts* (Chapel Hill, N.C., 1995), 257–58, 262–63; Dirk Hoerder, *Crowd Action in Revolutionary Massachusetts* (New York, 1977), 108.

76. Bernard to Halifax, August 15, 1765, in Morgan, ed., *Prologue,* 107–8.

77. Thomas Hutchinson to Richard Jackson, August 30, 1765, in ibid., 108–9.

78. Morgan and Morgan, *Stamp Act Crisis,* 157 and after.

79. Hutchinson to Jackson, August 30, 1765, in Morgan, ed., *Prologue,* 109.

80. Richard D. Brown, *Revolutionary Politics in Massachusetts: The Boston Committee of Correspondence and the Towns, 1772–1774* (Cambridge, Mass., 1970), 18–37; Morgan and Morgan, *Stamp Act Crisis,* 172–81; Bailyn, *Hutchinson,* 70–74.

81. Bernard to Halifax, August 31, 1765, quoted in St. George, *Conversing by Signs,* 246.

82. Jonathan Mayhew, *God's Hand and Providence to Be Religiously Acknowledged in Public Calamities* (Boston, 1760), 7, 11–12, 14, 22. Contemporary prints often depicted the devil standing at Hutchinson's side.

83. St. George, *Conversing by Signs,* 242, 280.

84. Ibid., 268–71.

85. Bernard to Halifax, August 15, 1765, in Morgan, ed., *Prologue,* 107; Hutchinson to Peters, August 30, in ibid., 108.

86. Thomas Moffat to Joseph Harrison, August 29, 1765, in ibid., 110.

87. The similarity to the Wilkes riots in England in the fall of 1763 cannot be missed. There, again, the object was to send a visible political message to the crown. Rudé, *Crowd in History,* 59–60.

88. Peter Oliver, *Origin and Progress of the American Rebellion* [1781], ed. Douglass Adair and John A Schutz (Stanford, Calif., 1967), 52.

89. Many in the mob were no doubt debtors, harmed by Hutchinson's advocacy of hard currency over paper emissions by the colony to relieve debtors. How much of the personal animus against him derived from this source, rather than his support of the government in the Stamp Act crisis, cannot be determined.

90. Thomas Moffat to Joseph Harrison, August 29, 1765, in Morgan, ed., *Prologue,* 112–13.

91. Jesse Lemisch, *Jack Tar vs. John Bull* (New York, 1997), 78–82; Edward Countryman, *A People in Revolution: The American Revolution and Political Society in New York, 1760–1790* (Baltimore, 1981), 38, 62. The street design is clear in "A Plan of the City and Environs of New York in 1743 . . . " [1813], New York City Historical Society.

92. But no mob would ever be successful if it did not have the tacit approval of some

of the leaders of the political and economic worlds, and more so, if some of these "better sort" were not among its leaders or at least its planners. Paul Gilje, *The Road to Mobocracy: Popular Disorder in New York City, 1763–1834* (Chapel Hill, N.C.,1987), 44; Maier, *From Resistance to Revolution,* 83–100.

93. [New York] *Mercury,* November 4, 1765.

94. Gilje, *Road to Mobocracy,* 48.

95. *Connecticut Courant,* August 26, 1765.

96. Lawrence Henry Gipson, *American Loyalist: Jared Ingersoll* (New Haven, Conn., 1971), 172–73.

97. Humphrey, "Crowd and Court," in Dennis, Newman, and Pencak, eds., *Riot and Revelry,* 112–14.

98. St. George, *Conversing by Signs,* 260–61. But it was not, as St. George suggests, the body parts of the effigies to which the notes were pinned that mattered; it was the underlying sensate imperative—you must look at this; you cannot avert your eyes.

99. Each of the riots had its own narrative, different leaders' voices were effective in directing the crowd at different times, and, on top of everything else, there is very little evidence about what happened within the crowd. See e.g. the disclaimers in Countryman, *People in Revolution,* 55, 63; and Rudé, *Crowd in History,* 12–14.

100. Benevolus to Colden, November 3, 1765, *Letters and Papers of Cadwallader Colden,* vol. 7, *1765–1775,* Collections of the New-York Historical Society (New York, 1923), 88.

101. Jonathan Sewall, "Massachusettensis, January 2, 1775," in *Novagnalus and Massaschusettensis* (New York, 1968), 159.

102. Moore, quoted in Edwin G. Burrows and Michael Wallace, *Gotham: A History of New York City to 1898* (New York, 1998), 202.

103. "Politeness in conversation meant an easy, mannerly and agreeable style of expression in good English." Shields, *Civil Tongues,* 28—but the mob's loud display was an insult to the ear and eye. Kimberly K. Smith, *The Dominion of Voice: Riot, Reason, and Romance in Antebellum Politics* (Lawrence, Kans., 1999), 22–23.

104. Otis, *The Rudiments of Latin Prosody* [1760], quoted in Gufstafson, *Eloquence Is Power,* 147. To be sure, when Otis acted the part of legal advocate, he bellowed and gesticulated to make his points. Ibid., 154.

105. Laurens quoted in Rediker and Linebaugh, *Many-Headed Hydra,* 211.

106. Sewall, "Massachusettensis," December 12, 1774, December 19, 1774, in *Novanglus and Massachusettensis,* 142, 146.

107. "An Act for Preventing Tumults and Riotous Assemblies," Pennsylvania, 1771.

108. Maier, *From Resistance to Revolution,* 54–55; Morgan and Morgan, *Stamp Act Crisis,* 187–204.

109. Gilje, *Road to Mobocracy,* 17, 26.

110. Carl Ubbelohde, *The Vice-Admiralty Courts and the American Revolution* (Chapel Hill, N.C.,1960), 117–19, notes that when the colonists attempted to rescue a ship seized by the customs officials for violating the Navigation Acts, the recaptors acted "under cover of night and silence." The tarring and feathering was the exact opposite.

111. Oliver, *Origin and Progress*, 94.

112. Gilje, *Road to Mobocarcy*, 65–66; Peter Shaw, *American Patriots and the Rituals of Revolution* (Cambridge, Mass., 1981), 7, 208–15, discusses rituals of parades and their origin in English customs. The mock funeral, the ridicule of the devil, and even the blackface of the marchers in "mummers" shows in England echoed in the American mobs' performances. But one must avoid the perils of historical omniscience; Shaw knows more about the English rituals than the Americans did at that time.

113. "Regulation" [1768], quoted in William S. Powell et al., "Introduction" to Powell et al., eds., *The Regulators in North Carolina: A Documentary History, 1759–1776* (Raleigh, N.C., 1971), xviii.

114. Richard Lyman Bushman, "Farmers in Court: Orange County, North Carolina, 1750–1776," in Christopher L. Tomlins and Bruce H. Mann, eds., *The Many Legalities of Early America* (Chapel Hill, N.C., 2001), 388–413. On the economic problems of these farmers with creditors and courts, see Marjoleine Kars, *Breaking Loose Together: The Regulator Rebellion in Pre-Revolutionary North Carolina* (Chapel Hill, N.C., 2002), 64–73.

115. Kars, *Breaking Loose Together*, 133–37.

116. There are widely differing interpretations of the origins and meaning of the North Carolina Regulation, including Hugh T. Lefler and William S. Powell, *Colonial North Carolina: A History* (New York, 1973), 217–39 (a sectional conflict, the Regulation representing the west, Tryon the east in the colony); A. Roger Ekirch, *"Poor Carolina": Politics and Society in Colonial North Carolina, 1729–1776* (Chapel Hill, N.C., 1981), 161–220 (a struggle between the country ideology and the court faction); Marvin A. Michael Kay, "The North Carolina Regulation, 1766– 1776: A Class Conflict," in Alfred F. Young, ed. *The American Revolution: Explorations in the History of American Radicalism* (De Kalb, Ill., 1976), 84–102 (lower-class farmers against upper-class planters and merchants), and most recently Kars, *Breaking Loose Together* (a combination of evangelical fervor and solid economic grievances), and Wayne E. Lee, *Crowds and Soldiers in Revolutionary North Carolina: The Culture of Violence in Riot and War* (Gainesville, Fl., 2001) (violence of the rioters limited by conventions of protest).

117. Alonzo Thomas Dill, *Governor Tryon and His Palace* (Chapel Hill, N.C., 1955), 111, 103, 114, 116, 118, 119, 120, 121; "Estimate of Expenses for Governor's Mansion, New Bern, 1767, in Williamson et al., "Introduction," Williamson et al., eds., *Regulators*, 39–40.

118. William McPherson deposition, April 23, 1770, in Williamson et al., eds., *Regulators*, 240.

119. On Fanning, see James P. Whittenburg, "Planters, Merchants, and Lawyers: Social Change and the Origins of the North Carolina Regulation," *William and Mary Quarterly*, 3d ser. 34 (1977), 230–31; Arthur Palmer Hudson, "Songs of the North Carolina Regulators," *William and Mary Quarterly*, 3d ser. 4 (1947), 477–78.

120. Regulus [Herman Husband], *A Fan for Fanning and a Touchstone to Tryon, Containing an Impartial Account of the Rise and Progress of the Much Talked about Regulation in North-Carolina* (Boston, 1771), 14. Husband claimed the authority of first-hand account, "he who has seen, and heard." Ibid., vii.

121. Herman Husband, "A Sermon" [1770], in Williamson et al., eds., *Regulators,* 238.

122. Quoted in Ekirch, *"Poor Carolina,"* 193.

123. Henderson to Tryon, September 29, 1770, in Williamson et al., eds., *Regulators,* 245–47.

124. Hudson, "Songs," 478.

125. Jingle quoted in Kars, *Breaking Loose Together,* 147.

126. Tryon, Speech to North Carolina Assembly, December 5, 1770, *Journal of House of Assembly of North Carolina* (New Bern, N.C., 1771), 3–4.

127. Williamson et al., "Introduction," in Williamson et al., eds., *The Regulators,* xxv.

128. Governor Tryon's Declaration to the Troops, May 17, 1771, in ibid., 457.

129. Husband, *A Fan for Fanning,* 54.

130. See e.g. Maier, *From Resistance to Revolution,* 76 (the riots led to a plan for "ordered resistance"); Bailyn, *Hutchinson,* 70 (the mobbing had created a new kind of popular politics).

131. [Samuel Adams], *An Appeal to the World; or, A Vindication of the Town of Boston* (Boston, 1769), 4, 5, 14, 18, 20.

132. John Trumbull, *M'Fingal: Canto First, the Town Meeting, A.M.* [1776], in Edwin T. Bowden, ed., *The Satiric Poems of John Trumbull* (Austin, Tex., 1962), 105.

133. John Dickinson, writing in 1781, quoted in Smith, *The Dominion of Voice,* 35.

134. Adams, "Novanglus, January 23, 1775," in *Novanglus and Massaschusettensis,* 11. A good lawyer as well as an astute observer, Adams' view of the mob had shifted from his 1770 defense of Captain Preston. See n. 137 below.

135. Oliver, *Origin and Progress,* 35, 41–42.

136. Hiller B. Zobel, *The Boston Massacre* (New York, 1970), 180–200.

137. Frederic Kidder, *History of the Boston Massacre, March 5, 1770 . . . Containing Unpublished Documents of John Adams* (Albany, N.Y., 1870), 255.

138. Josiah Quincy Jr. to the Jury, *The Trial of the British Soldiers . . .* (Boston, 1807) 41.

139. Forbes, *Revere,* 93–147; David Hackett Fischer, *Paul Revere's Ride* (New York, 1994), 15–29.

140. Forbes, *Revere,* 157–63; Clarence S. Brigham, *Paul Revere's Engravings* (New York, 1969), 52–70; Jay Fliegelman, *Declaring Independence: Jefferson, Natural Language, and the Culture of Performance* (Stanford, Calif., 1993), 169–70.

141. Hoerder, *Crowd Action,* 97. Liberty trees were symbols of tumult—but tumults were necessary now and then. As Thomas Jefferson wrote to Ezra Stiles in 1786, "If the happiness of the mass of the people can be secured at the expense of a little tempest now and then, or even of a little blood, it will be a precious purchase." Jefferson to Stiles, December 24, 1786, *The Papers of Thomas Jefferson,* ed. Julian Boyd et al. (Princeton, 1950), 10:629.

142. Always a danger with British troops nearby. Gilje, *Road to Mobocracy,* 54.

143. David Cressy, *Bonfires and Bells* (London, 1989), 22–23, 64, 171.

144. Gilje, *Road to Mobocracy,* 55–56.

145. Daniel R. Mandell, *Behind the Frontier: Indians in Eighteenth-Century Eastern Massachusetts* (Lincoln, Nebr., 1996), 131; Richard White, *The Middle Ground: Indians,*

Empires, and Republics in the Great Lakes Region, 1650–1815 (Cambridge, 1991), 368–69, 383–84; Ian Steele, *Betrayals: Fort William Henry and the Massacre* (New York, 1990), 149–60.

146. Zobel, *Boston Massacre,* 215.

147. Benjamin Woods Labaree, *The Boston Tea Party* (New York, 1964), 132–148.

148. Oliver, *Origin and Progress,* 102.

149. John Andrews to William Barrell, December 18, 1773, in Jack P. Greene, ed., *Colonies to Nation, 1763–1789: A Documentary History of the American Revolution* (New York, 1967), 201.

150. Oliver, *Origin and Progress,* 103.

151. Hoerder, *Crowd Action,* 257–64.

152. Hewes, quoted in Young, *The Shoemaker and the Tea Party,* 43.

153. Resolves of the New York Sons of Liberty, December 15, 1773, in Greene, ed., *Colonies to Nation,* 198–99.

154. John Adams, December 17, 1773, *Diary and Autobiography,* 1:85–86.

155. The full-scale rehabilitation of the Indians in the New England mind would wait upon their demise as a threat. Lapore, *Name of War,* 191–226. But dressing up (or down) as Indians allowed the mob to indulge in violent threats. See Alan Taylor, *Liberty Men and Great Proprietors: The Revolutionary Settlement on the Maine Frontier, 1760–1820* (Chapel Hill, N.C., 1990), 190–94.

156. John Adams to James Warren, December 17, 1773, Robert J. Taylor et al., eds., *Papers of John Adams* (Cambridge, Mass., 1977–), 2:2.

157. Isaac, *Transformation of Virginia,* 258.

158. *New Hampshire Gazette,* August 25, 1769.

159. Washington, quoted in Michael Zakim, "Sartorial Ideologies: From Homespun to Ready-Made," *American Historical Review* 106 (2001), 1556.

160. Ulrich, *Age of Homespun,* 178.

161. Pickering to Rebecca Pickering, July 8, 1778, quoted in Susan Klepp, "Rough Music on Independence Day: Philadelphia, 1778," in Dennis, Newman, and Pencak, eds., *Riot and Revelry,* 167.

162. James Thomas Flexner, *George Washington: The Forge of Experience (1732–1775)* (Boston, 1965), 332–37; McCullough, *John Adams,* 102–3; on the "sensuous vividness" of Adams' prose, see Bernard Bailyn, "Butterfield's Adams: Notes for a Sketch," *William and Mary Quarterly,* 3d ser. 19 (1962), 246–47.

163. *Scots Magazine,* October 1775, 562, quoted in Troy O. Bickham, "Sympathizing with Sedition? George Washington, the British Press, and British Attitudes during the War for Independence," *William and Mary Quarterly,* 3d ser. 59 (2002), 108.

164. Charles Royster, *A Revolutionary People at War: The Continental Army and American Character, 1775–1783* (Chapel Hill, N.C., 1979), 4–5, 25, 26 and after.

165. Garry Wills, *Cincinnatus: George Washington and the Enlightenment* (New York, 1984), 84.

166. Trumbull, *An Essay on the Use and Advantages of the Fine Arts* [1770], quoted in Joseph J. Ellis, *After the Revolution: Profiles of Early American Culture* (New York, 1979), 8–9.

167. Nathan O. Hatch, *The Sacred Cause of Liberty: Republican Thought and the Millennium in Revolutionary New England* (New Haven, Conn., 1977), 21–54.

168. Joseph Bellamy, "True Religion Delineated" [1750], reprinted in Alan Heimert and Perry Miller, eds., *The Great Awakening: Documents Illustrating the Crisis and Its Consequences* (Indianapolis, 1967), 553, 554.

169. Alan Heimert, *Religion and the American Mind* (Cambridge, Mass., 1966), 353–59; Cushing Strout, "Religion, Communications, and the American Revolution," *William and Mary Quarterly*, 3d ser. 34 (1977), 519–41; Isaac, *Transformation of Virginia* 243–69.

170. Mayhew abhorred the violence of the mob and the destruction it caused, and he wrote privately to Hutchinson to assure him of the same. But Mayhew equally abhorred the Stamp Act. Charles W. Akers, *Called unto Liberty: A Life of Jonathan Mayhew, 1720–1766* (Cambridge, Mass., 1964), 204–8. On the intellectual origins of Mayhew's ideas, see Bailyn, *Faces of Revolution*, 125–36.

171. Mayhew, *The Snare Broken* (Boston, 1766), 24, 25, 28, 31.

172. James Spear Loring, ed., *The Hundred Boston Orators Appointed by the Municipal Authorities . . . From 1770 to 1852; Comprising Historical Gleanings, Illustrating the Principles and Progress of Our Republican Institutions* (Boston, 1852), 64–65. I am grateful to Gustafson, *Eloquence Is Power*, 187–95, for introducing me to this source. She finds these orations an "imagery of voice," ibid. 192, while I see them as a voicing of imagery.

173. Tudor, in Loring, ed., *Hundred Boston Orators*, 137.

174. Quoted in Charles Royster, "'The Nature of Treason': Revolutionary Virtue and American Reactions to Benedict Arnold," *William and Mary Quarterly*, 3d ser. 36 (1979), 182.

175. Quoted in Pauline Maier, *The Old Revolutionaries: Political Lives in the Age of Samuel Adams* (New York, 1980), 289.

176. David A. McCants, *Patrick Henry; The Orator* (New York, 1990), 7, 8, 27, 29, 123.

177. William Wirt, *Patrick Henry: Life, Correspondence, and Speeches* (New York, 1891), 1:268.

178. Randolph, quoted in Isaac, *Transformation of Virginia*, 267–68.

179. McCants, *Henry*, 30.

180. Wirt, *Henry*, 1:263.

181. Jack Rakove, *The Beginnings of National Politics: An Interpretive History of the Continental Congress* ([1979], Baltimore, 1982), 78–86.

182. Newspaper pieces were often read aloud in taverns.

183. The work of the English Commonwealth Men greatly influenced the American Whigs. See e.g. Bailyn, *Ideological Origins*, 34 and after. But Paine was not one.

184. Robert A. Ferguson, *The American Enlightenment, 1750–1820* (Cambridge, Mass., 1997), 116.

185. [Thomas Paine], "Reflections on Titles," *Pennsylvania Magazine*, May 1775, in Moncure Daniel Conway, ed., *The Writings of Thomas Paine* (reprint ed., London, 1996), 1:46.

186. Thomas Paine, *Common Sense* [1776], ed. Isaac Kramnick (Baltimore, 1976), 67, 68, 77, 82, 88, 81.

187. Kramnick, "Introduction," ibid., 38; Eric Foner, *Tom Paine and Revolutionary America* (New York, 1976), 16.

188. Reid quoted in Fliegelman, *Declaring Independence,* 45.

189. Trumbull, *M'Fingal,* 124.

190. Thomas P. Slaughter, ed., "Introduction" *Thomas Paine, "Common Sense," and Related Writings* (Boston, 2001), 27, 40.

191. Fliegelman, *Declaring Independence,* 45–46, 79–80.

192. Paine, *Common Sense,* ed. Slaughter, 108.

193. *Virginia Gazette,* April 11, 1771.

194. Notes for James Duane Speech to Congress, September 8, 1774, in Paul H. Smith et al., eds., *Letters of Delegates to Congress, 1774–1789* (Washington, D.C., 1976), 1:52.

195. John Adams, diary entry for September 5, 1774, in ibid., 9.

196. John Adams to James Burgh, December 28, 1774, Adams to a "Friend in London," January 21, 1775, in ibid., 275–76, 297.

197. Silas Deane to Elizabeth Deane, September 5, 1774, in ibid., 15.

198. Ibid., May 12, 1775, in ibid., 345–46.

199. Adams to Tudor, October 7, 1774, in ibid., 157.

200. Samuel Adams, Draft of Letter to Thomas Gage, October 7, 1774, in ibid., 159.

201. Duane, "Propositions Before the Committee on Rights," September 22, 1774, in ibid., 40.

202. Richard Henry Lee, "Draft Address to the People of Great Britain and Ireland," October 11, 1774, in ibid., 178–79.

203. Samuel Ward, "Notes for a Speech in Congress, October 12, 1774," in ibid., 184.

204. Bailyn, *Ideological Origins,* 27–28.

205. Ward, "Notes for a Speech," in Smith et al., eds., *Letters,* 1:188.

206. John Dickinson, "Draft Memorial to the Inhabitants of the Colonies, October 21, 1774, in ibid., 215.

207. Dickinson, "Draft Letter to Quebec" October 26, 1774, in ibid., 239.

208. James Duane to Samuel Chase, December 29, 1774, in ibid., 279.

209. Silas Deane to Samuel Adams, November 13, 1774, and Richard Henry Lee to Patrick Henry, April 20, 1776, in ibid., 259, 3:564.

210. Oliver Wolcott to Samuel Lyman, April 17, 1776, in ibid., 3:553.

211. Patrick Henry to Congress, September 6, 1774, in John Adams' Notes on Debates, in ibid., 1:28.

212. Patrick Henry, Draft Address to the King, October 22, 1774, in ibid., 223.

213. John Dickinson, "Notes for a Speech in Congress, May 25, 1775, in ibid., 377, 380.

214. See e.g. John Hancock to Philip Schuyler, February 20, 1776, John Jay to Robert R. Livingston, February 25, 1776, in ibid., 3:288, 302.

215. Josiah Bartlett to Meshech Ware, March 2, 1776, in ibid., 319.

216. Pauline Maier, *American Scripture: Making the Declaration of Independence* (New York, 1997), 97–105.

217. Peter Charles Hoffer, *The Law's Conscience: Equitable Constitutionalism in America* (Chapel Hill, N.C., 1990), 66–79.

218. For the most recent and trenchant analysis, see Maier, *American Scripture,* 105–43.

219. John Adams to Abigail Adams, July 3, 1776, *Adams Family Correspondence,* ed. L. H. Butterfield et al. (Cambridge, Mass., 1963–), 2:30.

220. *Pennsylvania Journal,* July 9, 1777, quoted in David Waldstreicher, *In the Midst of Perpetual Fetes: The Making of American Nationalism, 1776–1820* (Chapel Hill, N.C., 1997), 35.

221. Ibid., 68. Of course, the newspaper accounts emphasized this quality, and for a reason. The actual events were undoubtedly rowdier and more debauched, but the image the newspapers wanted to project became the reality.

222. Simon P. Newman, *Parades and the Politics of the Street: Festive Culture in the Early American Republic* (Philadelphia, 1997), 87, 153. Waldstreicher agrees that "the critical period of the 1780s saw attempts to rein in these runaway representations. Celebrations and their circulation in print were key to this contest: they symbolically excluded particular groups." *Perpetual Fetes,* 55.

223. Steven Rosswurm, *Arms, Country, and Class: The Philadelphia Militia and the "Lower Sort" during the American Revolution* (New Brunswick, N.J., 1987), 152–53; Klepp, "Rough Music on Independence Day," 160–61.

224. Peter Thompson, *Rum Punch and Revolution: Taverngoing and Public Life in Eighteenth-Century Philadelphia* (Philadelphia, 1999), 154

225. Zakim, "Sartorial Ideologies," 1571–72; Klepp, "Rough Music on Independence Day,"163.

226. Shields, *Civil Tongues,* 313–18.

227. Thompson, *Rum Punch,* 191–92.

228. Tucker, quoted in Smith, *Dominion of Voice,* 49.

229. Thomas Welsh, "Oration Delivered at Boston, March 5, 1783, in Hezekiah Niles, ed., *Principles and Acts of the Revolution in America . . .* (Baltimore, 1822), 56, 57, 58, 59.

230. "The sentimental acts of celebration, which may appear to us distanced, secondhand, and unconnected to real life or politics, seemed at the time to open up a greater sphere of action for more and more citizens." Waldstreicher, *Perpetual Fetes,* 111. True— but these celebrations also dulled the senses, creating a mass political culture without texture and variety.

231. Nathan O. Hatch, *The Democratization of American Christianity* (New Haven, Conn., 1989), 24.

232. John Fenno, ed., in *Gazette of the United States* [1789], quoted in Waldstreicher, *Perpetual Fetes,* 109.

233. Hatch, *Democratization of Christianity,* 32.

234. Michael Merrell and Sean Wilentz, eds., *The Key of Liberty: The Life and Democratic Writings of William Manning* (Cambridge, Mass., 1993), 124–25.

235. Klepp, "Rough Music on Independence Day," 169, 171.

236. Timothy Dwight, "The Triumph of Infidelity" [1788], lines 21, 89, the poem re-

printed as the appendix to Colin Wells, *The Devil and Doctor Dwight: Satire and Theology in the Early American Republic* (Chapel Hill, N.C., 2002), 184, 186; Wood, *Radicalism of the American Revolution*, 215, 217, 221.

237. "Procession," Boston, October 19, 1789, Broadside, in Georgia B. Bumgardner, ed., *American Broadsides* (Barre, Mass., 1971), n.p.

238. Quoted in Newman, *Parades,* 51.

Coda

1. The Architect of the Capitol, *Art in the United States Capitol* (Washington, D.C., 1978), 130–45.

2. William J. Bennett, "Introduction," in Bennett, ed., *Our Sacred Honor: Words of Advice from the Founders in Letters, Poems, and Speeches* (Nashville, Tenn., 1997), 18.

3. See, generally, Bettina Drew, *Crossing the Expendable Landscape* (St. Paul, Minn., 1998).

4. Phil Patton, *Open Road: A Celebration of the American Highway* (New York, 1986), 139.

Index

Black (color) (*continued*)
  shades of, 141; and unity of slaves, 142–
  43; and "whiteness," 141, 292n. 22; in
  witchcraft cases, 117, 118
"Black Codes," 139, 148; in Maryland, 148;
  in New York, 139, 160; in South Caro-
  lina, 139, 147, 149–50, 159; in Virginia,
  139, 148
Blood oaths, 160, 161
Blue (color), 27
Bonfires, 44, 174, 212, 217
Books: devil's, in witchcraft cases, 123; of
  magic, 130
Boston, 206; merchants in, 207; unrest in,
  207
Boston Massacre, 225–27
Boyle, Robert: on demonic, 284n. 141; as
  scientist, 283n. 131; on supernatural, 78,
  283n. 13
Bradbury, Mary, suspected witch, 120
Bradford, William: on Pequots, 92; in Pe-
  quot War, 84; on the senses, 40, 92
Branding, 15
Bull, William, reaction to slave rebellion,
  153–54, 156
Burnet, William, 19
Burns, Anthony, 18
Burns, Ken, on documentary history, 8–9
Burroughs, George, suspected witch, 121–22
Byrd, William: on blackness, 141; on slavery,
  139

Cabeza de Vaca, Alvar Núñez, use of the
  senses, 5, 6
Caesar (slave), conspirator, 162, 164
Cahokia, 57
Calef, Robert, criticism of witchcraft trials,
  130
Campbell, William, on mobs, 191
Candles, 204
Cannibalism, 71, 85
Cannons: in England, 43; and fortification,

61; and Indians, 70; and provincial cel-
  ebrations, 200
Canonicus, in Pequot War, 84
Capitol (U.S.) Rotunda, 252
Captivity tales, 100–106, 122, 127
Carnival, 210–11
Carrier, Martha, examined, 114–15
Carter, Landon, on slavery, 144–45
Cartier, Jacques, on the senses, 4
Casas, Bartolomé de las, on autotopic vi-
  sion, 7
Catesby, Mark, on Indian languages, 49
Chauncy, Charles, opposes Great Awaken-
  ing, 180–81
Church, Benjamin, in King Philip's War, 98
Church membership, problem of, 169. *See
  also* Visible church, doctrine of
"Civil millennialism," 236
Clark, Stuart, on witchcraft, 118
Clarke, George, on slaves, 160
Cobb, T.R.R., on blackness, 140–41
Cognitive dissonance, 22–23
Colden, Cadwallader, and Stamp Act pro-
  tests, 214–15, 216
Cole, Nathan, on revival, 177–78
College of Wllliam and Mary, 199
Colonial Williamsburg (restoration), 8, 9;
  slavery discussed at, 10
Color: among Indians, 26–27; of animals,
  123; discernment in mammals, 133; and
  discrimination, 134; for Harriot, 37; in
  pre-modern world, 6; and race, 134,
  290n. 5. *See also specific colors*
Columbus, Christopher: and Indian lan-
  guages, 48; and naming, 50
Confabulation, 78
Conforti, Joseph, on New England, 9
Conspiracy, of slaves, 161, 162, 165, 302n.
  185
Continental Congress, 240, 242, 243, 245
Conversation: and gentility, 200; among
  Indians, 81